EU EXECUTIVE DISCRETION
AND THE LIMITS OF LAW

EU Executive Discretion and the Limits of Law

Edited by

JOANA MENDES

Professor of Comparative Administrative Law, University of Luxembourg

OXFORD

UNIVERSITY PRESS

UNIVERSITY PRESS

Great Clarendon Street, Oxford, OX2 6DP,
United Kingdom

Oxford University Press is a department of the University of Oxford.
It furthers the University's objective of excellence in research, scholarship,
and education by publishing worldwide. Oxford is a registered trade mark of
Oxford University Press in the UK and in certain other countries

Published in the United States of America by Oxford University Press
198 Madison Avenue, New York, NY 10016, United States of America

British Library Cataloguing in Publication Data
Data available

Library of Congress Control Number: 2018967699

ISBN 978–0–19–882666–8

Printed and bound by
CPI Group (UK) Ltd, Croydon, CR0 4YY

Preface

The project of this book started in 2015, as I was struggling with organizing my thoughts on administrative discretion in the EU. While a core concept of administrative law, discretion has been relatively neglected in EU legal scholarship (at least when it comes to the discretion of EU executive institutions and bodies), some noteworthy exceptions notwithstanding (such as Aude Bouveresse, *Le Pouvoir Discrétionnaire Dans l'Ordre Juridique Communautaire* (Bruyland, 2010) and various analysis on judicial review in competition law). The prominence that the political and administrative executive bodies acquired in the wake of the financial crisis required, in my view, an analysis that would transcend the specificities of one policy field and engage in a conceptual and normative discussion on the relationship between law and discretion. My first ideas on exploring the role of law in structuring the exercise of discretion by EU administrative actors were published in early 2016 (in the *Common Market Law Review*). But the topic required leaving the walls of my office. I was personally inclined to revisiting the legacy of administrative law doctrine on law and discretion, but doing so would risk losing sight of the transformations that had been shaking the EU financial, monetary and economic governance since at least 2010. Above all, it risked overlooking the specificities of EU law. I wanted to bring together scholars from different backgrounds and different generations, EU scholars and administrative law scholars alike, specialists and generalists, to test my ideas and learn from their work. Many of those I wanted to learn from, however, had not published on administrative discretion in the EU, or, at least, discretion as such had not been at the centre of their attention, even if some of their writings spoke to the concerns that motivated my research. The generous funding of *The Netherlands Organisation for Scientific Research (Nederlandse Organisatie voor Wetenschappelijk Onderzoek, NWO)* under a Veni grant, which I gratefully acknowledge, gave me the resources to bring some of them together in an exploratory workshop on understanding how law governs, and should govern, the EU executive's discretion.

We first met in Amsterdam in the Summer of 2016, still very much with the purpose of exploring ideas. The participants were bound neither to produce a paper ahead of the workshop, nor to any subsequent publication commitments. It worked and I am delighted it did. A second workshop followed up the first discussions. We met again in Luxembourg in the Summer of 2017, but this time to discuss papers with a view to publication. From those exchanges emerged the current structure of the book. A first part dedicated to concepts, problems and approaches establishes the basis for the more specific issues analysed in the second part that focuses on EU financial, monetary, and economic governance. The third part broadens again the analysis beyond the most recent developments in those fields to examine both the tools of judicial review and the role of selected legal principles in structuring the exercise of discretion, linking back to the first part's conceptual discussion. The various threads that run through the book are highlighted in the conclusion, which gives an account of the methodological challenges, conceptual difficulties and normative problems in searching for possible paths to secure the role of law in structuring discretion. It also proposes possible building blocks for a conceptual-normative framework on the relationships between discretion and law in the EU.

Absent from the book, but having provided generous comments to the first ideas jotted down in a preliminary introduction were Edoardo Chiti and Carol Harlow, to whom I am very grateful. Their critical remarks made me change direction on some crucial points (remaining errors are of course of my sole responsibility). Absent too are some of the participants to the first workshop, whose work and comments provided valuable input for collective reflection: Gareth Davies, Clemens Kaupa, Ian Harden, Anne Meuwese and Eljalill Tauschinski. I am very grateful to them. I am particularly indebted to the authors of the chapters of this book, for having been willing to think along and engage in a conversation, for their forbearance towards the succession of comments and organizational emails, for the time they dedicated to this project. And to Clara and Henrique, for their playful engagement in the choice of the book's cover, for them finally a sign that something colourful could come out of an insipid and uninspiring screen. Natalie Patey, at OUP, has been a wonderfully patient and supportive editor.

Whether the book has the coherence that is possible in an edited volume will be for the reader to judge. I hope nevertheless that the thought and work that went into it will be visible in its pages.

Joana Mendes
Hostert, 30 January 2019

Contents—Summary

PART IV. CONCLUSION

Contents—Detailed

Table of Cases

CJEU CASES

GENERAL COURT CASES

Table of Legislation

PART I

EU LAW AND EXECUTIVE DISCRETION—CONCEPTS, PROBLEMS, AND APPROACHES

1

Executive Discretion in the EU and the Outer Boundaries of Law

*Joana Mendes**

1. Crisis, Law, and Executive Discretion

In the aftermath of the 2008 financial meltdown, shifts in competences between the Member States and the European Union (EU) and among the EU institutions reinforced the powers of the EU's executive in ways that have strained the legal boundaries of their respective authority as it stood before the crisis. The Member States, the EU legislature, and the European Central Bank (ECB) first established the instruments intended to make the EU emerge from the crisis, thereby transforming the EU's economic and financial governance; then, the Court of Justice of the European Union (hereafter, the Court) cemented those changes, sanctioning with legal arguments deviations from the pre-existing legal norms.[1] Many have argued that this two-step change was part of a larger process that not only transformed the EU's constitutional framework, but also eroded the law's ability to constrain executive powers and further challenged the already-weak democratic foundations of

* Professor of Comparative and Administrative Law, University of Luxembourg. I gratefully acknowledge the discussions had with the contributors to this book and with the participants of two workshops that preceded its publication. The first workshop was held at the University of Amsterdam in 2016, with the generous support of the Dutch National Science Foundation (NWO). The second workshop took place at the University of Luxembourg in 2017. Work accomplished there contributed to the main lines of argument that emerge in this introduction and in the book's concluding chapter. I am indebted to Carol Harlow, Edoardo Chiti, and Vestert Borger for reading and providing their critiques of an earlier version of this introduction. I retain, of course, full responsibility for any remaining errors or imprecisions.

[1] Judgment in Case C-370/12 *Thomas Pringle v Government of Ireland and ors*, [2012] EU:C:2012:756 (hereafter *Pringle*); Case C-270/12 *United Kingdom v European Parliament and Council (ESMA)* [2014] EU:C:2014:18 (hereafter *ESMA*); Case C-62/14 *Gauweiler and Others* [2015] EU:C:2015:400 (hereafter *Gauweiler*). See, e.g. E Chiti and P Teixeira, 'The Constitutional Implications of the European Responses to the Financial and Public Debt Crisis', 50 *Common Mark Law Rev* 683 (2013), in particular 705–7; AJ Menéndez, 'Editorial: A European Union in Constitutional Mutation?', 20 *ELJ* 127 (2014), at 128–38; P Craig 'Economic Governance and the Euro Crisis: Constitutional Architecture and Constitutional Implications' in M Adams and others (eds), *The Constitutionalization of European Budgetary Constraints* (Hart, 2014), 19–40.

the Union.[2] A contrasting view, however, stresses that, as deep as the metamorphoses in the fields of economic, financial, and monetary policy may have been, the crisis-induced institutional changes did not lead to a major constitutional transformation outside the Eurozone, pointing out that other areas of EU law continued to operate as they had before the turmoil of 2008–2010.[3]

Limited or not to the policy areas impacted by the crisis, the adjustments to the EU's governance structures triggered developments that questioned law's ability to constitute and constrain public authority and, specifically, the exercise of discretion. EU executive authority in the fields of economic and financial policy was re-inforced by the Court's interpretation of the Treaties that allowed it to uphold the legality of the European Stability Mechanism (ESM) and its monetary transfers to those Member States in financial difficulty (in *Pringle*), as well as the legality of the ECB's role as the lender of last resort (in *Gauweiler*);[4] by the disruption of carefully crafted co-operative mechanisms between the Member States and the EU institutions, through the attribution to the latter of the power to monitor and discipline the national fiscal policies of the Eurozone Member States;[5] by the re-definition of the limits of the EU institutions' ability to delegate authority to European agencies (in *ESMA*) and the attribution of powers to agencies that changed the vertical al-location of powers between the EU and national competent authorities as well as the relative authority of such agencies and the European Commission;[6] and by the exercise of political discretion behind a veneer of technical-assessment accuracy for which executive institutions are competent.[7] More importantly, these different de-velopments involved the deployment of legal arguments giving the Court the means to accommodate the de facto changes to the ECB's legal mandate; the EU legislature the means to change the institutional position of both the Commission (in the field of economic governance) and the ECB (in financial regulation); and both the EU legislature and the Court the means to attribute important policy choices to the Commission and to some EU agencies. In some cases, those legal arguments weak-ened law's ability to shape and channel the exercise of the EU executive's discretion.[8]

---

[2] See, *inter alia*, M Dawson and F de Witte, 'Constitutional Balance in the EU after the Euro-Crisis' (2013) 76 *Mod L Rev* 817 ; M Ioannidis, 'Europe's New Transformations: How the EU Economic Constitution Changed During the Eurozone Crisis' (2016) 53 *Common Mark Law Rev* 1237 ; AJ Menéndez, 'The Crisis of Law and the European Crises: From the Social and Democratic *Rechtsstaat* to the Consolidating State of (Pseudo-)technocratic Governance' (2017) 44 *J Law Soc* 56.

[3] B de Witte, 'Euro Crisis Responses and the EU Legal Order: Increased Institutional Variation or Constitutional Mutation?' (2015) 11 *Eur Const Law Rev* 434.

[4] *Pringle* (n 1); *Gauweiler* (n 1).

[5] See, *inter alia*, K Tuori and K Tuori, *The Eurozone Crisis. A Constitutional Analysis* (CUP, 2014), 188–92.

[6] *ESMA* (n 1), paras 53, 105. On the impact of the rule-making powers of the financial agencies on the relative position of the Commission, see E Chiti, 'European Agencies' Rulemaking: Powers, Procedures and Assessment'(2013) 19 *ELJ* 93 and M Busuioc, 'Rule-Making by the European Financial Supervisory Authorities: Walking a Tight Rope' (2013) 19 *ELJ* 111.

[7] J Mendes, 'Discretion, Care and Public Interests in the EU Administration: Probing the Limits of Law' (2016) 53 *Common Mark Law Rev* 419; E Chiti, 'Is EU Administrative Law Failing in Some of Its Crucial Tasks?' (2016) 22 *ELJ* 576, 589–90.

[8] J Mendes, 'Bounded Discretion in EU Law: A Limited Judicial Paradigm in a Changing EU' (2017) 80 *Mod L Rev* 443, drawing on *ESMA* (n 1) and *Gauweiler* (n 1).

These developments prompt the question of how law may continue to structure and constrain the discretionary powers of the EU executive, i.e. to query the ability of legal norms, such as Treaty and statutory norms, and of legal principles to structure the executive choices that concretise normative programs in pursuit of legally protected public interests.[9] This question drives the various contributions to this book. A decade after the crisis-prompted restructuring of the EU's economic and financial governance, a shift in perspective is warranted that moves away from those constitutional issues that dominated the academic debate since the beginning of the crisis. That discussion, centred on whether the acquisition of new powers was lawful under the pre-crisis constitutional order and on the extent to which EU constitutional law has been challenged and changed, should now give way to an inquiry into the law's relationship to executive discretion. Specifically, the focus should shift to the challenges law faces when trying to frame executive discretion in a politically sensitive, highly complex, and constantly shifting reality. What are its limits in circumscribing discretionary choices? What are the limits of judicial review of the EU executive's discretionary decisions? Addressing these questions will probe law's ability to constrain public authority in the current stage of European integration.

This book, while revisiting and rethinking the law-discretion binomial against the backdrop of the post-2010 changes, examines the extent to which EU law can structure the rationality of expertise-based and policy-driven decisions by steering the deliberative political processes toward ensuring the accommodation, protection, and pursuance of competing public interests. It contributes to a better understanding of how law governs, and should govern, the EU executive's discretion, now that the crisis-driven changes have been consolidated. The book focuses on EU economic and financial regulation, but its scope is broader. The powers that the EU's executive institutions (in particular, the Commission, ECB, and EU agencies) have acquired in those policy fields since the crisis are a starting point for a more expansive reflection on law's relationship to the exercise of discretion, specifically on the concept of discretion, on the features of law in the context of EU integration that may condition its ability to structure discretion or place additional legal constraints thereon, and on the different approaches to contain and structure discretion via law.

This introductory chapter sets out and frames that analysis. It begins by outlining the general terms under which law may frame the exercise of discretion by executive institutions. What may appear as a misplaced, basic introduction to public law is an appropriate starting point to consider the blurred boundaries between a political executive and an administrative executive sphere in their relation to law in the EU. In national constitutional law, those boundaries are often grounded on formal criteria and conventionally refer to the possibilities of judicial control as well as to the consequent looser or stricter legal strictures that constrain executive action. In EU law, the lack of a formal constitutional delineation of those spheres leaves their delimitation much dependent on how the Court frames and reviews specific instances of

---

[9] See, further, Mendes, 'Bounded Discretion' (n 8). For an overview of different approaches to the concept of discretion, which also places it in its historical context, see Mattarella, Chapter 2 in this volume.

executive action (Section 2). That begs the question, addressed in the same section, of what constitutes the 'EU executive', the object of this book. That is one of the various conceptual challenges that one faces when addressing the relationship between discretion and the law in the EU, given its unique constitutional framework. This chapter then indicates some preliminary criteria that may delimit, in EU law, the instances where the role of law may be weaker in constraining discretion (Section 3). It argues that legal indeterminacy, combined with judicial deference, may invert the conventional relationship of discretion's subordination to law (a hypothesis that will be re-examined in the concluding chapter of the book, by reflecting on how the various contributions herein support or contest it). Finally, an explanation of the outline of the book and an overview of the different contributions closes this first chapter (Section 4).

2. Law, Executive, and Administrative Discretion: Blurred Boundaries in the EU

Executive discretion and its relationship to law is conventionally approached from an institutional, separation-of-powers perspective. In both national and EU law contexts, the subordination thereof to the law has mostly meant subordination to the courts' interpretation, application, and development of the relevant constitutional and legislative frameworks. Discussions about the limits of discretion and the limits of law have predominantly been about the relative boundaries of the spheres of policy and judicature.[10] Typically, in national legal systems, the degree of subordination—and, conversely, autonomy—of political executive bodies is different from that of administrative executive bodies. Political executive bodies derive their authority (and discretion) from their position in the constitutional system, in particular, from their democratic legitimacy or links of accountability to representative institutions. While bound by legal norms and general principles of law, executive bodies act, essentially, in a political role. Judicial oversight of such executive bodies is typically weaker by virtue of three combined factors: the theory of legal acts valid in each system; the correspondent avenues of judicial review that can exclude specific policy-making functions from the reach of courts; and the techniques of judicial review that can lead courts to recognize their broad scope of discretion. In contrast, administrative executive bodies—and political executive bodies acting in an administrative capacity—are typically more constrained. Their legal authority is grounded, essentially, on the legislative norms that define their mandates, the legal conditions, and their means of acting. In addition, they are typically subordinated to the political direction of democratically accountable governments. The scope of their discretion is also subject to these double-layered constraints. Courts will intervene—either curbing or enabling and structuring the exercise of discretion—to

---

[10] For a critique of this judicial perspective to understand discretion and its relation to law, see Mendes, 'Bounded Discretion' (n 8).

the extent that the legislature has established legal norms that limit the choices such administrative bodies can make, and to the extent that the available legal principles allow the judiciary to lend legal-normative rationality to such discretionary decisions. Discretion is justified insofar as the courts determine that the legislature gave the administrative decision maker the ability to make choices in accordance with political orientations grounded on their specific competence. The discretion inherent in the political decisions of the executive and in the discretion of the administration are, seemingly, distinct, as is their link to law.[11]

This stylized view expresses the two ends of the spectrum of law's capacity to structure discretion. At both ends, discretion is legally constituted, i.e. it expresses the authority to make a choice that law allows within the framework of the normative legal order. For this reason, public lawyers are likely to agree that regardless of 'the seriousness and urgency of the practical situations that may emerge, [executive authorities] can only address them by the means of action adopted within the established legal order by the texts in force' or, at least, by means that may be sanctioned by that legal order.[12]

In national legal systems, one main criterion differentiates the two ends of the spectrum: the means of scrutiny applicable to political executive or administrative executive action. Contrary to administrative action, political executive action may either be immune to judicial review—and subject only to political (parliamentary) control—or subject to judicial review—but by constitutional (as opposed to administrative) courts (in the legal systems where they exist). The result is that, even though both types of authority are constituted by law and must be exercised within the limits of the existing legal order, the political executive is not bound by the same strictures applicable to an administrative executive body.[13] Judicial intervention—whether directed at rights' protection or at the protection of the objective legality of an act—could hinder the fulfilment of the public interests that political executives are constitutionally competent to define, protect, and pursue. The legal normativity of their executive action is weaker than that of administrative decision makers, insofar as judicial review develops a set of parameters that instil such normativity. If courts—i.e. administrative courts—do not have jurisdiction over the actions of the political executive, the legal principles that they establish and develop to structure the exercise of discretion of administrative executive bodies either do not apply to political executive action or they are much looser in the way they constrain political executive bodies. That system of oversight opens up the potential for executive action to prevail over the underlying framing norms by virtue of an explicit constitutional choice expressed in the limits of the courts' jurisdiction.[14]

Such a distinction between the political executive and administrative executive spheres of action does not exist in EU law. The rationale for giving broad discretion to the EU executive in any given policy area or instance—i.e. to avoid a degree

---

[11] A Queiró, 'Teoria dos Actos de Governo' [1948], in *Estudos de Direito Público*, Vol 1 (Universidade de Coimbra, 1989) 519.

[12] R Carré de Malberg, *Contribution à la Théorie Générale de l'Etat* (Paris: Dalloz) 530.

[13] See also Mattarella, Chapter 2 in this volume.   [14] Queiró, 'Teoria' (n 11) 516–17.

of juridification that may be perceived as detrimental to policy choices and to the pursuit of the relevant public interests—may apply to executive entities, regardless of their political or administrative nature. Manifestly, reconciling divergent public interests that require complex assessments are not decisions that only the EU legislature makes.[15] The way the jurisdiction of the Court is generally defined subjects the actions of the EU executive to its review: any legal act of the EU institutions that, whatever its nature or form, is capable of producing legal effects vis-à-vis third parties is subject to judicial review.[16] The boundaries that, in national legal systems, one could draw—more on formal and organic, rather than substantive, grounds— between political executive and administrative executive action, therefore, are significantly blurred when applied to the EU institutions. So are the different ways in which law may structure the exercise of their discretion.

There are some instances where the jurisdiction of the Court is excluded. Those situations might provide an appropriate reference point for singling out an executive sphere less constrained by law. Most prominently, the Treaty excludes the jurisdiction of the Court in relation to provisions relating to the Common Foreign and Security Policy (CFSP). But, even here, two important exceptions—the Court is entitled to decide whether a particular CSFP measure should have been adopted pursuant to a non-CFSP Treaty provision, and, in addition, to review the legality of Council decisions that establish restrictive measures against natural or legal persons[17]—have ultimately allowed the Court to limit the reach of the Treaty derogation.[18] The Court mitigated the exceptionality of CFSP by embedding it in the EU constitutional framework, specifically, in the principles of the rule of law, the obligation to provide

---

[15] Judgment, Case C-355/10 *European Parliament v Council (Schengen Borders)* [2012] EU:C:2012:516, para 76, using this criterion to delimit the essential elements of an area that should be reserved to the legislature.

[16] On current challenges to this doctrine, see Tridimas, Chapter 3 in this volume, pointing out how the uncertainty regarding the author of the act combined with a formalistic reasoning may unduly limit the scope of judicial review (text accompanying footnotes 29–45).

[17] Arts 24(1)(2) and 40 Treaty on European Union (allowing the Court to ensure institutional balance, competence, and procedure) and Art 275 Treaty of the Functioning of European Union.

[18] The Court examined compliance with Treaty procedural rules for the conclusion of an international agreement adopted on the basis of a CFSP provision, upholding the right of the European Parliament to be involved (Case C-658/11 *European Parliament v Council (Mauritius)* [2014] EU:C:2014:2025, paras 69–74, 81–6 (hereafter *Mauritius*), and Case C-263/14 *European Parliament v Council (Tanzania)* [2014] EU:C:2014:2025, paras 68–94; hereafter *Tanzania*); it ruled on preliminary reference requests on the validity and interpretation of CFSP acts (Case C-72/15 *PJSC Rosneft Oil Company* [2017] ECLI:EU:C:2017:236, paras 65–76; hereafter *Rosneft*); it established jurisdiction to review compliance with EU public procurement rules and acts of staff management relating to staff members seconded by the Member States in the context of CFSP missions (Case C-439/13 P *Elitaliana v Eulex Kosovo* [2015] EU:C:2015:753, paras 41–50; C-455/14 P *H v Council and European Union Police Mission* [2016] EU:C:2016:569, paras 55–8; hereafter *H v Council*). See, further, P Van Elsuwege, 'Upholding the Rule of Law in Common Foreign and Security Policy: *H v Council*' (2017) 54 *Common Mark Law Rev* 841 and M Cremona '"Effective Judicial Review is of the Essence of the Rule of Law": Challenging Common Foreign and Security Policy Measures Before the Court of Justice' (2017) 2 *European Papers* 671, pointing out how the administrative law issues involved in CFSP matters enabled the Court to assert jurisdiction. On how the Treaty provisions define the role of the Court in CFSP, see, e.g. C Hillion, 'A Powerless Court? The European Court of Justice and the Common Foreign Security Policy' in M Cremona and A Thies (eds), *The European Court of Justice and External Relations Law. Constitutional Challenges* (Hart, 2014), 47–70.

effective jurisdictional protection, and democracy.[19] Nevertheless, the scope of judicial review in this policy field remains limited: the Treaty carves out a sphere of executive authority—albeit with blurred and evolving contours[20]—in which executive action prevails, presumably because the political nature of the relevant acts makes it too 'difficult to reconcile judicial review with the separation of powers'.[21]

The aforementioned jurisdictional criterion only gives a limited view of the spheres in which the law is relatively weak in providing a structure for the exercise of executive discretion. Beyond it, one may try to capture the different degrees of the law's circumscription of executive discretion by identifying those areas in which the Court recognizes the EU institution's broad scope of discretion. For example, the broad discretion of the Council in deciding whether an excessive deficit exists limits significantly the type of review that the Court may perform.[22] Moreover, in those segments of the CFSP in which the Court has asserted its jurisdiction, the Court has still emphasized the Council's broad discretion in view of the political, economic, and social choices, and complex assessments, that the Council must make when adopting CFSP measures.[23] Depending on the facts and issues brought before it in concrete cases, the Court may choose to apply the same procedural and substantive principles that it typically deploys when asked to assess the legality of discretionary acts (e.g. careful and impartial examination, proportionality). But, in cases involving the exercise of broad discretion, such principles may only serve to verify—in broad-brush terms—whether there is a 'reasonable relationship' between the content of the challenged act and its declared objectives.[24]

Within the areas of the Court's jurisdiction, an attempt to single out the way the discretion of the EU executive is bound by law—the instances in which it is possibly not subject, in the same degree, to general principles of administrative law that the Court itself developed to tame and frame discretion—stands on much shakier ground. It is a task handed over to judicial fiat. The extent to which the Court, within a given legislative framework and policy area, defers to the exercise of discretion by

---

[19] *Rosneft*, paras 72–5 (n 18); *H v Council*, para 41 (n 18); *Mauritius*, paras 80–1 (n 18); *Tanzania* 70–1 (n 18). Hillion, 'A Powerless Court?' 66–70 (n 18), and Cremona, 'Effective Judicial Review' (n 18).

[20] See Opinion 2/13 *Accession to the ECHR* [2014] EU:C:2014:2454, paras 251–2, where the Court, after noting the uncertain scope of the its limited jurisdiction in CFSP matters, stated that 'it is sufficient to declare that, as EU law now stands, certain acts adopted in the context of the CFSP fall outside the ambit of judicial review by the Court of Justice' (para 252). The more recent developments brought by the case law mentioned in note 16 confirm the evolving scope of the Court jurisdiction in the CFSP area (see also Opinion of AG Wathelet in *Rosneft*, para 3).

[21] Opinion AG Wathelet in *Rosneft*, para 52.

[22] The Treaty excludes the bringing of actions for infringement before the Court that deal with compliance with the various steps of the excessive deficit procedure (Article 126(10) TFEU). Yet, more than excluding judicial oversight, this clause limits the enforcement role of the Commission, since other judicial actions are possible against the legal acts and omissions of the Council within this framework (Case C-27/04 *Commission v Council* [2004] EU:C:2004:436). Here the limitation on the Court's jurisdiction comes mainly from the broad discretion that the institutions enjoy in this policy field.

[23] *Rosneft* (n 18), paras 113–16, 132, 146–7, and 150.

[24] Ibid., paras 115, 123–4, 132, 147. See Cremona, 'Effective Judicial Review' (n 18) 19–21. In *Rosneft*, the fact that the Court had just established its jurisdiction to hear a preliminary ruling on the validity and interpretation of a CFSP measures might explain (at least in part) the light judicial review.

an EU executive or administrative body is largely a decision the Court makes itself, subject only to the specific circumstances of the particular case before it and its own assessment of how to deploy the review tools at its disposal.[25] When faced with specific legal challenges, the Court decides the degree to which legal normativity and rationality ought to mould legal acts, deploying general legal principles and arguments in a variable way in each instance.[26] This casuistic approach in an evolving constitutional framework, itself co-defined by the Court, makes it harder to make a conceptual and normative differentiation between political executive and administrative executive action.

Against this backdrop, one may be inclined to ask what, then, does the term 'EU executive' mean in this book. The term is used, here, in a broad and somewhat imprecise sense to refer to EU institutions and bodies that combine two functions: on the one hand, they develop policies and programmes that, within looser or stricter legal constraints, shape the EU economy and society, by setting out the envisaged ends, the means to achieve those ends, or both (a function that is, in national settings, associated with the executive, *strictu senso*);[27] on the other hand, they implement previously defined policies enshrined in legislative regimes (a defining characteristic of the administrative function). These two layers are juxtaposed.[28] In each, the political and administrative functions of the executive can be woven into legal acts in which either the former or the latter dimension prevails.[29]

This way of characterizing the executive—i.e. blending the political and administrative functions—defies a basic tenet of public law: a neutral administration that implements and carries out previously determined policies is functionally different from the executive that makes such policy. This is a widely accepted convention, even by those who point out the difficulties or the impossibility of stripping the political element from the administrative function.[30] The problem, however, concerns more than just the difficulties of resorting to terms that have specific meanings in national law that do not necessarily apply to EU law. Opting for a broad notion of the EU executive—one that encompasses the Commission, the ECB, and the EU financial agencies—risks implying an artificially unitary concept of the executive; a

[25] D Ritleng, 'Le juge communautaire de la légalité et le pouvoir discrétionnaire des institutions communautaires' (1999) 55 *AJDA* 645. See, further, Nehl, Chapter 8 in this volume.

[26] On the varying degrees of deference, see P Craig, *EU Administrative Law* (OUP, 2012) 409–29. See also HCH Hofmann, GC Rowe, and AH Türk, *Administrative Law and Policy of the European Union* (OUP, 2011) 498–9.

[27] EU executive actors, even if bound by legal mandates that define policy objectives, may have the ability to define the substance of the policy that they pursue. See Moloney, Chapter 5 and Borger, Chapter 6 in this volume.

[28] For a detailed analysis of their composition, see D Curtin, *The EU Executive* (OUP, 2009).

[29] This approximation to the term 'executive' is not common to the contributions of the book. The contributors were not given pre-defined concepts to be used uniformly throughout the book. I will return in the conclusion to the conceptual difficulties associated with the use of this term, as well as of the concept of discretion, as evidenced in the various chapters of the book.

[30] See, e.g. Caillosse, according to whom this is 'a border that is as much blurred as it is necessary, because the territories that it crosses and divides are not subject to the same legal treatment or status'; J Caillosse, 'Les "principes généraux" de l'organisation administrative' in P Gonod and others (eds) *Traité de Droit Administratif*, Vol 1 (Dalloz, 2011) 154 (author's translation).

conceptual imprecision made possible by the lack of a formal and jurisdictional distinction in EU law between the administrative and the executive spheres.[31]

A broad and imprecise notion of the executive is a working definition that suits the purposes of the present inquiry: explore the outer boundaries of law in relation to discretion, i.e. those areas where the law's normative capacity appears to be challenged in a more significant way, due to its potential weakness in guiding the way the executive actors exercise their discretionary powers. This difficulty also occurs in areas in which the EU administrative entities implement political choices. There is, therefore, a methodological justification for resorting to the concept proposed here: it zooms in on the activities of those EU institutions and bodies in which policy definition and implementation are combined in a way that defies analytical–legal categories. The choice of the term 'executive' rather than 'administrative' has a similar justification: it suits the focus of this book on the limited structuring capacity of law, even in areas where discretion would appear sufficiently constrained by law's strictures and by heteronomous policy determinations. Despite its imprecision, the term 'EU executive' avoids losing sight of the significance of the grey zones that stand between legal categories and that might be overlooked if one continues, in EU law, to use distinctions that are too limited to capture its complexity. It also means that this choice does not deny that a functional difference between policy definition and policy implementation exists, which may require different legal tools and different legal treatment.[32] Rather, it stresses that is it by acknowledging such grey zones that lawyers can perpetuate the legal categories with which they work and which otherwise appear detached from the complex reality that they are intended to capture.

3. When Law Fades: Interpretation and Discretion

EU law often creates situations calling for the exercise of discretion whose legal limits can be quite loose. The legal regimes created in response to the Eurozone crisis demonstrate, perhaps with unprecedented force, that pursuing public interests can lead *de facto* to executive action, which appears to prevail over the framing norms *within* the areas that fall under the jurisdiction of the Court because of the way the latter exercises its control powers.[33] While law still formally frames the exercise of discretion, its constraining capacity significantly fades as the Court approaches discretion as a matter of cognition in the hands of executive decision makers. These instances of discretion are anchored in legal norms that may be highly specific due to the technical assessments they involve, but also highly undetermined due to the open-ended nature of the terms those norms use or to the contested nature of the

---

[31] I thank Edoardo Chiti for pointing out the limits of a conveniently broad concept of the executive.
[32] See Mattarella, Chapter 2 in this volume.
[33] D Chalmers, 'The European Redistributive State and a European Law of Struggle' (2012) 18 *ELJ* 5; M Dawson, 'The Legal and Political Accountability Structure of "Post-Crisis" EU Economic Governance' (2015) 53 *J Com Mar St* 5; P Leino and T Saarenheimo, 'Sovereignty and Subordination: On the Limits of EU Economic Policy Coordination' (2017) 40 *ELR*.

knowledge needed to make such technical assessments. For example, under the single supervisory mechanism, the ECB is entitled to determine whether there are 'particular circumstances' that justify a credit institution being considered 'less significant' by virtue of its size (thereby not applying the specific significance criteria set by the relevant regulation), and, as a result, subject that credit institution to supervision by the appropriate national competent authority under the ECB's oversight; or, conversely, if 'particular circumstances' do not exist, such that the credit institution must be classified as 'significant' and placed under the ECB's exclusive prudential supervision in accordance with the applicable regulation. The substantive conditions of 'significance' are set out in the Council regulation that established the single supervisory mechanism (as are the conditions under which a credit institution shall *not* be considered less significant),[34] while the ECB has been entrusted with specifying the meaning of 'particular circumstances'. The relevant ECB regulation defines it as follows: 'specific and factual circumstances that make the classification of a supervised entity as significant inappropriate, taking into account the objectives and principles of the [Single Supervisory Mechanism] Regulation and, in particular, the need to ensure the consistent application of high supervisory standards'.[35] The methodology to verify the existence or non-existence of such particular circumstances is also within the ECB's competence.[36] The ECB's assessment of whether the legally enshrined conditions for public action are met (i.e. whether there are or are not particular circumstances in a given case) is a decision that, arguably, entails discretionary choices.[37]

At this point, one is confronted with the grey zones of legal dichotomies. Discretion, as mentioned, refers to the ability of executive actors to make choices that concretise normative programmes in pursuit of legally protected public interests.[38] On the contrary, the interpretation of indeterminate legal concepts (such as 'particular circumstances') is about specifying the meaning of those concepts. Discretion and interpretation, therefore, are different concepts, refer to different phenomena, and are subject to different legal treatment (the former is a matter for executive or administrative entities to decide, while the latter is a matter in which courts have the final say). Yet, the two are intertwined: the interpretation of the enabling norm by the executive entity not only delimits its scope of choice, but also influences (or even determines) the choice eventually made and, hence, the ultimate legal solution adopted.[39] The General Court's judgment in *Landeskreditbank*

---

[34] Article 6(4) of Council Regulation (EU) 1024/2013 conferring specific tasks on the European Central Bank concerning policies relating to the prudential supervision of credit institutions; see *OJ L* 287.

[35] Article 70 of the ECB Regulation.

[36] Article 6(7) of Council Regulation 1024/2013.

[37] See, further, Mendes, 'Bounded Discretion' (n 8) 464–5.

[38] Text accompanying (n 9). The same observation made regarding the executive (n 27) applies here: this is the definition I adopt; see, in more detail, Mendes, 'Bounded Discretion' (n 8), but it is not necessarily endorsed by all the book's contributors (for a critique, see Borger, Chapter 6 in this volume). In Chapter 11, I discuss different aspects of the concept of executive discretion that feature in the contributions to the volume.

[39] Mendes, 'Bounded Discretion' (n 8) 464. Mattarella's analysis in Section 3 of Chapter 2 this volume indicates that the dichotomies are, in part, the product of history and of different conceptions of

illustrates this point.[40] At issue was the ECB's interpretation of the term 'particular circumstances', which can make the classification 'significant' inappropriate. Specifically, the disputed issue was whether the term must be understood as the circumstances that make supervision by national authorities better able to ensure the consistent application of high supervisory standards (the interpretation favoured by the ECB and upheld by the General Court), or as those that show that supervision by national authorities is sufficient to ensure the consistent application of high supervisory standards (the interpretation favoured by the applicant).[41] The interpretation that ultimately prevails determines which considerations are relevant for the purposes of applying the applicable norm and, hence, conditions the ability of the ECB to classify an institution as 'significant'.[42] The fact that the Court will settle the interpretation of the norm does not exclude the fact that the interpreter is delimiting the factors that can be considered relevant for the purposes of classification.[43] It also does not exclude that, regardless of whether or not the Court eventually rejects the ECB's interpretation, the interpreter is determining how the public interest will be concretely pursued. In fact, the interpretation the General Court upheld in *Landeskreditbank* depended also on this Court's and the ECB's view of how well the ECB is placed to pursue the objectives set by the Council in the SSM Regulation.[44] The relevance of public-interest considerations on the Court's interpretation of indeterminate legal concepts confirms that interpretation is not just a matter of legal argument. Overall, the conceptual distinction between the exercise of discretion and the interpretation of indeterminate legal concepts does not preclude a situation in which the executive decision maker defines, itself, the meaning of the legal conditions that delimit its discretionary power.[45] The way the interpretation of indeterminate legal concepts is interwoven with discretionary choices and how that may affect the intensity of judicial scrutiny may invert the conventional relationship of discretion's subordination to law. The General Court's *Landeskreditbank* decision arguably illustrates how that can happen within areas subject to the Court's jurisdiction. The determination of the legal conditions of action that delimit the powers of the ECB in this case is largely in the hands of the ECB itself, even if subject to judicial review. In addition, the procedural guarantees deployed to structure the exercise of discretionary powers (in this case, the duty to give reasons and the duty of careful and impartial examination) were also limited by the interpretation given to the indeterminate legal concept at issue.[46]

---

the place and role of the administration in the broader functions of government. Hofmann (Chapter 10 this volume) suggests that the interpretation of legal mandates can be either discretionary in nature or subject to similar treatment.

[40] Case T-122/15 *Landeskreditbank Baden-Württemberg—Förderbank v European Central Bank* [2017] EU:T:2017:337 (pending appeal at the time of the writing).

[41] Ibid. (n 40) respectively, paras 34, 80, on the one hand, and paras 35, 48, on the other.

[42] Ibid. (n 40) paras 101–05.   [43] Ibid. (n 40) para 149.

[44] Ibid. (n 40) paras 77–80.

[45] On the various choices implied in administrative decision-making and on the elusive character of the distinctions, see Mattarella, Chapter 2 this volume.

[46] *Landeskreditbank* (n 40) paras 130, 149, where the General Court held that 'since that argument is *clearly irrelevant in the light of the interpretation favoured by the ECB*, it cannot be held that the ECB

As the book shows in greater detail, the area of economic co-ordination provides many extreme examples of norm indeterminacy. For instance, within the framework of the surveillance of macro-economic imbalances, in order to open or close an excessive imbalance procedure, the Council, on the basis of a Commission recommendation, must establish that a Member State either is, or is not, affected by 'excessive imbalances'.[47] This notoriously vague notion ('severe imbalances, including imbalances that jeopardise or risk jeopardizing the proper functioning of the economic and monetary union') is dependent on the Commission's in-depth review of myriad economic variables and country-specific information.[48] That determination requires a wide scope of 'judgment' (to use the words of the Director General of Economic and Financial Affairs) as 'there are no obvious rules-based criteria for the identification and assessment of macroeconomic imbalances'.[49]

In instances such as these, the EU executive institutions and bodies are given the authority to determine whether and how the norm ought to be applied.[50] They have the capacity to establish whether the legal conditions for action are fulfilled or not. It is only by deploying the necessary technical knowledge (that they hold or are able to gather) that it is possible to assess the concrete verification of those conditions. In making those complex technical assessments, the decision makers also make value choices that define their powers and the substance of discretionary decisions based on them.[51]

Eventually, the use of indeterminate legal concepts to define the conditions for the exercise of authority may be combined with judicial deference to the exercise of discretion, if there is ever a resort to judicial action. The very nature of the public interests that executive bodies need to consider and the technical expertise that those assessments require may constitute a challenge to controlling legality via adversarial court procedures. The Court may consider that the matters at hand 'require complex economic assessments' and their review may be limited to examining whether procedural rules were complied with and whether an act contains a 'manifest error or constitutes a misuse of powers, or whether the authority did not clearly exceed

---

was bound to provide a detailed statement of reasons for its refutation' (emphasis added); and, regarding care, 'the circumstances which the ECB is criticised for having failed to take into account are irrelevant in the light of the wording of Article 70(1) of the SSM Framework Regulation[;] consequently, the ECB cannot be successfully criticised for having failed to take such circumstances into account in the application of that provision'.

[47] Articles 2(2), 7, and 11 of Regulation (EU) 1176/2011 of the European Parliament and of the Council of 16 November 2011 on the prevention and correction of macroeconomic imbalances; *OJ L* 306.

[48] Articles 2(2) and 5 of Regulation 1176/2011 (n 47).

[49] European Commission, Directorate-General for Economic and Financial Affairs, 'The Macroeconomic Imbalance Procedure - Rationale, Process, Application: A Compendium', November 2016, Foreword (available at <https://ec.europa.eu/info/sites/info/files/file_import/ip039_en_2.pdf>).

[50] Dawson, 'The Legal and Political Accountability' (n 33) 987. This may be disputed in the case of *Landeskreditbank* (n 40) and the Court's pending ruling may still invert this conclusion in this specific instance. Nevertheless, whatever the final outcome of this case, one should be mindful that instances in which primary decision makers interpret legal conditions of action in the absence of a Court ruling outweigh those that reach the Court.

[51] See, further, Mendes, 'Bounded Discretion' (n 8) 464–5. See, too, Borger, Chapter 6 in this volume.

the bounds of its discretion'.[52] Faced with legal challenges, the Court decides the degree to which legal normativity and rationality ought to mould those decisions by deploying general legal principles and arguments in a variable way in each instance.[53] While the legal principles and norms that they can deploy to check the legal rationality of discretionary decisions—proportionality, careful and impartial examination, reason-giving—may be tools of intense judicial scrutiny, the Court can also deploy them in a deferential way.[54] Arguably, if the public action that is subject to judicial scrutiny is successful in practice—a judgment that is not dependent on its legality—the Court may tend to be lenient regarding putative legal irregularities. If the Court places obstacles in the path of the functionally successful action, it would need to assume the cost thereof in situations in which an assessment of the legality of the particular action is codetermined by technical assessments and value judgments that the Court might not be well placed to assess.[55] In other instances, it might choose to interpret the constitutional and legal framework in a way that preserves the sphere of discretion that the legal norms attributed to executive actors.[56] Judicial scrutiny of the exercise of executive discretion is a fundamental cornerstone of legality and of the rule of law, in the EU as elsewhere. Yet, because of the very nature of discretion and of the institutional role of courts, that scrutiny—more deferent or more intense—is limited, as is an approach to the role of law in structuring discretion premised essentially on judicial review. Courts have a limited mandate when judging the conformity of executive discretion with the applicable law.

4. EU Executive Discretion and Law: Inversion and Subordination

Norm indeterminacy coupled with judicial deference, thus, may lead to an inversion of the relationship between executive discretion and law that deviates from the paradigm of implementation and the court-centric perspective from which such relationship was largely conceived.[57] However, this inversion does not necessarily lead to discarding legal normativity as an element that ought to structure the exercise of discretion. Rather, it invites a critical reflection on the ways in which law may structure executive discretion beyond that conventional paradigm.

Taking a step back from the specifics of the EU and adopting a general public law approach may provide the necessary critical distance to reflect on the limits of law in structuring discretion and to situate that analysis in a broader picture.

---

[52] For an earlier instance, see, e.g. Case C-55/75 *Balkan-Import Export GmbH v Hauptzollamt Berlin-Packhof*, EU:C:1976:8 [1976] para 8. See, further and in detail, Nehl, Chapter 8 in this volume.
[53] See Nehl, Chapter 8, Kosta, Chapter 9, and Hofmann, Chapter 10 in this volume.
[54] E.g. *Gauweiler* (n 1), *Landeskreditbank* (n 40). But, for an assessment of the Court's stringent review of manifest error, see Mendes, 'Discretion, Care and Public Interests' (n 7) 427–37.
[55] Drawing on *Gauweiler* (n 1), see M Goldmann, 'Adjudicating Economics? Central Bank Independence and the Appropriate Standard of Judicial Review' (2014) 15 *Ger Law J* 265. See, too, Borger, Chapter 6 and Kosta, Chapter 9 in this volume.
[56] Arguably the case in *ESMA* (n 1), where the Court revised the *Meroni* doctrine.
[57] Mendes, 'Bounded Discretion' (n 8) 459–62.

Thus, Chapter 2 by Bernardo Mattarella continues this first section on concepts, problems, and approaches by pointing out that the EU developments that form the background of this book are similar, in many respects, to those that have arisen in national legal orders facing the continuing growth of the administrative state. In fact, the problems of the relationship between law and discretion addressed in this book have a long-standing tradition in national legal orders. Mattarella's analysis brings the discussion back to national administrative law, exposing the continuity between how discretion and law are approached in national administrative law and in EU law, as well as the specificities of the problems of discretion in the EU. While the tools for limiting discretion in EU law and the reasons to preserve it are not different from those that have developed in national legal systems, discretion in EU law has additional layers of complexity, not least due to the fact that EU executive discretion contends not only with the protection of the autonomy of private parties, but also with the vertical allocation of power between the EU and the Member States. Mattarella talks about administrative discretion, distinguishing it from executive discretion in its subordination to law, in line with the observations in this chapter. Yet, he also argues that a proper assessment of the problem of discretion and its relationship to law in the EU must consider a complex matrix and may require public lawyers to move away from theories and concepts developed over the past two centuries in national law. Should, for example, the EU political executive actors be subject to constraints that have been developed to constrain the power of national (purportedly neutral) administrations? Mattarella does not address this question squarely, but this book suggests as much, given the scope of term 'EU executive' set forth above.

The complex matrix of factors one needs to consider when analysing law's ability to structure EU executive discretion ought not to lose sight of the specific characteristics of the EU as a polity and of its law. While norm indeterminacy and judicial deference are factors at play in both national and EU law, which, combined, may determine the inversion of the conventional relationship of subordination between discretion and law, norm indeterminacy in the EU may be one aspect of a deeper phenomenon that may decisively condition law's ability to structure discretion: EU law's high degree of constitutional fluidity fosters law's uncertainty. In Chapter 3, Takis Tridimas analyses various dimensions of this uncertainty, which include uncertainty regarding the sources of authority (stemming from the fusion between EU and collective Member State action, and from the intertwining between Member States' and EU institutions' actions, *inter alia*, in composite procedures and within EU agencies), recognition uncertainty (as to the very existence of a rule), content uncertainty, and ambiguity regarding the effects of rules. While uncertainty is present in any legal system and is an inevitable characteristic of government, Tridimas points out that, in important respects, the degree of uncertainty in EU law is unusual and, at times, particularly acute. His focus is on authority uncertainty and on effects uncertainty. Both lead to a mismatch between constitutional constraints and actual decision-making powers, which may condition the assertion that, even in weaker instances of legality, public authority in the EU is still legally constituted and discretion necessarily framed legally. Concluding the book's first part, in Chapter 4,

Mark Dawson steps in to explore different strategies that the EU political institutions can deploy to contain discretion in the context of economic governance. He analyses four strategies: deference in judicial review, prescription via soft law, proceduralism (i.e. the use of procedural rules to ensure deliberation and scrutiny, such as impact assessments), and inter-disciplinary justification. He discusses their respective advantages and normative weaknesses and the way they may facilitate or otherwise condition the role of the EU Courts in reviewing the exercise of discretion. The different assumptions and values behind these different strategies—likely to be combined in various instances of judicial review—point to the deeper issue of how to constrain EU executive discretion: choosing one or another strategy will shape not only what kind of judicial review develops in EU law, but also the role of the EU executive and the goals it should pursue.

No matter how one might conceive of law's ability to structure discretion, normative proposals should be assessed against concrete instances of discretion. The second part of the book focuses on specific relationships between law and discretion granted in EU financial and economic regulation, which may either reinforce or contest the doubts and problems raised earlier, as well as influence the possibilities for addressing them.[58] In Chapter 5, Niamh Moloney examines the discretion of the European Securities and Markets Authority (ESMA)—one of the European Supervisory Authorities (ESAs)—to highlight the 'hidden discretion' of these agencies and contrast it with the current constitutional and legal framework, which assumes that their scope of discretionary action is restricted. Behind the veneer of a dense thicket of norms, the normative implications of which may be difficult to assess or comprehend, lies a broad scope of discretion. Moloney analyses the specific constraints and limits of the agencies' discretion, by virtue of their position within the EU institutional set up. She argues that reconsideration of these constraints is necessary to secure the legitimacy of their actions. Such a reconsideration is warranted not only to adjust those constraints to the ESAs' present powers—they have not hitherto prevented ESAs from acting like autonomous financial regulatory authorities and making or determining public interest choices—but also in view of their possible expansion in an envisaged revision of the ESAs' governance framework.

The situation in which the holder of discretionary powers is an independent authority poses specific challenges to law's relationship to discretion. That the way discretion and independence are linked in the ECB's mandate has consequences for judicial review became clear in the Court's judgment in *Gauweiler*. In Chapter 6, Vestert Borger analyses the different approaches to discretion adopted by the German Constitutional Court in its reference decision in *Gauweiler* and by the Court in its ruling on that case. In doing so, he shows how, in instances of indeterminacy, it may be difficult to distinguish between the delineation of a competence and the exercise of discretionary power. This difficulty led the German Constitutional Court to conduct a stringent review that undermined the independence of the ECB. At the same time, the deferential approach of the Court, protective of the ECB's independence,

---

[58] See the conclusion of this book.

equated discretion with technicity leaving perhaps too much discretion to the ECB and minimizing the normative implications of the way the ECB exercised discretion. Could there be a middle way, in which the reviewing court could be more mindful of the value judgments that are a component of the exercise of discretion? In addressing this question, Borger turns to the unitary concept of discretion proposed by the editor of this volume and shows the potential as well as the difficulties of this conception to allow a degree of judicial review that preserves the independence of the ECB.

In Chapter 7, Päivi Leino and Tuomas Saarenheimo, in turn, examine the breadth of discretion that the EU executive has been granted in the framework of economic policy co-ordination. They analyse the powers of the Commission—whom they call the 'new (political) Commission'—in implementing the current Stability and Growth Pact (SGP) and the Macroeconomic Imbalances Procedure (MIP). Under rules with a high level of indeterminacy that are also qualified by numerous exceptions and flexibility clauses, or, in the case of the Macroeconomic Imbalances Procedure, in the absence of rules, the Commission's discretion seems to escape legal constraint. They stress an atypical situation in which discretion is exercised in relation to the Member States and potentially, but profoundly, impacts their policy choices in areas that, until recently, had been, and formally remain, the preserve of national parliaments and executives. In analysing the current powers of the Commission under the economic governance framework, they point out the mismatch between 'the faith in technocratic delegation' within the EU (to use their terms) and the political dimension of the delegated powers.

These sectoral analyses demonstrate the extent to which the specific legal contexts of executive discretion limit law's structuring ability. The limits are, perhaps, greater with regard to the Commission's discretion in the field of economic policy coordination, but they are also present, in a different way, in the case of the financial agencies and of the ECB. The analyses in the book's Part II seem to confirm the inversion argument mentioned above.[59] But, as demonstrated in Part III, that inversion hypothesis also depends on the role of judicial review, one of the possible avenues to shape law's relationship to discretion. It depends, more specifically, on the tools the EU Courts use when reviewing instances of the exercise of discretion; on how those tools have developed and functioned over the years, thereby enabling the Court to shape discretionary decisions according to the strictures of legal normativity; and on potential challenges the Court face in those areas where the law appears to fade. Part III examines both the tools of judicial review and the role of selected legal principles (i.e. care and proportionality) in structuring the exercise of discretion, and thereby, it broadens the analysis beyond the most recent developments in the fields of financial, economic, and monetary governance. Such tools and principles have been developed in other fields of law and are not sector specific. The way they have developed to structure the exercise of discretion in other policy fields and then applied to discretionary acts in the fields of economic, monetary, and financial regulation

---

[59] I return to this issue in the conclusion of the book.

highlights the extent to which the tensions between law and the exercise of discretion discussed in the first parts of the book are—or are not—specific to post-2010 developments.

In Chapter 8, Hanns Peter Nehl provides a rich analysis of the conceptual tools that the Court has used when reviewing discretionary decisions: 'manifest error of appraisal', standard of evidence and burden of proof, procedural guarantees (such as the duty to give reasons), fundamental rights, and principles of law (such as proportionality). He asks whether these are sufficient to strike a balance between effective judicial protection and the need to preserve the sphere of discretion of executive and administrative bodies, whether they have been consistently applied across different policy areas, and whether they require refinement. In doing so, he goes back to conceptual issues regarding law's relationship to discretion, showing the challenges they pose for effective judicial review in EU law. He highlights how, regardless of one's theoretical preconceptions on suitable balances between discretion and oversight, judges inevitably make value judgments about the relevant facts that ground the exercise of discretion. He shows how judges use and combine their tools of judicial review in a flexible way to reach what they deem to be an appropriate degree of oversight in each instance.

In Chapter 9, Vasiliki Kosta discusses the different dimensions of the principle of proportionality to tease out its ability to structure the exercise discretion, whether legislative or executive, and shape it according to legal–normative concerns. Of all the tools of judicial review, the principle of proportionality is perhaps the one most suited to structure according to legal standards the rationality of value judgments that are a component of discretion, because, as Kosta points out, proportionality always requires a set of conflicting interests that need to be 'balanced'. Premised on this idea, Kosta proposes a taxonomy of proportionality in EU law, based on the interest that it serves in each case. She argues that the legal interests worthy of protection in the exercise of discretion that proportionality is to serve are not always clear in the rulings of the Court when it is conducting a proportionality review. She also points out, however, that this does not mean that no interest is guiding the assessment of the Court. What she calls 'free-standing proportionality' to refer to the ambiguity of the protected interest may lead to a misapplication of the principle of proportionality, and may obscure the role of this principle in judicial review. This ambiguity has enabled the Court to make a strategic use of proportionality in reviewing the exercise of executive discretion. She shows how that played out concretely in the *Gauweiler* ruling.

In contrast to the principle of proportionality, the duty of careful and impartial examination has a distinctly administrative-law genesis. As Herwig Hofmann points out in Chapter 10, it is a procedural guarantee that emerged mostly to compensate the limited avenues for judicial review before the exercise of administrative discretion. Against the background of broader relationships between delegation, discretion, and procedural controls, Hofmann indicates the extent to which care and proportionality function as counterweights to discretionary power and how they have enabled the Court to extend its scope of review and their limits. In doing so, he also addresses the role and context of delegation of powers in EU law, in framing and constituting executive discretion, engages in the terminological ambiguity that pervades the case law on discretion, and argues that formal distinctions between technical and political aspects of decision making are inherently difficult to make.

Finally, Chapter 11 combines the different strands of arguments and the different themes that are discussed throughout the book. It both proposes building blocks for a conceptual–normative framework on the relationship between discretion and law in the EU, and assesses the possible paths to shape it, based on the book's contributions. In doing so, it shows the rich analysis that the book provides regarding the way law may structure discretion, its limits, and the specific challenges in the constitutional context of the EU.

2

Law and Discretion

A Public Law Perspective on the EU

*Bernardo Giorgio Mattarella**

1. Discretion and Administrative Decisions

The problem of administrative discretion arises in European law in a way that is substantially analogous to how it has arisen in the law of many Member States over the last two centuries. It is a problem of definition of the extent of the powers that legal provisions attribute to administrative bodies. Such a problem becomes more relevant in the historical moments in which administrative powers become more numerous or more important and, therefore, the demand for checks and balances increases. This is the situation that has occurred in recent years in the legal system of the European Union (EU), especially as a result of the 2008 financial crisis, which has led to the institution of new administrative bodies endowed with remarkable rule-making and adjudication powers (such as the European Security Markets Authority, ESMA) and the award of new powers to pre-existing administrative bodies (such as the European Central Bank, ECB), which imply a wide margin of appreciation.

In the legal doctrine of several Member States, different notions of administrative discretion have emerged over time, i.e. different ways of describing the margin of appreciation that statutory provisions leave to administrative bodies in the exercise of their powers: it has sometimes been described as a balancing of opposing interests,[1] sometimes as the application of indeterminate legal concepts or non-legal norms.[2] The conceptual tools that allowed the deepening of the judicial control over the discretionary choices have also been different in the different Member States: in France, the widening of the concept of legality; in Italy, the defect of misuse of power; in Germany, the principle of proportionality; in the United Kingdom (UK), the recognition of natural limits to administrative power.

---

* Professor of Administrative Law, Luiss Guido Carli University.
[1] This is the dominant thesis in Italy, dating back to M-S Giannini, *Il potere discrezionale della pubblica amministrazione* (Giuffrè, 1939).
[2] Especially in the German legal tradition. For a comparative overview, see J Mendes, 'Administrative Discretion in the EU: Comparative Perspectives', in S Rose-Ackerman and others (eds), *Comparative Administrative Law* (2nd edn, Edward Elgar, 2017) 632.

There are, however, at least two basic findings that are not contested. The first is that discretion is a characteristic of administrative power, i.e. the power recognized to an administrative body to make a decision that pursues the public interest, also affecting other interests, both public and private. The second is that such a power, like any legal power, is never totally free, nor totally bound: if there is a power, there is also a decision to be made, but this decision must be taken within the limits defined by the law. There is a continuous line between the two extremes of full freedom and the absence of power: according to its amount of discretion, every administrative power is placed in a different point of this line.

The theories of administrative discretion mainly address two problems. The first is how to identify the right point of that line, in which the single power must be placed, that is, the appropriate balance between predefined rules and appreciation on a case-by-case basis. These rules, as will be discussed later, can be of many different types. The picture is complicated by the fact that some of these rules are not set by statutory provisions, but instead are established by the courts, i.e. by those same subjects who have the task of verifying compliance with the rules by administrative bodies in the exercise of their powers.

The second problem is precisely that of judicial review of the decisions of administrative bodies and which has, in turn, two facets. One facet is the intensity of review, which translates into the number of rules, further than those imposed by statutory provisions, that courts can establish in order to verify the legality of single decisions: the intensity of review can come close to the point in which the court replaces its decision for that of the administration; the other facet is which types of choices are subject to the review of courts. The exercise of administrative powers implies the making of different types of choices.

For example, to establish if a bank has excessive exposures and its credits are risky requires a technical assessment, based on technical rules; identifying the powers of the supervisory authority is a legal issue, which must be addressed according to the law; defining the amount of the fine to be imposed on bank managers requires a purely administrative assessment, which must be reasonably made following a fair procedure; deciding whether to intervene with public money to save the bank is often a political decision, pertaining to governmental bodies. Which of these choices are subject to judicial review? It is often admitted that courts can replace their interpretation of legal provisions for that of the administrations;[3] it is less obvious that they can do the same with the value judgements; the case of technical assessments, that require the application of specialized rules, specific to certain sciences, techniques, or arts, is still different, as courts lack such knowledge. Furthermore, one can distinguish between the decisions concerning the assessment of the problem that the administration faces, and those concerning the choice of the most appropriate solution that it makes: when it comes to reviewing the conditions for the exercise of

---

[3] Although in the different legal systems there are different approaches to the problem of judicial review of questions of law, as shown by P Craig, 'Judicial Review of Questions of Law: A Comparative Perspective', in Rose-Ackerman and others (n 2) 389.

power, courts may have a different attitude to that of when they review the measure adopted by the administration.

The very distinction between these types of choice that the administration makes, in fact, is often elusive. Technical assessments and value judgements are continually intertwined. Administrative discretion concerns both the assessment of the conditions for the decision and the decision about its content, and both these choices are often a matter of interpretation of the law. The border between political and administrative assessments is clear only in theory, but extremely uncertain in the daily practice of public administrations, whose choices almost always affect different interests and are almost never exquisitely political or exquisitely executive. Similarly, the distinction between rule making and adjudication is clear in the abstract, but in practice every administrative power is placed on a different point of the continuous line between general and detailed choices. Moreover, administrative bodies often face new cases, not foreseen by the legislator. Finally, it is difficult for administrative bodies, even when they are supposed to make exclusively judicial or technical assessments, to ignore the relevant effects of their decisions on public and private interests.

It is often the law that undermines the distinctions discussed here. The enabling legislation is sometimes extremely detailed to the point that administrative bodies are deprived of any decisional autonomy. But legislation may also be sometimes so generic that leaves it up to those bodies to make fundamental policy decisions. At the same time, the legislative provisions governing administrative powers require the administrative bodies to carry out different types of assessment at the same time: e.g. certain provisions incorporate technical rules making the interpretation of the law coincide with the technical choices, while others refer to indeterminate legal concepts that call for evaluations of opportunities (such as 'the most appropriate measures') or technical evaluations (such as 'the state of the art').

The legal doctrine has begun to realize all these connections and the limited usefulness of those distinctions. In recent years, in the various legal cultures, scholars have increasingly recognized the difficulty of distinguishing between these types of choices and have proposed comprehensive theories that examine the problem of judicial review of discretionary decisions in unitary terms.[4]

This chapter examines the problems of discretion with reference to the legal system of the EU, which, in many respects, goes through a 'growth crisis' similar to those crossed by many national legal systems on the occasion of the institution of new types of administrative authorities and of the provision of new types of administrative powers. The subsequent sections deal with the following themes: the reasons and the tools to limit the discretion of administrative bodies (Section 2); the subjects to whom the law entrusts the task of limiting it (Section 3); the situations in which there are reasons not to limit it excessively (Section 4); the legitimacy of administrative powers and its relationship with the search for the right balance between discretionary powers and their limits (Section 5).

---

[4] For a comparative analysis and a critique of the 'segmented understanding of discretion', J Mendes, 'Bounded Discretion in EU Law: A Limited Judicial Paradigm in a Changing EU' (2017) 80 *Mod L Rev* 443.

2. The Case for Binding Discretion

The problem of administrative discretion arises because administrative powers are subject to much stricter limits than those to which private powers are subject. The reason, of course, is that administrative bodies manage public resources and exercise—according to the French term—'exorbitant' powers. Rules and controls are needed to ensure that public resources are used properly and that administrative powers do not produce injustice to citizens. In European law, the framework is often complicated by the interaction between the European and national administrations, which splits up administrative decisions and removes the correspondence between powers and review bodies. An example of such effect is provided by the decisions concerning the allocation of certain European funds, which are taken by European authorities on the basis of assessments by national administrative bodies. Another effect of this interaction is the possibility that European authorities' decisions affect previous decisions made by national ones, as in the case of state aid granted by the national administration. In such cases, peculiar problems may arise, such as the overlapping of different discretionary decisions and the identification of the reviewing court.[5]

The tools for limiting discretion in European law are not different from those developed in national laws: the limitation results from a combination of rules and controls.

The rules can be substantial, as they concern the content of the decision, or procedural, as they are related to the decision-making process. European administrative law also displays a peculiar complexity from the point of view of the rules aimed at limiting discretion. The complexity derives from the plurality of entities producing legal norms: the same administrative decision can consequently be subject to the limits and conditions laid down both by national law and by European law; the latter can overlap or replace the former. This happens, for example, for the annulment or revocation of national administrations' acts: European law requires these administrations to annul their provisions that violate European law, thus limiting the discretion often recognized by national law; or it authorizes the annulment of those measures, even in cases where national law would not allow it, thus eliminating a limit set by national law.[6]

Legislators often struggle to restrict administrative discretion with very detailed substantive rules. In European law there is an additional reason to produce detailed rules: EU institutions only apply the many rules they adopt to a limited extent, as implementation is mainly left to the Member States' administrations. For this reason, European law often undertakes to harmonize the laws of the Member States, so as to subject the powers exercised by the national administrative bodies to the

---

[5] G della Cananea, 'The European Union's Mixed Administrative Proceedings' (1997) 68 *Law Contemp Probl* 197.

[6] See, for example, Case C-453/00 *Kühne & Heitz* [2004] ECLI:EU:C:2004:17; and Case C-2/06 *Kempter* [2006] ECLI:EU:C:2008:78.

same substantive and procedural rules. Detailed rules are therefore an instrument with which the Union tries to ensure the uniform application of European law by a plurality of administrative bodies. The abundance of legal norms can be counter-productive, because it can cause uncertainty and compel frequent changes to the norms themselves, which in turn generates uncertainty and multiplies the choices regarding the identification and interpretation of the law to apply in the concrete cases. These dangers can be sighted in the impetuous regulatory production that characterizes sectors in which European regulators have repeatedly intervened in recent years, e.g. financial regulation and banking supervision.

It is not only the written statutory provisions that limit discretion, but also the principles developed by courts. Also, from this point of view, European administrative law does not differ from national law, as even the European courts have developed principles of substantive law (such as that of proportionality) and procedural law (such as that of the due process of law) and have imposed their respect to the European administrative bodies. Since the European courts were born after the national administrative courts had carried out this creative work for a few decades, European law benefited from the work done by them, incorporating many principles that had been developed at the national level. Moreover, European law has played a role of homogenization of national administrative laws: once those principles were incorporated into European law, they also spread to the Member States other than those in which they had been developed. The principle of proportionality is a good example of this dynamic: it was mainly developed by German administrative jurisprudence; European courts regularly apply it and have contributed to spread it in the domestic laws of other Member States. The principle of proportionality implies, inter alia, the prohibition of manifestly unreasonable decisions and the preference for the least detrimental solutions for the interested parties.[7] Another principle developed by the case law is the obligation of administrative bodies to consider carefully and impartially all the interests involved and the relevant circumstances, which is often coupled with the principle of proportionality.[8] As is evident, these are principles that are easily applicable to both legislative and administrative decisions: not by chance, they are extensively used by the Court of Justice of the European Union, which reviews both legislative and administrative acts.

In the absence of statutory provisions and in addition to the case law principles, administrative bodies themselves can limit their discretion in the concrete cases, establishing decisional criteria in order to predetermine the content of their subsequent decisions. Such criteria, in national legal systems, are not usually binding law; therefore, their violation cannot be qualified as violation of a legal provision. However, it can be considered a symptom of misuse of administrative power (which in some legal systems is called 'excess of power') or a violation of the principle of reasonableness and, therefore, can still cause the invalidity of an individual decision. This is also the case in European law, where such predetermination is a remedy

---

[7] On the principle of proportionality in EU law, see further Kosta, Chapter 9 in this volume.
[8] See Hoffmann, Chapter 10 in this volume.

for legislative provisions' breadth and vagueness, e.g. the regulation on prudential supervision requires the ECB to 'adopt guidelines and recommendations'.[9] This shows that administrative bodies can limit their own discretion, with soft law tools that reconcile the need for predictability of decisions and that of flexibility and, at the same time, shows the occasional inadequacy of command and control techniques.

Procedural rules are also a way to limit discretion, through the regulation of the way in which the decisions of the administrations are formed. In this regard, first and foremost the general principles of the administrative procedure must be considered, which are aimed at the adoption of adequately prepared and pondered decisions. The most important are those of reasonable duration, due process, statement of reasons, and right of access to administrative files. On these principles there is a great convergence at the European level and also among non-European legal systems. They are set out in the laws on the administrative procedure of several Member States. The EU has no general law on the administrative procedure,[10] but the principles mentioned are stated in Article 41 of the Charter of Fundamental Rights, which declares the right to a good administration, and in the Code of Good Administrative Behaviour drafted by the European Ombudsman. Even secondary law tends to refer to the same principles, as in the case of the proposal for a directive on national competition authorities, which, by way of protection of fundamental rights, establishes that 'the exercise of the powers referred to in this Directive by national competition authorities shall be subject to appropriate safeguards, including respect of undertakings' rights of defence and the right to an effective remedy before a tribunal'.[11]

These procedural principles can be applied to both rule-making and adjudication procedures, but of course there are differences in their application: the principle of due process, for example, gives rise to much more complex procedures for the former than for the latter. For rule making, there are further procedural mechanisms, also aimed at regulating the making of administrative decisions and limiting administrations' discretion. The regulatory impact assessment also figures among these mechanisms and imposes a decision-making method based on the evaluation of the various relevant aspects, on the balancing of costs and benefits, and on the involvement of stakeholders. Regulatory impact assessment has spread widely in many member states in the last thirty years for both primary and secondary legislation: it is not only an instrument for evidenced-based policy making, but also a means

---

[9] Art 4 of Council Regulation (EU) 1024/2013 conferring specific tasks on the European Central Bank concerning policies relating to the prudential supervision of credit institutions.

[10] In spite of two recommendations of the European Parliament and of a broad scientific debate on the subject. With reference to a codification project of the administrative procedure, drafted by a network of European academics, see DU Galetta, HCH Hofmann, O Mir Puigpelat, and J Ziller, 'Context and Legal Elements of a Proposal for a Regulation on the Administrative Procedure of the European Union's Institutions, Bodies, Offices and Agencies' (2016) *Rivista italiana di diritto pubblico comunitario* 313.

[11] Art 3 of the Proposal for a Directive of the European Parliament and of the Council to empower the competition authorities of the Member States to be more effective enforcers and to ensure the proper functioning of the internal market (2017) (COM 2017) 142 final), available at: <http://ec.europa.eu/transparency/regdoc/rep/1/2017/EN/COM-2017-142-F1-EN-MAIN-PART-1.PDF> accessed 22 May 2018.

to control the administrative bodies' regulations and to ensure their consistency with governmental policies.[12] It is not uncommon in European law in procedures leading to non-legislative acts, as shown by provisions as the regulation on banking supervision, which states that normally, 'before adopting a regulation, the European Central Bank will conduct open public consultations and analyse the potential related costs and benefits'.[13]

In addition to the general principles of the administrative procedure, it is necessary to consider the sectoral procedural rules contained in sectoral laws, which regulate the many administrative powers conferred by such laws. European law has traditionally been little interested in the detailed procedural rules, in relation to which it left a certain degree of autonomy to the Member States. However, the lack of procedural rules sometimes leads to differences in the implementation of European law, which consequently tends sometimes to limit that autonomy[14] and to regulate the structure of national administrative procedures: this happens quite prominently in the regulation of public contracts, which is essentially a procedural regulation.

The second type of instrument to limit discretion is controls, in relation to which the fundamental distinction is between judicial review, operated by the courts, and administrative remedies, managed by administrative bodies on their own decisions or on those of other administrative bodies. In some legal systems, the distinction is very rigid, while in others there are semi-judicial bodies of an ambiguous nature: this is especially the case of the UK, with its system of specialized administrative courts, which have progressively detached themselves from the administrative apparatus and approached the judicial system. In European law, courts are quite clearly separated from the administrations, so the distinction is quite clear.

Judicial review is obviously aimed at ensuring the respect of the law by administrative bodies. Its purpose is therefore to check whether the administrative decisions comply with legal rules. As discussed, however, such rules are partly elaborated by courts themselves. Courts, therefore, are not only guardians of the faithful application of the written legal rules, but also guardians of the rule of law in the broad sense. Judicial control is considered a fundamental right both in national and in European law, where it is stated by Article 47 of the Charter of Fundamental Rights.

Administrative remedies in many national legal systems are older than judicial review: the right to propose appeals to administrative bodies against the decisions of other bodies was recognized before the right to judicial protection and, in many continental European countries, administrative courts were born from the ashes of bodies in charge of administrative litigation. This is the case of the French Council

---

[12] For a comparative analysis, see *OECD Regulatory Policy Outlook 2015* (OECD Publishing, 2015) 93 ff.

[13] Art 4 of Council Regulation (EU) 1024/2013 conferring specific tasks on the European Central Bank concerning policies relating to the prudential supervision of credit institutions. On impact assessment as a means to control discretion, see Dawson, Chapter 4 in this volume.

[14] On the actual substance of such autonomy, see DU Galetta, *Procedural Autonomy of EU Member States: Paradise Lost? A Study on the 'Functionalized Procedural Competence' of EU Member States* (Springer, 2010).

of State, which, in the second half of the nineteenth century, switched from the 'retained justice' model to the 'delegated justice' one, as well as that of the Italian equivalent. During the second half of the twentieth century, however, the improvement of judicial review (due in part to European law, which, in some areas, requires Member States to have effective and timely redress procedures) has made administrative checks less important. The usefulness of administrative remedies has been questioned. In some states, such as Italy, this crisis depends on the lack of confidence in the effectiveness of these remedies and on the possibility of immediately proposing a judicial appeal, often considered a more effective instrument of protection.[15] Even in states, e.g. Germany, where administrative remedies have had an important standing (being in some cases a necessary passage before the appeal to the court), they are the object of debate, because it is sometimes observed that they are a complication in the path to judicial review.[16] In recent years, however, the growing complexity of administrative systems has led to the rediscovery of administrative remedies, entrusted, for example, to independent bodies set up within the regulatory authorities.

This trend is also reflected in European law, where, since the 1990s, various administrative appeals bodies have been established, especially in the European agencies, such as the European Chemicals Agency, the European Aviation Safety Agency, the Agency for the Cooperation of Energy Regulation, and the European Union Intellectual Property Office. In the last years, similar boards have been established in the areas of regulation and supervision of financial markets, after the reforms carried out following the 2008 financial crisis:[17] such boards face the problem of the intensity of control over broadly discretionary decisions.[18]

A further form of control over the conduct of administrative bodies, now widespread in many Member States, is administrative transparency, which allows all interested parties to know the facts and documents on which administrative decisions are based. There are different models of administrative transparency, but a fundamental distinction can be made between the case in which transparency is instrumental to the protection of a specific interest of an individual party, which may be affected by the administrative decision, and the case in which it is an end in itself and aims to allow all citizens to participate in public decisions and monitor the conduct of public officers. The first need is often addressed with laws that recognize

---

[15] R Caranta, 'Administrative Appeals in Italy' in JB Auby (ed), with T Perroud, *Droit comparé de la procédure administrative—Comparative Law of Administrative Procedure* (Bruylant, 2016) 795.

[16] A Jacquemet-Gauché and U Stelkens, 'Les recours administratifs en droit allemand', in Auby and Perroud (n 15) 741.

[17] For a general overview and an exam of several administrative remedies provided by European law, see B Marchetti (ed), *Administrative Remedies in the European Union. The Emergence of a Quasi-judicial Administration* (Giappichelli, 2017). See also S Cassese, *A European Administrative Justice?* Opening remarks for the Conference jointly organized by the Bank of Italy and the European Banking Institute on 'Judicial Review in the Banking Union and in the EU Financial Architecture', Rome, Bank of Italy, 21 November 2017 (forthcoming).

[18] See, e.g. concerning the Administrative Board of Review (ABoR) of the Single Supervisory Mechanism, C Brescia Morra, 'The Administrative and Judicial Review of Decisions of the ECB in the Supervisory Field' in R D'Ambrosio (ed), *Quaderni di Ricerca Giuridica*, Vol 81 (Bank of Italy, 2016) 7.

the right of access of interested parties to the administrative documents relating to them. Many states, a few years after adopting similar laws, have added other laws (sometimes called the Freedom of Information Act) to address the second need, recognizing the right of access of all citizens to public information or by stating the administrations' duty to publish certain information and documents.[19] The origin of the second form of transparency is Scandinavian. From this point of view, European law is less advanced than that of many Member States, because it has a regulation on access to administrative documents for the interested parties, but it does not have a Freedom of Information Act. In the European context, however, such a law would be less useful than in the national contexts, due to the limited size of the European administration and to the concentration of its offices in few physical places.

3. Discretion and the Balance of Powers

The previous section examined the reasons and the instruments of the limitation of discretion. It is now necessary to complete the analysis, considering that any limitation of the power of one party is to the advantage of other parties, and to whom the portion of power that is subtracted from the former is attributed. This suggests that the control of discretion has to do with the separation of powers.[20] Discretion is a typical feature of acts of the executive and of the administrative power. Limiting discretion means, obviously, recognizing a greater role for other public authorities. In fact, the history of administrative discretion in European states is a history of relationships: first, between administrations and courts and, subsequently, between administrations and the legislator.

The concept of administrative discretion was developed in France in the first half of the nineteenth century to indicate the acts of administrative bodies not subject to judicial review, in accordance with the principle of separation of powers. It expresses, therefore, the tension between the need to prevent courts from replacing the administration in the fulfilment of the choices reserved for it, and that of ensuring control over the administrative activity and of guaranteeing protection for citizens' interests, which can be sacrificed or not satisfied by administrative decisions.

The subsequent evolution of the concept, in France and in other European countries, was determined by the rule of law, which posed the problem of the magnitude of administrative powers in relation to the legislative provisions. The concept of discretion, which originally indicated the sphere of freedom reserved for administrative bodies, ended up indicating an assessment power that is not only limited, but must also be performed, on the basis of substantive and procedural rules such as those mentioned in Section 2.

---

[19] For a comparative overview, M Savino, 'The Right to Open Public Administration in Europe: Emerging Legal Standards' (2011) *Sigma Paper* 46; BG Mattarella and M Savino, *L'accesso dei cittadini. Esperienze di informazione amministrativa a confronto* (Editoriale scientifica, 2018) .

[20] The margin of autonomy of administrative bodies with respect to courts and to the legislator is a perennial object of debate: see, e.g. T Bingham, *The Rule of Law* (Penguin, 2010) 48 ff.

The role of statutory law as a limit to discretion has been accentuated by legal positivism and by the widespread concept of administration as execution of law. This concept does not correspond to the nineteenth-century origin of administrative law, which is linked to the emergence of few special rules, aimed at regulating the behaviour of administrative bodies, occasionally limiting the autonomy recognized by private law. It does not even correspond to the first decades of its evolution characterized by the elaboration of general rules of administrative action by the courts. However, in the second half of the twentieth century, in many national legal systems, the centrality of parliaments and the explosion of administrative legislation have often led to the view that statutory law constitutes the foundation and justification of all administrative activity and that the task of the administrative bodies is simply to execute the law. This notion has often produced some discomfort for administrative discretion and a tendency to circumscribe it as much as possible. If, instead, administration is conceived as care of public interests, in compliance with the law, discretion appears to be a natural feature of administrative powers.

Today, the concept of administration as execution of law is challenged by legislative provisions that define the conditions or the content of administrative decisions in a very vague, almost indefinite way. This occurs when the law provides for a certain measure to be adopted 'when the competent authority deems it appropriate' or 'in cases of serious need' and when the law defines the content of the decision by referring to the 'most appropriate measures' or to the 'suitable tools' to solve a problem. Such provisions, in European as well as national law, are the product of several factors: the complexity of some recently regulated sectors, such as certain food, industrial or financial matters; the novelty of the problems that they pose, and that the legislator is not able to predict; the need to adapt the regulation to the innovations introduced by private operators, which continually highlights the holes and defects in regulation; and the allocation of sectoral regulatory tasks to highly specialized authorities, who are asked to make assessments that the legislator is not able to make.

Legislative provisions of these types are all the more problematic, considering the implications of the principle of rule of law. In national law, even when it is accepted that the administration is not the only execution of law, this principle requires that administrative decisions, which have a restrictive effect on private interests, are expressly provided for by statutory law: the conditions and effects of the exercise of administrative powers must be defined by the legislator. Provisions such as those mentioned are critical from this point of view, because they make those assumptions or effects uncertain.

The problem of the legal basis of administrative powers is further complicated at the European level, due to the principle of conferral, which requires that the powers of the European institutions should be limited and expressly provided for. This suggests that, in the European law, the problem of discretion concerns not only the relations between administration, the judiciary, and the legislator, but also the relations between the EU and Member States. From this point of view, European law often raises a further problem, unknown to national laws. In national law, in fact, the legal provisions that grant powers to administrative bodies introduce limits to the freedom of individuals, which otherwise would not exist. The European legislative provisions that grant administrative powers to European bodies, on the other hand, often do not introduce new powers, but transfer powers from the national to the European administration: therefore, they are alternatives not to the absence of regulation, but to national regulations. In fact, European legislation does not usually regulate new matters not previously regulated: it intervenes in matters hitherto regulated by the laws of the Member States. This is the case, for example, for public procurement, for competition, for banking supervision, and for trade in pharmaceutical products. European law appropriates all or part of these matters, replacing national disciplines or, more often, inducing Member States to modify them for the purpose of harmonization: in this context, sometimes administrative competences, e.g. the power to make individual decisions, are in turn transferred in whole or in part to the European administrations. They are sometimes left to the national ones, but are subject to compliance with European legal norms. The transfer of administrative powers and the subjection to European legal norms produces significant effects, for example, by changing the conditions in which the persons concerned can take part in the procedure and by transferring to the European courts the jurisdiction over possible appeals.

The problem of discretion of European administrative bodies, therefore, is also a problem of the distribution of administrative powers between the EU and the Member States. The picture is further complicated by the fact that some discretionary powers that European law gives to European bodies are not exercised against private individuals, but against the Member States, which are no longer regulators and have become regulated.[21] Such powers inevitably have a certain political colouring: it is quite obvious, for example, that the decision to initiate an infringement procedure against a Member State implies a legal assessment, but is also influenced by the Commission's general policy guidelines; likewise, relevant decisions, such as those relating to the excessive deficit procedure, involve delicate assessments, which take into account, for example, the political cycle of the Member State concerned. The relations between supranational institutions and Member States can certainly not be assimilated to those between an administrative body and a private party: this justifies greater flexibility but exacerbates the problem of discretion.

It is not surprising, therefore, that the distinction between political discretion and technical discretion is upheld in the European case law.[22] Neither is it surprising that in the European law the problem of administrative discretion has widened after some recent reforms, especially in the banking and financial sectors, which have given considerable powers, including rule-making powers, to European administrative bodies.[23] Such powers put these bodies in a position of supremacy towards the national administrative authorities. These powers are often characterized by wide discretion or by the transfer of discretion from the national to the European

---

[21] On this problem, see Leino and Saarenheimo, Chapter 7 in this volume.

[22] See the opinion of AG P Léger of 17 February 2005 (Opinion Case C-40/03 *Rica Foods v Commission* [2005] EU:C:2005:93, para 48).

[23] See further Moloney, Chapter 5 in this volume.

level: e.g. the field of banking supervision, where the powers still left to the national authorities must be exercised within the framework of standards and guidelines set out at the supranational level.[24]

Furthermore, the discretion of the European administrative bodies also affects the relations between the EU and the Member States, since such bodies can assess the way in which the national ones perform their functions and also have substitutive powers towards them. A good example of this is the discretion which ESMA enjoys, in relation to the temporary ban on the marketing and sale of certain financial products or the performance of financial activities, in assessing whether the competent authority has taken appropriate measures.[25]

4. The Case for Unbinding Discretion

What has been observed so far shows that the reasons for limiting administrative discretion have to do with the relations between public powers and, in the European law, also with the relations between EU and Member States. There are, however, also reasons not to limit discretion too much, i.e. reasons to leave a certain margin of assessment to the administrative bodies, or at least reasons to use only some tools to limit it and not others. These reasons, too, are common to both national laws and European law.

To examine these reasons, one should reason in terms of discretionary powers. A short remark of general theory of law is necessary. Power is a technique of producing legal effects, which the law uses when it cannot directly produce the desired legal effect, because it cannot regulate all the situations that may occur in practice. Certain legislative provisions immediately produce their desired effects, without the need for further actions or decisions. This happens, for example, for the statutes that recognize a right, such as freedom of expression, or impose an obligation, such as that to compensate for the damage done to others: if everyone respects the law, such legislative provisions produce the desired effects without further legal action. In other cases, for the better protection of a certain interest, statutes do not directly produce the desired effect, but provide a certain person with the power to produce it. This may be in the interest of the holder of power (such as the employer who can decide to dismiss the employee who has committed a serious violation, but may also decide not to terminate the employment contract), or in the interest of others (such as the manager of a company, who can decide to hire a new employee or not). Administrative powers, of course, fall within the latter hypothesis, because they are always conferred to an administrative body for the best protection of the public interest.

---

[24] As established by various provisions of Council Regulation (EU) 1024/2013 conferring specific tasks on the European Central Bank concerning policies relating to the prudential supervision of credit institutions.
[25] Art 40 of the Regulation (EU) 600/14 of the European Parliament and of the Council on market in financial instruments and amending Regulation No 648/2012.

The legal technique that we call administrative power, therefore, is based on the deciding role of a party, which, in this case, is the public administration. When the law confers a power to an administrative body, it attributes to the administrative body a mediating role between the norm and the desired legal effect. Power, therefore, is often an element of flexibility, necessary for the effective application of the law. For example, administrative authorizations are necessary to produce the desired effect of the law (to allow a private activity, without risks for the public interest), as are administrative fines (whose desired effect is to impose a punishment proportionate to the gravity of the committed infringement): without the intervention of the competent administrative body, these effects could not be produced.

In some cases, European law tends to eliminate power precisely to eliminate this flexibility. This happens, for example, in the field of services, where European law tends to eliminate or neutralize administrative authorizations. For national law, as mentioned, authorizations are a useful instrument of flexibility to ensure more effective protection of the public interest. For European law, they are often barriers to market access, which can be used by national administrative bodies to favour national companies and to exclude those of other member states, i.e. to favour the national interest over the interest of the common market: flexibility is precisely what the European law seeks to eliminate in these cases. The services directive, therefore, allows for authorization schemes only if they are 'justified by an overriding reason relating to the public interest' and 'proportionate to that public interest objective'. Most notably, such schemes must 'be based on criteria which preclude the competent authorities from exercising their power of assessment in an arbitrary manner', and such criteria must have certain features (non-discriminatory, clear, and unambiguous objectives, made public in advance, transparent, and accessible) that neutralize discretion.[26]

In other cases, however, European law extensively utilizes this technique of producing legal effects. The conferral of administrative powers by European legislation is very frequent, in favour of European administrative bodies, in favour of national authorities, and also in favour of both, in the case of mixed procedures. The conferral of administrative powers to the European administration occurs in matters of direct execution, such as that of competition, and, from the point of view of discretion, does not raise problems different from those it raises in national law. The granting of administrative powers to national administrative bodies by European law occurs in many other fields, e.g. trade in pharmaceutical products and banking supervision, and raises peculiar problems, as these powers could be used to restrict access to the single market or to hinder its functioning. In order to prevent such use of administrative powers, their conferral is normally accompanied by legislative harmonization, which imposes common rules for the exercise of administrative powers by the administrative bodies of the various member states: this is clearly a way to limit discretion.

---

[26] Arts 9, 10 of the Directive (EC) 2006/123 of the European Parliament and of the Council of 12 December 2006 on services in the internal market.

Regardless of the subject who exercises it, the conferral of an administrative power means that some flexibility is necessary or useful. This implies that the administrative bodies must be able to make their decisions without excessive constraints, to ensure speed in carrying out their tasks. If discretion is too limited, the administration's action risks being inefficient. And, if the controls of courts and administrative bodies are too intense, the decision, which the law has attributed to a certain body, risks being transferred to the controlling authorities.

Thus, there are reasons to limit discretion and reasons not to limit it. The balance between the two depends on several factors, especially the type of decision, the authority that must make the decision, and the circumstances in which the decision is made.

The balance between discretion and limits depends, firstly, on the type of decision and, therefore, on the type of administrative power to be exercised. The need to limit discretion, in fact, is stronger for some types of power than for others, and the choice of tools to limit discretion is also affected by the type of power with which one is dealing. The need to limit discretion has arisen historically earlier for unfavourable decisions towards recipients, such as sanctions, and subsequently for favourable ones, such as authorizations and grants. The tools for limiting discretion may also vary: for unfavourable decisions, procedural requirements, such as the due process, are very important, while for favourable ones, substantial rules, such as that of equal treatment, may be more important. The due process principle is a good example: it corresponds to a particularly strong need in the procedures aimed at the imposition of fines, in which, similarly to what happens in the criminal trial, the accused should be given a right of defence. In such proceedings, this principle has been affirmed by the courts of various European states already at the end of the nineteenth century or at the beginning of the twentieth century[27] (and much earlier in the UK).[28] The principle of hearing the interested persons was then extended to various adjudication procedures or to all of them; during the twentieth century, it began to be applied to rule-making procedures (the US law on the administrative procedure of 1946 was a turning point in this respect), while the laws on the administrative procedure of some Member States continue to affirm due process principle only with reference to adjudication.[29] The distinction between rule making and adjudication, in fact, is often relevant: for example, the right of access to administrative documents is much more consolidated for the latter than for the former. This distinction is taken up by the Charter of Fundamental Rights of the European Union, which recognizes the right to be heard and the right of access to files only in adjudication procedures and not in rule-making procedures.[30]

---

[27] See, for example, for Italy and France, Consiglio di Stato, 17.5.1907, *Chiantera*; and Conseil d'Etat, 20.6.1913, *Téry*.

[28] King's Bench, *R v University of Cambridge* [1723] 1 Str 557.

[29] On the nonexistence of a general principle of due process in Italy, Germany, and France, see respectively G della Cananea, 'Administrative Rulemaking in Italy: Theories and Practice', A Jacquemet-Gauché and U Stelkens, 'La participation à l'élaboration des règlements administratifs en Allemagne', and J Richard and V Kapsali, 'La participation à l'élaboration des règlements administratifs en France', all in in Auby and Perroud (n 15) 246, 261, 317.

[30] Art 41 of Charter of Fundamental Rights of European Union.

A second factor influencing the need to mitigate or to select the limits to discretionary powers is the authority exercising discretion. From this point of view, two types of decision makers raise the most interesting problems: independent authorities and political bodies.

Regulatory authorities independent from political bodies have spread in the last few decades in various Member States and in recent years in the EU, particularly in the financial sector since the 2008 financial crisis. The two developments are linked, as the spread of such authorities in the Member States has sometimes been facilitated, sometimes imposed, by the European law: facilitated, because in many sectors, such as finance and public utilities, their establishment has been a consequence of the liberalization required by European law; imposed in areas in which European law requires each Member State to entrust certain tasks to a body independent of political power.[31] Both national and European law tend to entrust these authorities with the management of particularly complex sectors, which requires great technical expertise, and to grant them wide discretionary powers in the assessment of the conditions for the measures they adopt and in the definition of the content of their decisions. This discretion often entails technical judgements and, as explained in Section 5, this has often made it possible to overcome doubts about the legitimacy of their powers.

Independent regulators are a challenging test for theories on administrative discretion. As an example, the concept of discretion as a balancing of interests is challenged by laws establishing independent authorities with the task of pursuing a single public interest (e.g. financial stability of banks or fair processing of personal data) and giving these authorities wide discretion in the assessment of the conditions for their action and of the content of their decisions. The problems that these authorities have to face (e.g. in monetary matters) are so complex and unpredictable that there is no alternative to wide discretion. As a result, sometimes the law renounces placing substantial limits on their discretion and focuses on procedural rules and forms of control that are respectful of independence, such as internal redress mechanisms and transparency. All this can occasionally be found in European law, as demonstrated by the events of the Outright Monetary Transactions programme of the ECB.[32]

The need to preserve a reserved sphere of assessment, and therefore to not limit discretion too much, is even stronger when the decision is entrusted to a political body, such as the government or ministers in the national legal systems. The conception of governments and of their members varies greatly from one Member State to another: the nature of their acts can be considered political or administrative in nature, or both. The government and the administrative bodies can be considered as a unit, or as distinct authorities, each having its own responsibilities. However,

---

[31] See, e.g. two cases decided by the European Court of Justice, related to the telecommunications sector: Case C-424/07 *European Commission v Federal Republic of Germany* [2009] ECLI:EU:C:2009:749; and Case C-518/07 *European Commission v Federal Republic of Germany* [2010] ECLI:EU:C:2010:125.

[32] On the challenges that the independence of the ECB poses to discretion, see Borger, Chapter 6 in this volume.

there is a difference between the acts of the political bodies and those of the common administrative authorities. The latter must pursue the interests established by the laws or by decisions of political bodies. The former, instead, can choose not only the means, but also the ends: it is up to them to identify the public interests to be pursued. The democratic legitimacy that political organs enjoy affects in turn the extent of the powers and their methods of exercise. For example, the due process principle, which requires the involvement of the interested parties, may seem superfluous in the case of political bodies as it is often considered a sort of surrogate of the political process, useful for enabling the deciding administration to have a fair representation of the relevant interests: for political bodies, the political process to which they are subject may make a surrogate process superfluous.

The foregoing explains why, in national law, political acts are usually subject to a special legal regime often characterized by fewer procedural requirements, and sometimes by the exclusion of judicial control or by its weaker intensity. This legal regime must now be reconciled with the principles of the rule of law and of judicial protection, generally recognized in national and European law so that the total exclusion of judicial control now tends to be denied or admitted only in very rare cases. However, the decisions of the political bodies continue to be given greater discretion and, therefore, the courts often show an attitude of deference towards them. This does not mean that there are no rules and controls on such acts, but it means that there are fewer rules and less-intense controls, often based on very general standards, such as those of reasonableness and proportionality. However, rules and controls can concentrate on the administrative acts that come before or after the adoption of political decisions. For example, the governmental appointment of the manager of a state-owned company can be considered a political act, but the acts of the selection process of candidates, which precedes the appointment, may be subject to judicial review. Similarly, the government directives addressed to that manager may be political decisions, but the subsequent acts, put in place by the manager, may be subject to judicial review.

All this occurs also in European law as regards the decisions of the European Commission concerning the excessive deficit of the Member States. However, once again, the picture is complicated by the peculiarities of the European legal system: democratic legitimacy, at least for some European institutions, is less evident and the very distinction between political and administrative bodies is elusive.[33] The difference is not only due to the peculiarities of the EU's system of governance and to the absence of a clear distinction between political choices and administrative management, but also to historical and quantitative factors: national administrations are very large, diverse, and complex organizations, and they pre-exist political institutions, which therefore have a steering role but are not the *raison d'être* of administrations. In the EU, on the other hand, the political institutions predate the administrative apparatus of limited dimensions that developed to provide support to the institutions in carrying out their tasks. Moreover, this administrative

---

[33] See, further, Mendes, Chapter 1 in this volume.

apparatus often relies on forms of collaboration between different European bodies (for example, the Commission and ESMA) or the involvement of national administrations in the governance of European entities (such as the ECB and the European agencies). Thus, many of the problems discussed so far, such as the basis of the powers of the European administration, the ways of exercising discretionary power, and the technical evaluations, cross and overlap. For example, an administrative decision of an independent national authority raises a delicate problem of legitimacy if it is adopted on the basis of criteria established by an EU authority (usually the EU agency operating in the same field) that follows procedural rules different from those applicable to the national authority. Another peculiarity of the EU legal system derives from the distribution of tasks among the institutions and bodies asymmetrical to the allocation of tasks in national administrations. For example, in the field of competition, where in most Member States competition is the purview of an independent authority, in the EU it is a competence of the Commission. In this case, the reasons for recognizing discretion derive both from the political nature of the authority and from the technical nature of the task; these reasons, however, are opposed to the need to ensure protection to the private parties, on whose interests the Commission's decisions have a significant impact.

Finally, the reasons for avoiding excessive limitations of discretion may be related to the circumstances in which the discretionary decision is made. The relevant circumstances may include urgency, secrecy, and exceptional and temporary situations. Urgency is very often a cause of justification, which allows derogations from many substantive and procedural rules and thus limits the intensity of judicial control. All legal systems provide, for particularly urgent situations, powers to adopt extraordinary measures, inevitably characterized by greater discretion in the assessment of problems and in the identification of solutions. This holds true, even more so, in exceptional cases, where important public interests, such as security and economic stability, are at risk. Similarly, secrecy in matters such as public security and monetary policy may prevent the use or reach of tools to limit discretion like due process, access to documents, and judicial scrutiny. In European law, a good example is the regulation of crisis in credit institutions, which emphasizes the obligation of confidentiality for the public and private parties involved in the procedures.[34]

Recent European legislation offers several examples of cases in which some of the reasons discussed here determine the recognition of broad discretionary powers and may prevent the imposition of substantial limits on administrative discretion: e.g. the provisions that allow the European administration to adopt certain measures in 'particular circumstances'.

---

[34] Art 84 of the Directive (EU) 2014/59 of the European Parliament and of the Council of 15 May 2014 establishing a framework for the recovery and resolution of credit institutions and investment firms.

5. Discretion and the Balance of Legitimacies

The analysis carried out in Section 4 shows that administrative powers are inherently limited as they are functional in nature, being conferred for the best pursuit of the public interest. There are both reasons to limit administrative discretion and reasons to not constrain it excessively. We must now add that the balance between these opposing demands is influenced by the legitimacy of the holder of discretion. The need to limit discretion is inversely proportional to the 'degree of legitimacy' of the deciding authority: the greater the legitimacy, the less the need to limit discretion.

Public authorities can derive legitimacy from various sources. The strongest source in democratic systems is elections. Political bodies who are directly legitimated by elections have a wide power supported by the electorate's choice: this explains the particular legal regime of the decisions of the political bodies. The power of administrative bodies, on the contrary, is only indirectly legitimate from a democratic perspective and, accordingly, must be limited more intensively: from this factor derives a more complex system of rules and controls. The longer the chain of the representative democratic circuit, the greater the need to limit discretion. One way to limit administrative discretion, as discussed, is to set detailed rules introduced by statutory law: through them, political bodies steer the exercise of administrative powers, 'lending' their legitimacy to administrative bodies.

Not all decisions can be made by applying the democratic principle and detailed rules may not be possible or efficient. The reasons are well known: elected representatives are not able to make complex and structured decisions, which require special technical skills in different fields (e.g. legal, monetary) or in relation to which they are in conflict of interests (this is one reason why the European law requires Member States to set up independent authorities in certain fields). In this case, the source of legitimacy of the deciding authority is not (only) the election or oversight by elected officers, but is (also) technical competence. This source of legitimacy can be strong enough to become a limit to the application of the democratic principle itself (e.g. when a court can declare the unconstitutionality of a law and avoid applying it). In most cases, however, technical competence as a source of legitimacy requires constraints on discretion, among which are certain procedural requirements.

It can be inferred from the foregoing that the powers of ordinary administrative bodies have a lack of democratic legitimacy: from this perspective, their legitimacy derives only from the indirect connection with the democratic investiture. For independent authorities, this lack of legitimacy is even more serious, given their establishment at arm's length from political influence explained by their strong technical expertise. In both cases, the constraints to their discretion stem from this legitimacy conundrum. If the deciding authority sets out in advance the criteria for its decisions, consults the interested parties, states the reasons for its decisions (taking into account the alternative solutions), and allows access to its documents in the various stages of the procedures, the legitimacy of their decisions is strengthened. The procedure emerges as a source of legitimacy of public power.

This brief account of the legitimacy tensions underlying discretionary powers further exposes how the issue of discretion and its control is a complex one. This chapter has shown how a discussion on discretion and its control needs to take into account factors pertaining to the nature of the power to take an administrative decision, to the kind of body that exercises a discretionary power, to the subjects involved, and to the context in which discretion is exercised. The need of limiting discretion depends on many factors that must be balanced with opposing reasons and must be evaluated in the context of the relationships between public authorities and the sources of legitimacy of their powers. Scholars and courts often tend to oversimplify the analysis of the issue and to propose theories of administrative discretion that do not take this complexity into account. Indeed, certain traditional distinctions are of little help, such as the distinction between the evaluation of whether the legal conditions for administrative action are verified, on the one hand, and the choice of the measures to be taken, on the other; or that between exquisitely administrative judgments (involving the balancing of competing interests) and technical ones. It should instead be acknowledged that discretion involves many different factors, which, in the administrative reality, cannot be distinguished, and that condition its amplitude and its limitations.

Ultimately, the best lesson that comparative law can give to European law is that the discretionary powers of the European institutions must be analysed from different perspectives and that the problem of their limitation must be tackled with a variety of conceptual tools. One should consider the governance structure, the relations between political and administrative bodies, the characteristics of the deciding authority, the different types of administrative power and the different ways in which each of them can affect private interests, and the circumstances in which the decision are made. One should also consider the different types of assessment that the administration has to make (e.g. factual and legal findings, interest appraisal and technical evaluations, choice of times and ways of action), which are often intertwined with each other. Every kind of administrative power must be examined using all these perspectives and tools, partly abandoning the legacy of theories and concepts that no longer correspond to complex and innovative regulations, such as those of the EU.

3

Indeterminacy and Legal Uncertainty in EU Law

*Takis Tridimas**

1. Introduction

Successive treaty amendments and legislative developments have led to the increasing formalization of EU law through the express recognition of constitutional rights, the adoption of detailed rules in several spheres, and the concretization of norms and processes through administrative rule making. EU law has become more specific, more rule-bound, and more process-bound. Nevertheless, as a result of reforms or reactions to successive crises, it has also become more uncertain. This chapter seeks to explore the meaning, the reasons, and the effects of uncertainty in EU law. After attempting briefly a taxonomy of uncertainty, it examines constitutional fluidity, authority uncertainty, and uncertainty as to the effects of rules. Constitutional fluidity is generated, *inter alia*, by frequent treaty revisions, silent constitutional amendments, the plurality of legal sources, and growing asymmetry in the rules applicable to Member States. Uncertainty pertaining to the attribution of authority results, *inter alia*, from the fusion of EU and State action in many areas, and the remit granted to EU agencies. A distinct feature of contemporary EU law is that, in sensitive areas, it is difficult to ascertain whether action is attributable to the EU or the Member States which may leave citizens in a precarious state in relation to the protection of their interests. Ambiguity as to the effect of rules is illustrated by the widespread use of soft law instruments or hybrid measures, which sometimes appear to obfuscate intentionally the limits of normativity. The end result is a post-crisis legal edifice which increases EU discretion but may imperil individual rights.

Despite the importance that it attaches to legal certainty as a general principle of law,[1] EU law is rampant with dubiety and imprecision. In terms of positive law,

* Professor of European Law at King's College, London and Professor and Nancy A Patterson Distinguished Scholar at PennState University. I am grateful to Theodore Konstadinides and Marta Simoncini for comments on an earlier draft. The usual disclaimer applies.
[1] Legal certainty, and its sister principle of protection of legitimate expectations, are recognized as general principles of law of constitutional status breach of which can lead to annulment of a measure or liability in damages: See, e.g. the milk quotas cases: C-120/86 *Mulder v Minister van Landbouw en Visserij (Mulder I)* [1988] ECR 2321; Case C-189/89 *Spagl* [1990] ECR I-4539;

one could distinguish four types of uncertainty. Ambiguity may exist as to which entity has authority to act (authority uncertainty). Doubt may surround the partition of competence between the Union and the Member States or the distribution of powers among EU institutions. Secondly, uncertainty may surround the existence of a rule (recognition uncertainty). *Mangold*[2] and *Audiolux*[3] may be viewed as such cases of recognition uncertainty. In the former, the Court of Justice (ECJ) may be said to have recognized the existence of a general principle of law prohibiting discrimination on grounds of age while in the latter it rejected the existence of a general principle of equality of shareholders in the field of corporate law. Thirdly, uncertainty may exist as to the meaning of a rule, including its scope of application, the precise command that it entails, or its relations with other norms (content uncertainty). Finally, disagreement may emerge as to the effect of a rule, i.e. its binding effect, its capacity to grant rights, or the remedies available for its violation (effects uncertainty). The above categories are not intended to be exhaustive,[4] and may overlap, e.g. whether an entity has authority to take action may depend on whether a rule exists or what its meaning might be. Similarly, the boundaries between recognition and content uncertainty are not easy to draw. Ultimately, all legal disputes may be said to involve contestations of authority since the existence, content, or effect of a rule determine whether a party has authority to act in a specific way.

All types of ambiguity identified here are a feature of every legal system and, needless to say, do not as such amount to a breach of the general principle of legal certainty. Law is a living instrument that evolves as the polity that it governs changes. Written law cannot provide for every factual permutation. Constitutional rules, especially, tend to operate at a level of abstraction that facilitates political consensus but makes the intermediation of courts particularly necessary for the establishment of outcomes.[5] Although it would be difficult to assess the relative degree of uncertainty of EU law vis-à-vis that of its Member States, it deviates from established paths of dependency in a way which is commonly absent from the mature legal systems of European nation states. It is characterized by a high level of constitutional fluidity that may give rise to the types of uncertainty identified here.

Joined Cases C-104/89 and C-37/90 *Mulder II* [1992] ECR I-3061. The principle of legal certainty requires that the effect of EU legislation must be clear and predictable and that individuals must be placed in a position where they can assert and defend their rights: see Joined Cases 212–217/80 *Salumi* [1981] ECR 2735, para 10; Joined Cases C-203/15 and C-698/15 *Tele2 Sverige v Post-och telestyrelsen* [2016] EU:C:2016:970, para 121. It has also been used to guarantee the effective application of EU norms by the Member States: see, e.g. Case C-119/92 *Commission v Italy* [1994] ECR I-393.

   [2] Case C-144/04 *Werner Mangold v Rüdiger Helm* [2005] ECR I-9981.

   [3] Case C-101/08 *Audiolux v Groupe Bruxelles Lambert SA (GBL) and Others* [2009] EU:C:2009:626.

   [4] For other classifications and a theoretical discussion, see e.g. J Kammerhofer, *Uncertainty in International Law, A Kelsenian Perspective* (Rutledge, 2011) 3.

   [5] See CR Sunstein, *Legal Reasoning and Political Conflict* (OUP, 1996) at 35 et seq.

2. Constitutional Uncertainty

One may identify many sources of constitutional instability in EU law. First, it has an inherently dynamic character. The EU brings together separate political units with diverse preferences, which morph within heterogeneous political constituencies and evolve over time. If governance is complex at the level of a sovereign, it is particularly so at the level of the EU. While the integration process is telos-driven, consensus exists, at best, only at the most abstract level, and the objectives and priorities of Member States differ and shift over time. The integration bias of the EU Treaties is thus concretized, shaped, and qualified by the balance of national interests in a way which makes the future constitutional direction of the EU unstructured and unpredictable. It would have been difficult to predict, for example, the Banking Union, much less the precise legal framework governing it. The European Union (EU) remains a new legal order in the making and which, in its short history, has undergone many constitutional changes. Since the early 1980s, there have been no fewer than eleven treaty amendments. These include six waves of accession[6] and five substantive treaty amendments.[7] One needs to add the aborted constitutional treaty[8] and the impending withdrawal of the UK to complete a picture of constant constitutional adjustment.

Change and evolution is not exhausted in express constitutional revisions. EU law has also undergone silent amendments, namely, fundamental changes to the rules that underpin the constitutional bargain without formal treaty amendment. This is particularly the case in the field of European Monetary Union (EMU) and financial regulation following the financial crisis. The growth of EU agencies, the redefinition of the objectives of economic and monetary union, the introduction of conditionality as a *sine qua non* for granting assistance to ailing Member States, and the increasing presence of EU norms and institutions in the monitoring of state finances have redefined the fundamental paradigm of economic governance established by the Maastricht Treaty.[9] Such mutations may be inevitable, given especially how difficult it is to amend the EU Treaties, but make for an unstructured and opaque constitutional framework.

Ambiguity is further generated by the plurality of legal sources, especially the increasing use of international agreements concluded between Member States at the outskirts of EU law. Agreements have been concluded particularly, but by no means exclusively, in the field of Eurozone law.[10] The reasons for using international

---

[6] These have included the accessions of Greece (1981), Spain and Portugal (1986), Austria, Finland, and Sweden (1995), central and Eastern Member States together with Cyprus and Malta (2004), Bulgaria and Romania (2007), and Croatia (2013).

[7] These are the Single European Act (1986), the Treaty of Maastricht (1992), the Treaty of Amsterdam (1997), the Treaty of Nice (2001), and the Treaty of Lisbon (2007).

[8] The Draft Treaty establishing a Constitution for Europe, final draft of 6 August 2004, OJ 2004 C 310/1.

[9] See K Tuori and K Tuori: *The Eurozone Crisis. A Constitutional Analysis* (CUP, 2014).

[10] See the European Stability Mechanism (ESM) Treaty (2012), the Treaty on Stability, Coordination and Governance in the Economic and Monetary Union (TSCG or Fiscal Compact Treaty, 2012), and

law have not been the same in each occasion. Thus, the Fiscal Compact Treaty took the form of an international agreement as a result of the refusal of the British government to consent to treaty amendment. The ESM Treaty was seen as necessary in view of the express prohibition in the Treaty on the Functioning of the European Union (TFEU) barring the EU from providing financial assistance to Member States.[11] The Inter-Governmental Agreement on the Transfer and Mutualisation of Contributions to the Single Resolution Fund was seen as being both politically expedient and legally safer from the point of view of the available legal bases under EU law.[12] From the point of view of Member States, recourse to international agreements presents distinct advantages and is more suitable in areas of high political sensitivity. Nevertheless, it is not unproblematic. It may give rise to treaty-specific problems and encounters broader constitutional objections, since international treaties are liable to breach the unity and coherence of EU law, run counter to the distinct instrumentalities of EU integration, and may fall foul of the constitutional constraints of the EU Treaties. Furthermore, the relationship between such agreements and EU law proper is a source of intricate legal problems. It is ironic that, although the Lisbon Treaty did away with Article 293 EC, which provided for the conclusion of international agreements by Member States in certain areas, the use of such agreements to complement EU law has since intensified. Far from being an unsuitable tool to further integration, they have been instrumental in guaranteeing the survival of the European construct.

The fluid nature of the EU is further illustrated by growing constitutional asymmetry. There is a host of opt-outs, enhanced cooperation, or even de facto special arrangements,[13] which make the application of some parts of EU law applicable only to some Member States. Such fragmentation evokes the lack of political consensus on the optimum degree of integration. Differentiated integration is particularly prevalent in the EMU. One of the key features of the Banking Union is that it has accentuated the difference in treatment between Eurozone and non-Eurozone Member States. It fractures the supervision of financial institutions building on the fragmentation of the governance of public finances. The result is an imperfect sketch of a *two-speed* Europe.[14] While the Banking Union regime pursues equality as

---

the Inter-Governmental Agreement on the Transfer and Mutualisation of Contributions to the Single Resolution Fund (2014). For an example of a treaty concluded by some Member States outside the field of economic governance, see the Prüm Convention on the stepping up of cross-border cooperation, particularly in combating terrorism, cross-border crime and illegal migration signed on 27 May 2005, to which 14 Member States are currently parties.

[11] See Arts 123, 125 TFEU.

[12] The Inter-Governmental Agreement governs the obligation of Member States to transfer to the Single Resolution Fund established under the SRM Regulation contributions raised at national level. For a discussion of the legal basis of this obligation, see T Tridimas 'General Report on Banking Union' in G Bándi and others (eds), *European Banking Union, 2016 XXVIII FIDE Congress Proceedings Vol. 1* (Kluwer, 2016) 83 et seq.

[13] This is the case with Sweden which, although it fulfills the conditions for entry into the Eurozone and under the EU Treaties has an obligation to participate, remains outside the single currency.

[14] See, *inter alia*, J-C Piris, The *Future of Europe Towards a Two-Speed EU?* (CUP, 2012); Joishka Fischer 2000 Humboldt speech; G Majone, Rethinking European integration after the debt crisis, available at

a political objective and is constrained by the legal principle of non-discrimination, the application of the latter is heavily conditioned. An inevitable consequence of asymmetric integration is that the normative content of non-discrimination becomes more difficult to pin down. Equality of Member States is understood as a principle of inclusion, mutual respect, and the freedom to enter into and exit from the Banking Union, which is buttressed by process requirements governing decision making on regulatory standards.[15] The recognition of equality as an overarching principle in the Single Supervisory Mechanism (SSM) and the Single Resolution Mechanism (SRM) Regulations[16] bears legal consequences but, inevitably, the application of different rules to subsets of Member States leads to an uneven playing field. While some may see the resulting supervisory and regulatory incongruence as inherently destabilizing, others may view it as facilitating a meaningful framework of symbiosis.

A further cause of constitutional uncertainty is that treaty dispositions tend to be nebulous. Their vagueness allows plenty of scope for interpretation and can accommodate diverse integration models. In fact, the founding treaties themselves grant the Court of Justice of the European Union (CJEU) unusual power to shape the integration bargain.[17] This is true not only of the original treaties but also fundamental constitutional amendments. The creation of European Citizenship by the Treaty of Maastricht illustrates the point. The provisions on citizenship are vague and unclear as to their content. The same applies to the Charter of Fundamental Rights. The CJEU is entitled to assume that both sets of provisions were intended to be meaningful and that their authors intended them to be interpreted and given substance through a process of interpretation. In this respect, far from betraying mistrust towards the CJEU, the vagueness of treaty amendments has expanded its powers and revealed confidence in its role.

Finally, the application of EU law by national courts adds a further dimension of fragmentation. EU law is applied not only by the CJEU but also by the national courts which are, in fact, the primary venues for the assertion of EU rights by individuals. More generally, the dependence of EU law on the national legal systems and the national institutions for its application leads to variations in its understanding, enforcement, and effect.

<https://www.ucl.ac.uk/drupal/site_european-institute/sites/european-institute/files/working-paper-debt-crisis.pdf> accessed 10 March 2019, at 22.

[15] See the double majority voting system introduced for the decision making of EBA: Regulation (EU) No. 1093/2010 establishing a European Supervisory Authority (European Banking Authority), amending Decision No. 716/2009/EC and repealing Commission Decision 2009/78/EC, Art 44; and see XXVII FIDE Congress General Report on Banking Union, at 98.

[16] See Council Regulation (EU) No 1024/2013 conferring specific tasks on the European Central Bank concerning policies relating to the prudential supervision of credit institutions OJ 2013, L 287/63, Art 1(4); and Regulation (EU) No 806/2014 of the European Parliament and of the Council establishing uniform rules and a uniform procedure for the resolution of credit institutions and certain investment firms in the framework of a Single Resolution Mechanism and a Single Resolution Fund and amending Regulation (EU) No 1093/2010, OJ 2014, L 225/1, Art 6(1).

[17] The abbreviation CJEU is used in this article to refer to the EU judiciary as a whole, including the Court of Justice (ECJ) and the General Court (GC).

Constitutional fluidity increases at times or areas where national outlooks diverge on fundamental issues. The rule of law crisis currently unravelling in Poland and Hungary shows the fragility of the EU constitutional basis and also its dependence on national consensus. As Brexit shows, sometimes centrifugal forces cannot be contained within the constitutional boundaries of EU law and a definitive rupture occurs.

These features make for a constitutional design in a state of flux, which generates a considerable degree of authority, recognition, content, and effects uncertainty. It is not suggested here that uncertainty is necessarily a vice. For one thing, as already stated, ambiguity is the inevitable result of any governance system. For another, as a general principle of law, legal certainty is neither intended nor capable of eliminating the types of ambiguity identified here. In any event, it needs to be balanced with other principles, such as proportionality or the fundamental right to legal protection.[18] Elements of constitutional ambiguity are in fact salutary as they prevent the oscillation of the legal system, accommodate compromise, and avoid undue rigidity. It is, however, correct to say that contemporary EU law is characterized by an unusual degree of uncertainty in relation to the sources of authority and the nature and effect of rules.

3. Authority Uncertainty

3.1 The problem of attribution

While disputes pertaining to the division of powers are present in every polity, they are particularly acute in EU law. There may be argument about the horizontal allocation of powers between EU institutions or the vertical partition of competences between the EU and the Member States. Given that each EU institution occupies a distinct position in the national sovereignty–federalism spectrum, the two kinds of dispute are closely connected. Disagreements between the Council and the Parliament or the Council and the Commission in relation to the scope of their respective powers are a proxy war about the vertical allocation of competences. In recent years, such interinstitutional litigation has occurred, especially in the field of external relations and has attracted interventions by many Member States.[19]

Contestation may arise not only as to which entity has the competence to act, but also as to which entity action is attributable. The first type is a dispute about the scope of power, the second is a dispute about the source of authority. The second

---

[18] For conflicts between the two and their resolution in favour of the former, see, e.g. Case C-310/97 *Commission v AssiDöman Kraft Products AB and other (Woodpulp III)* [1999] ECR I-5363 reversing T-227/95 [1997] ECR II-1185; and Case C-263/02 P *Commission v Jégo Quéré* [2004] ECR I-3425 reversing on appeal Case T-177/01 *Jégo-Quéré v Commission* [2002] ECR II-2365.

[19] See, e.g. Case C-660/13 *Council v Commission* [2016] EU:C:2016:616; Case C-28/12 *Commission v Council* [2015] EU:C:2015:282; Case C-73/14 *Council v Commission (ITLOS)* [2015] EU:C:2015:490; Case C-425/13 *Commission v Council* [2015]EU:C:2015:483; Case C-244/17 *Commission v Council*, Opinion of Kokott AG [2018] EU:C:2018:364.

category of disagreement, if genuine and if it occurs frequently, reveals an unsettling level of constitutional ambiguity and a certain lack of quality in the law: the citizen faces objective difficulties in identifying the decision maker and is unable to locate from where authority emanates. The individual may find herself in an invidious position if there is blame shifting by each of the authorities involved where each authority denies ownership of an adverse measure.

In a number of areas, it is in fact difficult to ascertain whether a decision has been taken by the EU or the Member States. While such disputes appeared at an earlier stage in the development of EU law, they have become more prevalent. The boundaries between EU law and collective action by the Member States are porous in a way that serves to disguise the true source of authority. This occurs, for example, in the field of economic governance, especially in granting financial assistance to Member States, in the field of migration, and in mixed agreements. More generally, there are increasingly areas of law where the decision is a composite or joint one involving action by both EU and national authorities or action outside traditional hierarchical paths. This may occur, for example, in the field of Banking Union, Common Foreign Security Policy (CFSP), or Frontex action.[20] The growth and powers of EU agencies have also contributed to the confusion as to the true source of authority.

The fusion between EU and State action has been encouraged by two case law developments. First and foremost is the recognition in *Pringle* that, provided certain safeguards are respected, the EU institutions may carry out tasks on behalf of the Member States outside the framework of the Union.[21] This has opened the road especially for the Commission, but also the European Central Bank (ECB), to undertake tasks on behalf of the Member States acting collectively or through the auspices of an international organization such as the ESM, giving rise to issues pertaining to the attribution of authority and the law applicable. The second development is the shift of judicial emphasis from effects to objectives. In *Pringle* and *Gauweiler*, the ECJ held that, to determine whether a measure falls within monetary or economic policy, and therefore belongs to exclusive or shared EU competence, reference must be made principally to the objectives of the measure, the instruments which it employs also being relevant.[22] Thus, in *Gauweiler*, the ECJ drew a distinction between the purchase of governments bonds by the ESM and their purchase by the ECB in the framework of the Outright Monetary Transactions (OMT) programme. The difference lies in the objectives of the action. ESM purchase, subject to a condition of compliance with a macro-economic adjustment programme, aims to safeguard the stability of the euro area—an objective falling within economic policy and

---

[20] See Regulation (EU) 2016/1624 of the European Parliament and of the Council of 14 September 2016 on the European Border and Coast Guard and amending Regulation (EU) 2016/399 of the European Parliament and of the Council and repealing Regulation (EC) No 863/2007 of the European Parliament and of the Council, Council Regulation (EC) No 2007/2004 and Council Decision 2005/267/EC OJ 2016, L251/1 and for a brief comment, S Peers, 'Establishing the European Border and Coast Guard: All-new or Frontex Reloaded?' available at: <http://eulawanalysis.blogspot.com/2016/10/establishing-european-border-and-coast.html>, 16 October 2016, accessed 11 September 2018.

[21] See Case C-370/12 *Pringle v Government of Ireland* [2012] EU:C:2012:756, para 158.

[22] Case C-62/14 *Gauweiler and Others v Deutscher Bundestag* [2015] EU:C:2015:400, para 46; and Case C-370/12 *Pringle*, paras 53, 55.

not monetary policy.[23] By contrast, purchase in the framework of the OMT programme seeks to maintain price stability, and thus falls within monetary policy. Focusing on objectives rather than effects allows the same action to be considered either as part of economic or as part of monetary policy, depending on the entity that undertakes it and its objectives. This results in the fusion of the two policies and, as *Pringle* and *Gauweiler* indicate, grants immense discretion to the entity that undertakes the action. State and EU action appear to co-exist seamlessly. The interdependence between economic and monetary policy works mostly to the advantage of the ECB, whose broad powers to pursue monetary policy objectives may have substantial and widespread spillover effects on economic policy.[24]

3.2 Judicial tests and their limits

In determining the scope of judicial review, the case law has established sound rules under which the judicial inquiry relies on substance rather than formalism. Thus, the action for annulment is available against all measures adopted by EU institutions or bodies, whatever their nature or form, provided that they are intended to produce legal effects.[25] The label of the measure is not conclusive either as regards its binding effects or, importantly, as regards the authority from which it emanates.[26] The fact that a measure is presented as a decision of the Member States does not mean that it escapes legality review. It is necessary to determine whether, having regard to its content and all the circumstances in which it was adopted, the measure in question is in reality an act of an EU institution.[27] Thus, under the case law, to determine whether a measure is attributable to the EU or the Member States, it is necessary to examine whether the EU or the Member States have competence to adopt it, and the intentions of the author of the measure are not dispositive.[28] The Court may annul a measure on grounds of legal certainty on the basis of its signalling effect to the public even where its author denies that it is intended to have binding legal consequences.[29]

These principles however have come under strain. In *NM v European Council*,[30] the dispute centred on the authorship of action taken to counter the Syrian migration crisis. On 18 March 2016, in a public statement, the EU and Turkey agreed on

---

[23] Ibid., paras 63–4. Case C-370/12 *Pringle*, paras 56, 60.

[24] See, further, Borger, Chapter 6 in this volume.

[25] See, e.g. *Commission v Council*, 22/70 [1971] EU:C:1971:32, para 42, *Commission v Council*, C-114/12 [2014] EU:C:2014:2151, paras 38–9; *Commission v Council*, C-28/12 [2015] EU:C:2015:282, paras 14–15.

[26] See *Parliament v Council and Commission*, C-181/91 and C-248/91[1993] EU:C:1993:271 (*Bangladesh case*).

[27] See *Bangladesh case* (n 26) para 14; *Liivimaa Lihaveis*, C-562/12 [2014] EU:C:2014:2229, para 51.

[28] See *Bangladesh case* (n 26); Case C-316/91 *Parliament v Council (Fourth Lomé Convention Case)* [1994] ECR I-625.

[29] Case C-57/95 *France v Commission* [1997] ECR I-1627; Case T-496/11 *United Kingdom v ECB*, EU:T:2015:133.

[30] Case T-257/16 *NM v European Council* [2017] EU:T:2017:130.

a controversial resettlement plan for Syrian refugees arriving in Greece.[31] In *NM*, the General Court (GC) held that the statement and the commitments made thereto was attributable to the Member States and not the EU. There were strong elements to suggest the opposite. The press release in which the statement was announced specified that it was the result of a meeting between the members of the European Council and their Turkish counterpart and that it was 'the EU and Turkey' who agreed on the action points. The commitments were made under the framework of the joint action plan agreed between Turkey and the EU. The statement was published in the Council's website and was headed 'EU–Turkey' statement. The costs of the return operations of irregular migrants would be covered by the EU and the return of Syrian citizens would take place in full accordance with EU and international law. All the members of the European Council were present during the meeting of 18 March and the Council appeared to have been involved in its preparation.

The GC held that, 'notwithstanding [its] regrettably ambiguous terms', the statement was not attributable to the European Council as an EU institution, but the Governments of the Member States.[32] The GC accepted the Council's argument that the expression 'Members of the European Council' must be understood as a reference to the Heads of State or Government, since they make up the European Council.[33] References to the EU were the result of 'linguistic simplification' used for the general public in the context of a press release which serves only an informative purpose and has no legal value. This popularization of words cannot be used to proceed with legal and regulatory assessments.[34] The GC found that the official documents relating to the meeting of 18 March 2016 revealed the existence of two separate events—the meeting of the European Council as an institution and an international summit—that were organized in parallel in distinct ways from a legal, formal, and organizational perspective.[35]

It is not necessarily claimed here that the findings of the GC are incorrect. However, two objections may be made. First, the formalistic reasoning employed in the judgment is unpersuasive. It resolves ambiguity against the governed, and indeed against the most vulnerable categories of persons, and in favour of government. It is also unsatisfactory that the GC focused on the subjective intentions of the authors of the statement without examining the allocation of competences in the field of asylum. As stated, in determining whether an act is truly an act of the Member States or the EU, account must be taken of who had competence to adopt it. The intentions of the authors of the act are not conclusive. Secondly, more broadly, the rules governing the attribution of competences between the EU and the Member States are unclear. This, coupled with the licence given to the institutions in *Pringle*

---

[31] See the EU–Turkey Statement of 18 March 2016, International Summit EU Press Release, 144/16, 18/03/2016.

[32] *NM v European Council* (n 30) para 65. Having come to the conclusion that the Statement was attributable to the Member States, the GC rejected the action without examining whether it was binding. The case was dismissed on appeal for lack of clarity of the appellants' arguments: *NF et al v Council*, Joined Cases C-208/17 P to C-210/17 P, EU:C:2018:705.

[33] Ibid., paras 56, 68.   [34] Ibid., paras 57–8.   [35] Ibid., para 61.

to carry out tasks on behalf of the Member States, may result in obfuscating the true source of authority.

A further area where the attribution of authority becomes problematic is the granting of financial aid to ailing Eurozone Member States. The common pattern for granting such aid is the following. The decision to grant aid is taken by agreement at the Eurogroup whose status as an 'informal' body is recognized by Protocol 14.[36] The Eurogroup then mandates the Commission to agree on a Memorandum of Understanding (MoU) articulating the conditions for granting the aid. The formal decision to grant aid is taken by the Governing Council of the ESM, whose composition is exactly the same as that of the Eurogroup.[37] It is often the case that the Member State introduces changes to its law before the formal signing of the MoU paving the way for agreement at staff and formal level. The conditionality attached to financial assistance given to a Member State under the MoU is agreed concurrently with Council decisions adopted under Article 136 TFEU,[38] the intention being to ensure coherence and correspondence between intergovernmental and Union action.[39]

The Court has had the opportunity to examine some of the problems arising in the context of Eurozone aid in *Mallis* and *Ledra*, both of which concerned the Cyprus bail-in.[40] Following the Eurozone crisis, financial assistance was granted to a number of Member States but the support granted to Cyprus differed in one material respect. The Eurogroup agreement of 25 March 2013 made it an express condition that the funds must not be used for the recapitalization of the two banks at the centre of the crisis, requiring essentially a substantial diminution of bank deposits. The Eurogroup Agreement mandated the Commission to negotiate an MoU with Cyprus and led Cyprus to adopt a number of measures implementing the bail-in before the MoU was formally signed on 24 April 2013.

In *Mallis et al v Commission and ECB*,[41] the ECJ dismissed as inadmissible actions against the Commission and the ECB seeking the annulment of the Eurogroup

---

[36] Protocol 14 attached to the EU Treaties by the Treaty of Lisbon provides for the composition and function of the Eurogroup. Art 1 of the Protocol begins by stating that 'The Ministers of the Member States whose currency is the euro shall meet informally.' However, the very recognition of a body by primary law denies its informality. See also Art 137 TFEU.

[37] See Protocol 14 and Arts 5(1) to 5(3) of the ESM Treaty.

[38] Thus, for example, in relation to the financial assistance granted to Cyprus, Decision 2013/236 was adopted by the Council on 25 April 2015, a day after the ESM Board of Governors approved formally the conclusion of the MoU and a day before the MoU was concluded by the Commission. It was later repealed and replaced by Council Implementing Decision 2013/463, which is, in substance, identical to it.

[39] See Regulation No 472/2013 on the strengthening of economic and budgetary surveillance of Member States in the euro area experiencing or threatened with serious difficulties with respect to their financial stability OJ 2013 L 140/1. According to the regulation, "[f]ull consistency between the Union multilateral surveillance framework established by the TFEU and the possible policy conditions attached to financial assistance should be enshrined in Union law ... ' (Preamble, recital 3).

[40] See A Karatzia and M Markakis, 'What Role for the Commission and the ECB in the European Stability Mechanism?' (2017) 6 *CILJ* 232.

[41] Joined Cases C-105/15 P to C-109/15 P *Mallis and Malli v Commission and ECB* [2016] EU:C:2016:702. See at first instance: T-327/13 *Mallis and Malli v Commission and ECB* [2014] EU:T:2014:909.

Statement.[42] The ECJ held that the Eurogroup cannot be viewed as a configuration of the Council or a body or agency of the Union.[43] Although the scope of the ruling in *Mallis* remains unclear, the fact is that, at the very least, the decision-making process does not meet good governance standards. It appears that the Eurogroup Statement of 25 March 2013 determined not only the actions of Cyprus, but also the ESM. As stated, the composition of the Eurogroup and the Board of Governors of the ESM is the same. The Board of Governors is responsible for deciding, among others, to provide stability support by the ESM, including the economic policy conditionality as articulated in the MoU, and establish the choice of instruments and the financial terms and conditions of the assistance.[44] It is also responsible for deciding to give a mandate to the European Commission to negotiate, in liaison with the ECB, the economic policy conditionality.[45] The members of the Eurogroup who reached the agreement on Cyprus on 25 March 2013 were the same with the members of the ESM Board of Governors who approved formally the conclusion of the MoU on 24 April 2013 and the granting of assistance to Cyprus on 8 May 2013. Once the Eurogroup decided to grant assistance to Cyprus under the conditions provided in the Eurogroup Statement, the ESM had no option but endorse that decision. The members of the ESM Board of Governors could not have taken any action which would contradict their decision as members of the Eurogroup. It appears, therefore, that once the Eurogroup reached the agreement of 25 March 2013, no entity enjoyed real discretion to depart from the specific conditions for the granting of the aid imposed by that agreement. If the Board of Governors of the ESM wished to depart from the Eurogroup Agreement, it could not do so without the prior permission of the Eurogroup, whose crucial role was confirmed by the European Parliament.[46]

In *Ledra et al*,[47] the claimants were depositors in Cypriot banks who suffered a haircut in their deposits. They sought annulment of certain paragraphs of the April MoU and compensation for the damage that they had allegedly suffered by the diminution of their deposits. In dismissing their claims, the ECJ made a number of interesting findings. It first held that the participation of the Commission and the ECB in the procedure resulting in the signature of the MoU does not enable the latter to be classified as an act that can be imputed to them.[48] The ECJ then held that, under Article 17(1) TEU, the Commission has a duty to promote the general interest of the Union and must oversee the application of Union law. Furthermore,

---

[42] The applicants had argued that the Eurogroup Statement was to be imputed to the Commission and the ECB and that the Eurogroup constitutes the channel by which those institutions take decisions on specific questions linked to the ESM or to financial stability. This was dismissed by the GC: see para 40.

[43] Ibid., paras 57–61.   [44] See ESM Treaty, Art 5(6)(f).   [45] Ibid., Art 6(6)(g).

[46] See Parliament Resolution of 13 March 2014 on the enquiry on the role and operations of the Troika (ECB, Commission, and IMF) with regard to the euro area programme countries 2013/2277(INI).

[47] *Ledra Advertising Ltd et al v Commission and ECB*, Joined Cases C-8/15 P to C-10/15 P [2016] EU:C:2016:701. For first instance, see Case T-289/13 *Ledra Advertising Ltd v Commission and ECB* [2014], EU:T:2014:981; T-290/13 *CMBG v Commission and ECB* [2014] EU:T:2014:976.

[48] Ibid., para 52.

reiterating *Pringle*, it held that, under Articles 13(3) and (4) of the ESM Treaty, the tasks allocated to the Commission oblige it to ensure that MoUs concluded by the ESM are consistent with EU law.[49] Consequently, the Commission retains, within the framework of the ESM Treaty, its role of guardian of the EU Treaties, so that it should refrain from signing an MoU whose consistency with EU law it doubts. The ECJ also held that the Charter is addressed to the EU institutions, including when they act outside the EU legal framework,[50] thus allaying fears generated by its ruling in *Pringle* that when they carry out tasks on behalf of the Member States outside EU law proper, the EU institutions are not bound by the Charter. These findings are welcome and it must be accepted more generally that, where the Commission or another EU institution undertakes action on behalf of the Member States, even outside the confines of EU law, it is bound to ensure that such action is consistent with the fundamental rights guaranteed by the Charter. Nevertheless, while these aspects go some way towards bringing collective Member State action within the constitutional space of the EU, they do little to clarify the lines of authority attribution, which remain blurred.[51]

Authority disputes may also arise in the context of CFSP. In *H v Council*,[52] the ECJ held that a decision by the Chief of Personnel of the EU Police Mission in Bosnia-Herzegovina (EUPM) to redeploy to another post an Italian magistrate seconded to the EUPM was amenable to judicial review. Relying on the limitations imposed on the jurisdiction of the Court in the field of CFSP, Wahl AG agreed with the GC that the action was inadmissible. The Court however reversed the GC, holding that the limitations provided by Articles 24(1) TEU and 275 TFEU did not exclude the Court's jurisdiction. The EUPM consisted of staff seconded by the Member States and staff seconded by the EU. The ECJ held that, while decisions relating to the allocation of staff for the purpose of performing activities undertaken at theatre level have an operational aspect falling within the CFSP, they are also acts of staff management.[53] In relation to such decisions, personnel seconded by Member States had to be subject to the same rules as those applicable to personnel seconded by the EU, even though the EU staff regulations did not apply to the former. If it were otherwise, a staff management decision which concerned both categories of personnel might be subject to contradictory decisions by the ECJ and the national courts.[54] The Court also derived support from the fact that it had jurisdiction to rule on actions brought by national experts seconded to the European Defence Agency and those seconded to the European External Action Service, although the legal basis of its jurisdiction in those cases derives expressly from specific measures.[55]

---

[49] Ibid., paras 57–8; and see *Pringle*, C-370/12 [2012] EU:C:2012:756, paras 163–4.

[50] *Ledra Advertising Ltd.,* para 67.

[51] For another illustration of uncertainty surrounding the imputability of action and the powers of the Eurogroup, see the more recent judgments of the GC in Case T-680/13 *Dr K. Chrysostomides and & Co LLC et al v Council, Commission, ECB, Euro Group and European Union*, ECLI:EU:T:2018:486, and Case T-786/14 *Bourdouvali Eleni Pavlikka et al v Council, Commission, ECB, Euro Group and European Union*, ECLI:EU:T:2018:487.

[52] Case C-455/14 P, EU:C:2016:569.   [53] Ibid., para 54.   [54] Ibid., para 57.

[55] See Council Decision (CFSP) 2015/1835 and Decision 2012/C 12/04 of the High Representative of the Union for Foreign Affairs and Security Policy of 23 March 2011.

Another example of fusion between EU and collective Member State action is provided by the principles governing the location of EU agencies. Traditionally, location has been a political decision taken on a case by case basis by common agreement between the representatives of the governments of the Member States.[56] In the light of the proliferation of agencies, the Council, the Commission, and the Parliament agreed a common approach for future decisions in a non-binding statement, which laid down objective criteria to be taken into account for choosing an agency's seat.[57] Building on that framework, following the notification by the UK of its intention to withdraw from the EU, the heads of State or Government adopted a decision on the procedure for the relocation of EMA and EBA, the two EU agencies based in London. The decision was adopted in the margins of the Brexit European Council of 22 June 2017[58] on the basis of a proposal from the President of the European Council and the President of the European Commission.[59]

The Decision lays down detailed rules governing the procedure to be followed for the selection of the location of EMA and EBA, including the criteria for selection,[60] the time limit, and the specific procedure and voting rules to be followed for making the selection. The decision provided for a considerable degree of transparency compared with previous such decisions. The Commission was charged with assessing the offers and the decision was to be taken by a voting process, the outcome of which the Member States agreed in advance to respect. The decision on the location of EMA was taken on 20 November 2017 in the margins of the 3579th meeting of the General Affairs Council. Subsequently, the Commission put forward a proposal for a regulation amending the constitutive regulation of EMA specifying its new seat.[61] The Explanatory Memorandum accompanying the proposal states squarely that 'the issue of the location of the seat of the Agency falls within the exclusive competence of the Union.'

The process establishes a degree of hybridity that makes it difficult to determine the true source of authority and the link between the EU legislative process and ad

---

[56] See, for example, for a number of agencies including the EMI (later on ECB), the European Agency for the Evaluation of Medicinal Products (later on European Medicines Agency), OHIM, and the European Environmental Agency, Decision taken by common Agreement between the Representatives of the Governments of the Member States, meeting at Head of State and Government level, on the location of the seats of certain bodies and departments of the European Union and of Europol, OJ C 323/1 30.11.93.

[57] Joint Statement of the European Parliament, the Council and the Commission on Decentralised Agencies of 19 July 2012, available at: <https://europa.eu/european union/sites/europaeu/files/docs/body/joint_statement_and_common_approach_2012_en.pdf>, accessed 11 September 2018.

[58] See Procedure leading up to a decision on the relocation of the European Medicines Agency and the European Banking Authority in the context of the United Kingdom's withdrawal from the Union, Brussels, 22 June 2017, available at: <https://www.consilium.europa.eu/media/21503/22-euco-conclusions-agencies-relocation.pdf>, accessed 11 September 2018.

[59] Ibid., 1.

[60] The Decision lays down the following six criteria: the assurance that the agency can be set up on site and take up its functions at the date of the UK's withdrawal from the Union; the accessibility of the location; the existence of adequate education facilities for the children of agency staff; appropriate access to the labour market, social security and medical care for both children and spouses; business continuity; and geographical spread.

[61] COM(2017) 735 final, 2017/0328 (COD), Brussels, 29.11.2017.

hoc action by the same political actors acting outside the EU law framework. In particular, while the decision lays down criteria for the selection of the seat of the agencies, there is no obligation on the decision maker to decide on the location on the basis of those criteria. Furthermore, the Commission's assertion that the location falls within the exclusive competence of the EU sits at odds with Article 114 and 168(4)(c) TFEU as the legal bases of the proposal and the process for determining location, which was adopted outside the disciplines of EU law. The Parliament appears to have been presented with a fait accompli.

Related issues regarding the attribution of authority may occur not only at the constitutional and legislative level, but also at the administrative level. In the field of Banking Union, the SSM establishes essentially a system of joint supervision where the ECB provides the lead. One of the novel governance arrangements introduced is the responsibility of the ECB to apply national law. Under Article 4(3) of the SSM Regulation,[62] the ECB is charged with applying national law transposing EU directives, including therefore any national norms which Member States may have discretion to adopt thereunder. This gives rise to a host of issues. Which courts have jurisdiction to control ECB action in such a case? Is the ECB bound by the interpretation of national law given by national courts? Can it itself interpret national law? The EU system of judicial protection is based on a clear-cut distinction under which jurisdiction over EU and national action is respectively entrusted to the CJEU and the national courts. This jurisdictional separation however is under strain where EU and national action are interwoven or where the EU–national law boundaries break down through 'federal' enforcement of national rules. Ultimately, it will be for the ECJ to resolve those questions.

3.3 Agency power

The rise of EU agencies, a true 'headless fourth branch',[63] further obscures the source of authority. A distinct feature of the Union's institutional architecture has been the unprecedented growth in the number of independent EU agencies.[64] The main reason for their proliferation, which coincides with the increase in administrative rulemaking at Union level,[65] is found in the quest for expertise and specialization.

---

[62] Council Regulation (EU) No 1024/2013 conferring specific tasks on the European Central Bank concerning policies relating to the prudential supervision of credit institutions OJ 2013, L 287/63.

[63] The expression was coined by President Franklin Roosevelt's Committee on Administrative Management. See SG Breyer, RB Stewart, CR Sunstein, and ML Spitzer, *Administrative Law and Regulatory Policy* (Aspen Law & Business, 1999), 146.

[64] See, among others, P Craig, *EU Administrative law* (2nd edn, OUP, 2012), Ch. 6; M Scholten and M van Rijsbergen, 'The Limits of Agencification in the European Union' (2014) 15 *Ger Law J* 1223; HCH Hofmann and A Morini 'Constitutional Aspects of the Pluralisation of the EU Executive through "Agencification"' (2012) *ELR* 419; HCH Hofmann, GC Rowe, and AH Türk, *Administrative Law and Policy of the European Union* (OUP, 2011) 285 et seq; M Simoncini, *Administrative Regulation Beyond the Non-delegation Doctrine* (Hart, 2018).

[65] See R Dehousse, 'Misfits: EU Law and the Transformation of European Governance', *Jean Monnet Working Paper No. 02/02*. Available at: <http://www.jeanmonnetprogram.org/archive/papers/02/020201.html>

The growth of agency power is particularly evident in the field of financial regulation, where the multi-tier level of governance was already present in the pre-crisis era through the Lamfalussy structure.[66] Following the 2008 financial crisis, the EU embarked on a fundamental redesigning of the institutional architecture leading to the establishment of three new European Supervisory Authorities (ESAs), namely ESMA, EBA, and the European Insurance and Occupational Pensions Authority (EIOPA).[67] The ESAs enjoy more extensive powers than any other EU agencies. These include both executive and quasiregulatory functions. In addition to the ESAs, the Banking Union has led to the establishment of two powerful agencies, the Supervisory Board (SB)[68]—as part of the European Central Bank—and the Single Resolution Board (SRB).[69]

There is a tension between, on the one hand, the constitutional limitations on the remit of agencies and, on the other hand, the objectives which their establishment seeks to fulfil and their powers under their constitutive instruments. The challenge is how to ensure accountability, transparency, and good governance while enabling agencies to play a meaningful role in the regulation of economic affairs in a post-internal market era.[70]

In *Meroni*,[71] one of the most enduring precedents of the Court, the ECJ held that the Commission may not delegate to independent agencies discretionary powers involving a wide margin of appreciation which may make possible the execution of economic policy. The reason for that restrictive approach was to ensure observance of the principle of institutional balance. In the *ESMA case*,[72] the ECJ somewhat relaxed the *Meroni* doctrine. It found that the granting of power to ESMA to restrict or even prohibit short selling to safeguard financial stability did not exceed the permissible delegation of authority. The distinct aspect of delegation was that Article 28 of Regulation 236/2012[73] granted ESMA authority to adopt acts of general application and also decisions directed at specific market participants. The ECJ held that the exercise of powers conferred by Article 28 was circumscribed by various procedural conditions and substantive criteria and therefore it did not confer to ESMA any autonomous powers that went beyond the bounds of the regulatory framework

---

[66] See Final Report of the Committee of Wise Men on the Regulation of the European Securities Markets, 15 February 2001 (Lamfalussy Report), available at <http://ec.europa.eu/internal_market/securities/docs/lamfalussy/wisemen/final-report-wise-men_en.pdf>, accessed 11 September 2018.

[67] Regulation No 1095/2010 establishing a European Securities and Markets Authority [2010] OJ L 331/84; Regulation No 1093/2010 establishing the European Banking Authority [2010] OJ L 331/12; Regulation No 1094/2010 establishing the European Insurance and Occupational Pensions Authority [2010] OJ L 331/48.

[68] Council Regulation (EU) No 1024/2013 conferring specific tasks on the European Central Bank concerning policies relating to the prudential supervision of credit institutions OJ 2013, L 287/63.

[69] Regulation (EU) No 806/2014 of the European Parliament and of the Council establishing uniform rules and a uniform procedure for the resolution of credit institutions and certain investment firms in the framework of a Single Resolution Mechanism and a Single Resolution Fund and amending Regulation (EU) No 1093/2010, OJ 2014, L 225/1.

[70] On the discretion of ESMA, see Moloney, Chapter 5 in this volume.

[71] Case C-9/56 *Meroni v High Authority*, ECLI:EU:C:1958:7.

[72] C-270/12 *UK v Parliament and Council* (*ESMA case*), ECLI:EU:C:2014:18.

[73] Regulation (EU) No 236/2012 of the European Parliament and of the Council of 14 March 2012 on short selling and certain aspects of credit default swaps, OJ 2012 L 86/1.

established by the ESMA Regulation.[74] Although the ECJ's approach calls for a careful case by case analysis,[75] the *ESMA case* stands as authority that, provided an agency's discretion is carefully circumscribed and its powers are precisely delineated and amenable to review, the agency may adopt even rules of general application in a technical area.[76] The delineation of functions between the Commission and ESMA, however, is far from clear cut. The ECJ placed emphasis on the fact that it was for the Commission and not ESMA itself to specify criteria and factors to be taken into account by ESMA in determining when threats to financial stability arose. Those criteria and factors, however, are themselves drafted by ESMA (in the form of technical advice[77]) and the Commission's power to deviate from them is restricted.[78] One of ESMA's key functions, which gives it a quasiregulatory role, is to develop 'technical standards'. The other ESAs enjoy similar powers.[79] In view of the *Meroni* limitations, those standards do not acquire binding force unless they are adopted by the Commission. Thus, to use Justice Scalia's colourful language on agencies, ESMA 'may play the sorcerer's apprentice but not the sorcerer himself'.[80] Still, the apprentice can run the show. Regulation No 1095/2010 operates a framework of reverse accountability which brings ESMA's powers close to a regulatory competence: where the Commission decides not to endorse the standards submitted by ESMA or amends them, it must provide reasons for its decision.[81] Also, it can only bring into force rules that are at variance with those recommended by ESMA following a special procedure.[82] The system set up by the Regulation appears to satisfy

[74] The Court held that the exercise of the powers conferred on ESMA was circumscribed by various conditions and criteria limiting its discretion. Measures could only be adopted if a specific threat existed and to the extent that national competent authorities had not taken measures to address the threat. ESMA had to take into account the extent to which any measures it adopted (i) would significantly address the threat or improve the ability of national authorities to monitor it; (ii) would create a risk of regulatory arbitrage; and (iii) would have a detrimental effect on the efficiency of financial markets that was disproportionate to the benefits of the measure. The two kinds of measure that ESMA could take under Art 28 were strictly confined to those set out in Art 9(5) of the ESMA Regulation, namely imposing a temporary prohibition/restriction on certain activities. ESMA's discretion was further circumscribed by its duties to consult the ESRB and, if necessary, other relevant bodies; to notify national authorities of its proposed measure, together with the evidence supporting its reasons why it had to be adopted; and to review the measure at least every three months. The Court also drew attention to Art 30 of the Short-selling Regulation, which provided for the Commission (rather than ESMA itself) to specify criteria and factors to be taken into account by ESMA in determining in which cases the threats etc arose. See paras 44–53 of the Judgment.
[75] See M Chamon, 'The Empowerment of Agencies under the *Meroni* Doctrine and Article 114 TFEU: Comment on *United Kingdom v Parliament and Council (Short-selling)* and the Proposed Single Resolution Mechanism' (2014) *ELR* 380, 394.
[76] Cf. Case 98/80 *Romano* [1981] ECR 1241, where the Court held that an administrative commission could not be delegated by the Council power to adopt acts having the force of law. In *ESMA*, the Court distinguished *Romano* on somewhat dubious grounds: see *ESMA case* (n 73), paras 64–7.
[77] See ESMA's *Technical Advice on Possible Delegated Acts Concerning the Regulation on Short Selling and Certain Aspects of Credit Default Swaps*, ESMA/2012/263, pp. 65–7.
[78] Chamon (n 75) 395.
[79] See Reg 1095/2010, Arts 10 and 15 (ESMA); Reg 1093/2010, Arts 10 and 15 (EBA); Reg 1094/2010, Arts 10 and 15 (EIOPA).
[80] See *Alexander v Sandoval* 532 U.S. 275 (2001), 15 of the Opinion of the Court.
[81] See Reg 1095/2010, Art 10(1), sub-paragraph 6; and Art 15(1), sub-paragraph 5. Identical provisions are included in the corresponding articles of the EBA and EIOPA regulations.
[82] Ibid., Arts 10 and 15.

the *Meroni* standards since the final word rests with the Commission.[83] But the legal set up falls short of capturing the true influence of ESAs in decision making.[84]

Hybridity is also present in relation to the decision-making powers of the SB and the SRB in the context of the Banking Union. The concerns relating to the two agencies are, to some extent, different. The SRM Regulation provides for a resolution procedure of intense complexity. The main challenge here is to provide a workable decision-making process while striking the optimum division of competence between technocratic experts and politicians. Concerns have been expressed as to whether the discretionary powers of the SRB comply with the *ESMA case* criteria.[85] The SRM Regulation establishes a system of a negative resolution procedure with the Commission and the Council enjoying a power of objection, rather than a power of positive approval.[86] Unless the Commission or the Council object, the resolution scheme proposed by the Board stands. This gives to the EU institutions the role of exercising political oversight, rather than having full engagement. This mechanism is not novel as the same allocation of powers is provided for in relation to other EU agencies. But the time limits within which the Commission and the Council must react are asphyxiatingly short, which, in turn, raises doubts as to whether they can have a meaningful input. The less the time for the Commission and the Council to react and the more the technical expertise that the decision requires, the more likely that the agency will be the true author of the decision.

The challenges surrounding the SB are different and arise from its relationship with the ECB. The concentration of monetary policy and banking supervision on the ECB presents risks relating to conflicts of interest and central bank independence. Article 25 of the SSM Regulation uses peremptory language seeking to separate monetary from prudential decisions stating that, when carrying out its tasks under the SSM Regulation, the ECB must pursue only the objectives set out therein and that supervisory tasks of the ECB must neither interfere with nor be determined by its tasks relating to monetary policy.[87] The separation of tasks is supported by an elaborate process apparatus, political accountability mechanisms, and transparency obligations. Article 26 designs a governance architecture based on a separation between de jure and de facto decision making, where the former belongs to the SB but the latter to the ECB Governing Council. Article 25 essentially creates a system of Chinese walls granting power to take supervisory decisions on the SB. Such barriers are artificial since, ultimately, both monetary policy and supervisory decisions rest with the Governing Board and monetary concerns may trump supervisory needs.[88] The participation of the ECB to the appointment of the Chair of the SB furthers detracts from the independence of the latter. Still, conflicts are not necessarily avoided

---

[83] In Case T-311/06 *FMC Chemical SPRL* [2008] EU:T:2008:205, the General Court held that where an agency is charged with providing an opinion to the Commission from which the latter can depart, the Commission has not delegated the power to take binding decisions, since only its own final decision has binding effects vis-à-vis third parties.

[84] See, further, Moloney, Chapter 5 in this volume.

[85] For an extensive discussion, see T Tridimas, 'General Report on Banking Union' in G Bándi and others (eds) (n 12) 41–148.

[86] See Reg 806/2014, Art 18(7).   [87] Reg 1024/2013, Arts 25(1) and 25(2).

[88] See Art 26(8).

by entrusting monetary and prudential powers to different bodies since, ultimately, where the two conflict, a balance will need to be drawn at the political level. As a matter of governance design, it is not unreasonable to entrust the ECB with both functions, provided there is robust legal basis and a system of checks and balances ensuring accountability.

4. Uncertainty as to Legal Effects

4.1 Soft law, hybridity, and bindingness as a continuum

EU law is characterized by a considerable degree of uncertainty also as regards the legal effects of rules. The rise and influence of soft law is well documented.[89] It comes in an 'infinite variety'[90] of instruments and is 'omnipresent'.[91] It has grown both in volume and importance since the 1990s as a result of the expansion of EU competence and the growth of EU administration. It is commonly defined by way of contrast to hard law and refers to non-binding rules which may have practical or legal effects.[92] However, the plethora of informal or atypical sources of law is such that their influence and legal effect cannot be captured by the rigid hard–soft law dichotomy. Bindingness may best be seen as a continuum. To give but one example, acts of the representatives of Member States meeting within the Council are not EU acts and, in principle, are not subject to judicial review unless they meet substantive criteria of reviewability laid down by the ECJ.[93] Still, they are an integral part of the EU legal framework. They are part of the *acquis* to which new Member States must accede[94] and are treated as part of EU law by the Draft Withdrawal Treaty of the UK.[95] They may be interwoven with EU acts in a way that the true source of authority and the delineation of powers between different bodies is virtually impossible to draw.[96]

Soft law may be used to rein in and streamline the exercise of discretion,[97] supplement and concretize statutory rules in technical spheres,[98] or make up for the lack

---

[89] See O Stefan, *Soft Law in Court* (Kluwer, 2012); D Trubek, P Cottrell, and M Nance, ' "Soft Law", "Hard Law", and the EU Integration' in G de Búrca and J Scott (eds), *Law and New Governance in the EU and the US* (Hart Publishing, 2006); F Snyder, *Soft Law and Institutional Practice in the European Community in The Construction of Europe: Essays in Honour of Emile Noël*, 199–201(S Martin ed, Kluwer, 1994).

[90] R Baxter, 'International Law in Her Infinite Variety' (1980) 29 *ICLQ* 549.

[91] Stefan (n 89) 1.   [92] Ibid., 11.

[93] See this chapter (n 26) et seq and accompanying text.

[94] See e.g. Art 5(1) of the Act concerning the conditions of accession of the Czech Republic, the Republic of Estonia, the Republic of Cyprus, the Republic of Latvia, the Republic of Lithuania, the Republic of Hungary, the Republic of Malta, the Republic of Poland, the Republic of Slovenia, and the Slovak Republic, and the adjustments to the treaties on which the European Union is founded.

[95] See Art 2(a)(vi).

[96] See e.g. text to (n 56) re: the discussion of the selection of seats of EU agencies.

[97] This occurs for example in the field of state aid and competition law. For prime examples, see the Commission's Banking Communication (OJ 2013, C 216/1) in issue in Case C-526/14 *Kotnik v Državni zbor Republike Slovenije*, EU:C:2016:570, and the Commission's Leniency Notice: Notice on Immunity from fines and reduction of fines in cartel cases, 2006 OJ C 298/17. On the use of soft law as a strategy to constrain discretion, see Dawson, Chapter 4 in this volume.

[98] See, Section 4.2 re: the discussion of ESA guidelines.

of statutory powers.[99] It has been particularly prevalent in the governance frame-work that has resulted from the 2008 global financial crisis and the Eurozone crisis. Prime examples are provided by the Eurogroup Statements which, irrespective of their strict legal status, are of critical importance, the economic policy recommenda-tions that may be issued under the so-called Six Pack,[100] and the ECB OMT press release which, in terms of achieving its avowed objectives, proved to be particularly effective.[101]

4.2　ESAs and the legal effects of guidelines

A prime example of the ambivalence that may characterize the legal effect of EU instruments is provided by ESA guidelines. As stated, ESMA, EBA, and EIOPA are the most powerful EU agencies and play a key role in the governance of the fi-nancial sector. Article 16 of the ESMA Regulation confers to the agency power to issue guidelines and recommendations with a view to establishing consistent, effi-cient, and effective supervisory practices and ensuring the common, uniform, and consistent application of Union law.[102] Guidelines and recommendations may be addressed to the national competent authorities or to market participants. The com-petent authorities must make 'every effort' to comply, and there is a comply or ex-plain obligation: where an authority does not comply or does not intend to comply, it must state its reasons.[103] Similarly, where guidelines are addressed to financial institutions, they are under a duty to make every effort to comply and, where the guideline or recommendation so stipulates, to report in detail on their compliance or otherwise.[104] Identical powers are conferred to EBA and EIOPA by Article 16 of their constitutive regulations. All ESAs have made ample use of their authority adopting a plethora of guidelines.[105] In fact, the exercise of Article 16 powers has had a self-reinforcing effect as agencies appear to have entered into a fraternal com-petition seeking to outdo each other, as no agency wishes to be seen as falling behind in applying its authority.

---

[99] See, e.g. the Eurogroup Statements (n 43).

[100] See, e.g. Commission Communication of 23 May 2018, 2018 European semester—Country Specific Recommendations, COM(2018) 400 final.

[101] By a press release of 6.9.2012, the ECB announced that, under certain conditions, it was willing to purchase government bonds of ailing Eurozone Member States which were under a macroeconomic adjustment programme. The press release is a prime example of regulation by information. It had the ef-fect of calming financial markets and reducing the spreads of government bonds. See further T Tridimas and N Xanthoulis, 'A Legal Analysis of the OMT Case: Between Monetary Policy and Constitutional Conflict' (2016) 23 *Maastrich J Eur Comp Law* 17. For an evaluation of its positive economic impact of the OMT programme, see C Altavilla, D Giannone, and M Lenza, 'The Financial and Macroeconomic Effects of OMT Announcements', *ECB Working Paper, No 1707*/August 2014, available at: <https://www.ecb.europa.eu/pub/pdf/scpwps/ecbwp1707.pdf>, accessed 11 September 2018.

[102] Art 16(1).

[103] Art 16(3). Under that provision, ESMA must publish the fact that a competent authority does not comply or does not intend to comply and may also decide, on a case-by-case basis, to publish the reasons provided by the competent authority for not complying.

[104] Ibid.

[105] On how ESMA has used that authority, see Moloney, Chapter 5 in this volume.

The legal effects of EU guidelines cannot be captured by reference to a binary hard–soft law approach. Although they are not specifically mentioned in Article 288 TFEU, they are, at least on the ordinary meaning of the word, closer in nature to recommendations than to regulations or decisions.[106] They are generally considered to be instruments of soft law that lack binding legal effect. However, this by no means gives the full picture. Precisely because they are not recognized as a formal instrument in the EU Treaties, guidelines do not have a uniform nature. Their nature and effects are to be determined on the basis of an overall evaluation, taking into account the entity that issues them, their content, and the context in which they are adopted. The case law accepts that even non-binding legal acts, such as recommendations, may produce legal effects in that they may be important for the interpretation of a binding rule of EU law or national law.[107] Furthermore, it has recognized that guidelines may produce binding effects. Bindingness here may take several forms. A guideline may have a self-binding effect. Where the Commission adopts guidelines that explain how it will exercise its discretion in individual cases, it binds itself so that decisions which fail to abide by its own guidance are liable to be annulled. Examples abound in the field of competition and state aid law. In *BASF v Commission*,[108] the Court of First Instance (now the GC) found that the Commission's *Vitamins* cartel decision was 'vitiated by illegality' to the extent that the Commission had misapplied its Leniency Notice.[109] In *Spain v Commission*,[110] the ECJ annulled a Commission decision to the extent that it was incompatible with the Commission's *de minimis* aid notice.[111]

Nevertheless, the self-binding effect of guidelines does not mean that such instruments acquire the status of rules of law: instead, they are rules of practice from which the Commission may not depart without giving good reasons.[112] The rationale for the ECJ's approach is that, where the Commission acts inconsistently with the guidance it has adopted, it violates one or more general principles of law, namely legal certainly, the protection of legitimate expectations, or equal treatment.[113] Thus, in

---

[106] Cf the Opinion of AG Lenz in Case C-135/93 *Spain v Commission* [1995] ECR I-1651, para 31.

[107] See Case C-322/88 *Grimaldi v Fonds des maladies professionnelles* [1989] ECR 4407. The ECJ held that national courts are bound to take recommendations into consideration in order to decide disputes submitted to them, in particular where they cast light on the interpretation of national measures adopted in order to implement them or where they are designed to supplement binding EU provisions.

[108] Case T-15/02, [2006] ECR II-497 at para 541.

[109] At the time, the applicable guidance document was the *Notice on the non-imposition or reduction of fines in cartel cases* [1996] OJ C 207/4.

[110] Case C-409/00, [2003] ECR I-1487, para 73.

[111] At the time, the relevant notice was the *Commission notice on the de minimis rule for State aid* [1996] OJ C 68/9.

[112] See, e.g. Case C-189/02 *Dansk Rørindustri v Commission* [2005] ECR I-5425, para 209.

[113] In the words of one commentator, the Court here recognizes 'binding effects of soft law not as the result of some intrinsic feature of the instrument—as in the case of instruments endowed with legally binding force, hard law—but through the mediation of certain mechanisms judicially constructed … these mechanisms rely on general principles stemming from the rule of law and the national constitutional traditions of Member States …': O Stefan, *Soft Law in Court* (Kluwer, 2012) 181.

Kotnik,[114] where in issue was the Commission's Banking Communication, the ECJ held that, where the Commission adopts guidelines to establish the criteria on the basis of which it proposes to assess the legality of state aid, it cannot, as a general rule, depart from them. It self-limits its discretion so that, if a Member State notifies proposed State aid which complies with the guidelines, the Commission must, as a general rule, authorize it. On the other hand, the Member States retain the right to notify the Commission of State aid which does not meet the criteria laid down in the guidelines and, in exceptional circumstances, the Commission may authorize it. The ECJ concluded that the Banking Communication was not capable of imposing independent obligations on the Member States, but did no more than establish conditions designed to ensure that State aid granted to the banks in the context of the financial crisis is compatible with the internal market.[115]

In addition to such self-binding effect, the ECJ has recognized that, in certain cases, guidelines and other soft law instruments are capable of producing binding effects vis-à-vis third parties and are thus susceptible to challenge under Articles 263, 267, and 277 TFEU.[116] This is especially[117] the case where guidance is construed by the ECJ as introducing a new obligation or as adding to a Treaty provision or an EU measure. In *France v Commission* (*Financial Transparency Directive case*),[118] the ECJ was asked to annul the Commission's Communication on the application of the Financial Transparency Directive to public undertakings in the manufacturing sector on the ground that it went beyond the obligations placed on Member States by that directive.[119] In response to the Commission's challenge to the admissibility of the action, the ECJ held that it could not assess admissibility divorced from the substance of the action: if France was right, then the Communication was liable to have legal effects and so the challenge would be admissible.[120] It appears that the wording of the instrument will be an important factor in this respect. In that case, the ECJ noted the imperative language of the communication in question; and in the *Pension funds case*,[121] the Court noted that provisions of the communication in question[122] were 'characterised by their imperative wording'; this supported the ECJ's view that the communication was intended to have legal effects of its own.

A further example of the CJEU's approach is provided by *United Kingdom v ECB*.[123] The UK challenged the ECB Eurosystem Oversight Policy Framework, a statement published in the ECB's website which provided that, in the interests of

---

[114] *Kotnik* (n 97).   [115] Ibid., paras 40–4.

[116] For an exposition of the justiciability of soft law instruments, see the Opinion of AG Tizzano in *Dansk Rørindustri* (n 112) paras 54–64. See further J Scott, 'In Legal Limbo: Post-legislative Guidance as a Challenge for European Administrative Law' (2011) 48 *CML Rev* 329, 340–2.

[117] Another such case is where Member States are bound by a specific (legislative) obligation of co-operation with the Commission in circumstances where guidelines are adopted as one element of that cooperation: see Case C-311/94 *Ijssel-Vliet Combinatie BV v Minster van Economische Zaken* [1996] ECR I-5023, paras 37, 44.

[118] Case C-325/91, [1993] ECR I-3283.

[119] Directive 80/723/EEC on the transparency of financial relations between Member States and public undertakings, [1980] OJ L 195/35.

[120] *France v Commission* (n 118) para 11.   [121] *France v Commission* (n 29) para 18.

[122] Commission Communication on an Internal Market for Pension Funds [1994] OJ C 360/07.

[123] *United Kingdom v ECB* (n 29).

promoting the smooth operation of payment systems and managing systemic risk, entities that clear euro-denominated transactions should be legally incorporated in the euro area. In response to the ECB's claim that the Policy Framework was not an act having legal effects, the GC held that, in determining whether an act is binding, account must be taken of the way in which the parties concerned could reasonably have perceived that act to be assessed. If the act is perceived as only proposing a course of conduct and, therefore, as being similar to a mere recommendation, it should be concluded that it does not have legal effects. If, on the other hand, the parties concerned will perceive the act as one which they must comply with, despite the form or designation favoured by its author, then it would be subject to annulment.

It follows from the discussed case law that, to determine whether a guideline has binding effects, the CJEU will not rely on the label of the measure but will undertake a substantive examination looking at the circumstances of its adoption, its substantive content, its peremptory or otherwise language, and the way it is perceived by those to whom it is addressed and those who are affected by it.[124] It will also take account of the intentions of the author of the guideline, but the apparent intentions of the author are not conclusive.[125] Where, following the discussed analysis, it is established that a measure is binding, it will be susceptible to judicial review, and it will be annulled if the authority that adopted it lacks legal basis to do so under EU law.

Turning specifically to the guidelines that may be adopted by ESMA and the other ESAs under their constitutive regulations, their precise legal status will depend on their content. At the level of principle, however, it appears that they are binding in the following respects. First, they give rise to a procedural duty to comply or explain.[126] Secondly, they give rise to a 'best efforts' obligation.[127] This goes beyond a mere procedural duty and imposes also duties of substance.[128] Breach of these obligations may give rise to an enforcement action by the Commission under Article 258 TFEU.[129] It could be argued that the obligations outlined here derive not from the guidelines themselves, but rather from Article 16. It is that provision which gives rise to the comply or explain and the best efforts obligations. It is doubtful, however, whether this is correct. These obligations arise upon the adoption of a guideline. Article 16 makes the process and substantive obligations outlined here an attribute of guidelines, just as Article 288 TFEU attributes different kinds of binding effect on regulations and directives.

Furthermore, the application of the case law may lead to the conclusion that ESA guidelines have binding effects. If the perceptions of interested parties matter, as

---

[124] Note that the legal effects of a guideline may reach further than its addressees: Case C-410/09 *Polska Telefonia Cyfrowa v Prezes Urzędu* [2011] ECLI:EU:C:2011:294.

[125] *Bangladesh case* (n 26); Case C-57/95 *France v Commission (pension funds case)* [1997] ECR I-1627.

[126] See Art 16(3) (n 103).   [127] Ibid.

[128] In relation to market participants, guidelines give rise to a best efforts obligation (Art 16(3), first sub-paragraph) and a reporting obligation: where so provided by a guideline, financial institutions must report, in a clear and detailed way whether they comply. See Art 16(3), fourth sub-paragraph.

[129] Breach of a guideline might also lead to enforcement action against a national authority or against a financial institution as provided for in Art 17 of the ESMA Regulation to the extent that it is considered as breach of the EU acts which the guidelines are intended to concretize.

they can be identified by an ex post facto objective analysis,[130] ESA guidelines may be viewed as binding. It is a common secret that in their overwhelming majority national authorities perceive them to be binding and also transpose them through the adoption of binding national measures. In those circumstances, it is difficult to avoid the conclusion that affected parties, whether national authorities or market participants, should have the right to judicial redress.

Finally, to the extent that guidelines impose on national authorities or individuals obligations that go beyond the obligations to which they are subject by virtue of EU legislation, they will be invalid. This is because the ESAs do not have general power to adopt legally binding rules of general application and also because guidelines cannot impose obligations going beyond legislation.

5. Conclusion

While legal certainty is elevated to an overarching principle of EU law, it cannot capture the ambiguity characterizing the source of authority, the scope of competence, and the content and effect of EU rules. The complex division of powers among various entities within the EU legal system may disguise the true source of authority and make it difficult to identify the proper defendant or the proper judicial forum. In particular, the boundaries between EU law and collective action by the Member States are porous in a way that serves to disguise the true source of authority. The capacity of the same actors to act either as EU institutions or *qua* representatives of sovereign States may operate in a constitutional vacuum, which may foreclose access to justice and fall short of rule of law standards. A well-governed polity, like the EU aspires to be, cannot tolerate a situation where the source of authority on important issues is subject to genuine doubt. Hybridity should not be allowed to breed arbitrariness. EU law is also characterized by a considerable degree of ambiguity as regards the legal effects of rules. Instead of examining such effects under a binary hard–soft law dichotomy, it is best to view bindingness as a continuum. Article 16 of the ESMA Regulations suggests that, sometimes, the obfuscation of legal effects is encouraged by the legislature.

Many of the deficiencies identified here have resulted from EU intervention necessitated by responses to crises, especially the 2008 global financial crisis and the ensuing Eurozone crisis. Those crises highlighted the mismatch between constitutional constraints and the need for extensive, both legislative and executive, decision-making powers at EU level. Crisis management has led EU institutions to an apologetic narrative of justification making a virtue out of necessity. However, from the point of view of the citizen, this narrative misses the point. It seeks to provide a rational explanation but there is little quest for legitimization by reference to a coherent system of governance structures and democratic principles. The discussion

---

[130] See (n 123).

here also illustrates the limits of judicial contribution. Many deficiencies in EU decision making can simply not be remedied by the courts. In that respect, it would be complacent to view the ECJ's active jurisprudence on the protection of rights, welcome and noble as it might be, as offering by itself an adequate counter-weight to the expansion of EU competence.

4

How Can EU Law Contain Economic Discretion?

*Mark Dawson**

1. Introduction

'The better part of valor is discretion.'[1] Those who are wise avoid unnecessary risks. In legal systems, however, discretion is unavoidable. Law is plagued, as catalogued by the American critical legal studies movement, with indeterminacy.[2] It is left to judges to fill the gaps produced by technological change, legislative ambiguity, and diverse factual circumstances. What is interesting, therefore, is not whether legal systems produce discretion—all of them do—but how discretion is controlled. By answering that question, a whole host of further questions; about the role of judges in our societies, about their techniques of interpretation, and about the accountability of our legal and political systems; are revealed. Through analysing the management of discretion we reveal some of the fundamental components of legal orders.

This chapter focuses on the control of discretion in one particular system of rules: EU economic governance. By focusing on the EU, and on the economic example, two further potential amplifiers of discretion are introduced. On top of the inevitable indeterminacy of all legal texts, EU legal sources are complicated by the multi-level nature of the EU legal order. Many EU legal sources are of a particularly vague and contested character, from the abstract norms of EU primary law to the confusing and potentially contradictory rules of secondary law (the product of compromises and competing views between 28 Member States). As also outlined in other chapters in this volume, EU policy making is a highly discretionary space. In EU economic governance, the intersection of different social systems must be added to that mix. Norms in economic governance attempt to regulate a field—the EU economy—that is governed largely via economic concepts and mechanisms, which are not easily reducible to legal categories. Economic governance expands the EU discretionary space even further.

* Professor of European Law and Governance, Hertie School of Governance. This research received funding from the ERC under the EU's Horizon 2020 programme (grant agreement no. 716923).
[1] W Shakespeare, *1 Henry IV*, Act V, sc. iv.
[2] See R Unger, 'The Critical Legal Studies Movement' (1980) 96 *Harv L Rev* 570.

To this extent, there seems little point in writing an analysis evidencing the prevalence of discretion in the application of the rules of EU economic governance. The evidence—discussed briefly in Section 2—is indisputable.[3] While authors may disagree on the extent of freedom that policy makers in the economic field enjoy, few would contest the idea that the control of economic decision makers is a perilous and difficult task.

This chapter's purpose is therefore a different one. Assuming that the basic rules of EU economic governance provide policy makers with an extremely large margin of manoeuvre, what kind of strategies can the European judiciary, and other actors such as the EU's political institutions, use to control discretion? How can they ensure adherence to a basic level of legal accountability, i.e. faithfulness to the overall 'rules of the game' in the economic field? The chapter therefore aims to be inductive, exploratory, and forward looking. Rather than critique a particular judicial approach to the control of economic policy making over others, its purpose is to categorize and lay out different methodologies to control discretion in the economic field. The rationale, advantages, and disadvantages of each approach will be examined as openly as possible. It is ultimately for judges and policy makers to determine which of these approaches to choose.

Having discussed the main causes and challenges of economic discretion in Section 2, the chapter then examines four strategies for the control of discretion. Section 3 discusses strategies of deference; functional varieties of what in the human rights field is termed a 'margin of appreciation' in policy making. Section 4 discusses prescription, i.e. the idea of containing discretion through the production, via soft law or other instruments, of more detailed rules to prescribe economic conduct. Section 5 covers proceduralism, i.e. subjecting economic decision makers to forms of process-based and political accountability. Finally, Section 6 discusses interdisciplinary justification—the use by judicial actors in particular of (economic) knowledge as a means of limiting the space for discretionary action. The chapter concludes by analysing the political and constitutional values that underpin each of these strategies. As argued there, the choice of one strategy over another is likely to reflect back on the weight particular actors give to one value over another.

2. Discretion in EU Economic Governance

From where does discretion in EU economic governance emerge? While this is a complex question that could be approached from many angles, much of the answer derives from the complexity and dynamism of the economic system that EU economic governance attempts to regulate. Part of the core vocabulary of European

---

[3] For other examples cataloguing this phenomenon, see D Chalmers, 'The European Redistributive State and a European Law of Struggle' (2013) 18 *ELJ* 5; A Menendez, 'The Crisis of Law and the European Crisis: From the Social and Democratic Rechtsstaat to the Consolidating State of Pseudo-Technocratic Governance' (2017) 44 *J Law Soc* 1; P Leino and T Saarenheimo, 'Sovereignty and Subordination: On the Limits of EU Economic Policy Coordination' (2017) 42 *ELR* 166.

Monetary Union (EMU) is the extent to which it ought to be 'rules-based'. In this debate, the German finance minister has been a particularly stout advocate of strict rule following in banking and fiscal regulation.[4] This, however, is a peculiar form of rule following. The rules to be adhered to are not universal and abstract rules of conduct, but often quantitative, state-specific targets, the fulfilment of which depends on meeting particular economic criteria.[5] These criteria are themselves contested between actors and depend on fluctuating economic cycles. As such, the idea of a 'rules-based' EMU is rather misleading. For most of the EMU's rules, there is no 'automaticity' that easily connects a state's fiscal performance with a clear outcome. Instead, we have a complex system of decision making and evaluation.

This can be illustrated through the commonly cited example of the excessive deficit procedure (EDP). While the secondary legislation governing this procedure seems to carry relatively clear quantitative boundaries—for example, the 3 per cent deficit target, or the setting of Medium-Term Budgetary Objectives (MBTOs) for states—this certainty is illusory. The terms of the applicable legislation, for good reasons, do not specify in precise detail what does or does not 'count' for the purposes of calculating deficits. Where they do—for example, via the definition of a 'structural deficit'—they rely on economic concepts with unclear boundaries.[6] Which items of expenditure, then, should count as 'structural' and which are fluctuations or one-off investments that can be expected as part of the economic cycle?[7] The same difficulty applies to the question of whether states are making adequate progress towards MBTOs in the context of the EDP's corrective arm. The legal framework allows the Commission to take into account a number of vague factors in determining 'progress' towards MTBOs, from whether a state is implementing 'major structural reforms'[8] to whether 'temporary measures' apply. What do these terms mean?

As Damian Chalmers has argued, these provisions seem less like rules than 'decisions': norms which are of a sufficiently vague character to allow the actor executing them unfettered discretion in determining how they might be applied to a concrete

---

[4] See, e.g. 'Germany's Schäuble says Eurozone Must Stick to Fiscal Rules', *Wall Street Journal*, 28 October 2016, <https://www.wsj.com/articles/germanys-schauble-says-eurozone-must-stick-to-fiscal-rules-1477658559> accessed 17 May 2018.

[5] On this point, see Leino-Sandberg and Saarenheimo, Chapter 7 in this volume, and P Leino-Sandberg and T Saarenheimo, 'Sovereignty and Subordination: On the Limits of EU Economic Policy Coordination' (2017) *ELR* 2.

[6] A further example is the definition of 'macro-economic imbalances' given in Art 2 of Regulation (EU) 1176/2011 of the European Parliament and of the Council of 16 November 2011 on the prevention and correction of macroeconomic imbalances (OJ L 306 [2011]), which is 'means any trend giving rise to macroeconomic developments which are adversely affecting, or have the potential adversely to affect, the proper functioning of the economy of a Member State or of the economic and monetary union, or of the Union as a whole'. It is difficult to identify the outer limits of such a broad definition.

[7] See also M Dawson, 'The Legal and Political Accountability Structure of "Post-Crisis" EU Economic Governance' (2015) 53 *J Common Mark Stud* 5, 987–8.

[8] See Art 5 of Council Regulation (EC) 1466/9 of 7 July 1997 on the strengthening of the surveillance of budgetary positions and the surveillance and coordination of economic policies (amended): 'When defining the adjustment path to the medium-term budgetary objective[..] the Council and the Commission shall take into account the implementation of major structural reforms which have direct long term positive budgetary effects.'

case.[9] They also rely on a complex determination of effects, e.g. of whether a particular structural reform really is 'major', and if so, whether it will have a positive budgetary effect. In this sense, while the 'Six-Pack' and 'Two-Pack' regulations were heralded as 'tightening' fiscal regulation, they had little option but to create a significant discretionary decision-making space into which a diverse array of Eurozone economies, and a highly fluctuating economic environment, could fit. For judicial actors, this discretionary space creates a real quandary. If the rules of the EDP, like other rules of economic governance, are open, nested in economic concepts, and reliant on uncertain future effects, how can judges ensure that economic decision makers (in the EDP case, the Commission) have exercised their functions faithfully?[10] Law seems to be playing catch-up with an economic and fiscal decision-making system able to easily evade its control.

3. Strategy 1: Deference

One answer to the quandary is not to play the game of 'catch-up' at all. Typically, when reviewing the actions of the EU institutions when engaging in policy making, and particularly when making complex technical assessments, the CJEU has adopted a highly deferential approach. This often involves checking merely whether a 'manifest error of assessment' or 'abuse of power' can be observed.[11] As Joana Mendes argues, a more expansive understanding of the CJEU's approach in cases involving the supervision of executive discretion would involve anchoring judicial review in a (thin) conception of the public interest.[12] When making decisions of an economic nature, the Commission carries a duty of care to examine all of the relevant facts impartially, to accurately state those facts and to base their decisions on 'the fullest information possible'.[13] The EU executive is thus provided with a broad margin of discretion, provided that it can demonstrate that it had adhered to principles of sound administration—based on accurate information and orientated towards the public interest. Once this basic threshold of reasonable conduct has been met, the Courts are prepared to give the institutions the benefit of constitutional doubt.

It is not challenging to read recent case-law in the field of economic governance in this light. In the infamous *Gauweiler* judgment, the CJEU's response to a reference by the German Constitutional Court allowed the ECB a high margin of discretion.[14] This allowance concerned two aspects of the judgment—firstly, the determination of whether the OMT programme of the European System of Central Banks (ESCB) had lain within the ECB's monetary and price stability mandate, and

---

[9] Chalmers (n 3) 682–4.   [10] Dawson (n 7) 888.

[11] E.g. Case C-42/84 *Remia and Others v Commission* [1985] ECLI:EU:C:1985:327; Case T-13/99 *Pfizer Animal Health v Council* [2002] ECLI:EU:T:2002:209.

[12] J Mendes, 'Discretion, Care and Public Interests in the EU Administration: Probing the Limits of EU Law' (2016) 53 *CML Rev* 419.

[13] See also Hofmann, Chapter 10 in this volume.

[14] Case C-62/14, *Gauweiler and Others v Deutscher Bundestag* [2015] ECLI:EU:C:2015:400 (hereafter *Gauweiler*).

secondly, the proportionality of the programme. The *Gauweiler* judgment illustrates starkly some of the difficulties of adjudicating economic governance discussed in Section 2. Assessing whether OMT lay within the price stability mandate required a close analysis both of the purpose of the OMT programme and its likely effects.[15] For the CJEU, the purpose of OMT was to ensure the smooth functioning of the Monetary Transmission mechanism, i.e. the ability of central interest rate setting to filter into the wider economy, and into pricing and lending practices in particular.[16] Addressing whether or not the OMT programme was necessary to ensure the proper functioning of this mechanism is clearly an empirical question. Was the ECB's argument—that widening bond yields between EU states and economic uncertainty was acting as a decisive hindrance to the ability of monetary policy to be effective—convincing and observable?

This speaks to the most powerful argument for favouring deference as an approach to dealing with economic discretion. Clearly, empirical questions require empirical answers. For all the qualities of the CJEU Justices, they are not economists and are unlikely to carry as sophisticated an understanding of the transmission mechanism as the institution entrusted with this task under the EU Treaties.[17] The CJEU therefore—in answer to the question of whether OMT was within the ECB's mandate—largely takes the ECB at its word, accepting the objectives and justification of the programme given by the ECB itself. In its proportionality review, the Court follows many of the traditional steps mentioned here, arguing that the OMT programme requires the making of complex technical assessments for which the ECB and ESCB are themselves competent, thus demanding a broad margin of discretion.[18] As there was no obvious error of assessment, as there was evidence that evidence-based, reasoned decisions had been given, and as limitations on the programme's scope had been made, the ECB's programme was consistent with Treaty rules.[19] Deference in this sense could be seen as a tool to preserve institutional balance, and the proper demarcation of institutional functions in the EU constitutional order.[20] A court that went beyond the limited thresholds demanded in *Gauweiler* could lay accused of over-stepping its constitutional mandate to apply rules of law, rather than to second-guess the judgments of institutions with explicitly non-legal tasks.

The difficulty of course—a long-held obsession of administrative law[21]—is that such reasoning tends to make a mockery of the very purpose of judicial review of

---

[15] On effects-based reasoning in *Gauweiler*, see A Steinbach, 'Effects-Based Analysis in the Court's Jurisprudence on the Euro Crisis' (2017) 2 *ELR* 254.

[16] *Gauweiler* (n 14) 51–2.

[17] The judgment has been defended on this basis, i.e. as allowing for a pluralist form of what Mathias Goldmann has playfully termed 'mutually assured discretion'. See M Goldmann, 'Constitutional Pluralism as Mutually Assured Discretion: The Court of Justice, the Federal Constitutional Court and the ECB' (2016) 23 *Maastricht J Eur Comp Law* 1.

[18] *Gauweiler* (n 14) 68.   [19] Ibid., 82–92.

[20] See Goldmann (n 17); see also M Goldmann, 'Adjudicating Economics? Central Bank Independence and the Appropriate Standard of Judicial Review' (2014) 15 *Ger Law J* 2.

[21] See, for a classical account, JL Mashaw, 'Structuring a "Dense Complexity": Accountability and the Project of Administrative Law' (2005) 5 *ILS* 1.

administrative action, which is to ensure that executive actors remain within *their* constitutional mandates. In simple terms, if the legality of the ESCB's action rests on a determination of the OMT programme's effects, and only the ESCB is competent to assess those effects, judicial review of its action seems a formalistic and perhaps even pointless exercise. Examining manifest errors and evidence gathering, and requiring a statement of reasons, seems to do little to mitigate this concern. A powerful and well-tasked EU institution seems unlikely to be careless enough—when conducting a programme of the size and significance of the OMT programme—to commit the kind of egregious mistakes judicial checks of this nature could remedy. Similarly, one need not be a cynic to suppose that the ECB's Governing Council consulted its legal service before issuing the press releases and other documents signalling the objectives of the OMT programme. By this reading, strategies of deference do not protect but rather upend the institutional balance by abrogating the role of the CJEU in ensuring that this balance is maintained (e.g. by checking substantively, and not merely procedurally, whether EU institutions have respected the limits of their powers).[22]

The purpose of this analysis is not to criticize deference or the *Gauweiler* judgment, but rather to point to the trade-offs that deferential approaches to economic discretion pose. The uneasiness of these tensions may demand other strategies, including more extensive use of ex ante rule-making (a practice to which the next section now turns).

4. Strategy 2: Prescription and Soft Law

The short analysis of *Gauweiler* discussed in the previous section makes the case seem much easier than it in fact was. The ESCB is not only bound by its formal Treaty mandate, but also by a plethora of other rules and standards.[23] Such standards—in both hard and soft law forms—abound in economic governance and could be seen as a further means of limiting the discretion of the actors who apply them.

A useful example is the one introduced in Section 2—the rules surrounding the EDP. Many of the vague standards referenced there, e.g. the definitions of a structural deficit or progress towards MBTOs—have been clarified by more detailed rules in delegated acts or soft law instruments. An example is the Commission's publication in 2015 of a Communication clarifying some of the main rules of the Stability and Growth Pact (SGP).[24] As the Commission acknowledges, many of the SGP's rules are unclear and hence carry the potential to create unpredictability and opacity.[25] In this light, the Communication provides some key criteria determining

---

[22] C Joerges, 'Pereat Iustitia, Fiat Mundus: What is Left of the European Economic Constitution after the OMT Litigation' (2016) 23 *Maastricht J Eur Comp Law* 1.

[23] On soft law in banking and financial regulation, see, J Schemmel, 'The ESA Guidelines: Soft Law and Subjectivity in the European Financial Market: Capturing the Administrative Influence' (2016) 23 *Ind J Global Legal Stud* 455.

[24] Commission Communication, 'Making the Best Use of the Flexibility within the Existing Rules of the Stability and Growth Pact', COM (2015) 12.

[25] Ibid., 5.

the circumstances under which the Commission will enforce provisions of the SGP without, the Commission insists, 'changing or replacing the existing rules'.[26]

In respect to, for example, some of the vague provisions of the EDP discussed in Section 2, the Communication clarifies that significant structural investments or payments to European investment funds, such as the European Fund for Strategic Investments (EFSI), will not 'count' towards assessing thresholds for the activation of sanctioning procedures.[27] Equally, when measuring progress towards MTBOs, the Commission will take into account whether Member States have implemented recommendations made under the European Semester and will consider closing a deficit procedure early if any excess is due to structural reforms with likely positive budgetary effects.[28]

The Communication is a form of 'soft law'. It nevertheless could be seen as an example—pursued by the Commission itself—of placing what would otherwise be unfettered discretion within particular bounds. By defining or providing criteria for terms that are unclear in legislative acts, i.e. what constitutes a 'one-off payment' or a 'major structural reform'[29], guidance is given to the addressees of the SGP (i.e. the Member States) and to citizens on how particular rules will be applied. If the problem of discretion in economic governance is one of how to assess executive conduct ex post, a solution could in this sense be encouraging executive actors to produce more detailed rules of conduct to guide their action ex ante.

Such rules or norms could be seen as 'self-binding' standards that could then be used to assess the limits of executive action by reviewing Courts. While the SGP Communication is a soft law instrument, some of its content could be seen as sufficiently precise to create legal obligations.[30] In recent case-law, the CJEU has significantly limited the ability of the EU institutions to avoid judicial review on the basis that obligations were laid out in non-binding policy instruments. In *UK v ECB*,[31] on the Euro area clearing system, the UK had challenged before the General Court (GC) elements of an ECB policy framework, particularly rules that credit institutions holding certain product categories denominated in euros had to be incorporated in Euro area. Was this an annullable act? According to settled case-law, regardless of the form in which an act appears, 'an action for annulment is available in the case of all measures adopted by the institutions, whatever their nature or form, which are intended to have legal effects.'[32] As this act was published, used words of a mandatory nature, and carried specific content and a specific addressee, it was deemed an act of hard rather than soft law and hence was reviewable. By establishing a policy framework that was relied upon by those to whom it was addressed, the

---

[26] Ibid., 3.   [27] Ibid., 5–7.   [28] Ibid., 13.

[29] See, e.g. the tests for this listed under page ten of the Communication: that structural reforms must be major, must have long-term budgetary effects and must be implemented (including via a submitted structural reform plan).

[30] On the judicial review of soft law in the EU more generally, see O Stefan, 'Helping Loose Ends Meet: The Judicial Acknowledgement of Soft Law as a Tool of Multi-Level Governance' (2014) 21 *Maastricht J Eur Comp Law* 359

[31] Case T-496/11 *United Kingdom of Britain and Northern Ireland v European Central Bank (ECB)* [2015] ECLI:EU:T:2015:133.

[32] Ibid., para 30.

ECB had bound its own discretion (even if such a framework would not bind other EU institutions). Perhaps, in this way, soft law can be used to address the challenge of discretion by encouraging economic actors to create more detailed standards for themselves (i.e. standards that Courts could later patrol).

There remain, however, profound difficulties with the use of prescription or soft law to meet the challenge of discretion in economic governance. Some of these challenges are simply new variants of long-held problems with regard to rationale attempts to codify legal standards. One of the core concerns of efforts to codify continental civil law in the nineteenth century was to rationalize disparate legal standards and place the political branch at the centre of legal reform.[33] More detailed rules, covering a wide range of circumstances, would better guide judges and administrators and avoid unwarranted discretion.

The difficulty was the mismatch between the complexity of social relations and the goal of 'simplicity' in rule making.[34] As technologies and social circumstances changed, drafters of legal codes had two options: either they had to create increasingly detailed rules to proscribe conduct—rules which began to conflict with each other, to grow, and ultimately to defeat the goals of rationale simplification; or, they were forced to couch rules in broad language and categories—duties of care or 'reasonableness' that did little to meaningfully constrain administrative or judicial discretion. Either way, new pathways of discretion were revealed.

While the current corpus of soft law in economic governance is limited, such a dilemma is not unimaginable in the economic governance case. To take the example given here, while the Euro clearing case provided some criteria regarding when a policy framework would tie the ECB's hands, it remains unclear how these criteria could be transferred to other cases. To apply the CJEU's criteria to the example of the Commission's Communication on the SGP, this guidance is public and has a specific set of thresholds and addressees (Member States). However, the Commission also repeatedly states that it does not intend to 'change or replace existing rules' and that the guidance is tied to the political guidelines for the new Commission and hence part of policy making.[35]

While the Communication narrows the Commission's discretion, it is still likely to be overtaken by new events (e.g. changes in EU programmes such as the EFSI, or an altered economic landscape), requiring new guidelines to which the obligations are unlikely to be clear. As the body of soft law governing economic governance grows, so will grow the ability of economic decision makers bound by one rule to simply point to another more favourable to their chosen decision. The growth of soft law is thus just as likely to create a morass of unclear obligations, unknowable to the ordinary public, as it is to lead to the precision and clarity which animated the original rationale stated in the Commission's SGP Communication.

---

[33] On this rationale, see the earlier justifications put forward by Bentham in *Of Laws in General*, HLA Hart (ed), (Athlone Press, 1970), Ch. 19.

[34] For an overview of some of these criticisms, see M Reimann, 'The Historical School Against Codification: Savigny, Carter and the Defeat of the New York Civil Code' (1989) 37 *Am J Comp L* 1.

[35] On the latter, see SGP Communication (n 24) 3.

Finally, one could wonder what kind of incentives a shift towards prescriptive rule making, particularly a form of rule making policed by the European Courts, will create. By judicially reviewing acts, such as the ECB's policy framework or the SGP Communication, we may encourage institutions not to create such norms in the first place. In the case of the SGP Communication, the Commission had already been applying many of its provisions in practice in any case[36]; adopting a relatively flexible and hands-off approach to the corrective arm of the SGP in particular. By adopting the Communication, the Commission made transparent the norms guiding its activities; at the same time, by raising the spectre of judicial review of these norms, a future Commission may be reluctant to publicize such evaluative frameworks again, on the basis that policy documents could tie its hands in future activities. By using soft norms to limit discretion, transparency in policy making may, in fact, be reduced, encouraging the EU institutions to keep private and away from public view the detailed criteria guiding its decision making.[37] Like strategies of deference, the use of prescription may also involve trade-offs between limiting discretion and encouraging open and transparent policy making.

5. Strategy 3: Proceduralism and Political Accountability

Section 3 analysed deference as a means of dealing with economic discretion. It described how forms of deference create a dilemma between, on the one hand, the need to respect the principle of institutional balance and, on the other hand, the need to ensure that Treaty rules are properly fulfilled. One question is whether procedural requirements, particularly those guaranteeing greater political scrutiny and deliberation of economic decisions, could provide a way out, or a compromise position, regarding this dilemma.

To sketch the compromise requires making a detour to other areas of EU policy. One of the key developments in EU policy making in 2015–16 was the announcement by the Commission of an extensive 'better regulation' package.[38] While extensively watered down in the eventual inter-institutional agreement on better law-making agreed between the three political institutions,[39] the purpose of the agenda was to simplify the EU regulatory process and agree on a common method for forming, evaluating, and implementing EU proposals. A central tool in this regard has been the generalization of impact assessment (IA) as a means of measuring the costs and benefits of EU policy and its effects on different actors. For its proponents, IA is a means of rationalizing policy making, ensuring that EU policies

---

[36] On the Commission's lenient application of the SGP, see, D Adamski, 'Economic Policy Coordination as a Game Involving Economic Stability and National Sovereignty' (2016) 22 *ELJ* 2.

[37] On potential trade-offs between transparency and judicial review in EU law, see D Adamski, 'Access to Documents, Accountability and the Rule of Law: Do Private Watchdogs Matter?' (2014) 20 *ELJ* 4.

[38] Commission Communication, 'Better Regulation for Better Results: An EU Agenda', COM (2015) 215.

[39] Inter-institutional Agreement of 13 April 2016 on Better Law-making (OJ 2016 L 123/1).

are based on evidence and incorporate different viewpoints in the decision-making process.[40] For sceptics, IA also carries a political purpose: while its emphasis on costs and benefits places an undue burden on social and environmental proposals with high implementing costs, IA could also be used as an instrument to make amendment of Commission proposals by the other EU institutions more difficult.[41]

One of the more interesting aspects of the discussion over better regulation is whether IA could be used by the European Courts as a tool to control executive discretion and to ensure compliance requirements demanded by EU primary law.[42] For example, one demand of the Commission's package is that IAs provide a clear assessment of the legal basis for EU action, including an account of how requirements of subsidiarity and proportionality have been met.[43] This requirement—as the inter-institutional agreement on Better Regulation states—extends to all 'legislative and non-legislative initiatives, delegated acts and implementing measures which are expected to have significant economic, environment or social effects'.[44] Other elements of the better regulation package are also of relevance in this regard: the Commission's better regulation guidelines require a minimum 12-week stakeholder consultation period for EU measures, widening the scope of consultation requirements to include delegated and implementing acts.[45] These elements of better regulation could be seen as significantly contributing to the ability of EU officials to meet constitutional requirements, such as the duty to give reasons protected under Article 296 TFEU or the commitment under Article 11 TEU to participatory democracy.

Importantly for our question, better regulation also provides Courts with tools to assess whether constitutional requirements have been fulfilled.[46] IAs have increasingly found their way into the CJEU's case-law.[47] For example, in *Vodafone* the CJEU accepted that the Commission had demonstrated via its IA that variations in roaming charges constituted a meaningful barrier to the internal market and that harmonization of these charges constituted a proportionate measure without obvious alternatives.[48] Similarly, in *Afton*, while the CJEU acknowledged that IAs were not binding on the Council or Parliament, they could act as an indicator of the evidence base used by the Commission when proposing legislative measures.[49] The

---

[40] On this academic debate over IA in the context of better regulation, see M Dawson, 'Better Regulation and the Future of EU Regulatory Law and Politics' (2016) 53 *CML Rev* 5, 1214–28.

[41] See, e.g. Corporate Europe Observatory, ' "Better Regulation": Corporate-friendly Deregulation in Disguise' (2016) <https://corporateeurope.org/power-lobbies/2016/06/better-regulation-corporate-friendly-deregulation-disguise > accessed 17 May 2018.

[42] See A Alemanno, 'A Meeting of Minds on Impact Assessment: When Ex Ante Evaluation Meets Ex Post Judicial Control' (2011) 17 *EPL* 3.

[43] Commission Staff Working Document, European Commission, 'Better Regulation Guidelines' (SWD, 2015) 111: 29.

[44] Inter-institutional Agreement (no 39), 13.   [45] Ibid., 52.

[46] See, on this question, A Meuwese and P Popelier, 'Legal Implications of Better Regulation: A Special Issue' (2011) 17 *EPL* 455

[47] See for a fuller account, D Keyaerts, 'The Impact of Better Regulation in the Case-law of the European Court of Justice' (2012) 2012 *Eur J Risk Regul* 241

[48] Case C-58/08, *Vodafone and Others* [2010] ECLI:EU:C:2010:321, para 45.

[49] Case C-343/09, *Afton Chemical Limited v Secretary of State for Transport* [2010] ECLI:EU:C:2010:419.

President of the Court himself has argued that IAs could form the basis of a 'process-oriented' form of judicial review in which the European Courts do not 'second guess the intentions of the legislator' but confine themselves to assessing whether basic procedural requirements of good governance have been met.[50] In this sense, IA and better regulation could be part of an enhanced form of the strategies of deference discussed earlier: while the substantive decisions of policy makers should not be assessed judicially, the EU Courts should enlarge their review of the procedural and political steps decision makers undertake prior to adopting policy. Law thus acts, under this model, as a guarantor of a rigorous and pluralistic decision-making process.[51]

How could this apply to the economic governance example? A thin reading of procedural review in economic governance may simply be a beefed-up version of the existing requirement that decision makers give reasons for their decisions and base them on impartial evidence. The CJEU could require, for example, that actors such as the ECB demonstrate the necessity of their policies, or their link to the ECB's Treaty-based mandate, through more than mere press releases and abstract reasons; rather, it could insist on more detailed forms of evidence, e.g. IAs (which would then be necessary to establish a presumption for more lenient forms of judicial review based on the notion of 'manifest error'). A thicker reading would be the requirement for decisions to be based not only upon evidence, but also upon the integration, depending on the type of economic decision, of affected stakeholders. This radical departure could involve the development of an EU equivalent to the American interest representation model of administrative review, whereby Courts require decision makers to demonstrate the inclusion in policy making of either directly affected actors or public interest advocacy groups able to demonstrate a legitimate interest in decision making.[52] Discretion is narrowed not by demanding responsiveness to substantive legal standards per se, but rather through demanding the inclusion in economic decision making of a wider range of affected actors.

What would be lost if the 'thin' or 'thick' models of procedural review were adopted? Taking the thin model first, it potentially falls into exactly the same trap—of reducing judicial review to formal 'box-ticking'—as strategies of deference. It is notable that the Commission itself, when providing guidance to policy officers on IA, explicitly points to the use of IA as a method to guard against judicial challenges to the validity of EU policy.[53] IA, just as it could assist the judge in checking executive discretion, could also act as a shield against judicial scrutiny.[54]

[50] See K Lenaerts, 'The European Court of Justice and Process-Oriented Review' (2012) 31 *YEL* 3.

[51] Lenaerts relies in his article on broader theories of judicial review particularly the defence offered by the American constitutional theorist, John-Hart Ely. See J-H Ely, *Democracy and Distrust* (Harvard University Press, 1980).

[52] See RB Stewart, 'The Reformation of American Administrative Law' (1975) 88 *Harv L Rev* 1711.

[53] 'Properly assessing any impact on fundamental rights in the preparatory stages of new legislation will therefore not only contribute to finding the most appropriate solution to a given problem, but will also strengthen the defence of EU legislation against legal challenges before the European Court of Justice.' Commission Staff Working Document, European Commission, 'Operational Guidance on Taking Account of Fundamental Rights in Commission Impact Assessments', (SEC, 2011) 567, 5.

[54] Dawson (n 40).

The danger, unacknowledged in Lenaerts' conception of process-orientated review, is that the mere presence of IA becomes an indicator that compliance with constitutional requirements has been fulfilled and thereby that judicial scrutiny of economic decisions, such as whether they carry a legal base or meet subsidiarity and proportionality requirements, is unnecessary (or can be conducted under a lower threshold of scrutiny).

At the very least, the incorporation of IA into judicial review places greater pressure on the adequacy of the IA process itself. The better regulation package contains some measures to improve IA, e.g. creating a regulatory scrutiny board, staffed by external members, to review the IA process and veto poor-quality assessments.[55] At the same time, the IA process carries plenty of critics, not least those who accuse it of carrying a deregulatory bias,[56] or of being easily 'gamed' by evidence constructed around a policy decision that has already been hierarchically agreed (and therefore is immutable to consultation or change via the IA process itself).[57] These criticisms seem to suggest that, rather than rely on IA as a tool to limit discretion, the EU's judiciary needs to play a role in scrutinizing, rather than deferring to, the IA process.

The thicker version of procedural review faces challenges of its own. Some of these can be discerned from the US debate.[58] While stakeholder and public interest inclusion can provide a new circle of actors to check and hold accountable administrative action, it is questionable whether courts carry the tools to properly police this process. One question, for example, is whether economic decision makers will include a fair balance of affected interests and whether those unfairly excluded can remedy their exclusion.[59] Another is the balance of power, resources, and knowledge between civil society actors, which may narrow discretion but does so in favour of more privileged and resourced participants.[60] Finally, there is the always uncertain relation between participatory and representative models of democracy: what should economic decision makers, and judges checking administrative actors, do when duties towards civil society participants and towards general electoral processes (in the EU case, the views of the European Parliament, for example) conflict?

Other challenges more specifically relate to the EU, and economic governance, case. The final problem—of a conflict between representative and participatory

[55] See Decision on the Establishment of an Independent Regulatory Scrutiny Board, C (2016) 3263, <https://ec.europa.eu/info/sites/info/files/decision-on-the-established-of-an-independent-regulatory-scrutiny-board_may2015_en.pdf> accessed 17 May 2018.

[56] See, e.g. the view of organized labour on the better regulation agenda and the use of IA, 'ETUC Declaration on Better Regulation', 18 June 2015, <https://www.etuc.org/documents/etuc-declaration-better-regulation#.WN4tsYXl04A> accessed 17 May 2018.

[57] See K Wegrich, 'Which Results? Better Regulation and Institutional Politics' (2016) 6 *Eur J Risk Regul* 369.

[58] On some criticisms and alternatives to the US public interest model, J Freeman, 'Private Parties, Public Functions and the New Administrative Law' (2000) 52 *Adm Law Rev* 3

[59] See, by analogy, the role of the EU judiciary in policing representativeness in the context of the European social dialogue in N Bernard, 'Legitimising EU Law: Is the Social Dialogue the Way Forward? Some Reflections Around the UAEPME Case' in J Shaw (ed), *Social Law and Policy in an Evolving European Union* (Hart, 2000).

[60] On this critique in the EU context, see P Magnette, 'European Governance and Civic Participation: Beyond Elitist Citizenship?' (2003) 51 *Political Stud* 144.

democracy—does not apply in the case of many aspects of economic governance, principally because economic decision makers may be intentionally insulated from both forms of democratic input. To take *Gauweiler* as an example, the ECB's mandate provides, with good reason, a high level of political independence from other institutions, and from national political opinion. To what extent, therefore, should one expect or want actors in the banking field to be responsive to, or include, civil society input in their decision making? By providing the ECB with a fixed mandate via the Treaty, its writers seemingly excluded the responsiveness of that mandate to the accountability of interest groups (with ECB accountability restricted to formal dialogue mechanisms, with no sanctioning measures, such as the Monetary Dialogue undertaken between the ECB and the European Parliament).[61] 'Thick' proceduralism simply sits uneasily with the very functions and design of the system of EU economic governance (or at least particular aspects of it).

Procedural forms of judicial review and political accountability offer some mechanisms for judges to use political institutions as intermediaries in narrowing economic discretion; at the same time, they carry the risk of doing too little or too much—either of retreating into formal box-ticking or conflicting with the very *raison d'etre* of the EU's economic functions. A final alternative may be to look elsewhere—at the process via which economic decisions are justified and defended.

6. Strategy 4: Interdisciplinary Justification

To illustrate the fourth and final approach, it may be useful to again return to the *Gauweiler* decision. At the decision's heart was the Court's acceptance that the OMT programme was a necessary element of the ECB's monetary transmission mechanism and therefore part and parcel of the ECB's core monetary policy mandate. As those who have defended the decision have argued, how could the Court have done otherwise? To deny the centrality of the OMT to the transmission mechanism would have been to substitute the judgment of the Court for that of the ECB on a fundamentally economic question: one which lawyers are ill-equipped to judge.

How well does this reasoning hold up? For all their limitations, judges rule on empirical and economic questions all the time. The EU's judiciary is no different. In determining whether national regulation constitutes a barrier to the four freedoms, the EU Courts face no choice but to wade into the questions of what constitutes a market barrier, and how such a barrier may be proportionality designed.[62] In competition law, the Court must ask, when adjudicating Articles 101 and 102 of the Treaty, whether certain agreements 'distort' the market or constitute an 'abuse' of a dominant position. In doing so, they are inevitably drawn into the domain of

---

[61] On this form of ECB accountability, see S Collignon and S Diessner, 'The European Central Bank's Monetary Dialogue with the European Parliament: Efficiency and Accountability during the Euro Crisis?' (2016) 54 *J Com Mar St* 6.

[62] See Nehl, Chapter 6 in this volume.

general economics. 'The market'—essentially an economic concept—may also be a central, if not *the* central, concept of substantive EU law.[63]

The behaviour of judges in domains like competition law may in this sense offer a guide as to how judges may seek to limit discretion in the field of economic governance. In competition law, too, the EU judiciary often limits its engagement with general economics. Tools to do this include the idea that certain practices or agreements necessarily distort competition regardless of their substantive effects on competitors.[64] Many cases, however, are not so easy. Given the immense power the Commission, in particular, wields in this field—as a first instance arbiter of competition infringements—the Courts require tools to check whether the Commission itself may be abusing its own position, or overstepping the mandate that Articles 101 and 102 provide.

One of the tools the Courts use to police the Commission's enforcement powers is to demand that the Commission justify its enforcement decisions. Decades of judicial prodding of the Commission to give transparent reasons for competition decisions has led the Commission to itself adopt standards to guide its decisions under Articles 101 and 102.[65] While these standards could be seen as akin to the soft law guiding the SGP mentioned in Section 4, they also incorporate standard economics into the process of competition review. This 'more economic approach' is particularly used to prioritize intervention. In its 2009 paper on priorities for the enforcement of competition infringements, the Commission promises to intervene to prohibit anticompetitive and exclusionary conduct only 'where the conduct concerned has already been or is capable of hampering competition from competitors which are considered to be as efficient as the dominant under-taking.'[66] Via the 'as-efficient' comparator approach, the Commission must utilize evidence, drawn from standard welfare economics that, absent the practice deemed illegal, an efficient competitor would be able to compete with the pricing or marketing strategy of the dominant market actor.

Some scholars have considered whether such a test should also inform judicial review.[67] Even if judges are not economists, mainstream economics can act as a means of guiding judicial review of Commission discretion. The Courts in this sense should check which impacts an anticompetitive practice surveyed by the Commission is likely to have on consumers, and assess whether tests like the 'as-efficient comparator' have been adequately fulfilled. Certain features of the EU Courts, such as the concentration of competition cases in the GC, could assist this

---

[63] On the EU Court's evolving and contested conception of the market, see C Kaupa, *The Pluralist Character of the European Economic Constitution* (Hart, 2016).

[64] See, e.g. exclusivity rebates as such an example in Case T-286/09, *Intel v European Commission* [2014] ECLI:EU:T:2014:547 (as rejected by the subsequent opinion of A-G Wahl on appeal).

[65] See Commission Communication on the Commission's Enforcement Priorities in Applying Article 82 of the EC Treaty to Abusive Exclusionary Conduct by Dominant Undertakings, COM (2009) 45.

[66] Ibid., 23

[67] See, e.g. M Albert and S Voigt, *The More Economic Based Approach to Competition Law* (Mohr, 2007); P Ibanez-Colomo, 'Beyond the More Economics-based Approach: A Legal Perspective on Article 102 Case-law' (2016) 53 *CML Rev* 5.

function, encouraging the selection for competition cases of judges with familiarity with the essential requirements of competitive markets. By incorporating standard economics into judicial reasoning, the Courts could send a simple message: while the Commission carries discretion, that discretion is not unlimited, with substantive economic knowledge used as a baseline from which the Commission's use of discretion can be assessed.

The fourth strategy for dealing with economic discretion would involve generalizing the 'more economic-based' approach to the broader economic governance case. To return to *Gauweiler*, if the crux of the case is the ECB's insistence that OMT is a necessary element of the monetary transmission mechanism rather than a tool of general economic policy, we require an EU judiciary that carries the disciplinary tools to verify that claim. This requires, for example, reasoning in the alternative— what would be the likely impact on the euro area, and on the ability of interest rate setting to affect prices, were an OMT scheme absent? The Court's approach would move from one of deference to what Ronald Reagan once dubbed, 'trust but verify', i.e. the assumption that other EU institutions act in good faith combined with the requirement that empirical claims are vigorously assessed and evidenced.

Clearly, such an approach would require more than a change in judicial reasoning. It may require further tools or institutional reforms. One could be providing judges with heightened training in the economics of Monetary Union. Another could be permitting greater use of *amicus curiae,* i.e. briefings from high-level economists and think tanks (the Bruegels or Institutes for Fiscal Study of this world), providing up-to-date economic knowledge to scrutinize the empirical claims forming the basis of economic decisions.[68] Finally, a more radical approach would be to make use of the possibility, envisaged under Article 257 of the TFEU, to attach judges to a specialized tribunal of the Court. The rationale for such a tribunal would be to assess decisions under EU economic governance via judges with a narrower background and specialization in the law and economics of EU economic governance. Such an approach would have a single aim: to bridge the gap between the legal and economic worlds. By doing so, it would narrow the enormous discretion that this gap currently affords to actors such as the ECB.

Clearly, such an approach would not be plain sailing. Even in the field of competition law, the 'more economics-based' approach faces plenty of criticisms, particularly as it applies to judicial review. One is that such an approach encourages a disinterested weighing of costs and benefits to consumers, undervaluing process-based elements of Treaty rules (e.g. in the competition field, the idea of equality of opportunity between competitors regardless of any 'pro-competitive effects' of actions by dominant undertakings).[69] Similarly, in the economic governance field, Treaty rules, such as the 'no bail-out clause' of Article 125 TFEU, may serve certain

---

[68] On this more dialectical approach to judicial reasoning in the EU Courts, see V Perju, 'Reason and Authority in the European Court of Justice' (2009) 49 *Va J Intl L* 307.

[69] See WPJ Wils, 'The Judgment of the EU General Court in *Intel* and the so-called "More Economic Approach" to Abuse of Dominance' (2014) 37 *World Competition* 4.

goals—like avoiding moral hazard—irrespective of their overall impact on the welfare of citizens.

A further difficulty is that—by using mainstream economics to control discretion—we treat mainstream economics as natural and uncontested. The EU Courts could end up forcing the EU's institutions to adopt a mainstream approach to economics even where evidence points to its failure in dealing with regulatory problems. One criticism of judgments like *Gauweiler* or *Pringle* is that it engages in *too much* mainstream economics, rather than too little.[70] By elevating austerity and conditionality in these cases to the status of a constitutional principle, the Court legalizes an economic approach to Article 125 in particular that has caught Greece in a vicious spiral of stagnation and debt.

If we accept that economics, like law, is a pluralist discipline, and that different economists may have different views on how something like the monetary transmission mechanism or the 'no bail-out' rule ought to be applied, we also might accept that the ECJ should not privilege one approach of economics over others.[71] At the very least, a justification-based approach based on mainstream economics would place the ECJ itself at the centre of a battle between economists (in a world where many EU citizens distrust the notion of economics as a neutral scientific discipline, able to objectively resolve particular social problems). By distancing judges from the task for which they are qualified—the 'objective' application of rules—an approach based on economic justification could also distance the EU judiciary from two of the central planks of their legitimacy: their expertise in the law and their ability to apply that expertise impartially. Justification seems the most rigorous means of limiting economic discretion; at the same time, it seems the most radical and risky approach of all four approaches to tackling the adjudication of discretion in the EU economy.

7. Conclusion

This chapter has presented four alternative methods of limiting economic discretion that have been forwarded as alternatives. Certainly, there are tensions and trade-offs between them. At the same time, the European Courts are likely to mix and combine methods, and to do so differently in different areas of EU policy. To take the first approach—deference—as an example, a more deferential approach may be justified precisely in circumstances where the conditions present in other approaches have been met (e.g. where ex ante procedural or political requirements have been fulfilled). There seem good reasons to be less demanding of the ECB, for example, in circumstances where it is acting in an area of high complexity yet has consulted relevant actors and interests than in those where it explicitly contradicts its own established guidelines or has failed to justify and consider alternatives to its economic decisions.

---

[70] On this, see M Bartl, 'Contesting Austerity: On the Limits of EU Knowledge Governance' (2017) 44 *J Law Soc* 1.
[71] Kaupa (n 63).

To conclude, it is worth reflecting precisely on the assumptions and values lying behind different approaches to controlling discretion. In the case of deference, we have already discussed its rationale, namely, to protect the values of institutional balance, and of a division between legal and policy-making bodies, established by the Treaty. In the case of the strategies of prescription and proceduralism, quite different rationales present themselves (to which different actors may attach varying importance). Here an assumption may be that Courts should allow less discretion where economic decision makers are acting alone and are therefore more likely to make error-laden or biased decisions. Another assumption may be that Courts should be more active in policing economic authority where that authority strays into politically sensitive areas where bodies closer to the preferences of the general public should have greater input in decision making. More broadly, these strategies place a high value on inclusivity and principles of good governance within the political process, positing EU law as a mechanism to ensure that the policy process meets standards of democratic and political accountability.[72]

Finally, the strategy of interdisciplinary justification, by grounding its review in welfare economics, places a stronger emphasis on the need for policy makers to make economically rational decisions. The value sought under this form of review is less inclusivity or respect for the Treaties than high-quality output, capable of objective justification. To this extent, while this chapter merely attempts to offer some 'options' for the control of economic discretion, choosing between these options requires a clear understanding of what kind of economic executive the EU is building and what kind of priority the EU should give to one rationale for judicial review over others.[73]

Those who place a high value on institutional balance, for example, may posit executive actors in the economic field, such as the ECB, as authoritative and legitimate actors in their own right whose decisions carry an intrinsic legitimacy.[74] Alternatively, those who place value on political inclusivity may see ECB action as authoritative only insofar as it can be tied to other forms of authority, provided via national governments, via electoral processes, or via the direct participation of those affected by its decisions. Alternatively, those who see the role of judges in policing discretion in terms of rationale outputs may be less open to using judicial review to tie economic decision makers to predefined 'mandates' and more open to seeing those mandates as incomplete tasks to be refined as the EU economy evolves and according to institutional judgment as to what the European economy requires to develop and thrive in the future. Each strategy is, in this sense, also tied to an idea of what judicial review in EU law, and in the EU economy, should be trying to achieve.

---

[72] On such a conception of the role of the EU Courts in EU governance more broadly, see J Corkin, 'Constitutionalism in 3D: Mapping and Legitimating our Lawmaking Underworld' (2013) 19 *ELJ* 5.

[73] See, e.g. A Vauchez, 'Fielding Supranationalism: The European Central Bank as a Field Effect' (2016) 64 *Sociol Rev* 2.

[74] See, on this, the opinion of AG Cruz Villalon in *Gauweiler* (n 14).

Developing a fuller theory of judicial review of economic discretion require something beyond the scope of this chapter—a theory of political authority and accountability in European economic governance, and an idea of why one rationale for judicial review ought to be chosen over another.[75] The EU Courts need both better strategies and better criteria for determining which strategy to choose.

[75] This constitutes one of the broader goals of the Leviathan project based at the Hertie School of Governance. See: <https://www.hertie-school.org/en/research/research-directory/research-project-pages/leviathan/> accessed 17 May 2018.

PART II

EU LAW AND EXECUTIVE DISCRETION IN FINANCIAL, MONETARY, AND ECONOMIC GOVERNANCE

5

The European Supervisory Authorities and Discretion

Can the Functional and Constitutional Circles be Squared?

*Niamh Moloney**

1. Agencies, the ESAs, and Legitimation—The Discretion Problem

The European Supervisory Authorities (ESAs) are reaching an inflection point some eight years or so after their establishment in 2011 as part of the crisis-era restructuring of EU financial governance. Three themes are suggested by empirical observation. The ESAs are gaining in credibility and in regulatory capacity. They are becoming more entrepreneurial and opportunist. Finally, they are increasingly being deployed by the EU institutions, often in an ad hoc manner, to address weaknesses and gaps in EU financial governance and as 'fixes' to emerging issues.[1] These three developments are placing pressure on the ESAs' original governance settlement as set out in their founding 2010 Regulations[2] and supported by relevant EU administrative and constitutional law. The Commission's September 2017 ESA Proposal represents the first serious attempt since 2010 to update the ESAs' governance framework, but may generate more problems than it solves, as discussed later in this chapter.[3]

This inquiry focuses on one pressure point: discretionary ESA action. The ESAs are designed, in their financial governance sphere of operation, to use their delegated powers to achieve expert, technically sound outcomes that are protected from short-term political interference—in the classic formulation of the need for and technical role performed by EU administrative agencies.[4] As the ESAs mature, and as they

---

* Professor of Financial Markets Law, London School of Economics and Political Science (LSE).
[1] See further N Moloney, 'EU Financial Governance after Brexit: The Rise of Technocracy and the Absorption of the UK's Withdrawal' in K Alexander and others, *Brexit and Financial Services. Law and Policy* (Hart, 2018).
[2] All three ESAs operate under three similar (but not identical) founding regulations. This chapter draws in the main on the ESMA Regulation (Regulation (EU) No 1095/2010 OJ [2010] 331/84).
[3] COM (2017) 536.
[4] For a survey of the extensive literature on EU agencies, see B Rittberger and A Wonka, 'Introduction: Agency Governance in the European Union' (2011) 18 *J Eur Public Policy* 780. For the classic account of the need for technocratic agencies in EU governance, see G Majone, *Regulating Europe* (Routledge, 1996). For an examination of the forces which have shaped their evolution, see recently

edge away from technocratic action and closer to making discretionary choices, involving a weighing of public interests, pressure is being placed on their legitimation arrangements. Accordingly, while the concept of discretion discussed across this book has a number of dimensions, for the purposes of *this* discussion it is considered in terms of the constraints and limits on authority which should apply, in order to secure legitimation,[5] where a legislature has delegated power to a non-majoritarian, independent administrative actor/agency[6]—in this case, the ESAs.

While agencies, despite their technical function and mandates, can and often must balance different public interests and can have redistributive effects in making expert/technical decisions, as independent actors they are not subject to direct political control/legitimated by representative institutions.[7] Agencies are non-majoritarian, technocratic, and bureaucratic institutions, possessed of specialized public authority but neither directly elected nor directly managed by elected officials;[8] their actions as public authorities are not directly legitimated by representative actors and so challenge representative democracy.[9] The constraints and relating oversight regimes imposed on agencies and that support legitimation and the related 'license to operate', can flow from various sources.[10] These include legislative rules that define and delimit the mandates and powers of agencies (thereby structuring and confining the legal space within which agency action is taken);[11,12] related veto, oversight, and review powers, exercised by the legislature;[13] judicial review;[14] mandated procedural

M Egeberg and J Trondal, 'Researching EU Agencies: What Have We Learned and Where do We Go to from Here?' (2017) 55(4) *J Common Mark Stud* 675 and, for the earlier developmental phase of EU agencies, M Thatcher and A Stone Sweet, 'Theory and Practice of Delegation to Non-Majoritarian Institutions' (2002) 25 *West Eur Polit* 1.

⁵ While legitimacy in the regulatory/agency context can be characterized in various ways, it is effectively captured by Black's identification of legitimacy in terms of a social and political license to operate. See, e.g. J Black, Constructing and Contesting Legitimacy and Accountability in Polycentric Regulatory Regimes, *LSE Law Society and Economy Working Papers* 2/2008, available at <http://ssrn.com/abstract=1091783>, accessed 11th September 2018.

⁶ As considered by Paul Craig in the context of EU administrative governance and in relation to the constraints imposed by the Court of Justice of EU. See P Craig, *UK, EU and Global Administrative Law, Foundations and Challenges* (OUP, 2016) 377–8.

⁷ On the 'crisis of democracy' which can accordingly be associated with such agencies see K Yeung, 'The Regulatory State' in R Baldwin and others (eds), *The Oxford Handbook of Regulation* (OUP, 2010) 64.

⁸ Thatcher and Stone Sweet (n 4).

⁹ F Amtenbrink and R Lastra, 'Securing Democratic Accountability of Financial Regulatory Agencies—A Theoretical Framework' in R de Milder (ed), *Mitigating Risk in the Context of Safety and Security—How Relevant is a Rational Approach* (OMV, 2008) 115, 121.

¹⁰ See Craig (n 6) 679–82, in the context of administrative regulatory power, and highlighting legal control (legislative specification of principles governing regulation), political control (legislative veto or power to amend), and judicial review. Similarly, Chiti has identified the EU's mechanisms of control as including the administrative rule of law, institutional control by the EU institutions, and judicial review, see E Chiti, 'Is EU Administrative Law Failing in Some of its Crucial Tasks' (2016) 22(5) *ELJ* 576, 590.

¹¹ J Mendes, 'Discretion, Care and Public Interests in the EU Administration: Probing the Limits of Law' (2016) 53 *Common Mkt Law Rev* 419.

¹² Amtenbrink and Lastra describe the legal basis of an agency as providing the 'basic legitimacy of the institutional set up'; see (n 9) 122.

¹³ Craig (n 6) 679, identifying the specification of the principles governing regulatory action, veto powers, and amending powers as control devices.

¹⁴ Craig (n 6) 404, noting, in the EU context, that judicial review served as the vehicle through which the courts 'elaborated the structural, substantive, and procedural conditions on which [such] regulatory power was exercised in order thereby to help legitimate it'.

requirements directed to supporting the achievement of the mandated outcomes and including consultation obligations; and reporting and review-orientated accountability devices. They can also stem from the wider normative order of constitutional provisions and general principles that binds public authority generally, and which should be respected by administrative action.[15]

These constraints and oversight regimes can come under pressure from agency discretion. Agencies are designed to fulfil technical and efficiency-orientated functions, but the establishment of an agency typically and unavoidably involves some degree of discretion being conferred so that the agency can meet its objectives[16]—and the more contingent, uncertain, and complex the area in which the agency operates, the greater the need for discretion. It is almost impossible to confine agency action within a technical box—discretionary choices, with normative policy implications and political content, almost inevitably arise.[17] As agencies exercise their discretion and so 'fill the institutional setting with life',[18] legitimacy strains can arise. Although agencies are designed to take technical decisions and to operate within a legally constrained environment, discretionary action is susceptible to multiple influences beyond the benchmarks set by the legislature. [19] Further, in exercising discretion agencies can and often *must* balance different public interests, and can have redistributive effects, making the need for effective legitimation acute.[20] In the EU, as agency influence has burgeoned, the legitimacy and related accountability of agencies has come under closer scrutiny[21] resulting in offers of reform prescriptions.[22]

[15] Mendes (n 11).

[16] D Curtin, 'Delegation to EU Non-Majoritarian Agencies and Emerging Practices of Public Accountability' in D Geradin and N Petit (eds), *Regulation through Agencies in the EU. A New Paradigm of European Governance?* (Routledge, 2005) 88.

[17] As has been repeatedly acknowledged. See, e.g. noting that, in relation to regulatory power, seemingly technical issues can also be deeply political, engaging the allocation of resources and contestation over values: P Lindseth, 'Equilibrium, Demoi-cracy, and Delegation in the Crisis of European Integration' (2014) 15(4) *Ger Law J* 529, 537 and, in the context of EU agencies, noting that it is 'doubtful whether a useful definition of "technical" as opposed to "political" issues can be developed', see S Griller and A Orator, 'Everything under Control? The "Way Forward" for European Agencies in the Footsteps of Meroni' (2010) 25 *ELR* 3, 22.

[18] E Ruffing, 'Agencies between Two Worlds: Information Asymmetry in Multilevel Policy-Making' (2015) 22 *J Eur Public Policy* 1109.

[19] Mendes has highlighted that, while the legal space within which administrative actors take discretionary decisions can be structured, the decisions made, while guided by conditions set by the legislature, are shaped by different factors, including political dynamics, expert judgment, and the moral/ ideological preferences of decision makers (n 11).

[20] On the 'crisis of democracy' which can accordingly be associated with such agencies, see Yeung (n 7).

[21] A vast legal and political science literature examines the legitimacy of agencies and the related accountability arrangements which can apply. For an early assessment, prior to the establishment of the ESAs, see D Geradin, 'The Development of European Regulatory Agencies: What the EU Should Learn from the American Experience' (2005) 11 *Columbia J Eur Law* 1. For a recent political science perspective, see M Buess, 'European Union Agencies and their Management Boards: An Assessment of Accountability and *Demoi*-cratic Legitimacy' (2015) 22 *J Eur Public Policy* 9 and, for a legal perspective, I Chiu, 'Power and Accountability in the EU Financial Regulatory Architecture: Examining Inter-agency Relations, Agency Independence and Accountability' (2015) 8 *European Journal of Legal Studies* 67.

[22] See, in particular, the work of Eduardo Chiti, calling for common reforms to EU agencies, including a stronger accountability framework, based on common principles for all agencies; greater

Legitimation issues are acute in relation to financial regulators given the extensive discretionary powers they typically wield and the extent to which their actions can have distributive consequences in the form of taxpayer burdens.[23] Financial agencies/regulators internationally represent a classic expression of the need for a 'regulatory state.' They are designed to deliver expert, technically-informed decision-making in a highly complex area in relation to which, given the long-term and societal nature of the risks and consequences engaged and the dangers of short-term political interference given the strength of related private interests, an independent technocracy is deemed appropriate to support the public interest.[24] The delegation of discretionary regulatory, supervisory, and enforcement power to financial regulators is a long-standing feature of financial system governance. In parallel with the exponential growth in financial markets since the early 1980s, and the related and increasing dependence of national fiscal stability and individual financial welfare on the financial system, governments worldwide have expanded the administrative structures which oversee the financial system. This expansion in the administrative state reflects the strong and ever-deepening public interest in a stable and productive financial system. This public interest is usually characterized in terms of the triumvirate of the protection of financial stability, consumer protection, and market efficiency which must be balanced by financial regulators.[25] Since the financial crisis and the retreat from iterative 'new governance' (broadly, governance through partnership between regulator and regulated) to 'command and control' intervention, financial regulators have seen their powers increase internationally and in the EU. But given the scale of the discretion typically afforded to financial regulators, legitimation risks arise, including in relation to the potential for 'bureaucratic drift' away from mandates and objectives, industry capture, and agency engagement with issues that can be highly politicized and have distributive consequences.[26] The scale of the delegation to financial regulators implies that the main legitimating constraints imposed on regulators' discretionary powers are usually directed to the ex-ante,

---

proceduralization of soft law; and stronger consultation practices: Chiti (n 10) and E Chiti, 'European Agencies' Rulemaking: powers, procedures and assessment' (2013) 19 *ELJ* 93.

[23] As has been repeatedly emphasized in the context of the financial crisis. From the US debate see, e.g. S Omorova, 'Bankers, Bureaucrats and Guardians: Towards Tripartism in Financial Services Regulation' (2012) 37 *J Corp Law* 622 and A Levitin, 'The Politics of Financial Regulation and the Regulation of Financial Politics' (2014) 127 *Harv L Rev* 1991.

[24] For a survey of the role of financial regulators see E Ferran, 'Institutional Design: The Choices for National Systems' in N Moloney and others (eds), *The Oxford Handbook of Financial Regulation* (OUP, 2015) 97.

[25] One of the classic balancing points relates to how to balance financial stability with consumer protection where large fines for non-compliance with consumer protection rules might, for example, weaken the capital position of a regulated actor. Similarly, where a financial regulator has a growth-related objective (which is unusual) or a mandate to promote competitiveness (more common), its pursuit can come into tension with the transaction costs associated with stability, market efficiency, or consumer protection-related action.

[26] E Hüpkes, M Quintyn, and M Taylor, The Accountability of Financial Sector Supervisors: Principles and Practice, *IMF Working Paper* WP/05/51 (2005), in the context of the uneasiness with which legislators typically approach the delegation of powers to financial regulators.

legislative structuring of the exercise of delegated powers within defined mandates and specified powers (input-orientated legitimacy); and to related procedural as well as ex-post accountability mechanisms, which provide a means for directing the exercise of powers and assessing how those powers are exercised (procedural/output-orientated legitimacy).[27] Input-orientated legitimacy devices in the form of detailed legislative mandates and specification of operating powers and conditions, designed to frame the legal space within which the regulator operates and to set objectives, are common. Given the need to allow financial regulators a significant degree of operational freedom, however, procedural/output legitimacy-orientated mechanisms are most strongly associated with financial regulators. These include the procedural impact assessment requirements and related data-gathering and interrogation requirements as well as consultation obligations, which apply in particular to (quasi-)rule-making activities by financial regulators. For example, the ESAs are required under their founding Regulations to carry out impact assessments when preparing draft administrative rules and soft guidelines (unless to do so would be disproportionate); they are also usually mandated by the Commission (when providing it with technical advice on administrative rules) to carry out impact assessments. Chief among the output legitimation devices in common use, however, are accountability mechanisms, linked to the input-orientated legal mandates that structure the space within which discretion can be legitimately deployed by the regulator, and which hold the regulator to account with respect to its actions.[28] Output legitimation, and the related 'trust in technocracy' it implies, is not without challenge in the financial regulation context. Beyond the well-charted difficulties in insulating technical decisions from political implications,[29] financial regulation is not a science and regulators operate under conditions of significant uncertainty and contingency. Despite the increasingly empirical and data-driven quality of regulatory intervention, data remains incomplete, indicators of market stress can be unclear, and regulators frequently struggle to identify which behavioural change is necessary and how it can be achieved.[30] Bureaucratic drift can also threaten output legitimation. For output legitimation to be effective, accordingly, related accountability mechanisms must deliver informed and purposeful review of the regulator and legislative constraints must allow for meaningful assessment.

The agencification of financial governance that has taken place in the EU, notably through the 2011 establishment of the ESAs, forms part of a wider pattern of greater

---

[27] On legitimacy and accountability in relation to financial regulators, see generally P Iglesias Rodríges, *The Accountability of Financial Regulators: A European and International Perspective* (Kluwer, 2014) and Amtenbrink and Lastra (n 9).

[28] For an analysis of the regimes which apply to financial regulators in the UK, US, and Spain, see Iglesias Rodríges (n 27).

[29] See Mendes (n 11).

[30] See, e.g. on the difficulties posed by stress tests, an increasingly important tool for managing stability risks, M Goldman, Stress Testing Stress Tests. Challenging the Authority of Indicators of Indicators (2012), available at <http://ssrn.com/abstract=2083594>, accessed 11th September 2018.

national reliance on agencies, as well as of greater EU engagement in market governance, which is extending beyond traditional agency/administrative governance and extending to the classic governmental functions of stabilization and distribution through the management of fiscal policy.[31] But ESA discretion is structured and limited in a different way to the manner in which the discretion of national financial regulators is managed. The ESAs are functionally designed to deliver the independence, technical competence, and expertise typically associated with national financial regulators. But the legal constraints that shape the space within which powers can be delegated to the ESAs, and in which they can take discretionary action, are significantly greater than those that apply to their counterparts at national level—albeit that the powers exercised by the ESAs are significantly weaker than those of their national counterparts. These additional constraints derive from the ESAs' distinct position as single-market agencies based in EU legislation and designed to support the administration of the single market. The ESAs are subject to constraints in the form of defined mandates and powers, procedural requirements, accountability mechanisms, and oversight/judicial review, which are, in their essentials at least, similar to those that apply to national financial regulators (in the EU and internationally) and that are broadly directed to accountability-orientated output legitimacy. But additional constraints apply, which derive from the ESAs' distinct constitutional and single-market setting. The first is legal: the *Meroni* ruling only permits the delegation of executive powers, the exercise of which can be subject to strict review in light of objective criteria determined by the delegation authority; the delegation of discretionary powers, implying a wide margin of discretion that may make possible the execution of actual economic policy, is prohibited.[32] In effect, action engaging discretionary choices that require a weighing of different public interests and which may have distributive consequences is prohibited (and reserved to the EU's legislative bodies). The 2014 *Short Selling* ruling has since then emphasized that, if appropriate conditions apply to the exercise of discretion by the ESAs and support effective judicial review, the *Meroni* requirement is met.[33] While the implications of the ruling are contested,[34] it is hard to read it other than as a loosening of the *Meroni* constraint and a widening of the operating space of the European Securities and Markets Authority (ESMA, the ESA in question),[35] particularly as the conditions which bounded ESMA's exercise of the relevant powers

---

[31] J Caporaso, M-H Kim, W Dirrett, and R Wesley, 'Still a Regulatory State? The European Union and the Financial Crisis' (2015) 22 *J Eur Public Policy* 889.

[32] *Meroni v High Authority of the European Coal and Steel Community* [1958] ECLI:EU:C:1958:7.

[33] *UK v European Parliament and Council* [2014] ECLI:EU:C:2014:18.

[34] See CF Bergstrom, 'Shaping the New System for Delegation of Powers to EU Agencies: United Kingdom v European Parliament and Council (Short Selling)' (2015) 52 *Common Mkt Law Rev* 219; P Van Cleynenbrueguel, 'Meroni Circumvented? Article 114 TFEU and EU Regulatory Agencies' (2014) 21 *Maastrich J Eur Comp Law* 64; E Howell, 'The European Court of Justice: Selling us Short' (2014) 11 *Eur Co Financ Rev* 454; and M Scholten and M van Rijsbergen, 'The ESMA Short Selling Case: Erecting a New Delegation Doctrine in the EU upon the Meroni-Romano Remnants' (2014) 41 *Legal Issues of Economic Integration* 389.

[35] See Craig (n 6) 539, and N Moloney, *EU Securities and Financial Markets Regulation* (OUP, 2014) 998–1003.

in this case were general and high level, and the particular decision-making power delegated to ESMA engaged a balancing of public interests. The *Meroni* constraint is not only legal, however; it is also political. It is clear from the negotiations on the ESAs, and as they have developed, that the limits *Meroni* imposes on delegations to administrative actors have been deployed to achieve political aims. Many Member States remain ambivalent in relation to ESA power,[36] while the Commission's preferences have long been to control the ESAs, given the threat they pose to its executive power,[37] although the September 2017 ESA Proposal outlines an incremental but material extension of ESMA's direct supervision powers, which suggests a weakening of the Commission's resistance to empowering the agencies. The Commission has, for example, proposed that ESMA be given exclusive, direct supervisory powers over a limited set of regulated actors (of small population admittedly—including certain 'EU-labelled' funds such as the European Long-term Investment Fund, data services providers, and certain benchmarks), but these powers, if granted, would mark a notable strengthening of ESMA's current direct supervisory powers.

Notwithstanding *Meroni*, in practice the ESAs are increasingly behaving like autonomous financial regulatory authorities making public interest choices—both formally, as their delegated powers expand, and informally, as they shape their operating environments in a frequently entrepreneurial manner. Functionally, this development could be regarded as a triumph of ESA ingenuity and diplomacy; the outputs of the ESAs, measured against their objectives and the wider functions of EU financial governance, can be regarded as providing appropriate legitimation.[38] But ESA ingenuity has limits (legal and political) and *Meroni*, which conflates legal prescription and political interests, can increasingly be regarded as an obstruction to functionally useful ESA action. Conversely, the expansion in the ESAs' powers can be regarded as undermining the rule of law within which the ESAs operate and as leading to a situation in which discretionary choices are not appropriately legitimated.[39] This is noteworthy, as the constraints that currently apply to ESA power are not based on the ESAs exercising extensive discretionary powers and may not, accordingly, deliver sufficient legitimation.

Thus far, the current ESA organizational settlement has 'muddled by', notwithstanding the ambiguities as to the constraints on discretionary action. But an inflection point is on the horizon. The fate of the September 2017 ESA Proposal is difficult to predict given its acute political salience, but in its current form it, as noted

---

[36] Notably Germany. In February 2016, the Bundestag adopted a resolution which called for the German federal government to ensure adequate scrutiny of the ESAs. It has also stated that where soft ESA Guidelines do not correspond to the Bundestag's objectives they should not be adopted in Germany. Centre for European Policy, European Supervisory Authorities. Room for Improvement at Level 2 and 3. Study on Behalf of the fpmi Munich Financial Centre Initiative (2016) 42.

[37] Moloney (n 35) 994–1003 and 1007.

[38] For a functional case for ESMA empowerment, see E Howell, 'The Evolution of ESMA and Direct Supervision: Are There Implications for EU Supervisory Governance?' (2017) 54 *Common Mkt Law Rev* 107 and N Moloney, 'Institutional Governance and Capital Markets Union: Incrementalism or a 'Big Bang'? (2016) 13 *Eur Co Financ Rev* 376.

[39] E.g. Griller and Orator (n 17).

earlier, suggests a material expansion of ESA power;[40] the UK's withdrawal from the EU is prompting calls for the ESAs to be empowered in order to support the single market in financial services against any Brexit-related risks and, in the case of ESMA, has led to a proposal for it to be conferred with new supervisory powers over 'third country' actors.[41] And changing political conditions, notably in France, may lead to stronger Member State support for supranational financial governance and for a strengthening of the ESAs' functions—although changes to political preference can be difficult to predict in this area. Any related significant empowerment of the ESAs will require that the nature of the *Meroni* constraint is addressed. Specifically, if, as the CJEU has indicated, *Meroni* can be met by the imposition of general legislative/administrative conditions on ESA action (as was the case in the *Short Selling* ruling), reforms to ESA governance will be needed to ensure appropriate legitimation of any material enhancement of ESA powers. The current trajectory of the ESAs and the evidence as to how they are, de facto, strengthening their ability to shape and make public interest choices also suggest that reforms are necessary. Current accountability and legitimacy controls are not sufficiently strong to take the weight of any new powers or of the ESAs' de facto capacity to exert technocratic influence.

Subsequent sections of this chapter seek to expose the hidden nature of ESA discretion[42] and to probe the implications. This chapter takes the position that the functional effectiveness of the European System of Financial Supervision (the institutional location of EU financial governance since the crisis and in which the ESAs operate, outlined later in the chapter) requires a loosening of *Meroni*, and an acknowledgement that the ESAs exercise discretionary powers and balance public interests, but that stronger output legitimacy, delivered through strengthened accountability arrangements, is required.[43] In addition, the constitutive legislation shaping ESA discretion must make a stronger attempt to identify the outcomes to be sought by the ESAs: both as an input means of structuring their discretion and, potentially, of making judicial review more meaningful; and as an output means for strengthening legitimation through accountability. In taking this position, the analysis is located in a multidimensional literature. It primarily adopts a legal/institutionalist approach to examine the nature of the ESAs' current powers, how they are developing, and

---

[40] The September 2017 ESA Proposal is primarily concerned with expanding and strengthening the ESAs' soft supervisory convergence powers. It also, however, proposes new binding powers for all three ESAs to request information from financial market participants and to impose sanctions for non-compliance, as well as a discrete suite of new binding supervisory powers for ESMA (only), albeit just in relation to a small cohort of regulated actors with distinct cross-border reach (including certain EU funds, benchmark administrators and data services providers) (n 3).

[41] Over summer 2017, the Commission proposed that ESMA be empowered to supervise directly third country 'central clearing counterparties' (CCPs), financial market infrastructures of critical importance to the operation of the EU derivatives market, as a means for addressing the risks and competitive tensions posed by the post-Brexit 'offshoring' of a significant component of the CCP market in the UK: COM (2017) 331. See further Moloney (n 1).

[42] Chiti (n 10) has argued in the context of EU administrative law generally that the discretionary nature of its decentralized administrations is not being openly recognized but hidden in relevant legislation.

[43] This chapter does not address the wider issue as to whether the *Meroni* constraint should be removed and EU agencies liberated to take discretionary choices. On this debate, see Craig (n 6) 540–4.

the related pressure being placed on *Meroni*, but is informed by the political science/
regulatory governance literature on agency development and legitimation. ESMA,
the most advanced of the ESAs in terms of the suite of delegated powers it deploys,
is the major concern of the analysis.

2. ESMA and EU Financial Governance

ESMA forms part of the European System of Financial Supervision (ESFS) which
was constructed as part of the EU's response to the catastrophic weaknesses in EU
financial governance, and the related exposure of EU financial stability to cross-
border contagion risks, revealed by the financial crisis.[44] The ESFS is composed
of the national competent (supervisory) authorities (NCAs) which, through their
'home' supervision of locally registered regulated actors, and through their co-
ordination with the 'host' supervisors in whose jurisdictions cross-border regulated actors operate, ground the ESFS; the three co-ordinating ESAs—for banking
(European Banking Authority—EBA); securities and markets (European Securities
and Markets Authority—ESMA); and insurance and occupational pensions
(European Insurance and Occupational Pensions Authority—EIOPA); and the
European Systemic Risk Board (ESRB, charged with scanning for systemic risks to
the EU financial system). The ESAs operate through their Boards of Supervisors,
the decision-making members of which are representatives of all the Member States'
relevant national financial regulators—giving the Boards an intergovernmental flavour, although their tasks are supranational (the Board must act in the 'sole interest of
the Union as a whole').[45] A QMV is required for quasi-regulatory decision making,
but the ESAs typically operate through consensus. All three ESAs are independent
and are formally accountable to the European Parliament and the Council.[46]

The ESAs are charged with an array of co-ordination-orientated responsibilities.
These are primarily directed to two areas. First, administrative rule making, where
a relevant mandate is given in a related legislative measure (through the ESAs' proposal of administrative 'Binding Technical Standards' (BTSs), which are adopted by
the Commission, and the giving of 'technical advice' to the Commission on other
Delegated Acts). Second, supervisory co-ordination and convergence (including
through the adoption of soft law Guidelines, FAQs, templates, and similar measures; peer review; support of co-ordinating 'supervisory colleges'; the collection and
interrogation of market data; and stress testing). Additionally, all three ESAs have
the power to direct national regulators and market participants to act in three specified and prescribed circumstances relating to breach of EU law; failure of mediation
between national regulators; and in emergency conditions. Furthermore, the ESAs

---

[44] For an examination of ESMA in EU financial governance, see N Moloney, *The Age of
ESMA: Governing EU Financial Markets* (Hart Publishing, 2018).
[45] E.g. 2010 ESMA Regulation, Art 42.
[46] E.g. 2010 ESMA Regulation, Arts 1 (ESMA is to act independently and objectively and in the
interests of the EU alone), and 3 (accountability).

are conferred with limited direct intervention powers, which have been conferred in a piecemeal, ad hoc manner over the period since the ESAs were established. In the case of ESMA (unusual among the three ESAs in the extent to which direct intervention powers have been granted), the most significant of these intervention powers cover ESMA's exclusive supervisory and enforcement jurisdiction over rating agencies and trade repositories (the latter being data collection vehicles for the EU derivatives market); last resort intervention powers in relation to short selling; and last resort intervention powers in relation to the prohibition of services and product distribution. EBA and EIOPA also have last resort intervention powers in relation to deposit-related and insurance-related products, respectively. All these powers, delineated in the ESAs' founding Regulations and, in the case of the intervention powers that have followed their establishment, in relevant sectoral legislation,[47] are to be exercised in accordance with the ESAs' objectives. In the case of ESMA, this is to protect the public interest by contributing to the short-, medium-, and long-term stability and effectiveness of the financial system and to contribute to a series of subsidiary objectives.[48]

The fast-maturing ESAs have significantly enhanced the EU's regulatory capacity, or its ability to achieve outcomes through the adoption, monitoring, and enforcing of rules,[49] and the EU's related ability to support the public interest in a stable and productive EU financial market, in particular, through the protection of financial stability, consumer protection, and market efficiency. Empirical observation suggests that the ESAs have provided, through their quasi-rule-making powers, extensive technical support to the massive expansion in the EU's administrative rulebook since the financial crisis and have significantly deepened supervisory co-ordination arrangements.[50] Formally, however, the ESAs are not legislators and cannot, reflecting the *Meroni/Romano* constraint,[51] adopt rules. Additionally, with regard to supervision, as EU agencies their supervisory powers are circumscribed (under the *Meroni* ruling they are not empowered to take discretionary decisions unless appropriate conditions are placed on the relevant powers). But by virtue of the significant enhancement that they have brought to the EU's regulatory capacity, they have come to exert a material technocratic influence on EU financial governance, often shaping how public interest choices are made, either by making those choices, or by

---

[47] ESMA's short selling powers, e.g. are set out in the 2012 Short Selling Regulation (Regulation (EU) No 236/2012 [2012] OJ L86/1).

[48] Including in relation to: improving the functioning of the single market; ensuring the integrity, efficiency, transparency and orderly functioning of financial markets; strengthening international supervisory coordination; preventing regulatory arbitrage; and enhancing consumer protection (ESMA Regulation, Art 1(5)).

[49] Regulatory capacity is a term typically associated with political economy and relates to the ability of a state to formulate, monitor and enforce rules. See, e.g. D Bach and A Newman 'The European Regulatory State and Global Public Policy: Micro-Institutions, Macro-Influence' (2007) 14 *J Eur Public Policy* 827.

[50] Reviews of the ESAs from market, institutional, and political stakeholders have been broadly positive. See, e.g. stakeholder reaction to the Commission's 2017 ESA Review: Commission, Feedback Statement on the Public Consultation on the Operations of the ESAs (2017).

[51] The *Romano* ruling prohibits agencies from adopting normative measures: Case 98/90 [1981] ECR 1241.

means of the very significant technical influence they exert on how those choices are shaped and made.[52] Strains are accordingly being placed both on *Meroni*—in the form of the pressure it is placing on the development of the EU's regulatory capacity—and on ESA legitimation—as their powers and capacity develop, as the following sections discuss.

3. ESMA as a Maturing and Entrepreneurial Actor: Meroni Pressure and Legitimation Strains

3.1 Expanding powers and deepening influence

Since ESMA's establishment in 2011, the EU institutions have repeatedly strengthened its delegated administrative powers.[53] Subsequently, almost every legislative reform relevant to EU securities markets has strengthened ESMA in some way. To take only three examples: the 2012 Short Selling Regulation conferred on ESMA direct intervention powers in relation to short selling; the 2011 Credit Rating Agency Regulation made ESMA the exclusive EU supervisor of rating agencies;[54] and the 2014 Markets in Financial Instruments Regulation conferred on ESMA direct intervention powers in relation to EU investment product markets (the power to ban products). Less dramatically, every new securities market legislative measure has brought with it new mandates for delegated rule making, increasingly in the form of administrative BTSs, over which ESMA has more control as proposer to the Commission of the standard, rather than standard administrative Delegated Acts, on which ESMA gives technical advice to the Commission;[55] mandated ESMA to develop soft Guidelines in often operationally critical areas; required ESMA to gather and interrogate data; empowered ESMA to host market-critical databases; and enhanced ESMA's supervisory co-ordination and co-operation powers.

---

[52] On the ESAs strengthening capacity to shape EU financial governance through technocratic means, see further Moloney (n 38).

[53] The extent to which the ESAs' administrative powers in relation to supervision are formally 'delegated' by a principal is contestable. While their quasi-regulatory powers are delegated from the Commission, it is not clear that the Commission is the location of financial market supervision which is currently a Member State competence, if one shared at the supranational level to different degrees—the more accurate term accordingly might be 'conferred'. Busuioc, e.g. has considered whether the growth of agency power is a function of delegation or rather of a 'Europeanization' of the relevant functions: M Busuioc, *European Agencies* (OUP, 2013) 19. Similarly, agency powers can be regarded as being delegated from multiple co-principals, including the Council, the Commission, Parliament, and the Member States; see Curtin (n 16). For the purposes of simplicity, however, and to underscore the legitimation issues which arise with administrative powers, the term delegation is used.

[54] Directive 2014/65/EU [2014] OJ L173/349 and Regulation (EU) No 513/2011 [2011] OJ L145/30.

[55] This was particularly marked in the case of the cornerstone Markets in Financial Instruments Directive II/Markets in Financial Instruments Regulation 2014 (MiFID II/MiFIR), leading to the Commission lodging a reservation on the final adoption of the regime which underlined its concern as to the over-use of these rules where Delegated Acts (in relation to which the Commission has more control) would be more appropriate.

ESMA's evolution has also been a function of its strengthening credibility and capacity in EU financial governance, and its related opportunism and entrepreneurialism. Empirical observation of ESMA reveals it to be an increasingly agile and ambitious actor, pushing against the limitations of its *Meroni*-bound suite of powers and thereby engaging in, or at least significantly shaping, public interest choices.

3.2 Regulatory governance

In relation to regulatory governance, ESMA, which is embedded within the process governing administrative rule making for financial markets, has been the dominant influence on the massive administrative rulebook which now forms part of the single rulebook for EU financial markets. It has also begun to shape the legislative process, although ESMA, as an administrative actor, is not formally engaged in the level 1 legislative process.[56] ESMA has, for example, recently begun to shape the legislative Markets in Financial Instruments Directive II/Markets in Financial Instruments Regulation (MiFID II/MiFIR) regime (a behemoth measure providing the EU's single rulebook for trading and investment services).[57] For example, reflecting its privileged position as the repository of a vast bank of EU market data, it recently warned the Commission of market developments that suggested that the new MiFID II/MiFIR rules regarding trading venues may be circumvented, calling for legislative revisions, prompting the adoption of revisions by the Commission, and taking remedial action in the form of related soft law.[58] It has also long used its soft power to adopt soft Guidelines and similar measures to address ambiguities and weaknesses in legislative texts.

Binding rules aside, ESMA has also used soft measures to drive market action. ESMA is having a material influence on financial market governance by means of its now-immense body of soft law, whether in the form of formal Guidelines (which must follow the procedural requirements set out in the ESMA Regulation[59]), Opinions, Public Statements, Q&As, templates, and a host of other soft materials. Two examples from a multitude underline the extent to which ESMA is shaping market behaviour outside the confines of the formal Commission-located process for administrative rule making. First, ESMA's extensive Q&A on the complex

---

[56] EU financial governance is based on the 'Lamfalussy model' of level 1 legislative rules; level 2 administrative rules; level 3 soft supervisory convergence measures; and level 2 enforcement action by the Commission.

[57] Regulation (EU) No 600/2014 [2014] OJ L173/84.

[58] Letter from ESMA Chair Maijoor to Commission, 1 February 2017, highlighting ESMA's concerns that the rules that prevent a particular form of trading venue from engaging in certain activities were being circumvented by emerging market arrangements. ESMA's intervention led to two letters from the Parliament to the Commission in which the Parliament called for a legislative response and was followed by ESMA adopting soft guidance to the market to address the related arbitrage risk. The Commission adopted an administrative rule change over summer 2017 (Com Ares (2017)3070825).

[59] Under Art 16 of the 2010 ESMA Regulation, ESMA is empowered to adopt Guidelines which are subject to a 'comply of explain' requirement imposed on its member regulators (and, where relevant, regulated actors), which has a 'hardening' effect. Art 16 Guidelines can be mandated by the co-legislators or adopted by ESMA under its own initiative and are subject to consultation requirements.

2012 European Market Infrastructure Regulation (EMIR), the pillar measure for the regulation of EU derivatives markets,[60] has come to attain the de facto status of binding law given the extent to which it is followed by the market and supervisors, as have the suite of Q&As which ESMA has adopted on the massive 2014 MiFID II/MiFIR regime.[61] Second, ESMA is typically quick to seize the agenda on emerging issues by means of its soft law powers. It has, for example, recently adopted soft 'Public Statements' on the practices it encourages banks to follow in their market disclosures as they implement the major new international financial reporting standard (IFRS), IFRS 9.[62] The implementation of IFRS 9, which came into force in January 2018, is one of the biggest operational challenges currently faced by the EU banking sector; the standard transforms how banks report credit risk and loan losses. It is primarily of concern to EU bank regulators and EBA. ESMA nonetheless seized the agenda, adopting Public Statements setting out how it expects banks to report to the market on IFRS 9 issues.

ESMA is also increasingly influencing the 'upstream' rule-making/policy process through informal channels by advising the Commission or producing own-initiative policy measures and soft Guidelines.[63] This is particularly apparent from the Commission's current Capital Markets Union (CMU) agenda, which, along with 'completing Banking Union,' defines the EU's financial governance agenda at present. ESMA has been consistent and transparent in its support of CMU,[64] which has the potential to be politically contested given persistent divergences in economic/market models across Member States (and has been particularly forceful since the Brexit referendum),[65] and has advocated for CMU before the European Parliament.[66] It is also shaping how key Commission CMU policies are developing;[67]

---

[60] Regulation (EU) No 648/2012 [2012] OJ L201/1.

[61] E.g. the Q&As in the MiFID II/MiFIR Investor Protection/Intermediaries Q&A, which address ESMA's interpretation of whether certain forms of research in the debt market might not constitute 'research' for the purposes of the new MiFID II/MiFIR rules which apply to payment for research by asset managers and so could fall outside the new and highly contested restrictions relating to the establishment of research payment accounts, have been used by some asset managers to work around the new MiFID II/MiFIR rules; others have adopted a more conservative approach, following the spirit rather than the letter of the new rules. See L Noonan, 'Investment Banks to Clash over MiFID II Rules on Free Research,' *Financial Times*, 11 September 2017.

[62] ESMA, Public Statement on Implementation of IFRS 9 (ESMA/2016/1563) (2016) and ESMA, Public Statement on European Common Enforcement Priorities for 2017 IFRS Financial Statements (ESMA32-63-340) (2017).

[63] As it is empowered to do under the ESMA Regulation (Arts 16 and 34).

[64] ESMA, Response to the Commission Green Paper on Building a Capital Markets Union (2015/ESMA/856) (2015).

[65] See, e.g. ESMA, Response to the Commission Consultation Document on CMU Mid-Term Review (ESMA31-68-147] (2017), highlighting the 'urgency' of completing CMU given the Brexit decision.

[66] ESMA Chairman Maijoor has underlined the importance of CMU both informally (Speech to European Parliament ALDE Seminar on the European Supervisory Authorities, 8 February 2017) and formally (in his September 2016 annual report to the European Parliament (Statement of ESMA Chair Maijoor, ECON Hearing, 26 September 2016 (ESMA/2016/1392)).

[67] ESMA has, e.g. engaged in extensive preparatory work on loan origination (or lending by investment funds—a key aspect of the CMU agenda), setting out the necessary technical elements for a common European framework (ESMA, Opinion, Key Principles on a European Framework on Loan Origination by Funds (ESMA/2016/596) (2016)). To take another example, the Commission

calling for certain reforms;[68] acting as a data source for the Commission;[69] and supporting supervisory co-ordination and convergence in relation to aspects of the CMU agenda.[70]

These developments, however technocratically appealing from an efficiency and expertise perspective, are placing pressure on *Meroni*. For example, it is difficult to square the extent to which ESMA shapes the administrative rule-making process with the *Meroni/Romano* formality that it is prohibited from adopting rules/making discretionary choices. Recent experience with MiFID II/MiFIR in relation to administrative rule making is illustrative. MiFID II/MiFIR, which came into force in 2018, recasts and reforms the earlier MiFID I and significantly expands the scope of EU financial market regulation to reflect the global crisis-era consensus that the reach of financial market regulation needed to be significantly extended, as well as EU-specific regulatory policies. Massive in itself, it is supported by a dense 'level 2' administrative rulebook, composed of over 40 sets of lengthy and complex administrative rules.[71] ESMA, operating under MiFID II/MiFIR mandates, either proposed these administrative rules as BTSs or advised the Commission where the rules took the form of Delegated Acts. Reflecting the immense complexity of many of these rules, and the extent to which they were heavily data-driven,[72] the Commission accepted the vast bulk of ESMA's proposals/advice. There were flashpoints where the Commission over-ruled ESMA,[73] but ESMA has, in effect, written the vast new administrative rulebook. Legitimation issues accordingly arise: this rulebook, the construction of which involved highly technical choices, is nonetheless predicted to bring transformative change to the EU financial market, reordering business models in the pursuit of financial stability, and has generated significant market concern.[74]

has highlighted its commitment to working with ESMA and the other ESAs on developing a policy response to fintech (Commission, Fintech: A More Competitive and Innovative European Financial Sector (2017)), in relation to which ESMA has engaged in a number of related activities.

[68] ESMA was an early proponent of the need for reforms to the EU venture capital fund regime (now a component of the CMU agenda), addressing the uncertainties generated by the fund rules in a 2014 Q&A, and calling for legislative reform in its response to the Commission's 2015 Green Paper on CMU: ESMA, Response to the Commission Green Paper on CMU (ESMA/2015/856) (2015).

[69] This is particularly the case in relation to SME finance where the Commission has engaged in a host of fact-finding, consultation, and ESA-based co-ordination efforts: Commission, Capital Markets Union—Accelerating Reform (COM (2016) 601) (2016), Annex, State of Play.

[70] A key example relates to its activities as regards crowdfunding (another key element of the CMU agenda) in relation to which ESMA has engaged in a range of co-ordination-based activities, including: an Opinion on the regulatory challenges (Opinion, Investment-based Crowdfunding (ESMA/2014/1378)(2014)), a review of national approaches (Investment-based Crowdfunding, Insights from Regulators in the EU (ESMA/2015/856) (2015)), and an examination of the regulatory implications in relation to money laundering and terrorist financing rules (Q&A, 1 July 2015 (ESMA/2015/1005)).

[71] Many were published in [2017] OJ L87, 31 March 2017.

[72] ESMA engaged in an unprecedented series of market consultations, empirical assessments, and data modelling in advising on/proposing the new MiFID II/MiFIR rules.

[73] Notably in relation to aspects of the new trading transparency regime which now applies to EU bond markets and which has the capacity to generate significant unintended effects. The Commission requested ESMA to make changes to certain of its proposed rules in this area which, after robust expression of its disagreement with the Commission's position, ESMA did. See ESMA Opinions ESMA 2016/666, 2016/668, and 2016/730.

[74] Much of the concern relates to the risk that the new rules may reduce the incentives of key market actors such as investment banks to 'deal' in securities, given the increased cost of such activities, and

Accordingly, while the construction of the rulebook by ESMA involved the exercise of technical discretion, it also engaged public interest choices as to the nature of the EU market.[75] Certainly, it cannot be stated that neither the Commission's review of ESMA's BTS proposals/technical advice nor the Council/Parliament's oversight of the Commission in adopting the related administrative rules[76] is a formality.[77] Nonetheless, given the scale of ESMA's influence it is difficult to make the case against it being a de facto rule maker. Formal *Meroni* challenges and wider challenges for legitimation accordingly arise.

Guidelines and related measures pose particular challenges.[78] Functionally, ESMA's soft law measures fulfil a critical role in clarifying legislative and administrative rules and supporting legal certainty, minimizing opportunities for regulatory arbitrage, and supporting supervisory convergence. But *Meroni* and related legitimation challenges are acute here. Guidelines adopted under Article 16 of the ESMA Regulation are the only form of ESMA soft law subject to procedural requirements, notably the obligation for market consultation. All other soft measures are, formally at least, only constrained by ESMA's scope and mandate constraints. But Article 16 Guidelines and other soft measures are troublesome in terms of *Meroni*, given their direct impact on how markets and regulators behave; and also in terms of legitimation more generally, given the weaknesses in ESMA's wider legitimacy mechanisms (Section 5.2)—a recurring complaint from market stakeholders is that ESMA's Guidelines, while nominally in the form of soft law that does not have binding effect, are treated as having a binding effect by national regulators, can impose significant costs, can shape subsequent legislative action by the EU, and are not always based within a secure mandate.[79]

Similar themes emerge in relation to ESMA's policy/legislative support activities. The CMU agenda noted earlier is designed to have transformative effects, seeking to weaken the EU's current dependence on bank funding and strengthen market-based

---

thereby reduce liquidity and increase stability risks. See, e.g. European Systemic Risk Board, Market Liquidity, and Market-Making (2016).

[75] Exemplifying accordingly that it is neither empirically possible nor normatively desirable to disaggregate 'technical discretion' and 'discretion proper' in the area of financial governance. See Mendes (n 11).

[76] Administrative rules are adopted either under Art 290/291 TFEU or under the related procedures which apply to BTSs under the ESMA Regulation, Arts 10–15.

[77] There have been occasions when ESMA resisted changes requested by the Commission to its proposals for BTSs, but the Commission prevailed. These are, however, rare when considered in light of the vast corpus of rules in relation to which ESMA has proposed BTSs since 2011; see further Moloney (n 38). Similarly, the Parliament, which holds veto powers in relation to most BTSs and Delegated Acts, has in the past signalled its intention to veto (although the Commission has typically been able to address its concerns) and, for the first time did so in September 2016. The Parliament exercised its veto powers in relation to the administrative rules proposed by the Commission (advised by all three ESAs) in relation to certain highly contested investment product disclosures: European Parliament, Objection to a Delegated Act: Key Information Documents for Packaged Retail and Insurance-based Investment Products (P8_TA(2016)0347), 14 September 2016.

[78] On the legitimacy challenges posed by soft law in EU governance generally see L Senden, 'Soft Post-Legislative Rulemaking: A Time for More Stringent Control' (2013) 19 *ELJ* 57.

[79] See further the 2017 ESA Review: Commission, Consultation on the Operating of the European Supervisory Authorities (2017).

funding. Its amplification demands multiple and complex policy choices relating to, for example, the structure of national economies, the extent to which risk should be diversified, and the extent to which households should be 'financialized'.[80] ESMA, which is exerting very significant influence on how the CMU agenda is developing, is shaping how these choices are framed and addressed.

Functionally, it is relatively easy to make the case for ESMA's strengthening capacity and in support of its entrepreneurial approach. ESMA's efforts to clarify and strengthen the single rulebook, for example, can serve to reduce transaction costs, limit regulatory arbitrage, increase legal certainty, and deepen national supervisory capacity, while its technocratic support of developing policy initiatives should reduce the risk of short termism and poor legislative design. Nonetheless, ESMA is sailing very close to setting out policy choices and to balancing different public interests in a manner troublesome not only from a *Meroni* perspective, but also more generally. ESMA is not, however, subject to the legitimation which would typically be required of a financial regulator in relation to its rule-making powers (notably in relation to governance). Neither does it, as considered in Section 4, have the formal powers to adjust and refine rules as necessary.

3.3 Supervisory governance

A similar narrative emerges from ESMA's parallel supervisory mandate. ESMA has up to now been primarily focused on its quasi-regulatory activities given the weight of the crisis-era administrative rule-making mandates. But as it increasingly turns to its supervisory co-ordination/convergence mandate,[81] similar trends can be identified in relation to supervisory convergence and co-ordination, and in relation to direct supervisory intervention. Here, also, ESMA's activities are increasingly taking it close to the territory of making policy choices and of balancing different public interests.

ESMA has as yet to exercise its direct intervention powers under its founding Regulation to direct national regulators and market actors in relation to breach of EU law, failed mediation, or in emergency circumstances. But even allowing for the conditions that apply to all these powers, it is still difficult to claim that they will not require a weighing of the public interest or will not potentially lead to consequences that could have significant economic/distributive effects, given that these powers allow ESMA to direct national regulators and market participants to take particular action. ESMA has also yet to exercise the specific Short Selling Regulation intervention powers that the CJEU, even in the face of evidence as to the significant economic consequences that ESMA intervention could generate, found to be *Meroni*-compliant—but the legitimation difficulties remain. ESMA has, however,

---

[80] See, e.g. L Quaglia, D Howarth, and M Liebe, 'The Political Economy of European Capital Markets Union' (2016) 54 *J Cap Mark Stud* 185 and N Moloney, 'Capital Markets Union: "Ever Closer Union" for the EU Financial System' (2016) 41 *ELR* 307.

[81] This change in direction is clear from, e.g. ESMA, Supervisory Convergence Work Programme (2017).

already deployed its controversial new product intervention powers under MiFIR, following their coming into force in early 2018.[82] Notwithstanding the very significant conditionality framing the exercise of these powers, it is difficult to argue that their exercise by ESMA, involving, in this epochal first case, a temporary pan-EU prohibition on the marketing to retail investors of one type of complex derivative (binary options) and restrictions on the retail marketing of another (contracts for differences) on investor protection grounds, does not take ESMA closer to the territory of making public interest choices.

Similar, if less acute, difficulties emerge with ESMA's softer supervisory co-ordination/convergence powers, particularly given ESMA's increasingly muscular approach to these powers. For example, ESMA's founding Regulation confers it with peer review powers but it has, since its establishment, become ever more robust and hierarchical in its approach to peer review, increasingly highlighting departures from best practice and exerting soft pressure on its member supervisors to take distinct supervisory approaches.[83] Steering national supervisory behaviour across the EU, however, almost inevitably brings ESMA into the territory of shaping and making different policy choices. More specifically, policy choices are difficult to avoid in one of the newest elements of ESMA's supervisory co-ordination toolkit—the co-ordination of national supervision of central clearing counterparties (CCPs), the oft-termed 'nuclear power plants' of the EU financial system that contain risks relating to derivatives transactions. ESMA has, for example, been conferred under the European Market Infrastructure Regulation (EMIR) with the power to co-ordinate the stress testing of CCPs. CCP stress testing is a relative novelty to financial governance internationally as CCPs only came to the fore as risk management mechanisms over the financial crisis, and ESMA is only in the very early stages of developing its approach; the first stress test took place over 2015–2016 and ESMA is refining its approach.[84] But it is difficult to argue against the reality that the design choices ESMA makes as to how to conduct a CCP stress test, the indicators to deploy, and the adverse scenarios to test could have material public interest consequence, if a failed stress test (as per ESMA's design) generates market anxiety, impacts asset prices, or increases risk or, alternatively, if an insufficiently demanding stress test fails to capture emerging risks.

---

[82] ESMA exercised its MiFIR product intervention powers in relation to the marketing of certain complex derivatives products to retail investors in March 2018; the related temporary restrictions and prohibitions came into effect over summer 2018 and were, at the time of writing, extended to apply into 2019.

[83] ESMA took an assertive and direct tone in its 2016 peer review of how national regulators were approaching a key element of the EU's investor protection regime: ESMA, MiFID Suitability Requirements. Peer Review Report (2016).

[84] ESMA carried out its first stress test of CCPs over 2015–16 (ESMA, EU-Wide CCP Stress Test 2015 (ESMA/2016/658)) and is developing methodologies as its experience develops (ESMA, Methodological Framework, 2017 EU-Wide CCP Stress Test Exercise (2017) and ESMA, Risk Assessment, Work Programme 2017 (2017) 3).

3.4 A strengthening actor

These trends are likely to strengthen given the indications that ESMA's credibility, and its related regulatory capacity, is being enhanced. ESMA has emerged from the massive exercise of developing the EU administrative rulebook that accompanies the legislative crisis-era reforms, with its reputation broadly enhanced. It has also acquired a very significant capacity to gather and interrogate data,[85] which further strengthens its position in EU financial governance. Environmentally, its institutional position within the ESFS is strengthening in response to wider governance reforms. It has, for example, since the establishment of Banking Union's Single Supervisory Mechanism (SSM) and the related empowerment of the ECB as direct supervisor within the SSM of Banking Union's 'significant banks,' come to act as a conduit through which national financial markets regulators can co-ordinate with the ECB in relation to areas of supervision where market supervision and banking supervision overlap.[86]

More generally, as EU financial governance has come increasingly to rely on ESMA, institutional support has, with some flashpoints, remained strong. The 2017 ESA Proposal, while, at the time of writing, still at an early stage in the legislative process and a somewhat unreliable indicator of future developments accordingly— particularly in light of the political and market salience of Brexit-related effects— underlines that the Commission's previous suspicions about ESA/ESMA empowerments are receding. The Commission has proposed significant empowerment for all three ESAs in relation to their soft supervisory convergence powers, including that they be empowered to adopt three-yearly 'Strategic Supervisory Plans' against which national regulators would be required to align their activities and that would give the ESAs significant opportunities to review the exercise of day-to-day supervisory powers by national regulators. It has also proposed a suite of new direct empowerments for ESMA in relation to the direct supervision of an additional cohort of regulated actors, in part driven by a perceived need to strengthen the single market against Brexit risks and to support the CMU agenda.[87]

This evolutionary trajectory of intensifying ESMA influence and power, which is increasing legitimation risks, is predicted by the literature on regulatory governance generally. EU financial governance has recently been associated with an 'experimentalist' form of governance in its intensifying reliance on administrative governance through the ESAs. Experimentalist governance[88] identifies as experimentalist those governance arrangements which supplement (or displace) the traditional 'command

---

[85] ON ESMA's extensive data collection, hosting, management, and interrogation activities, see ESMA, Risk Assessment Work Programme (2017).

[86] Most notably in relation to a concerted supervisory approach by national regulators to how the disclosure to the market of SSM-required bank supervisory measures (which can have market-moving effects and so are of concern to market supervisors) should be managed. See, e.g. ESMA Board of Supervisors Meeting, Minutes 12 July 2016.

[87] 2017 ESA Proposal (n 3).

[88] See J Zeitlin (ed), *Extending Experimentalist Governance? The EU and Transnational Regulation* (OUP, 2015) and C Sabel and J Zeitlin (eds), *Experimentalist Governance in the European Union. Towards a New Architecture* (OUP, 2010).

and control' model of EU governance based on binding legal rules set through the institutional/political process. It assumes the setting of general framework goals through legislative rules but adds the deployment, at lower levels of governance (typically administrative governance levels), and with a degree of flexibility and discretion, of different forms of implementing rule, of monitoring devices, including peer review, and of mechanisms for revising goals and rules.[89] Experimentalist governance is associated with a form of governance which is fluid and iterative, and co-ordination-orientated. While much of post-crisis EU financial governance can be associated with traditional 'command and control' style regulatory governance, there are elements of experimentalism in how the ESAs support the EU rulebook at the administrative level, most notably as regards their supervision-related functions, but also as regards their soft amplification of the rulebook.[90] And as the ESAs become more experienced with such 'bottom-up' governance techniques (including the adoption of soft law, peer review, the support and co-ordination of supervisory colleges, the collection and management of data, the monitoring of risk, and the management of stress tests)[91] they are also, as experimentalist governance predicts, increasingly developing the capacity to produce, and also to shape the resolution of, policy questions.

4. Emerging Pressure for ESMA Empowerment: Meroni Pressure and Functional Strain

ESMA's current trajectory and its de facto pressing on the boundaries of *Meroni* generate legitimacy difficulties. But it also generates functional difficulties.

Administrative rule making is increasingly coming under strain as rules become, first, ever more complex and data-driven and, second, given their transformative effects. There are a number of difficulties with the current process and with the *Meroni/Romano* prohibition on ESA rule making, not least among them the significant delays which can arise. After an ESA proposes a BTS or provides technical advice, the Commission can be very significantly delayed in adopting the related rules, although formally timelines apply to the Commission; transaction costs can accordingly increase as regulated actors wait for the relevant rules (which they can anticipate through the ESA consultation process) and are prevented from finalizing internal processes. Two additional pressure points can be identified. The first relates to the inability of the ESAs, and of ESMA in particular, to adopt changes to administrative rules where necessary in response to market developments. This has emerged as a particular difficulty with the complex new administrative rules governing the

---

[89] See 'Learning from Difference: The New Architecture of Experimentalist Governance in the EU', in Sabel and Zeitlin (n 88) 1, 2–3.

[90] For an experimentalist analysis of EBA, see E Ferran, 'The Existential Search of the European Banking Authority' (2016) 17 *Eur Bus Organ Law Re* 285.

[91] ESMA's 2017 report on its supervisory convergence activities, e.g. underlines the growing scale and ambition of its activities in these primarily soft/coordination-based areas of intervention: ESMA, Supervisory Convergence. Work Programme (2017).

transparency requirements that apply to trading in non-equity instruments (bonds, derivatives, and other instruments). These MiFID II/MiFIR administrative rules are designed to improve market transparency and strengthen supervisory oversight, but they are also, as noted, projected to have significant market effects as they are likely to change incentives and behaviour as trading counterparties become required to disclose their trading positions and intention; a reduction in trading activity (or liquidity) is emerging as a potential risk to financial stability and efficiency from these rules. The current suite of related MiFID/ II/MiFIR administrative rules is heavily based on ESMA's empirical assessments (made over the development of these rules) and is also tied closely to related ESMA-developed benchmarks and metrics relating to, for example, trading volumes. But ESMA cannot change these rules easily or quickly if any market dislocation erupts that alters earlier empirical assessments or disturbs the highly technical metrics on which the rules are based: the standard process for amending administrative rules, which engages the Commission, must be followed. Similar difficulties arise in relation to the pivotal rules governing the derivative instruments that must be 'cleared' through CCPs and that have, in effect, restructured the EU derivatives market. Under EMIR, the market-shaping decisions governing the classes of derivatives that must be cleared through CCPs are taken by the Commission, but these decisions are proposed by ESMA (under the BTS process). ESMA identified at an early stage of EMIR's development that the BTS process could lead to significant market dislocation as it does not accommodate speedy suspensions or reversals of clearing decisions where they are required because of rapid and severe changes in market conditions, such as a major contraction in liquidity.[92]

A second set of difficulties relates to technical efficiency. As the administrative rulebook becomes ever more complex, it is also becoming increasingly operationalized. Administrative rules now cover, for example, the highly detailed reporting templates regulated actors are required to return to their national supervisors. These templates are governed by administrative rules, leading to the sub-optimal result that even the most technical, data cell change is, in theory, subject to the standard Commission-located administrative rule-making process, notwithstanding the technical inefficiency which follows. The formalities of administrative rule making have become a material obstruction for EBA, which has proposed that it be given the power to adopt these highly technical rules relating to bank financial reporting.[93]

Fixes are being proposed to these difficulties, but on an ad hoc basis. An 'early legal review' process has been agreed between the Commission and ESMA, and is designed to ensure that any legal issues (relating to, for example, scope or mandate) that could subsequently slow the administrative process are identified at an early stage and resolved between the Commission and ESMA.[94] More specifically, the

---

[92] ESMA, EMIR Review Report No 1 (ESMA/2015/1251) (2015).

[93] EBA, Opinion on Improving the Decision-making Framework for Supervisory Reporting Requirements under Regulation (EU) No 575/2013 (EBA/Op/2017/03) (2017).

[94] Letter from ESMA Chairman Maijoor to Commission, 11 May 2015 (ESMA/2015/841) and Commission Response, 12 May 2015.

Commission has proposed a new 'suspensive' mechanism under EMIR which will empower the Commission to speedily remove or suspend an administrative decision it has previously made to the effect that a class of derivatives be cleared through a CCP, following ESMA's advice. [95] This proposed change to the administrative decision-making process underlines the adaptive capacity of the EU in relation to the ESAs, but it also exposes the increasingly pivotal role of the ESAs as technocratic actors in EU financial governance and the need for a fuller reconsideration of their role. The Commission has not, however, supported EBA's proposals relating to bank financial reporting, although it has indicated its willingness to consider whether technical reporting requirements be reconfigured by their taking the form of general legislative requirements, supported by ESA guidelines (which could be revised by the ESAs), rather than of administrative rules. These solutions are, however, only ad hoc fixes to specific problems.

The more eye-catching source of strain, however, comes from the intensifying calls for the ESAs, and in particular ESMA, to be given additional supervisory powers. Proposals for ESMA to exercise direct supervisory powers over particular market segments are not new, but they are increasing in frequency. The European Parliament, a supporter of ESMA having direct supervisory powers from the outset,[96] recently proposed that ESMA have supervisory powers in relation to two specialist forms of EU-regulated funds,[97] proposals which were incorporated by the Commission in the 2017 ESA Proposal. The 'Five Presidents' earlier called for more centralization of financial market supervision, in the form of a 'Financial Union' in order to complete EMU. [98] These developments could be dismissed as simply signals and nudges indicative of the evolutionary dynamics of EU financial governance; over time, institutional templates get refined and reworked, leading to changes to institutional governance. Change to EU financial governance can, however, also be a function of market disruption, as exemplified by the financial crisis and the related establishment of the ESAs within the ESFS. Accordingly, it is not unexpected that the confluence of the CMU agenda and of Brexit intensified calls for ESMA to be reconfigured as a more traditional financial regulator in relation to EU securities markets, in order to ensure that the stability and efficiency of the EU capital market at a time of change be secured and strengthened. There is, for example, some market support for ESMA to exercise supervisory powers over certain wholesale market actors and services, given the disruption which the withdrawal of the UK, which acts as vital pipeline to the

---

[95] Commission, Report on EMIR (COM (2016) 857) (2016), 6. The new mechanism has been proposed in the Commission proposal for a new resolution regime for CCPs (COM (2016) 856) and empowers the Commission to suspend a clearing decision within 48 hours, following a request from a relevant supervisor and ESMA issuing an opinion that the suspension is necessary to avoid a serious threat to financial stability.

[96] The Parliament's initial set of revisions to the proposal for what became the 2010 ESMA Regulation included proposals for wide-ranging ESMA supervisory powers. These proposals foundered on *Meroni* grounds but also given Member States' resistance to losing supervisory autonomy to the ESAs while retaining any fiscal risks consequent on ESA supervisory decision making.

[97] Briefing, EU Legislation in Progress, Reviving Risk Capital. The Proposal to Amend EuVECA and EUSEF, 19 January 2017.

[98] The Five Presidents' Report: Completing Europe's Economic and Monetary Union (2016).

EU in relation to such actors and services, could generate;[99] centralized supervision could, for example, reduce transaction costs at a time of potential disruption, provide stronger financial stability oversight, and limit disruptive supervisory arbitrage. There have also been calls for ESMA to play a supervisory role in relation to third-country actors operating in the EU as a means for smoothing UK (third-country) access to the EU market.[100] Stronger ESMA powers in relation to third-country actors have also been called for by ESMA itself, in the specific context of CCP supervision. ESMA currently registers third-country CCPs, once the regulatory/supervisory regime of their state of establishment is found to be 'equivalent' under EMIR, but it does not exercise supervisory control; this, ESMA has argued, leaves the EU vulnerable, given ESMA's inability to intervene where difficulties arise.[101] The Commission appears open to reconsidering ESMA's role in light of the potential risks posed to the EU capital market, and to the CMU agenda, by Brexit; the 2017 CCP Supervision Proposal and the 2017 ESA Proposal both suggest material (if specific) empowerments for ESMA in relation to supervision.

Whether or not there is a strong functional case for ESMA to be granted additional supervisory powers is not clear. EU capital markets remain fragmented (remediation is being sought through the CMU agenda) and national supervisors are likely to be the most effective supervisors in most cases. In particular, capital market supervision is strongly associated with conduct supervision, which requires proximity to market actors—prudential supervision (as carried out by the ECB/SSM within Banking Union) can be carried out more easily at a distance. Further, the extent to which Brexit could disrupt EU financial stability, and of any related imperative for remediation in the form of supervisory centralization, is not clear—certainly, there is little evidence yet of the type of market shock which drove the construction of Banking Union. On the other hand, it is possible to make a functional case for different pockets of supervision to be carried out by ESMA, particularly in response to Brexit-related risks. The potential dependence of the EU capital market on the UK for some 70 per cent of its clearing arrangements (for certain derivatives), and the related 'offshoring' of a significant element of its capital market accordingly to the UK,[102] makes discussions on centralized EU supervision of third-country CCPs reasonable, and ESMA a natural, if not necessarily optimal,[103] candidate. Any decision to further empower ESMA will not only be a matter of functional effectiveness,

---

[99] E.g. a single market regulator has been identified as means for addressing any Brexit-related capital market fragmentation (R Moghadam, 'How a Post-Brexit Redesign Can Save the Capital Markets Union,' *Financial Times*, 31 February 2017).

[100] On the discussions, see Moloney (n 1).

[101] ESMA has warned that it has very few powers to intervene in an emergency and that the EU market may accordingly be at risk. ESMA Chairman Maijoor, Keynote Speech, Prime Finance Conference, 23 January 2017.

[102] On the many issues raised by the current dominance of the UK in the EU clearing market see International Regulatory Strategy Group, CCPs post Brexit: Implications for the Users of Financial Markets in the UK and EU 27 (2017).

[103] Assuming appropriate political support, the ECB could be empowered (outside the SSM's legal arrangements) to supervise CCPs. This would have the advantage of locating EU-level supervision in an institution which already provides last resort liquidity support to euro area CCPs.

however; political preferences will be determinative. These are currently very difficult to predict. While the Member States have been supportive of some ESMA-based supervision so far, they are likely to resist any significant ESMA empowerment which implies risk-sharing, given the current difficulties the 'completing Banking Union' agenda is experiencing, or which significantly constrains their ability to compete for Brexit-related relocation business.

Meroni further obscures what is already highly complex territory. Assuming a functional/political case can be made, at least for a limited empowerment of ESMA and perhaps only in relation to third-country supervision, the *Meroni* prohibition on agency discretionary action will pose difficulties. Supervision is a granular, operational activity, which requires from the supervisor nimble responsiveness to firm-specific and market-level conditions.[104] It cannot be hedged about by multiple constraining conditions, as is clear from Banking Union's SSM Regulation, which does not place the ECB within the SSM in an operational straitjacket.[105] The 2017 ESA Proposal does not suggest a material expansion of ESMA's supervisory powers. Nonetheless, it imposes significant conditionality and proceduralization on the proposed new suite of powers (such as the procedural conditions proposed for the application of ESMA's suggested new supervisory and enforcement powers over certain funds, data services providers, and benchmarks, which include conditions governing, for example, the carrying out of investigations and the imposition of financial penalties), reflecting the *Meroni*-influenced templates earlier used for ESMA's supervision of rating agencies and of trade repositories under the legislative rating agency regime and EMIR. The proposed supervisory powers for ESMA over third-country CCPs (under the 2017 CCP Proposal) are similarly constrained and confined. If any other future empowerment of ESMA, if deemed politically expedient and functionally necessary, was to take a more maximalist approach—and so to engage a wider set of supervisory powers and embrace a wider group of regulated actors—a set of suitably open-ended conditions, designed to structure the legal space within which ESMA's new supervisory discretion was to be exercised, could be designed. But any such open-ended constitutive measure, while necessary to allow ESMA to act in a functionally optimal manner, could be legally unstable and lead to challenges to ESMA's powers as not being *Meroni*-compliant—particularly as supervision inevitably brings costs and is likely to generate industry (and related political) incentives for challenge—all the more so if market conditions become more competitive on Brexit. And even if legal challenges could be minimized, difficulties would persist in relation to legitimation, given the current weaknesses in ESMA's accountability arrangements and the scale of its capacity to exercise discretion, as discussed in Section 5.

---

[104] An extensive literature and policy discussion underlines the importance of an adaptive and flexible approach to regulatory intervention, which reflects changing behaviours in the regulated community. Among the initial and most influential discussions is: I Ayres and J Braithwaite, *Transcending the Deregulation Debate* (OUP, 1992).

[105] Regulation (EU) No 468/2014 [2014] OJ L141/1.

5. Addressing the Legitimation Challenge

5.1 ESMA's legitimation architecture

The legitimation of ESMA's administrative functions is primarily a function of output-orientated accountability requirements, but not entirely. The legal space within which ESMA can deploy its delegated powers and exercise discretion is bounded by ESMA's constitutive 2010 Regulation and the subsequent legislative measures that have expanded its powers; the *Meroni* doctrine; and the location of ESMA (and the other ESAs) in a Treaty competence (Article 114 TFEU) that confines its legal operating space.[106] In practice, the constraints—primarily in relation to scope and mandate—imposed by ESMA's constitutive legislative measures are relatively loose, while its related powers, particularly in relation to soft law and supervisory convergence, are sufficiently elastic to allow it to exert significant soft influence over the EU capital market. Similarly, ESMA's constitutive legislative objectives are high level and couched in very general terms.[107] Further, there has been only limited judicial policing of how these constitutive legislative measures (and the background Treaty requirements) apply; judicial review provides only a thin form of constraint here. To date, the only material CJEU ruling is the *Short Selling* ruling, which suggests a significant deference by the EU courts to ESA operational discretion and a sensitivity to not disrupting the institutional apparatus of EU financial governance.[108] As a functional matter, however, intensive ex post judicial review of how ESMA interprets its mandate in a live operational context might fetter ESMA's discretion in a manner that could prejudice its ability to deliver its legislative mandate. Law still matters, however, and, specifically, considerable pressure is being placed on how ESMA's constitutive legislative measures design and structure ex post accountability as a legitimating mechanism for discretionary ESMA action.

The accountability of ESMA is supported by an array of formal and informal mechanisms directed to output legitimacy. ESMA is formally accountable to the European Parliament and Council, and subject to related annual reporting requirements.[109] ESMA's different organizational components are similarly subject to reporting and review requirements, including that the ESMA Chairperson may be invited to answer questions before the European Parliament and Council.[110] Beyond these formal reporting and review channels, ESMA is subject to a range

[106] On legal bases as forming part of legitimacy and related accountability controls, see Amtenbrick and Lastra (n 9).

[107] As indicated, ESMA is to protect the public interest by contributing to the short-, medium-, and long-term stability and effectiveness of the financial system and to contribute to a series of subsidiary objectives, including improving the functioning of the single market; ensuring the integrity, efficiency, transparency, and orderly functioning of financial markets; strengthening international supervisory coordination; preventing regulatory arbitrage; and enhancing consumer protection (ESMA Regulation, Art 1(5)).

[108] Reflecting Mendes' analysis of the degree of latitude which the EU courts allow in the case of discretionary action and their reluctance to engage in substantive review (n 11).

[109] E.g. 2010 ESMA Regulation, Arts 3 and 47.   [110] E.g. Ibid., Art 50.

of procedural/consultative obligations which provide 'softer' accountability channels, but which also provide for a degree of input legitimacy. Its quasi-regulatory activities, for example, including the adoption of Guidelines, are subject to consultation and impact assessment requirements,[111] the results of which are published, and ESMA has developed extensive feedback protocols through which it explains how it has engaged with the results of consultations.[112] ESMA, like all the ESAs, must also have a representative 'Stakeholder Group' (composed of representatives of the industry, the consumer sector, and independent experts), which it must consult on a regular basis.[113]

There are gaps in this accountability-based, output-orientated approach to legitimation. For example, ESMA's legislative objectives, which define the public interests that ESMA is mandated to pursue, are very widely drafted and so do not easily support the development of appropriate output indicators that can ground accountability review.[114] ESMA's annual reporting tends, accordingly, to be narrative in style and is not usually linked to the achievement of particular benchmarks or metrics. In terms of accountability fora, to date, the Council has paid little attention to ESMA in terms of holding it to account; its preference for the securing of legitimacy by means of a material degree of national control and representativeness is clear from ESMA decision making being reserved to the national regulators who sit on the Board of Supervisors.[115] The European Parliament, the other institution to which ESMA is accountable, has been more active. The annual ESMA review sessions with the European Parliament's Economic and Monetary Affairs Committee (ECON) can be challenging but are more usually occasions at which ESMA presents its priorities and raises concerns.[116] ECON regularly engages with

---

[111] E.g. Ibid., Arts 10, 15, and 16.

[112] All three ESAs follow 'Statements on Consultation Practices'. For the ESMA version see ESMA/2011/11.

[113] E.g. 2010 ESMA Regulation, Art 37.

[114] The objectives set out for ESMA under Article 1(5) of its founding Regulation (n 107) are high-level, open-textured, and malleable. They contrast sharply with the detailed operational objectives imposed on the UK FCA, alongside its 'strategic objective' of ensuring relevant markets function well. These operational objectives relate to: consumer protection (to secure an appropriate degree of protection for consumers); integrity (to protect and enhance the integrity of the UK financial system); and competition (to promote effective competition in the interests of consumers in the markets for identified services) (Financial Services and Markets Act 2000, section 1B(3), 1C, 1D, and 1E). The nature of these objectives is also amplified in detail under the Act (sections 1C-1E), including with respect to the matters to which the FCA is to have regard to in achieving its objectives. The Australian Securities and Investments Commission (ASIC) Act 2001, to take another example, imposes a range of statutory objectives on ASIC, the Australian financial markets and conduct regulator, including that it maintain, facilitate, and improve the performance of the financial system (ASIC Act 2001, section 1(2)), while the Australian government annually sets outs its 'Statement of Expectations' for ASIC.

[115] The Council's preferences in relation to national representation were particularly marked over the ESA negotiations, given the incentives at that time for Member States to protect their national financial systems from supranational incursion and any related fiscal costs, but the Council's general concern to ensure national representation on and control over agencies is longstanding: J Christensen and V Nielsen, 'Administrative Capacity, Structural Choice and the Creation of EU Agencies' (2010) 17 *J Eur Public Policy* 176.

[116] This reflects agency behaviour generally. Busuioc has found that EU agencies often use Parliament accountability mechanisms as a lobbying platform and a means for increasing their visibility; see n 53, 128–9.

ESMA, however, including through informal workshops on issues of emerging concern.[117] More generally, the European Parliament has monitored ESMA's exercise of its powers through resolutions and budgetary discharge decisions, and by means of written questions from MEPs. The latter are fairly sporadic and tend to reflect national interests.[118] The former can be more robust as an accountability mechanism. The Parliament's 2015 Resolution reviewing EU financial governance generally is indicative.[119] The Parliament called generally for better quality and cross-sector coordination in relation to the ESAs' quasi-rule-making activities, warned against the administrative process taking political decisions reserved to the level 1 process, and called on the ESAs, when developing administrative rules and Guidelines, to 'stick to the empowerments laid down in the basic acts' and 'regretted' that the ESAs had not always respected the mandates for administrative rules set out in the related legislative act.[120] Similarly the Parliament asked the ESAs to take a 'careful approach' to the number and extent of Guidelines they adopted, particularly where they were not expressly mandated by legislation.[121] In addition, the Parliament's budgetary discharge decisions relating to ESMA have, on occasion, been assertive in signalling parliamentary concern. In 2017, for example, the Parliament called on ESMA to 'carefully adhere' to the tasks assigned to it by the co-legislators; to ensure that it exercised all prerogatives in its legal mandate, warning that a closer focus on its mandate could result in a more efficient use of resources; and to keep the Council and Parliament informed, particularly in relation to the preparation of administrative rules, in a timely, regular, and comprehensive manner.[122] Overall, however, the European Parliament acts as a high-level political check on ESMA and does not provide more granular accountability.[123] Further, its main concern is usually with protecting its prerogatives in relation to administrative rule making generally, rather than with holding ESMA to account against its objectives. The European Parliament can also, however, indirectly hold ESMA to account in relation to its quasi-rule-making activities through the veto powers it can exercise over certain forms of BTSs (Regulatory Technical Standards)[124] and Delegated Acts. But this is a weak form of accountability check as by the time a proposal reaches the Parliament it has been

---

[117] E.g. the early 2017 ALDE workshop at which ESMA Chairman Maijoor, in the context of the UK's withdrawal from the EU, set out ESMA's concerns relating to third country CCPs: ESMA Chairman Maijoor, Address, ALDE Seminar on the Review of the European Supervisory Authorities, 8 February 2017.

[118] Reflecting European Parliament practice generally. See N Font and I Perez Duran, 'The European Parliament Oversight of EU Agencies Through Written Questions' (2016) 23 *J Eur Public Policy* 1349, which notes the limited number of questions directed to EBA.

[119] European Parliament, Resolution on Stocktaking and Challenges of the EU Financial Services Regulation (P8_TA(2016)0006), 19 January 2016.

[120] Ibid., para 49.   [121] Ibid., para 54.

[122] European Parliament Resolution on Discharge of the 2015 ESMA Budget, 27 April 2017 (P8_TAPROV(2017) 177), Observations.

[123] This reflects the Parliament's approach to agency accountability generally which has been characterized by Busuioc as a 'fire alarm' check; see n 53, 133.

[124] Regulatory Technical Standards have a legislative colour and deal with substantive matters; Implementing Technical Standards, by contrast (which are not subject to a Parliament veto), are highly technical, usually dealing with templates, formats, and reports.

agreed by the Commission and may be substantially altered from the ESMA version, and as it is very rare for the Parliament to exercise its veto powers.[125] In practice, although the Commission is not a formal accountability forum for ESMA, it is the most assertive and challenging of the EU institutions in constraining ESMA, as is clear from its approach to ESMA's quasi-regulatory powers, its posture as a (non-voting) member of ESMA's Board of Supervisors, and its adherence to *Meroni* in its interactions with ESMA.[126] The Commission has, however, distinct institutional interests to protect in its interactions with ESMA. Overall, given the range of EU institutions engaged and their different institutional interests/preferences and related levels of engagement, it is not clear that ESMA is being appropriately held to account in relation to how it balances the distinct public interests raised by EU financial governance within the space structured by law within which it can exercise discretion.

More granular forms of accountability, tied to more precisely delineated mandates and objectives, are usually provided within domestic financial regulators by their boards or similarly constituted bodies, which usually contain independent members who are charged with holding management to account against the regulator's objectives. The ESA boards, however, are not configured in this way. They are designed to accommodate inter-institutional interests and different intergovernmental/supranational preferences, rather than to provide optimal challenge and accountability. Thus, ESMA's board is composed of the (voting) representatives of the relevant national regulators, the (non-voting) permanent Chair, and non-voting representatives of the Commission, the ESRB, and the two other ESAs (EBA and EIOPA).[127] It acts as a decision-making body rather than an accountability forum. Certainly, proposed rules and actions are discussed at the Board, as is clear from the publicly available minutes, but there is little sense of the Board acting as an accountability forum, challenging ESMA action and holding it to account; to do so would, of course, require a 'double-hatted' approach, given that the Board is also the ESMA decision maker.

Agency accountability mechanisms are not easy to design given, in particular, the need to secure agency independence, and are all the more troublesome in the ESMA context, given the range of different 'delegating' actors (loosely termed) to which ESMA could be regarded as accountable (potentially, the Council, Parliament, Commission, Member States, and national regulators).[128]

---

[125] While it has in the past threatened to veto, the Parliament has only done so once in relation to securities market measures advised on/proposed by ESMA (in September 2016 in relation to administrative rules on investment product disclosure).

[126] The Commission has, e.g., challenged Board of Supervisor decision making where it has regarded the Board as overstepping its legislative mandate (for an example, see the Commission's questioning of ESMA's position in relation to the administrative rules developed under the EMIR regime: Board of Supervisors Meetings, 14 March 2013 (ESMA/2013/BS/30) and 6 November 2012 (ESMA /2012/BS/143)).

[127] EEA members participate as observers.

[128] Further, Busuioc has argued that, as accountability does not imply control, in the form of an ability to direct (which flows from a principal/agent relationship), accountability fora, which are rather concerned with ex post control, can accordingly take multiple forms. See n 53, 48.

Nonetheless, taken in the round, the devices contained within ESMA's constitutive legislative measures and that seek to legitimate ESMA's activities as an administrative actor in line with a liberal interpretation of *Meroni* are not, at present, sufficiently robust to accommodate either ESMA's current trajectory and entrepreneurial orientation, or any new powers which may be conferred on it, in line with a liberal interpretation of *Meroni*. The ongoing ESA reform process provides the opportunity for constructing a new toolkit. Two modest proposals are offered here.

5.2 Strengthening legitimation: board-located accountability

First, the role of the Board of Supervisors as a legitimating mechanism should be strengthened. Recent thinking in EU constitutional theory suggests that agency legitimation in the EU context can be characterized as extending beyond the EU's representative institutions and as relating to the EU as a multi-faceted 'demoi-cracy.' The notion of 'demoi-cracy' is based on including the Member States (and the national regulators to which they delegate power), rather than exclusively citizens, within the EU polity, and on recognizing the scale and importance of the interdependence between Member States in the EU constitutional settlement[129] and, accordingly, the related role of Member States as legitimating actors. Legitimacy is then not just a function of delegation (loosely termed) from direct representative actors, primarily the European Parliament and, less directly, the Council. For the EU, as a demoi-cracy, to function optimally and to be legitimated, and also given the difficulties in characterizing the Parliament and Council as representative democratic institutions, Member States and their non-state institutions, including agencies, must be recognized as having a transformative role in EU law and policy and as accordingly forming part of the legitimation process.[130] The demoi-cratic analysis emphasizes the interplay between the EU and domestic institutions, and, in particular, the potential for vertical (in relation to national democratic institutions) and horizontal/transnational (in relation to peer regulators) legitimacy arrangements.[131] ESMA legitimation can accordingly be a function of horizontal peer accountability relationships between national regulators on ESMA's Board of Supervisors, as well as of vertical accountability from those national regulators to their national political systems in relation to their ESMA activities.[132] The notion of demoi-cracy, and of such vertical/horizontal legitimation, has resonances with the related conceptualization of EU governance

---

[129] K Nicolaïdis, 'European Demoicracy and Its Crisis' (2013) 51 *J Common Mark Stud* 351.

[130] Nicolaïdis (n 129) has suggested that for the EU, as a demoi-cracy, to function optimally, non-state institutions, including agencies, 'must use their margin of manoeuvre to translate, transform, and own collective EU disciplines'.

[131] See Buess (n 21).

[132] Buess has suggested that as the vertical links between EU institutions and the Member States are of crucial importance in assessing the demoi-cratic quality of EU institutions and their legitimacy, EU agencies should be politically accountable to the Member States and their political institutions; see Ibid., 98.

as a supranational extension of the recent and strong development of national administrative governance, and the related diffusion and fragmentation of regulatory power beyond 'strongly legitimated' representative bodies at national level to agencies. Viewed through this perspective, the source of horizontal and vertical legitimacy for EU agencies can be national in character and located within the national agencies that sit on EU agencies.[133] The productive notion of horizontal/vertical peer accountability as forming part of ESMA's governance arrangements also has resonances with ESMA's characterization as an experimentalist actor. Experimentalist governance supports new ways of thinking about legitimation given its assumption that an agency acting in an experimentalist manner is not following a tightly prescribed mandate for delegated action, but has the freedom to adjust and revise in response to experience. Experimentalist governance can accordingly be associated with 'dynamic' or 'forward-looking' accountability,[134] which requires that the actor 'diligently and responsibly' exercise its operational freedom to meet its mandates.[135] This way of considering legitimacy acknowledges the limitations of, for example, EU legitimation through European Parliament oversight, particularly in highly complex and contingent areas like financial regulation. It relates legitimation to the accountability of the agency for experimenting, searching for solutions, and revising in light of experience, and to the ability of the agency to provide related mechanisms for self-review.[136] ESMA's Board of Supervisors also supports this understanding of accountability. The ESMA peer review process, for example, opens up a channel for horizontal and vertical accountability. It allows national regulators to engage in horizontal mutual monitoring, review, and learning, but it also provides a means through which the ESMA Board of Supervisors can monitor compliance by its member national regulators and thereby signal vertically to its delegating (EU and national) principals that it is operating within and achieving its mandate. This analysis does not seek to suggest that this form of accountability can bear a great deal of legitimation weight, particularly as ESMA's legislative objectives are not, as noted, particularly granular. But nonetheless, the Board of Supervisors does have some potential as an accountability forum and should be supported in this regard, particularly through the application by the EU legislature of more granular objectives to ESMA's activities.

Two governance reforms are suggested here to strengthen horizontal and vertical accountability through the ESMA Board of Supervisors. First, mechanisms should be deployed to ensure active Board oversight of ESMA decision

---

[133] Lindseth (n 7) 534–5, showing how an administrative interpretation of EU governance leads to a characterization of EU governance in terms of delegation from national principals to EU supranational agents, and of shared national oversight.

[134] E.g. G de Burca, RO Keohane, and C Sabel, 'Global Experimentalist Governance' (2014) 44 *Br J Political Sci* 477, finding that experimentalist governance, with its emphasis on mutual monitoring, peer review, and consultation, supports new patterns of accountability.

[135] C Sabel and J Zeitlin, 'Experimentalism in the EU: Common Grounds and Persistent differences' (2012) 6 *Regul Gov* 410, 411.

[136] Ibid., 418–20.

making, avoid bureaucratic creep, and reduce the risk of Board inertia and 'rubber stamping'. While there are reasonable grounds for suggesting that the Board can support vertical and horizontal peer accountability, its large format (28/27 voting national regulator members) reduces its effectiveness as an accountability forum given in particular the risks of inertia, particularly where certain national regulators have less experience with the issues at hand. The adoption by the Board of an oversight committee structure, akin to the committee structure operated by corporate boards (banks typically have, for example, audit, risk, remuneration, and appointment committees composed of a small number of board members), which would ensure that certain ESMA decisions were reviewed in depth by such committees before formal adoption by the Board but also before subsequent and final execution by ESMA, should create incentives and opportunities for stronger oversight by national regulators. While Board decision making is currently supported by a number of Standing Committees, organized on policy lines, these Committees are primarily ex ante, policy preparation committees and are not usually composed of Board members, but of senior representatives of the national regulators that sit on the Board. A small number of Board of Supervisor committees composed of Board members and accountable to the Board, and charged with ensuring that, in identified areas, ESMA decisions were thoroughly reviewed prior to Board adoption and, after Board adoption and prior to final ESMA execution, should enhance vertical and horizontal accountability through the Board. Second, ESMA's governance should be further recast to include some form of independent 'Monitoring Board', which sits above the decision-making Board of Supervisors and its proposed new oversight committees. This Monitoring Board could include independent experts, representatives of the supranational interest (the Commission and Parliament), and representatives of national interests (perhaps in the form of representatives from different groups of Member States, grouped by, for example, market size or structure). Its role would be to receive reports and challenge ESMA management and the Board of Supervisors, and to set strategic objectives and priorities—and not to subvert operational or strategic decision making nor to adopt the proposals and actions which are the prerogatives of management and the Board.

The 2017 ESA Proposal, however, subverts the notion of the Board of Supervisors as an accountability forum, and so deepens legitimation risks. It suggests that the decision-making powers of the Board be reduced, with operational supervisory decision making, and decision making where Board conflicts may be acute (for example, the Board's powers to proceed against a defaulting national regulator or to impose binding mediation on national regulators), being located in a new, bureaucratic 'Executive Board'. This Board would be composed of the relevant ESA Chairperson and five other independent members, appointed by the Parliament/Council from a Commission short list. The Proposal does not provide for oversight of this new Executive Board. This proposed reform, because it draws power and accountability away from the Board of Supervisors, is accordingly regressive from a legitimation perspective, limiting the potential of the Board to act as an accountability forum.

5.3 Strengthening legitimation: thicker normative direction

Second, ESMA's constitutive legislative measures should include a thicker set of objectives. Accountability presupposes the existence of objectives, established in constitutive legislative measures, against which the actor is assessed. In the financial governance area, it presupposes the identification of measurable financial market outcomes, whether in terms of the classic objectives of financial stability, market efficiency, or consumer protection—or other objectives. ESMA's objectives are, as noted, couched in very general terms and are ill-suited to support the construction of required outcomes or to act as benchmarks for accountability in themselves. In practice, ESMA has responded to this ambiguity by determining its own set of objectives against which it must be held to account. The open-textured nature of ESMA's formal legislative mandate has allowed it to set a 'mission' for itself—which it regards as to enhance investor protection and promote stable and orderly financial markets; and to recast the lengthy objectives set for it in the ESMA Regulation as three high-level objectives—investor protection, orderly markets, and financial stability.[137] While this somewhat opportunistic claiming of mission and objectives might generate some queasiness in relation to legitimacy,[138] it can also be regarded as a reasonable response to a diffuse set of objectives, allowing ESMA to impose priorities and set specific objectives, and so as supporting accountability. Similarly, ESMA's reporting style has evolved over time to become more granular. ESMA's first annual report on 2011 was primarily narrative and historic in nature, setting out in detail its activities over its first year, but not linking its activities to particular objectives or outcomes, beyond general statements linking its work to the ESMA Regulation.[139] By 2017, ESMA's Annual Report on 2016 was significantly more detailed, providing extensive coverage of ESMA's activities in relation to the single rulebook, risk assessment, supervisory convergence, and supervision, as well as comprehensive disclosures on how ESMA operated as an organization. Of particular significant to accountability, however, is that the 2016 Report, in sharp contrast with the 2011 Report, set out the objectives set for particular 'workstreams' in ESMA's related Work Programmes for 2016 and also how those objectives were met in practice. While, as is also the case with the related Work Programmes, the reporting on objectives was broadly narrative and high level

---

[137] E.g. ESMA, 2017 Work Programme, 5 and Annual Report on 2016, 9 and 10, describing its mission 'based on its Regulation' as 'to enhance the protection of investors and promote stable and orderly markets in the EU' (at 9) and its objectives as 'investor protection: to have the needs of financial consumers better served and to reinforce their rights as investors while acknowledging their responsibilities; orderly markets: to promote the integrity, transparency, efficiency, and well-functioning of financial markets and robust market infrastructure; and financial stability: to strengthen the financial system in order to be capable of withstanding shocks and the unravelling of financial imbalances while fostering economic growth' (at 10). ESMA's sense of its mission has not changed materially since its first expression in ESMA's initial 2011 Annual Report, in which it described its mission as to enhance the protection of investors and promoted stable and well-functioning markets: see, ESMA, Annual Report on 2011, 9.
[138] The self-articulation of, e.g. its investor protection objective by ESMA in its Annual Report on 2016 introduces notions of consumer responsibility which are contested and which are more typically associated with legislative amplification (as in the case of the UK FCA's consumer protection objective).
[139] ESMA, Annual Report 2011.

in style,[140] it nonetheless provided some form of benchmark against which account-ability oversight could be exercised. By contrast, however, the UK Financial Conduct Authority produces a detailed annual report that assesses its performance against its statutory objectives (strategic and operational), contains detailed outcomes for each objective and related outcome indicators, and examines how each outcome has been achieved and to what extent.[141]

The setting by the EU legislative process of statutory objectives for ESMA, and the related identification of outcomes, , is, as it is in financial regulation generally, a complex task. Objectives, although normatively attractive, can conflict—the trade-off between financial stability and investor protection (both statutory objectives for ESMA under its founding Regulation) can be a complex one for a financial regulator and have distributional consequences. Objectives can also be overly open-ended—for example, to what extent should consumer protection be pursued, given the costs of such regulation? By contrast with the metrics often deployed for central banks (for example, the ECB's inflation target), objectives can also generate significant measurability difficulties, given, for example, the preventative nature of much of a fi-nancial regulator's mandate and also the need to accommodate regulatory judgment and discretion, including, e.g. the deploying of risk-based models for intervention. The elusive quality of objective setting underscores, however, the need for efforts to be made to ensure clearer specification if legitimation is to be more secure, as is re-flected in the IOSCO (the International Organization of Securities Commissions, the international standard-setter for financial markets) requirement that the re-sponsibilities of financial regulators should be clear and objectively stated.[142] In the ESMA context, specification is all the more necessary given ESMA's entrepreneurial and dynamic quality and a certain fuzziness in its legitimation arrangements. ESMA has, as mentioned, sought to amplify its legislative objectives, but the setting of ob-jectives, and the identification of the qualifications which apply, is a legislative task as its engages political choices with distributional and public interest consequences. With greater specification, in the form of a significantly more granular set of object-ives, more clearly specified outcome/performance indicators can be required of, or developed by, ESMA; reporting can be more evidenced based; and accountability monitoring can be tied to the achievement of specified benchmarks. The risk of accountability being, as it currently is, a function of protecting the distinct institu-tional prerogatives of the co-legislators should also be reduced.

This analysis does not underestimate the challenges in setting more granular object-ives for ESMA. It would require a major effort on the part of the EU's legislative pro-cess, which has always struggled with setting objectives, reflecting the piecemeal nature of EU financial regulation as well as the myriad preferences and interests which have shaped it. In the consumer financial protection sphere, for example, EU regulation

---

[140] ESMA's single rulebook 'workstream', e.g. included a MiFID II/MiFIR sub workstream, the ob-jective for which was the delivery of between 15 and 18 BTSs and one item of Technical Advice, against which objective ESMA reported in a narrative but also quantitative manner: ESMA, Annual Report on 2016, 18–19.

[141] E.g. FCA, Annual Report 2015–16, 13.

[142] IOSCO, Objectives and Principles of Securities Regulation (2010), Principle A.1.

has developed in a piece-meal manner and has never articulated the type of consumer behaviour which is sought or the exact outcomes that regulation seeks: firm behaviour is regulated, but the nature of the outcomes sought is typically not expressed beyond platitudes relating to investor protection and confidence, and to the efficiency of the single market. The relevant questions range from the macro (for example, what level of household participation is optimal?) to the structural (which forms of distribution structure are, ultimately, to be privileged, and how is this to be assessed?)—none of these questions are easy to answer, and many more and equally complex questions are generated by other spheres of financial regulation. But some form of objective identification through legislative prescription, which can support the development of related metrics for assessing progress, is necessary if accountability mechanisms are to carry the legitimation weight required of them in the ESMA arena.

This is not to suggest that open-ended normative directions, such as the promotion of market efficiency and consumer protection, should be reduced to a legislative list of operational targets. Not only would this be almost impossible to achieve, but also it would prejudicially shackle ESMA's ability to respond to a highly dynamic market context. But there is a need for a clearer legislative articulation of the general aims ESMA should be pursuing and also of their relative importance. Further, ESMA's objectives should include prescription of what is to be avoided— whether excessive regulatory costs, disproportionate action, threats to competition, or similar. Greater legislative specification would structure ESMA's discretion more clearly, and thereby support not only legitimation through accountability, but also legitimation through judicial review.

6. Conclusion

The notion of discretion, and how its exercise by non-majoritarian actors operating within legislative mandates can be legitimated, poses distinct challenges in the context of EU financial governance, and specifically in relation to the burgeoning technocratic influence of the three ESAs. This chapter explores how one of the ESAs, ESMA, has come to exercise a degree of discretion which its current legitimating arrangements, including its constitutive legislative measures, are struggling to contain. Discretion is, however, essential to the functional effectiveness of financial regulators generally, and of the ESAs, and of ESMA in particular, given the highly complex and contingent environment in which they operate and in relation to which they must deliver their politically conferred mandates for delegated action. What role accordingly for law?

This chapter suggests that the degree of discretion exercised by ESMA should be acknowledged, along with the limited capacity of law, and, in particular, of the *Meroni* constraint, to contain ESMA discretion. ESMA's accountability arrangements should be recognized as carrying the bulk of the weight in relation to legitimation and strengthened accordingly, including through governance reform. The chapter identifies a specific and related role for law, however, in the form of a thicker specification by the EU's legislators of the objectives ESMA should pursue when applying its delegated powers.

6

Central Bank Independence, Discretion, and Judicial Review

Vestert Borger[*]

1. Introduction

Discretion does not always manage to capture the minds of lawyers. It is easily seen as a by-product, as the unavoidable consequence of the textual vagueness and ambiguity that accompanies much of the law.[1] But it does not need to be. Discretion can also be the result of intentional design, an asset entrusted by the lawmaker to another actor—administrative or political—which the latter needs to discharge its tasks.[2] The European Central Bank (Bank) forms a case in point. When the currency union was being negotiated in the early 1990s, treaty drafters ensured the Bank would have great discretion.[3] This attribution of discretion first of all formed a recognition of the fact that monetary policy is a highly complex, context-dependent matter requiring considerable freedom for those charged with its formulation and implementation. Perhaps even more important was that discretion was considered necessary in view of the need for central bank independence.[4] Granting central bankers a certain

[*] Assistant Professor, the Europa Institute of Leiden Law School. This contribution builds on earlier work by the author, in particular V Borger, 'Outright Monetary Transactions and the Stability Mandate of the ECB: *Gauweiler*' (2016) 53 *CML Rev* 139, and V Borger, *The Transformation of the Euro: Law, Contract, Solidarity* (Doctoral dissertation, Leiden University, 31 January 2018). The author thanks the participants in two workshops linked to this book, which were initiated and organized by Joana Mendes. The usual disclaimer applies.

[1] See, famously, HLA Hart, *The Concept of Law* (OUP, 1994) 136.

[2] DJ Calligan, *Discretionary Powers: A Legal Study of Official Discretion* (Clarendon Press, 1990) 1.

[3] For detailed analyses, from various angles and disciplines, of European monetary integration, the negotiations on the Treaty of Maastricht, and their influence on the mandate of the Bank, see T Padoa-Schioppa, *The Road to Monetary Union in Europe: The Emperor, The Kings and the Genies* (OUP, 1994); D Gros and N Thygesen, *European Monetary Integration* (2nd edn, Longman, 1999); A Szász, *The Road to European Monetary Union* (Macmillan Press, 1999); K Dyson and K Featherstone, *The Road to Maastricht: Negotiating Economic and Monetary Union* (OUP, 1993); K McNamara, *The Currency of Ideas: Monetary Politics in the European Union* (Cornell University Press, 1998); A Moravcsik, *The Choice for Europe: Social Purpose and State Power From Messina to Maastricht* (Cornell University Press, 1999) 379 ff.

[4] On the relation between central bank independence and price stability see, e.g. V Grilli, D Masciandaro, and G Tabellini, 'Political and Monetary Institutions and Public Financial Policies in the Industrial Countries' (1991) 13 *Econ Policy* 341; A Alesina and L Summers, 'Central Bank Independence

autonomy over the definition of their policy objectives as well as the instruments needed to achieve them was thought to boost their 'functional' independence and ultimately their capacity to safeguard monetary stability.[5]

Article 127(1) TFEU shows how these considerations have influenced the mandate of the Bank and how closely related are discretion and functional independence.[6] The provision determines that price stability is the Bank's primary aim, yet leaves it up to the Bank itself to operationalize the notion.[7] In doing so, it bestows on the Bank considerable discretion.[8] At the same time, it is this indeterminacy of the notion of price stability that also enhances the Bank's independence and its ability—at least in theory—to realize this very stability.

In the first decade following the launch of the euro, the Bank's discretion did not raise serious problems. What is more, the Bank was praised for its ability to keep inflation close to its official target of 'close to, but below 2% over the medium term',[9] an impressive achievement for a young central bank without a track record of stability on which to rely.[10] But things changed when all hell broke loose in the financial sector with the fall of Lehmann Brothers in September 2008, and even more so when panic spread to sovereign bond markets at the end of 2009. With the single currency under heavy attack in the markets, the Bank had to take measures that, until then, had been considered impossible. Its purchases of government bonds were regarded especially as pushing, or even exceeding, the boundaries of its mandate. Those sceptical of the purchases consequently no longer considered the Bank's discretion to be an *asset*, but a *liability*.[11] It had enabled the Bank to morph into a very different institution than

---

and Macroeconomic Performance: Some Comparative Evidence' (1993) 25 *J Money Credit Bank* 151; T Havrilesky and J Granato, 'Determinants of Inflationary Performance: Corporatist Structures vs. Central Bank Autonomy' (1993) 76 *Public Choice* 249. For critical analyses questioning the causal connection between the two see, e.g. B Hayo, 'Inflation Culture, Central Bank Independence and Price Stability' (1998) 14 *Eur J Polit Econ* 241; K McNamara, 'Rational Fictions: Central Bank Independence and the Social Logic of Delegation' (2002) 25 *West Eur Polit* 47, 58–9.

[5] For a discussion of the various dimensions to central bank independence and how these show up in the mandate of the Bank, see F Amtenbrink, L Geelhoed, and S Kingston, 'Economic, Monetary and Social Policy' in PJG Kapteyn and others (eds), *The Law of the European Union and the European Communities* (Kluwer Law International, 2008) 951–63; R Smits, *The European Central Bank: Institutional Aspects* (Kluwer Law International, 1997) 151–78; RM Lastra, 'The Independence of the European System of Central Banks' (1992) 33 *Harvard Intl LJ* 475, 482–96.

[6] See also Art 282(2) TFEU.

[7] Following the launch of the currency union the Bank defined price stability as 'a year-on-year increase in the Harmonised Index of Consumer Prices (HICP) for the euro area of below 2%' for the medium term. See European Central Bank, (*ECB Monthly Bulletin,* January 1999) 46. As this led to fears that this could lead to a policy of deflation the Bank subsequently redefined price stability as a year-on-year increase in the HICP 'below, but close to 2%'. See European Central Bank, 'The Monetary Policy of the ECB' (ECB 2004) 50–1.

[8] Not all lawyers would necessarily qualify this as discretion. Joana Mendes gives the example of Germany where 'undertermined legal concepts' (*unbestimmte Rechtsbegriffe*) such as price stability are distinguished by some from true discretion (*Ermessen*). See J Mendes, 'Bounded Discretion in EU Law: A Limited Judicial Paradigm in a Changing EU' (2017) 80 *MLR* 443, 454–5. For Mendes' critique on such a 'segmented' approach to discretion see text to (n 62).

[9] See the text and references in (n 7).

[10] P De Grauwe, 'The Euro at Ten: Achievements and Challenges' (2009) 36 *Empirica* 5, 6.

[11] For critical legal views on the purchases, see e.g. D Murswiek, 'ECB, ECJ, Democracy and the Federal Constitutional Court: Notes on the Federal Constitutional Court's Order From 14 January

the one that had been put in place two decades earlier—an institution that did not simply target price stability, but functioned as a 'lender of last resort',[12] propping up financially distressed states all across the currency union.

This contribution takes a closer look at the Bank's discretion, in particular how it has been approached by the *Bundesverfassungsgericht* and by the European Court of Justice (ECJ), when the bond purchases became the subject of a legal challenge in *Gauweiler*.[13] It consists of three parts. The first shows that the German Constitutional Court can be seen as an exponent of the view that the Bank's discretionary power poses a liability and that its exercise should consequently be subject to intense judicial review. This approach has its roots in a desire to strictly delineate the Bank's mandate and not only has negative repercussions for the discretion of the Bank, but above all for its independence.

The second part shifts attention to the ECJ. It shows that the latter's approach to discretion is much more deferential, even too much. Underlying this approach is a technical conception of discretion, one that reduces discretion to the deployment of expertise. Although this approach, reinforced by the need to protect the Bank's independence, enabled the ECJ to hold the bond purchases compatible with Union law, it also portrays discretion as largely disconnected from this law. As a consequence, little is being asked of the Bank in terms of motivating how, from the various interests that the law requires it to protect, it weighs and selects those that provide the basis for its exercise of discretionary power.

The third part examines whether and to what extent a unitary conception of discretion, as proposed by the initiator and editor of this volume Joana Mendes,[14] could steer a middle course between the above two approaches. In particular, it attempts to see whether such a unitary conception could allow courts to review whether and how the Bank has directed its discretionary power to the public interests making up its mandate, while avoiding a full-blown competence review with its negative consequences for central bank independence.

Finally, two remarks. First, some may argue that *Gauweiler* should not be used as a basis for discussing judicial review of central bank action, if only because the reasoning of both the German and European courts was strongly influenced by the

---

2014' (2014) 15 *GLJ* 147; G Beck, 'The Court of Justice, the Bundesverfassungsgericht and Legal Reasoning during the Euro Crisis: The Rule of Law as a Fair-Weather Phenomenon' (2014) 20 *EPL* 539.

[12] On the Bank (trying to act) as lender of last resort for states, see e.g. P Krugman, 'Currency Regimes, Capital Flows, and Crises' (2014) 62 *IMF Econ Rev* 470, 473–5; D Gros, 'On the Stability of Public Debt in a Monetary Union' (2012) 50 *JCMS* 36, 37–8; W Buiter and E Rahbari, 'The European Central Bank as a Lender of Last Resort for Sovereigns in the Eurozone' (2012) 50 *JCMS Annual Review* 6, 6–8, 18; P De Grauwe, 'The European Central Bank as Lender of Last Resort in Government Bond Markets' (2013) 59 *CESifo Econ Stud* 520. Note, however, that the notion 'lender of last resort' is an economic, not a legal, one. Qualifying the Bank as such a lender does therefore not necessarily mean that it acts in violation of Union law. See V Borger, 'Outright Monetary Transactions and the Stability Mandate of the ECB: *Gauweiler*' (2016) 53 *CML Rev* 139, 152.

[13] Case C-62/14 *Peter Gauweiler and others v Deutscher Bundestag* [2015] ECLI:EU:C:2015:400 (hereafter *Gauweiler*).

[14] Mendes (n 8); J Mendes, 'Discretion, Care and Public Interests in the EU Administration: Probing the Limits of Law' (2016) 53 *CML Rev* 419.

exceptional, crisis-driven nature of the case. There is certainly truth in that argument. What is more, there are good reasons for arguing that the courts should not have entered into the merits of the case at all due to the existential importance of the bond programme for the euro and the Union.[15] The fact is, however, that they did and, in doing so, used techniques whose relevance exceeds the confines of the case itself.[16] Even though the way these techniques were applied may have been influenced by the case's exceptional nature, this does not preclude a more fundamental reflection on their suitability as a tool to review central bank discretion. Second, this contribution does not necessarily subscribe to the unitary conception of discretion discussed in the third part. It rather aims to contribute—and only modestly—to the thinking about this conception by examining it in the context of central bank action.

2. Karlsruhe: Competence, not Power

The Bank's motivation for its Outright Monetary Transactions (OMT) programme is by now well known.[17] In the summer of 2012, when the crisis had reached its absolute peak, the difference in interest rates—the so-called 'spread'—between bonds of states in the currency union was extremely high. The rates for states in the currency union's 'periphery' had reached such heights that the Bank considered them no longer to reflect their fundamental economic condition.[18] Instead, markets, driven by fear and panic, had lapsed into a 'bad equilibrium' and seemed to factor in a 'currency redenomination risk premium', i.e. that they were anticipating a break-up of the euro area as a consequence of which the bonds would be redenominated in a new, devalued currency.[19] Apart from the fact that the Bank judged the bond rates excessive, they also negatively affected its ability to safeguard price stability. Under normal conditions, the Bank exercises control over the price level through the setting of official interest rates. But due to the financial instability resulting from high bond rates, the policy 'signals' flowing from these official rates no longer were 'transmitted' throughout the currency union.[20] With its OMT programme, the Bank

---

[15] See V Borger, *The Transformation of the Euro: Law, Contract, Solidarity* (Doctoral dissertation, Leiden University, 31 January 2018).

[16] In general, on techniques of judicial review of discretion, see Nehl, Chapter 8 in this volume.

[17] For extensive analyses of the Bank's motivation see European Central Bank, 'The Determinants of Euro Area Sovereign Bond Yield Spreads' (*ECB Monthly Bulletin*, May 2014) 67–83; P Cour-Thimann and B Winkler, 'The ECB's Non-standard Monetary Policy Measures: The Role of Institutional Factors and Financial Structure' (2012) 28 *Oxf Rev Econ Policy* 765, 774–83.

[18] For a solid explanation of the currency union's susceptibility to 'multiple equilibria' and the fact that this may lead to bond rates being disconnected from economic 'fundamentals', see P de Grauwe and Y Ji, 'Mispricing of Sovereign Risk and Macroeconomic Stability in the Eurozone' (2012) 50 *JCMS* 866; P de Grauwe and Y Ji, 'Self-fulfilling Crises in the Eurozone: An Empirical Test' (2013) 34 *J Int Money Finance* 15. For a legal analysis of the OMT programme in light of the theory on multiple equilibria, see C Gerner-Beuerle, E Kücuk, and E Schuster, 'Law Meets Economics in the German Federal Constitutional Court: Outright Monetary Transactions on Trial' (2014) 15 *GLJ* 281; Borger (n 12).

[19] ECB, 'The Determinants' (n 17) 77–8.

[20] For a discussion of the various transmission 'channels' that were not working properly due to the high interest rates for certain government bonds, see Cour-Thimann and Winkler (n 17) 774–6.

sought to restore the transmission mechanism by bringing interest rates for government bonds back to normal levels through targeted purchases on the secondary market. It formed the practical follow-up to the pledge made in July 2012 by the president of the Bank, Mario Draghi, 'to do whatever it takes to preserve the euro'.[21]

Critics, however, argued that there was more to the bond programme than the Bank would admit. With the programme the Bank would position itself as a 'lender of last resort' for states in the currency union, ensuring that they would always have enough liquidity at their disposal to honour their financial commitments. In doing so, it would act outside its monetary policy mandate, instead conducting economic policy, and violate the prohibition on monetary financing in Article 123 TFEU.

These two issues—the mandate and monetary financing—were at the heart of the *Bundesverfassungsgericht*'s reference decision in *Gauweiler*.[22] What matters most for present purposes is the mandate.[23] Set out in Article 127(1) TFEU, it determines that the Bank should first and foremost target price stability, and that it can only support economic policy to the extent this does not conflict with this primary goal. In the eyes of the judges in Karlsruhe, this arrangement makes up the core of the currency union's legal set-up which, as stated in the *Maastricht* judgment of 1993, guarantees that the currency union constitutes a *Stabilitätsgemeinschaft*, 'a community based on stability'.[24] This focus on stability forms 'the basis and subject matter' of Germany's accession to the currency union and, if abandoned, could ultimately force the state to withdraw.[25]

No wonder, therefore, that when the OMT programme became the subject of an *ultra vires* challenge in *Gauweiler* the *Bundesverfassungsgericht* took great care in delimitating the Bank's mandate. But in doing so it made a questionable move from the perspective of discretion.[26] At the basis of that move lies a reasoning about the relationship between the Bank's mandate and its independence. The German court recognized the importance of this independence, but denied that it should influence the delineation of the mandate. The independence guarantees laid down in the Treaties, it argued, only concern the Bank's 'actual powers', not 'the determination of the extent and scope of its mandate'.[27] In fact, a strict delineation of the mandate

---

[21] Verbatim of the remarks made by Mario Draghi at the Global Investment Conference in London, 26 July 2012.

[22] BVerfG, 2 BvR 2728/13, 14 January 2014 (hereafter *BVerfG OMT reference decision*).

[23] See, however, text to (n 54).

[24] BVerfG, Cases 2 BvR 2134/92 & 2159/92, 12 October 1993 (as translated in [1994] 1 CMLR 57), para 80 (hereafter *BVerfG Maastricht*).

[25] *BVerfG Maastricht* (n 24), paras 89–90. During the euro crisis the *BVerfG* issued several judgments in which it reflected on this notion of *Stabilitätsgemeinschaft*. Particularly interesting is its judgment on a temporary injunction concerning the European Stability Mechanism (ESM) and the Treaty on Stability, Coordination and Governance. In that judgment, the German court indicated that the currency union's stability arrangements were not written in stone. The introduction of Art 136(3) TFEU, which indicates that the member states in the currency union can establish a mechanism like the ESM, amounted to a 'fundamental reshaping of the existing economic and monetary union', yet was nonetheless acceptable. At the same time, however, the *BVerfG* indicated that the acceptability of this reform was tied to the fact that 'essential parts of the stability architecture' remained 'in place', in particular, the mandate of the Bank. See BVerfG, 2 BvR 1390/12, 12 September 2012, paras 128–9.

[26] See also Borger (n 12) 170–4, 192–5.

[27] *BVerfG OMT reference decision* (n 22), para 60.

was required precisely because of this independence, so as to make sure the Bank did not have the ability to expand it 'at will'.[28]

The *Bundesverfassungsgericht* then went on to define the mandate on the basis of the test the ECJ had developed in *Pringle* to determine the policy nature of the European Stability Mechanism (ESM).[29] Without discussing this test in great detail, one can say that it attributes over-riding importance to a measure's objectives. The *Bundesverfassungsgericht* now similarly looked at objectives to determine the policy nature of the OMT programme and, by extension, the scope of the Bank's mandate.[30] And in doing so it did not hold back. Instead of accepting the official objective put forward by the Bank—purchasing government bonds to bring down their interest rates to levels justified by the economic condition of the issuing state—the German court stated the OMT programme aimed to 'neutralize' interest rate spreads in the currency union across the board.[31] To the extent it did take into account the official objective, it relied on the opinion of the *Bundesbank* that it was impossible to determine a correct or 'rational' level for bond rates and that any attempt to do so was therefore 'meaningless'.[32] One should consequently not justify bond market intervention on the basis of the alleged 'irrationality' of these rates and the problem this may pose for the transmission of monetary policy.[33]

This reasoning about objectives formed the basis for the *Bundesverfassungsgericht*'s conclusion that the OMT programme constituted economic policy and fell outside the monetary policy mandate of the Bank.[34] More importantly, it shows the difficulty, from the point of view of discretion, of distinguishing between the delineation of a competence and the exercise of discretionary power.[35] Distinguishing between 'mandate' and 'power' may work on paper, yet in practice this distinction is hard to maintain. Indeed, the German court only managed to define the scope of the mandate through an extensive review of the bond programme adopted on the basis of that very mandate; both in relation to the *definition* of the programme's objective and its *feasibility*, the court substituted its own assessment for that of the Bank, ignoring the latter's discretion.

Karlsruhe's contention that it respects the independence of the Bank is consequently deeply problematic.[36] As mentioned, the discretion of the Bank to a great extent resides in the indeterminacy of its mandate, in particular the notion of price

---

[28] Ibid.

[29] Case C-370/12 *Thomas Pringle v Government of Ireland and others* [2012] ECLI:EU:C:2012:756, paras 55–7.

[30] On the inappropriateness of using this test for delineating the mandate of the Bank, see Borger (n 12) 179.

[31] *BVerfG OMT reference decision* (n 22), para 70.   [32] Ibid., paras 71, 97–8.

[33] Ibid., para 98.

[34] For an extensive analysis of its entire reasoning, see T Beukers, 'The Bundesverfassungsgericht Preliminary Reference on the OMT Program: "In the ECB We Do Not Trust. What About You?"' (2014) 15 *GLJ* 343; M Wendel, 'Exceeding Judicial Competence in the Name of Democracy: The German Federal Constitutional Court's OMT Reference' (2014) 10 *EuConst* 263.

[35] Borger (n 12) 192–3.

[36] Ibid., 193–4; S Baroncelli, 'The *Gauweiler* Judgment in View of the Case Law of the European Court of Justice on European Central Bank Independence' (2016) 23 *MJ* 79, 87.

stability. This indeterminacy is also the source of its functional independence.[37] By entering the discretionary space of the Bank and contradicting it on the bond programme's objective the *Bundesverfassungsgericht* undermined this independence. Judging by the German court's own standards, this cannot but be seen as a cynical result. Back in 1993, in its *Maastricht* judgment, the German court tied its acceptance of the monetary union to the condition that it would be a community based on stability.[38] The independence of the Bank is a central pillar of, as well as a key guarantee for, such a community. Yet, this independence now was threatened by the *Bundesverfassungsgericht* itself due to its intrusive review of the bond programme.

3. Luxembourg: Discretion as Technicity

The ECJ similarly distinguished between mandate and power. But contrary to the *Bundesverfassungsgericht* it instead stressed the importance of the Bank's independence and concentrated its analysis on the exercise of power, not on the mandate.[39] Even though it also used the *Pringle* test to chart the limits of this mandate, and consequently attributed great importance to objectives, it easily followed the Bank's reasoning that its bond purchases served to safeguard the transmission of its interest rate decisions—and ultimately price stability—and therefore fell within its mandate.[40]

Real engagement with this reasoning only occurred after the ECJ had shifted its focus to the exercise of power, which allowed it to explicitly recognize the Bank's discretion. This recognition took place within the broader framework of an analysis of the bond programme's proportionality, in particular its suitability.[41] As a programme like OMT requires the Bank 'to make choices of a technical nature and to undertake forecasts and complex assessments', the ECJ considered it had to be allowed broad discretion.[42] At the same time, and precisely because of this broad discretion, the ECJ emphasized the importance of reviewing compliance with procedural guarantees like the duty of care and the duty to state reasons.[43]

---

[37] Interestingly, neither the *BVerfG* nor the ECJ explicitly recognized the various dimensions to central bank independence, in particular the political and functional ones, nor the overlap between functional independence and discretion. Advocate General Cruz Villalón did. See Opinion of Advocate Cruz Villalón in *Gauweiler* (n 13), paras 107–11. See also Baroncelli (n 36) 90–1.

[38] See text to (n 24).

[39] See *Gauweiler* (n 13), paras 40–1, in which the ECJ first underscores the importance of central bank independence before it states that the Bank can only 'act within the limits of the powers conferred on it'. See also Baroncelli (n 36) 83, 89.

[40] *Gauweiler* (n 13), paras 46–56.

[41] Ibid., paras 66–80. There is, of course, a problematic element to this strategy of the ECJ. The *BVerfG*'s reference decision dealt with an *ultra vires* complaint. Its concerns about several aspects of the bond programme related to the question whether or not they showed it fell outside the mandate of the Bank. By discussing many of these concerns only in the context of a proportionality analysis, the ECJ changed their nature and took the sting out of them. They no longer served as indicators potentially showing the programme's *ultra vires* nature, but only its disproportionality. On this specific use of proportionality, see Kosta, Chapter 9 in this volume.

[42] *Gauweiler* (n 13), para 68.   [43] Ibid., para 69.

The ECJ subsequently went into the merits of the motivation for the bond programme. It accepted the Bank's observation that, in the summer of 2012, bond rates for certain states in the currency union no longer reflected their economic condition but had spiralled out of control, heavily impairing its ability to have its policy signals transmitted throughout the currency union. While the ECJ recognized that this observation had been 'subject to challenge'—a subtle acknowledgment of the criticism voiced by the *Bundesbank*—this did not suffice to conclude that the Bank had wrongfully employed its discretion.[44] 'Questions of monetary policy are usually of a controversial nature', it reasoned, and given the Bank's broad discretion 'nothing more' could be asked of it 'apart from that it use its economic expertise and the necessary technical means at its disposal' to deal with these questions 'with all care and accuracy'.[45] The ECJ consequently found that the Bank's reading of the situation in sovereign bond markets was not 'vitiated by a manifest error of assessment' and provided an adequate justification for the bond programme.[46]

By focusing on the exercise of power instead of the mandate, the ECJ could take into account the Bank's discretion and consequently pay tribute to its functional independence. But this approach to discretion can be criticized as well, on two counts notably. The first concerns its practical implementation, where the second is more fundamental and relates to the understanding of discretion on which it is based.

First, practical implementation. When reviewing the exercise of discretion, in particular the factual assessments on which it is based, two standards come into play.[47] On the one hand, there is 'the standard of proof required of the primary decision taker', in this case the Bank.[48] This is the standard that the Bank needs to meet concerning the facts before it can act. As Paul Craig explains, the standard can be more or less demanding depending on the nature of the action and the particulars of the case, ranging from 'a high degree of probability', 'possibility', or simply 'sufficiency'.[49] On the other hand, there is the 'standard of judicial review', which the ECJ applies to establish whether the primary decision taker has met the standard of proof.[50] This standard may be more or less stringent—'substantial evidence', 'sufficient evidence', etc.—as long as it does not lead the ECJ to put its own assessment for that of the primary decision-maker.

How did the ECJ employ these standards? Scantily, to say the least.[51] By reasoning that 'nothing more' can be required of the Bank than that it uses its expertise 'with all care and accuracy', the ECJ did not distinguish between the two standards,

---

[44] Ibid., para 75.
[45] Ibid. The formula is repeated in the Opinion of Advocate General Wathelet in the *Weiss* case on the Bank's quantitative easing programme. See Opinion of Advocate General Wathelet in Case C-493/17 *Heinrich Weiss and others* [2018] ECLI:EU:C:2018:815, para 152.
[46] *Gauweiler* (n 13), paras 74, 76–80.
[47] As P Craig, *EU Administrative Law* (OUP, 2012) 431 ff, explains, one can distinguish between 'judicial review for factual error' and 'judicial review of discretion'. In *Gauweiler*, however, the ECJ does not clearly separate the two, instead carrying out its review for factual error under the umbrella of reviewing discretion. See in this regard also the text to (n 66), which discusses Mendes' unitary account of discretion and her criticism of attempts to strictly separate the deployment of technical expertise from discretion proper.
[48] Craig (n 47) 432.   [49] Ibid.   [50] Ibid., 433–4.   [51] Borger (n 12) 194.

let alone substantiate their stringency. It failed to indicate the standard of proof required of the Bank to reach the conclusion that government bond markets suffer from a bad equilibrium and hamper the transmission of monetary policy, just as it did not set out the standard of review applicable to itself when verifying whether the Bank has met this standard of proof. As a result, the ECJ's finding that the Bank's reading of the economic situation in the currency union was not 'vitiated by a manifest error of assessment' loses much of its meaning.[52]

Regarding the understanding of discretion, the view that emerges from the ECJ's reasoning is one equating discretion with technicity.[53] A proper exercise of discretion is dependent on the correct use of technical expertise, in this case concerning government bond markets and monetary policy transmission. But is that really all there is to discretion? As Joana Mendes explains, by adopting the OMT programme, the Bank did more than merely deploying its monetary policy expertise.[54] It took a decision with policy implications reaching far beyond price stability, stretching out to the operation of bond markets, fiscal policy as well as its own institutional position, in particular its political independence vis-à-vis member states.[55] These are all interests enjoying protection under Union law. Articles 119(2) and (3) TFEU make clear that monetary policy needs to be in accordance with the principles of 'an open market economy with free competition' and 'sound public finances', whereas Articles 130 and 282(3) TFEU stipulate that the Bank enjoys 'independence in the exercise of its powers'.

Now, these interests did feature in the reasoning of the ECJ, especially when it reviewed compliance with the prohibition on monetary financing. The ECJ examined, for example, whether the bond programme respects the market mechanism by ensuring that secondary market purchases do not have an equivalent effect as those carried out on the primary market.[56] It also ascertained whether the programme does not contain incentives for fiscal imprudence.[57] Yet, at such instances the interests served a similar function as they did in the reasoning of the *Bundesverfassungsgericht*: to verify whether the Bank had stayed within the limits of its mandate.[58] When the ECJ reviewed the exercise of discretionary power on the basis of that mandate they were largely absent; it did recognize that adopting the programme required the Bank to 'weigh up' interests, yet only in the context of assessing the bond programme's

---

[52] See also T Tridimas and N Xanthoulis, 'A Legal Analysis of the *Gauweiler* Case: Between Monetary Policy and Constitutional Conflict' (2016) 23 *MJ* 17, 31: 'The key point that emerges from the judgment is the enormous discretion left to the ECB. Although its power is restricted by a number of conditions, none of those conditions are firm and the determination of whether they are fulfilled invariably entails complex technical assessment in relation to which the Court of Justice left the ECB with broad discretion.' Even more critical in this respect is C Joerges, '*Pereat Iustitia, Fiat Mundus*: What is Left of the European Economic Constitution after the Gauweiler Litigation?' (2016) 23 *MJ* 99, 106–7. More permissive are P Craig and M Markakis, 'Gauweiler and the Legality of Outright Monetary Transactions' (2016) 41 *EL Rev* 4, 19–20.

[53] Mendes (n 8) 449.   [54] Ibid.

[55] For a discussion of the difference between political and functional independence, see references (n 5).

[56] *Gauweiler* (n 13), paras 97, 103–8.   [57] Ibid., paras 98–101, 109–21.

[58] A prohibition like the one on monetary financing can, after all, be read as a competence negatively construed.

proportionality *stricto sensu*.[59] That such weighing of interests may actually be a defining feature of discretion, and should be treated as such in the context of judicial review, was not discernible in the reasoning of the ECJ.

It consequently almost seems as if the German and European courts occupy two opposite ends on the spectrum of discretion. The judges in Karlsruhe say to concentrate efforts on demarcating the mandate of the Bank but nonetheless *de facto* review the exercise of its discretionary power up to the point that they substitute their own normative assessment for that of the Bank. Those in Luxembourg explicitly acknowledge the Bank's discretion, yet approach it as a technical construct that involves the use of expert knowledge but is devoid of any normativity. This raises the question whether a 'thicker' understanding of discretion, one that acknowledges its normative dimension, has the potential to bridge the divide between these approaches by allowing courts to take into account the interests the Bank is required to pursue by law, yet without forcing them to engage in a competence review with its negative repercussions for functional independence.

4. A Unitary Conception of Central Bank Discretion

To explore this question it serves to bring to mind Ronald Dworkin's well-known account of discretion. 'Discretion', says Dworkin, 'like the hole in a doughnut, does not exist except as an area left open by a surrounding belt of restriction. It is therefore a relative concept. It always makes sense to ask, "Discretion under which standards?" or "Discretion as to which authority?" '.[60] According to Dworkin, discretion, at least in its *strong* sense, is characterized by the fact that its possessor is not controlled by any standards introduced by the authority at issue.[61] Taking law as authority, Dworkin argues that judges do not have such discretion, given that in all cases, even hard ones, they will be governed by legal standards, be it rules or principles.[62]

Interestingly, the ECJ creates the impression that the Bank does have strong discretion. According to Mendes, the technical conception of discretion in *Gauweiler*, which equates discretion with the deployment of expertise, has its origin in a perspective on law and discretion centred around the judiciary.[63] Characteristic of this perspective is that it holds a 'negative' understanding of discretion in the sense that it aligns discretion with legality and judicial review.[64] Discretion is seen as situated beyond the law, out of reach of rules or principles that, once interpreted by courts, could indicate the proper course of action. It is 'what is left outside of judicial

---

[59] *Gauweiler* (n 13), para 91. See also Mendes (n 8) 449, according to whom ' ... public-interest appraisals and technical assessments appear logically separate moments in the Court's reasoning'.

[60] R Dworkin, 'Is Law a System of Rules?' in R Dworkin (ed), *The Philosophy of Law* (OUP, 1977) 38, 52–3.

[61] Ibid., 53.

[62] See also SJ Shapiro, 'The Hart-Dworkin Debate: A Short Guide for the Perplexed'. Michigan Law School *Public Law and Legal Theory Working Paper Series, Working Paper No. 77*, March 2007) 12.

[63] Mendes (n 8) 459.   [64] Ibid., 461.

control'.[65] In *Gauweiler*, the ECJ could consequently review the Bank's deployment of technical expertise, but not the balance struck by the latter between the public interests covered by its mandate, even if it had explicitly acknowledged this normative, value-laden dimension to the Bank's discretion.

This perspective on law and discretion also helps to explain the approach of the *Bundesverfassungsgericht*. It takes the view that it is in charge of interpreting the rules that both make up the Bank's mandate and carve out the space of its discretion. What subsequently happens within that discretionary space, especially from a normative dimension, is largely outside the scope of its control.

Mendes, however, stresses that such a 'segmented' view on executive action, distinguishing between the interpretation of rules, technical assessments, and normative discretion, fails to recognize their intricate relationship.[66] The theoretical difference between technical assessments and normative discretion, or between 'cognition' and 'volition', denies the ontological connection between the two. For example, regarding the OMT programme, factual expertise about the functioning of euro area government bond markets, in particular their susceptibility to bad equilibria, led the Bank to carry out targeted purchases of government bonds on secondary markets so as to remedy the transmission of monetary policy. This expertise, in other words, influenced how the Bank balanced various public interests enjoying protection under Union law; it considered an intervention in the market mechanism, protected under Articles 119(2) and 127(1) TFEU, acceptable in view of the need to safeguard price stability.

This interplay between cognition and volition also shows how the exercise of discretion impacts on the interpretation of rules.[67] In 1993, when the Treaty of Maastricht entered into force, few would have considered targeted purchases of government bonds to bring down their interest rates as falling within the mandate of the Bank. At that time, however, technical knowledge about the tendency of euro area government bond markets to lapse into a bad equilibrium, as well as the resulting risks for financial stability, was largely absent. According to Cour-Thimann and Winkler, 'the concept of "ensuring the financial stability of the euro area as a whole" had to be "invented" in the crisis'.[68] The need to safeguard this stability in view of the transmission of monetary policy and ultimately price stability consequently led to a reinterpretation of the mandate of the Bank and the actions it allows.

Given the close inter-relation between the interpretation of rules, technical expertise, and normative discretion, Mendes argues in favour of a 'unitary' conception of discretion.[69] At its basis lies a change in perspective on discretion from the

---

[65] Ibid., citing R Caranta, 'On Discretion' in S Prechal and B van Roermund (eds), *The Coherence of EU Law: The Search for Unity in Divergent Concepts* (OUP, 2008) 185.

[66] Mendes (n 8) 458, 461–2.

[67] See also Baroncelli (n 36) 88: 'Since Maastricht, however, the role of the ECB has grown and the economic and legal context has changed ... the mandate of the ECB as described in the Treaties has remained vague, as shown by the fact that it was down to the Governing Council of the ECB to decide upon the content of price stability; this shows that it was endowed with a technical discretion to decide upon the extent of monetary policy'.

[68] Cour-Thimann and Winkler (n 17) 767.   [69] Mendes (n 8) 462 ff.

judiciary to the primary decision maker. The latter possesses discretion when it has 'the authority ... to choose between different alternatives when concretising legal norms with a view to achieving the ends that those norms identify'.[70] It receives this authority from the rules that bestow upon it the power to achieve the public interests set out in them. When exercising this discretionary authority, it engages in a process in which interpretation, expert judgment, and normative balancing intertwine.

Instead of portraying the exercise of this authority as *detached* from legal standards, characteristic of the judicial perspective on discretion, Mendes stresses that it remains *bound* by them.[71] The primary decision maker possesses a certain autonomy in virtue of its discretionary authority, yet it employs this in pursuit of particular legally protected public interests from which it derives that very authority. It is consequently misplaced to argue that its discretion is somehow situated beyond the confines of law; by exercising discretion, the decision maker is specifying the law while at the same time being bound by it.

As the unitary conception of discretion no longer has the perspective of the judiciary at its basis, Mendes argues that the role of courts as guardians of its proper exercise takes a back seat.[72] It is rather by means of safeguards incorporated into the decision-making process itself that this should be secured, in particular through procedural instruments like the duty of care and that to state reasons. They should function as 'self-reflective tools' allowing decision makers to verify and make insightful how relevant public interests interact with technical assessments and inform the actions they consider permissible in light of their mandates.[73]

Even if a unitary conception of discretion causes courts to take a back seat, denying them any role would be wrong. Standing aloof would be an option if courts were to face strong discretion in the sense used by Dworkin, given that such discretion is characterized by the absence of standards. But the unitary conception of discretion rather makes the opposite claim that discretion is always exercised with a view to legally protected public interests and consequently bound by law. Mendes herself raises the possibility that courts could 'signal' the relevant procedural instruments for a correct exercise of discretion while refraining from enforcing them, as this would amount to 'a type of review that only internal administrative bodies should perform'.[74] Yet, one can imagine courts going one step further and operationalizing procedural instruments like the duty to state reasons to review the exercise of discretion, including that of the Bank.

This review would go beyond a 'rationality check' that some regard as the proper instrument for reviewing central bank action.[75] Such a check enables courts to verify whether in the exercise of its discretion the Bank has respected the pragmatic, ethical, and moral considerations that make up the 'law-generating discourse' informing the choice for the substance and form of its mandate.[76] Judicial review on the basis of

---

[70] Ibid.   [71] Ibid., 464.   [72] Ibid., 465–70.   [73] Ibid., 468–79.
[74] Ibid., 469.
[75] M Goldmann, 'Adjudicating Economics? Central Bank Independence and the Appropriate Standard of Judicial Review' (2014) 15 *Ger Law J* 265, 272–4.
[76] Ibid., 273.

a unitary conception of discretion would be more demanding. The duty to state reasons would allow courts to penetrate the discretionary space of the Bank in as far as they may require it to show not only that is has respected the limits of the discursive basis for its mandate, but also that it has interpreted and exercised that mandate in a manner that takes account of the various public interests that make it up.

What would this kind of review mean for the functional independence of the Bank? It would certainly be more stringent than the current approach of the ECJ, as it not only verifies the deployment of technical expertise, but also its interaction with public interests, thereby covering the normative dimension to discretion. Yet it would fall short of the intrusive competence review of the *Bundesverfassungsgericht*. There is a subtle yet real difference between putting one's own normative assessments on monetary policy in the place of the Bank's or asking the latter to motivate how it has directed its powers to the public interests it needs to serve. Precisely because of the intricate relationship between technical expertise, value judgements, and the interpretation of rules—which may lead to different decisions by several actors, as exemplified by the *Bundesbank* and the European Central Bank in *Gauweiler*, or over time—reviewing compliance with a duty to motivate does not equal substitution of judgment.

The real difficulty therefore does not lie in the independence of the Bank, but instead in the identification and demarcation of the interests it is expected to serve. Where to draw the line? At the objectives explicitly mentioned in Article 127(1) TFEU, the guiding principles in Article 119 TFEU or perhaps those on which the Union is founded and which it strives to attain in Articles 2 and 3 TEU? This difficulty is not so much one of judicial review, but one bound up with the unitary conception of discretion itself. Mendes pursues that conception to its conclusion by arguing that discretion concerns choosing 'the options that best fulfil the public interests that are legally protected, all in accordance with the founding values and legal principles that ground the legal order of which they are a part'.[77] Respecting that standard in practice will be a challenge for the primary decision maker as well as the reviewing court.

5. Conclusion

The independence of the European Central Bank to a great extent resides in the indeterminacy of 'price stability'—the primary goal of monetary policy. In virtue of that indeterminacy, the Bank enjoys a certain autonomy, or discretion, to operationalize this goal, which fits the idea—popular at the time of the drafting of the Treaty of Maastricht—that monetary policy is best left to skilled technocrats. But the crisis forced the Bank out of its technocratic comfort zone to act on the fringes of its mandate, especially through targeted purchases of government bonds. Both the *Bundesverfassungsgericht* and the ECJ grappled with the discretion of the Bank

---

[77] Mendes (n 8) 463.

when they were called upon to assess the legality of these purchases in *Gauweiler*. The former sought refuge in a distinction between 'mandate' and 'power'. Whereas this distinction holds in theory, in practice it is hard to maintain, with the result that the *Bundesverfassungsgericht* only managed to delimit the mandate of the Bank at the expense of a full review of the exercise of discretion, up to the point that it redefined the objective of the bond purchases. The ECJ found a way out of its predicament by reducing discretion to a technical construct that requires the use of expert knowledge, but that is devoid of normative judgment.

Both approaches create the impression that discretion is situated beyond the law, out of reach of legal standards that, once interpreted by courts, may indicate how to act. A unitary conception of discretion challenges this idea. Changing the perspective of the judiciary for that of the primary decision maker, it holds that discretion is always exercised in pursuit of legally protected public interests and consequently bound by law. When the decision maker draws on its discretion, it engages in a process in which technical expertise, value judgment, and the interpretation of rules intertwine. Focusing on one of these elements in isolation, as did both the *Bundesverfassungsgericht* (rules) and the ECJ (expertise) in *Gauweiler*, oversimplifies discretion.

Switching to this unitary conception arguably would be easier for the ECJ than it would be for the *Bundesverfassungsgericht*. The former primarily has to upgrade procedural tools like the duties of care and to state reasons, whereas the latter needs to do some real soul-searching. In its final judgment on the OMT programme, the *Bundesverfassungsgericht* accepted the ECJ's approval, yet it did not budge from its original position that it is possible to delineate the mandate of the Bank without affecting its independence. In fact, it criticized the ECJ for not having acknowledged the argument that a 'particularly strict judicial review' of this mandate is warranted precisely because of the Bank's independence.[78] The mantra is repeated in its reference decision on the Bank's quantitative easing programme.[79] A unitary conception of discretion learns, however, that one better think twice before sacrificing central bank independence on the altar of *ultra vires* control.

---

[78] BVerfG, 2 BvR 2728/13, 21 June 2016, paras 187–8.
[79] BVerfG, 2 BvR 859/15, 18 July 2017, paras 102–5.

7

Discretion, Economic Governance, and the (New) Political Commission

Päivi Leino and Tuomas Saarenheimo*

1. Introduction

This is a story about EU economic governance, and how a relentless quest for better rules eventually led to a system that is, for practical purposes, entirely discretionary. We argue that successive reforms of the Stability and Growth Pact (SGP) have transformed the economic governance framework from a narrow, rules-based system geared towards avoiding gross fiscal errors into a broad and discretionary process that seeks to guide Member States towards good policies in practically every economic policy field. In parallel, the framework has expanded far beyond mere fiscal policy into questions of macro-economic, structural, and social policies, where no Treaty rules exist to guide the Union's exercise of power. This expansion in scope has led to a substantial increase in the discretionary powers of the Commission. With its broader application and loftier ambition, the framework no more lends itself to easy parametrization and automatic application. In some parts of the framework, no rules exist and the Commission's discretion is constrained only by some very high-level principles. Even in those parts of the framework that still formally remain rules-based, the rules relate to unobservable variables and are qualified by numerous exceptions and flexibility clauses. National budgetary authorities are left in a maze of alternative or even conflicting rules, part legislative, part non-legislative, which few understand. This chapter explains how, as a practical consequence of the framework's complexity, the Commission's task to navigate this maze and assess compliance has become an exercise of nearly unlimited discretion, the outcome of which is very difficult to predict and almost impossible to contest. We also discuss the downstream implications of the expanded discretionary powers of the Commission; how the fundamentally political nature of the decisions the Commission is today tasked with

* Päivi Leino is Professor of Transnational European Law at the University of Helsinki. Tuomas Saarenheimo is the Permanent Undersecretary responsible for international and financial matters at the Finnish Ministry of Finance. The paper reflects the authors' personal views. We thank Carol Harlow for brainstorming discretion with us.

sits uncomfortably with its traditional technocratic identity and has contributed to a mutation of its genetic makeup from a technocratic into an openly political body.

The recent reforms of the governance framework were driven by two implicit assumptions. First, that States, like any economic agents, respond predictably to incentives, and thus could be effectively compelled to comply with rules. Second, that the strict administration of these rules could be ensured by allocating responsibility for the enforcement to the Commission, which would act in an objective and technocratic manner as the Guardian of the Treaties.[1] As a result of the first assumption, the traditional EU regulatory mode of integration was extended to matters that reach deeply into Member State democratic structures. This latter assumption was the motivation for the introduction of the Reverse Qualified Majority voting rule into the SGP,[2] entailing that the Commission's proposal will stand unless it is voted down by a qualified majority within the Council. The Fiscal Compact further qualified the decision-making procedure by committing the euro countries to vote *en bloc* in support of the Commission, unless a qualified majority among them oppose its proposal.[3] Strengthening the role of the technocratic and objective Commission vis-à-vis the politicized Council was intended to make the adoption of decisions more automatic and thereby enhance enforcement.[4]

Some margin of decisional leeway is largely considered necessary in order to transpose abstract general provisions into more concrete individual decisions.[5] The context in which the Commission exercises its new executive discretion is, however, in many ways atypical. Discretion is, in most cases, exercised by a public authority with respect to technical questions, in relation to individuals or other private agents,[6] and within a framework that enables the courts to monitor that its exercise remains within the specified limits.[7] In the context we study, the legislature has chosen to define discretion so broadly that any possible constraints are political, rather than legal, in nature.

Discretion begins where law ends.[8] In economic governance law ends early and gives little substantive guidance to the exercise of executive discretion. What is more,

---

[1] See in greater detail, P Leino and T Saarenheimo, 'Sovereignty and Subordination: On the Limits of EU Economic Policy Coordination' (2017) 43(5) *European law Review* (2018) 623–47.

[2] See Arts 4(2), 5(2), and 6(2) of Regulation (EU) 1173/2011 on the effective enforcement of budgetary surveillance in the euro area [2011] OJ L306/1; Arts 6(2) and 10(2) of Council Regulation (EC) 1466/97 on the strengthening of the surveillance of budgetary positions and the surveillance and coordination of economic policies [1997] OJ L209/1 as amended by Regulation (EU) 1175/2011 [2011] OJ L306/12; Art 10 (4) of Regulation (EU) 1176/2011 on the prevention and correction of macroeconomic imbalances [2011] OJ L306/25; Art 3 Regulation (EU) 1174/2011 on enforcement measures to correct excessive macroeconomic imbalances in the euro area [2011] OJ L306/8.

[3] Treaty on Stability, Coordination and Governance in the Economic and Monetary Union, Brussels (1 February 2012), Art 7.

[4] While the motivation behind the RQMV was explicitly stated, the preamble of Regulation No 1174/2011 was laconic in its justifications: 'The Commission should have a stronger role in the enhanced surveillance procedure'. See Regulation 1174/2011 (n 2) recital 10.

[5] HCH Hofmann, GC Rowe, and AH Türk, *Administrative Law and Policy of the European Union* (OUP, 2011) 492.

[6] See, e.g. KC Davis, 'Discretionary Justice' (1970) 23 *J Legal Educ* 56.

[7] For classic accounts, see, e.g. GE Treves, 'Administrative Discretion and Judicial Control' (1947) 10 *MLR* 276, which includes a comparative analysis of the matter in the English and French legal system.

[8] KC Davis, *Discretionary Justice: A Preliminary Inquiry* (Louisiana State University Press, 1969) 3.

discretion is exercised in relation to sovereign States, in matters that form the heart-land of national political decision-making. Little or no research exists on the use of executive discretion in such contexts.[9] In the plans for developing the European Monetary Union (EMU), both the Five Presidents and the Commission argue for broadening the European Semester to a number of new policy questions to be ad-dressed through enforceable but highly discretionary convergence standards in the areas of public spending, products and services markets, and tax and benefit systems, backed up by sanctions and strengthened conditionality to EU funds.[10]

The point that we wish to make is this: Settling these kinds of questions is not a technical, but rather a deeply political, exercise. In managing the framework, the Commission necessarily enters into the realm of political judgment and cannot but act politically. Commission President Juncker recognized this in his 2016 State of the Union speech in calling for more politics in the implementation of the SGP, with a promise to 'continue to apply the Pact not in a dogmatic manner, but with common sense and with the flexibility that we wisely built into the rules'.[11] While the portrayal of the Commission as the 'politically independent and neutral trustee of the European common interest'[12] was always a bit of a fairy tale, and politics has always played a role in certain areas of its deliberations, e.g. its use of legisla-tive initiative, the enforcement of the SGP was generally thought to be primarily a technocratic exercise. Yet, the political nature of enforcing the SGP is now openly acknowledged.

That the application of the SGP is and should be a political exercise is something we agree on. However, we are concerned about the appropriateness of the use of such a highly discretionary framework in matters that substantively fall under national competence and involve the substantive core of democratic decision making. We see that these governance choices may also affect the legitimacy of the European project as a whole. In a political system, uniformity of rights and obligations is often crucial for conceiving of the system as fair; because, indeed, 'a system that is shot through with exceptions may not command authority or even autonomy'.[13] In our view, at the heart of democratic decision making, this kind of experimental government models come with too many risks.

In this paper we first demonstrate how discretion has entered the economic gov-ernance framework, in particular, through the most recent Six-Pack and Two-Pack reforms (Section 2).[14] Discretion exists 'whenever the effective limits [on the power

---

[9] See J Mendes, 'Discretion, Care and Public Interests in the EU Administration: Probing the Limits of Law' (2016) 53 *CMLR* 419, 426.

[10] J-C Juncker and others, 'Completing Europe's Economic and Monetary Union' (Five Presidents' Report) (2015) <https://ec.europa.eu/commission/sites/beta-political/files/5-presidents-report_en.pdf> accessed 29 November 2017; Commission, 'Reflection Paper on the Deepening of the Economic and Monetary Union' (2017) <https://ec.europa.eu/commission/sites/beta-political/files/reflection-paper-emu_en.pdf> accessed 29 November 2017 (Commission Reflection Paper).

[11] J-C Juncker, State of the Union 2016, 14 September 2016, available at <http://europa.eu/rapid/attachment/SPEECH-16-3043/en/SOTEU%20brochure%20EN.pdf>.

[12] FW Scharpf, 'Political Legitimacy in a Non-optimal Currency Area' (2013) MPIfG Discussion Paper 13/15 <www.mpifg.de/pu/mpifg_dp/dp13-15.pdf> accessed 29 November 2017.

[13] D Beetham and C Lord, *Legitimacy and the European Union* (Longman, 1998) 120.

[14] We have mapped this development in greater detail in Leino and Saarenheimo (n 2).

of a public officer] leave him free to make a choice among possible courses of action or inaction'.[15] Schwarze defines discretion as 'freedom of decision',[16] while Galligan understands it as 'autonomy in judgment and decision'.[17] Such autonomy may exist at various points of the decision-making process: first, in finding facts; second, in settling the standards; and third, in applying the standards to the facts.[18] In our context, discretion exists in relation to all three stages. We discuss the basic presumptions concerning discretion and its exercise found in literature and Court jurisprudence and consider their relevance in the particular context that we study (Section 3). We evaluate how the Commission has used its discretion and what its broader consequences have been, not only for the application of the governance framework, but also for the Commission's own institutional role and self-identity (Section 4).

Our subject stands at the crossroads of economic, legal, and also political considerations and cannot be analysed merely from a legal viewpoint. What might look discretionary from a legal perspective may, in fact, be structured from the economic perspective, and decisions that in legal analysis appear closely rule-bound may, in reality, be heavily discretionary.[19] And whether framed in economic or legal reasoning, the eventual decisions are thoroughly permeated by political considerations. For all these reasons, our analysis invokes legal, economic, and political perspectives. We close with some thoughts on the lessons that should be drawn from managing the framework when designing the future Economic and Monetary Union (Section 5).

2. Discretion Enters the Framework

The EU's economic co-ordination framework started out as a narrow, rules-based exercise focused on fiscal policies. Its solid core consisted of the Excessive Deficit Procedure (EDP) (Article 104c TEC; now Article 126 TFEU), which established limits for public deficits and gross debts (3 and 60 per cent of GDP, respectively), with limited discretion and few escape clauses. The Treaty also established a well-defined path of escalation from a Council recommendation to non-interest-bearing deposits until the excessive deficit was corrected and eventually, in the absence of effective action, to fines 'of an appropriate size'. The objective of the EU fiscal rules was essentially to function as an emergency brake to protect against major fiscal transgressions. Within the allowed limits, Member States were more or less free to choose their own fiscal path.

Beyond the fiscal, the economic pillar originally relied only on soft modes of co-ordination. The Treaty placed Member States under an obligation to consider their economic policies as a 'matter of common concern', essentially encouraging them to mind the spillover effects of their national choices on other euro states. Article 103 TEC

[15] For the classic definition, see Davis (n 8).
[16] J Schwarze, *European Administrative Law* (rev edn, Sweet & Maxwell, 2006) 298.
[17] On this, see also D Galligan, *Discretionary Powers: A Legal Study of Official Discretion* (Clarendon Press, 1986) 16.
[18] Ibid.   [19] Ibid, 19.

(now Article 121 TFEU) laid down the multilateral surveillance procedure, under which the Council adopted a recommendation on the broad guidelines of the economic policies of the Member States, the observance of which the Commission monitored on the basis of information provided by the States. In case of infractions, the Council could adopt recommendations and—as the ultimate form of peer pressure—make them public.

The original framework did not last long. Already in 2002, the President of the European Commission Romano Prodi famously described EMU fiscal rules as 'stupid' and 'rigid', lacking intelligence and flexibility.[20] At a purely factual level, Prodi's assessment was fundamentally accurate, if a little exaggerated. The simple framework did not—and could not—prescribe the optimal fiscal response to the wide variety of possible economic circumstances. However, its rigid and inflexible nature was the key to a credible, mechanistic implementation, intended to minimize the risk of political interference. The expectation was that a credible threat of sanctions would persuade governments to conduct prudent policies and maintain a safe distance from the Maastricht limits.

Reality turned out differently. Many Member States treated the Maastricht requirements not as ultimate limits but as policy targets in their own right, leaving little safety margins and practically no room for manoeuvres when their economy faltered. In 2003, when the two largest Member States found themselves in violation of the SGP in an economic downturn, the choice was either to force those Member States—and, by implication, the whole euro area—to engage in procyclical fiscal policies, or instead to introduce additional flexibility to the framework. Not surprisingly, the EU chose the latter, triggering a fundamental rethinking of the EU fiscal framework, which culminated in 2005 in the first major overhaul of the SGP.[21] The 2005 reform divided the SGP formally into the *corrective arm* (for those Member States identified as having excessive deficits) and the *preventive arm* (for those not in excessive deficit). The euro area debt crisis prompted the adoption of the Six-Pack legislation, followed by the Two-Pack legislation two years later.[22] The cumulative effect of these reforms was a fundamental transformation of the way the Union

---

[20] A Leparmentier and L Zecchini, 'La France sera en minorité si elle n'est pas le levain de l'Europe' *Le Monde* (18 October 2002) <www.lemonde.fr/archives/article/2002/10/17/la-france-sera-en-minorite-si-elle-n-est-pas-le-levain-de-l-europe_294558_1819218.html?xtmc=romano&xtcr=1> accessed 29 November 2017.

[21] Council Regulation (EC) 1467/97 on speeding up and clarifying the implementation of the excessive deficit procedure [1997] OJ L209/6 as amended by Council Regulation (EC) 1056/2005 [2005] OJ L174/5.

[22] The Six-Pack adopted in November 2011 to improve budgetary discipline, on the one hand, and economic surveillance, on the other, includes Regulation 1175/2011 (n 2); Regulation 1177/2011 amending Regulation 1467/97 on the EU's excessive deficit procedure [2011] OJ L306/33; Regulation 1173/2011 (n 2); Regulation 1176/2011 (n 2); Regulation 1174/2011 (n 2); and Directive 2011/85/EU on requirements for budgetary frameworks of the Member States [2011] OJ L306/41. The Two-Pack includes Regulation 472/2013 on the strengthening of economic and budgetary surveillance of euro states experiencing or threatened with serious difficulties with respect to their financial stability [2013] OJ L140/1, and Regulation 473/2013 on common provisions for monitoring and assessing draft budgetary plans and ensuring the correction of excessive deficit of the euro area Member States [2013] OJ L140/11.

controls the public finances of its Member States. This happened along at least two dimensions.

First, the SGP revisions considerably broadened the range of situations in which and the means by which the EU may interfere—through recommendations, instructions and, ultimately, monetary sanctions—in a Member State's fiscal policies. In addition to actual breaches of the Treaty-based fiscal limits, the reformed SGP granted the EU powers to interfere if it considered that a Member State is not building a large enough safety margin vis-à-vis those limits. Depending on the economic situation, the required distance to the limits may be large. In some cases, a country may be found to be in violation of the SGP even if even if it technically has a budgetary surplus. Together with the beefed-up framework came new procedures to ensure its implementation. These procedures are aimed at monitoring and assessing the Member States' budgetary processes in every phase.[23] The annual cycle of reporting and monitoring was organized as the European Semester. With the successive revisions, the SGP morphed from an emergency brake to be applied when a Member State's policies pose a direct threat to the stability of the single currency, into a broad vehicle for guiding Member States towards good fiscal policies on a continuous basis.

The second notable departure from the original Maastricht vision brought about by the successive revisions of the SGP was largely unintentional but, in retrospect, a logical consequence of the vastly increased sophistication described here: the move from a rules-based towards increasingly discretionary coordination. The attempt to codify good fiscal policies necessitated a much higher degree of sophistication, since, by its very nature, such a goal does not lend itself to easy parameterization. The key analytical concepts of the framework—output gap and structural deficit—are unobservable and their estimates notoriously contested among economists.[24] Also, a wide variety of exceptional circumstances, temporary factors, and measurement issues come into play. Over the last decade, the EU has made considerable efforts to formalize the handling of many kinds of circumstances. Exceptions or flexibility clauses have expanded so that today, Member States may be excused on the basis of at least bad economic times,[25] investments,[26] structural reforms,[27] solidarity operations,[28] costs of refugees,[29] and low

---

[23] Regulation 473/2013 (n 22) Arts 6–8.

[24] To resolve chronic differences on the measurement of output gap, a dedicated EU working group was established, see <https://europa.eu/epc/output-gaps-working-group_en> accessed 29 November 2017. Although a common methodology has been established, the issue remains a constant object of criticism among Member States. A fundamental difficulty is that the estimate of output gap is subject to very sizeable revisions for years afterwards.

[25] Regulation 1467/97 (n 21) as amended by Regulation 1056/2005 (n 21) and Regulation 1177/2001 (n 22) Art 2(2).

[26] Commission, 'Commission Communication – Making the Best Use of the Flexibility Within the Existing Rules of the Stability and Growth Pact' COM(2015) 012 final, 7.

[27] Regulation 1466/97 (n 3) Art 5.

[28] Regulation 1467/97 (n 21) as amended by Regulation 1056/2005 (n 21) and Regulation 1177/2011 (n 22) Art 2(3).

[29] Commission, 'Communication from the Commission, 2016 Draft Budgetary Plans: Overall Assessment' COM(2015) 800 final, 3.

inflation.[30] Regulation No 1467/97 as amended by the Six-Pack places the Commission under an obligation to:

give due and express consideration to any other factors which, in the opinion of the Member State concerned, are relevant in order to comprehensively assess compliance with deficit and debt criteria […].[31]

An even clearer example of the trend towards discretionary economic governance can be found in the Macroeconomic Imbalances Procedure (MIP), created as part of the Six-Pack legislation package.[32] Here, the legislative constraints on the exercise of discretion are even more limited. The introduction of the MIP was motivated by the recognition that the fiscal difficulties experienced by some euro countries (particularly Ireland and Spain) during the crisis had their origins in a boom fuelled by the uncontrolled accumulation of private sector debt which, when followed by the inevitable burst, led to financial instability and large fiscal costs. The conclusion was that, to be effective, the EU fiscal framework needed to be complemented by a broader framework aimed at preventing macro-economic imbalances. That framework is the MIP, which 'sets out detailed rules for the detection of macroeconomic imbalances, as well as the prevention and correction of excessive macroeconomic imbalances within the Union'.[33] What actually counts as an 'imbalance' is defined in remarkably wide terms as 'any trend giving rise to macroeconomic developments which are adversely affecting, or have the potential adversely to affect, the proper functioning of the economy of a Member State or of the economic and monetary union'.[34] There are very few significant macro-economic phenomena that could not be said to have such a potential, through some conceivable sequence of events. While the Regulation provides indications about the variables which the Commission should (*inter alia*) consider when preparing the scoreboard for the Alert Mechanism, intended to provide an early warning on emerging imbalances, the actual enforcement and sanctions revolve around the In-depth Reviews, where the Regulation leaves full discretion to the Commission. For all practical purposes, the MIP Regulation leaves the reach of the new procedure essentially up to the interpretation of the Commission. In principle, the MIP opened nearly all areas of Member States' economic policies to EU scrutiny, advice, and, as explained later, even sanctions.

Given its ambitions, the MIP cannot be organized other than as a highly discretionary mechanism. There are a multitude of conceivable macro-economic imbalances and, since there is no simple one-to-one mapping from macro-economic imbalances to policy responses, there is an even greater multitude of possible policy responses to them. Such a vast policy space simply cannot be nailed down by formal rules. The assessment has to take into account the 'extremely divergent,

---

[30] Commission, 'Report from the Commission; Italy, Report prepared in accordance with Article 126(3) of the Treaty' COM(2016) 305 final, 21.

[31] See Regulation 1467/97 (n 21) as amended by Regulation 1056/2005 (n 21) and Regulation 1177/2011 (n 22) Art 2(3).

[32] Regulation 1176/2011 (n 2) and Regulation 1174/2011 (n 2).

[33] Regulation 1176/2011 (n 2) Art 1(1).   [34] Regulation 1176/2011 (n 2) Art 2.

highly contingent, and extremely variable conditions in individual member-state economies'.[35] To have any chance of success, the MIP 'must be allowed to respond flexibly, even opportunistically and unequally to highly diverse and uncertain problem constellations'.[36] Implementing the MIP framework is left to the Commission, which prepares a scoreboard to be used as a basis for assessments, runs the alert mechanism, undertakes in-depth reviews in conjunction with surveillance missions to the Member State when necessary, and makes proposals under the EIP.

To support the enforcement of the new, wider co-ordination framework, the possibility to invoke sanctions, initially foreseen only under the excessive deficit procedure of the SGP, was extended to also cover the preventive arm of the SGP and the MIP. Sanctions were introduced to 'ensure fair, timely, graduated and effective mechanisms for compliance' by Member States.[37] Yet the instrument established in the Treaty for use in these procedures is a Council recommendation, which logically follows from the Treaty's choice of leaving economic policy largely under Member State competence. These recommendations are, according to the Treaty, non-binding, and according to the Court's case law 'not intended to produce binding effects'.[38] Stronger sanctions in the fiscal field were seen as 'necessary to make the enforcement of budgetary surveillance in the euro area more effective' and 'enhance the credibility of the fiscal surveillance framework of the Union'.[39] As to the MIP, the sanctions were to incentivize Member States suffering from macro-economic imbalances to 'establish corrective plans before divergences become entrenched', and in case of a failure to do so, ' . . . application of the sanctions to those Member States [sh]ould be the rule and not the exception'.[40] It is noteworthy that, unlike the EDP sanctions, which are explicitly foreseen in the Treaty, the sanctions under the preventive arm of the SGP and the MIP were established by secondary legislation under the multilateral surveillance procedure, for which the Treaty does not expressly provide such a possibility. The European Structural and Investment Funds Regulations of 2014, adopted on the basis of Article 177 TFEU, broadens conditionality in accessing structural funds to cover cross-sectoral issues by linking the effectiveness of ESI funds to the implementation of the SGP.[41] Considering the complexity and degree of discretion built into the framework, many of the core provisions gain their interpretation only ex post. Therefore, Member States have limited means to anticipate what is required from them to comply with the economic governance framework, making it an unorthodox setting for the use of sanctions.

---

[35] FW Scharpf, 'After the Crash: A Perspective on Multilevel European Democracy' (2014) MPIfG Discussion Paper 14/21 <www.mpifg.de/pu/mpifg_dp/dp14-21.pdf> accessed 29 November 2017.
[36] Ibid.   [37] Regulation 1173/2011 (n 2) recitals 13–14.
[38] For the classic reference, see Case C-322/88 *Grimaldi v Fonds des maladies professionnelles* [1989] ECLI:EU:C:1989:646, paras 13 and 16.
[39] Regulation 1173/2011 (n 2) recital 13.
[40] Regulation 1174/2011 (n 2) recital 6 and 1.
[41] Regulation (EU) 1303/2013 laying down common provisions on the European Regional Development Fund, etc (ESI Regulation) [2013] OJ L347/320, Art 23.

3. Economic Governance: An Atypical Context for Discretionary Decision Making

In all modern legal systems, executive actors are often allocated broad discretionary powers. Discretion and its limits have been discussed in particular in the US in the 1980s, in the context of the rise of a nondelegation doctrine. John Hart Ely criticized the US Congress for a 'refusal to legislate' by leaving the politically controversial matters to non-elected bodies to solve and take on the 'inevitable political heat':[42] 'How much more comfortable it must be simply to vote in favor of a bill calling for safe cars, clean air, or nondiscrimination, and to leave to others the chore of fleshing out what such a mandate might mean'.[43] Resolving issues of policy is often politically inconvenient; much can be lost by taking a clear stand on a controversial issue of social or economic policy.[44] And yet, legislative action is often deemed necessary, and passing vague statutes preferred by all the opposing groups to no action at all, even though the winners and losers might only be determined by administrative action.[45] However, the US debate also recognized that sometimes broad discretion is justified: detailed legislative specification might be beyond the legislature specifically because it requires investigation, decision, and revision of specialized and complex issues.[46] Discretion may also exist because it is preferred to any rules, or because it is needed to tailor results to unique facts and circumstances.[47] While discretion is often treated as a residue left by the absence of rules, it may also exist within and in relation to rules:

discretion occurs on deciding the importance of rules, on their relationship to other rules, on whether exceptions should be made to them, or whether they should be ignored altogether. In short, discretion is as much a product of rules as of their absence.[48]

Ely's main point of criticism was directed at the way in which much of the law is effectively left to 'legions of unelected administrators' with a duty to offer operative meanings to broad delegations contained in legislation. His main concern was not that the bureaucrats would 'do a bad job' as legislators. Instead, his unease related more to how these actors are neither elected nor re-elected, and are only sporadically controlled by officials who are politically accountable for their actions.[49]

These earlier, more theoretically orientated, approaches offer a useful background to think about discretion in the context of economic governance. The 2011 reforms fell into a long tradition of depoliticization and delegation to a technocratic body, which has been the EU's standard response to problems of policy co-ordination and implementation. More than two decades ago, Majone, in his criticism of the

---

[42] JH Ely, *Democracy and Distrust: A Theory of Judicial Review* (Harvard University Press, 1980) 131–4.
[43] Ibid, 131.
[44] R Steward, 'The Reformation of American Administrative Law' (1975) 88 *Harv L Rev* 1669, 1695.
[45] JL Mashaw, 'Prodelegation: Why Administrators Should Make Political Decisions' (1985) 1 *J Law Econ Organ* 81, 85.
[46] Steward (n 44) 1695.   [47] Davis (n 8) 15–17.   [48] Galligan (n 17) 19.
[49] Ely (n 42) 131.

discussion on the EU's 'democracy deficit', proposed that the EU is, and should be, essentially a 'regulatory state',[50] where policy goals are more effectively achieved by delegating day-to-day decisions to non-elected professionals, constrained by politically set mandates, who are free from the biases and distortions of democratic and electoral politics.[51] In Majone's view, '"short-termism" and poor credibility are intrinsic problems of democratic governance', and often an objective, technocratic agency was best equipped to produce Pareto (non-redistributive) improvements that would win popular support in all Member States. In most cases, the natural body to delegate to has been the European Commission,[52] which has a Treaty-based mandate to promote the general interest of the Union, ensure the application of the Treaties, and be 'completely independent' in the exercise of its duties (Article 17(2) TEU).

In the CJEU jurisprudence on the matter, the general justification for delegating broad policy-framing responsibilities—usually to the European Commission—has been 'complexity', 'a shorthand for the requirement of undertaking a decision balancing up a combination of various factors, of evaluations and prognoses of future factual developments, and of interests and rights.'[53] It is settled case law that the legislature enjoys a considerable power of discretion in circumstances where it is necessary to evaluate a complex economic situation. Its discretion is not limited solely to the nature and scope of the measures to be taken but also, to some extent, to the finding of basic facts.[54]

The Court has persistently upheld the EU legislature's broad discretion to delegate authority.[55] The appropriateness of delegations is thus, to the extent they are properly reasoned, a legislative prerogative. Administrative decision making is never totally bound or without any limits, but the appropriate standards can be so vaguely defined that they require a great deal of interpretation.[56] Therefore, when discussing discretion, the major issue is that of 'fine-tuning the extent and nature of the control over substantive decision-making by administrative actors'.[57] In the EU, the control of discretion is usually discussed in the context of possible judicial review. In cases where the institutions enjoy a significant freedom of evaluation, Court review remains limited to 'a manifest error or misuse of power or whether the authority in

---

[50] G Majone, 'The Rise of the Regulatory State in Europe' (1994) 17 *West Eur Polit* 77. See also PL Lindseth, 'Democratic Legitimacy and the Administrative Character of Supranationalism: The Example of the European Community' (1999) 99 *Colum L Rev* 628.

[51] Beetham and Lord (n 13) 17.

[52] G Majone, 'The Regulatory State and its Legitimacy Problems' (1999) 22 *West Eur Polit* 1, 6. Habermas takes a far less enthusiastic view of technocratic delegation and speaks of 'the temptation to bridge, in a technocratic manner, this gulf between what is economically required and what seems to be politically achievable, only apart from the people.' J Habermas, 'Democracy, Solidarity and the European Crisis' in A-M Grozelier and others (eds), *Roadmap to a Social Europe* (Social Europe, 2013), 6.

[53] Hofmann, Rowe, and Türk (n 5) 494–5. For a critical assessment of "complexity" and its ambiguity, see Nehl, Chapter 8 in this volume.

[54] Case C-120/99 *Italy v Council* [2001] ECLI:EU:C:2001:567, para 44.

[55] See, e.g. Case C-203/12 *Billerud Karlsborg AB* [2013] ECLI:EU:C:2013:664, para 35. See also Case C-343/09 *Afton Chemical Limited* [2010] ECLI:EU:C:2010:419, para 28.

[56] Galligan (n 17) 16.

[57] Hofmann, Rowe, and Türk (n 5) 493. See also Mattarella, Chapter 2 in this volume.

question has clearly exceeded the bounds of its discretion'.[58] In particular, courts 'cannot substitute their own evaluation of the matter for that of the competent authority but must restrict themselves to examing [sic] whether the evaluation of the competent authority contains a patent error or constitutes a misuse of power.'[59] An evaluation of complex facts and accounts also requires a 'considerable measure of latitude'.[60] After all, in addition to making substantive choices, identifying the relevant facts often determines who wins and who loses; and selecting the cases that 'are important enough to pursue entails policy discretion of the broadest sort.'[61]

The room for manoeuvre allocated to the Commission in the area of economic governance is largely in line with these more general findings. The delegations have been made in response to an acute crisis, where the legislator has preferred action to non-action, and involve broad discretion to be exercised in situations that are both not only economically complex but also invariably politically loaded, and are to be used in challenging economic times when the political choices are difficult to make and ideological cleavages wide. Therefore, economic governance undoubtedly involves a significant degree of 'complexity' and, considering the current scope of the framework, requires a strong discretionary element. Against this background, it is unlikely that the Court would question the legislature's choice to allocate a broad discretion to the Commission.

The degree of discretion is not only dependent on grants of authority to administrators but also on what the latter do to confine, structure and enlarge their own powers.[62] While the Commission's discretion in the area of economic governance is the result of explicit legislative choices, the way it plans to use this discretion has also caused anxiety among Member States. Post-legislative guidance has in particular attempted to respond to these worries: to alleviate legal uncertainty and provide guidance on the scope of vaguely drafted legal provisions.[63] A sizeable body of soft law has gradually emerged, including Codes of Conduct, Common Understandings, Commission Communications, and a thick application manual called the Vade Mecum.[64] However, the existence of guidance does not necessarily

---

[58] Case *Italy v Council* (n 54) para 44. See further, Nehl, Chapter 8 in this volume.

[59] Case 57/72 *Westzucker GmbH v Einfuhr und Vorratsstelle für Zucker* [1973] ECLI:EU:C:1973:30, para 14.

[60] Case T-81/00 *Associação Comercial de Aveiro v Commission* [2002] ECLI:EU:T:2002:118, para 50.

[61] Mashaw (n 45) 97.

[62] Davis (n 8) 15. Guidance might sometimes fall short of capturing what the text or objectives of legislation actually require. J Scott, 'In Legal Limbo: Post-legislative Guidance as a Challenge for European Administrative Law' (2011) 48 *CMLR* 329, 330. Guidelines can, for example, indicate how the Commission assesses compatibility with certain criteria. See Case C-526/14 *Tadej Kotnik and Others v Drzavni zbor Republike Slovenije* [2016] ECLI:EU:C:2016:767.

[63] See H Marjosola, 'Regulating Financial Markets under Uncertainty: The EU Approach' (2014) 39 *ELR* 338, 355.

[64] Commission, 'Vade Mecum on the Stability and Growth Pact 2016 Edition' (2016), Institutional Paper 021 <https://ec.europa.eu/info/sites/info/files/file_import/ip021_en_2.pdf> accessed 29 November 2017. For a selection of other soft-law documentation, see Commission, 'Commission Communication – Making the Best Use of the Flexibility within the Existing Rules of the Stability and Growth Pact' COM(2015) 012 final; Commission, 'Two-Pack Code of Conduct: Specifications on the Implementation of the Two Pack and Guidelines on the Format and Content of Draft Budgetary Plans, Economic Partnership Programmes and Debt Issuance Reports' (2016) <http://ec.europa.eu/economy_finance/economic_governance/sgp/pdf/coc/2014-11-07_two_pack_coc_amended_en.pdf>

exhaust Commission discretion, since even other alternatives may need to be examined.[65] While post-legislative guidance is used to increase clarity, effectiveness, and transparency, it often has the opposite effect,[66] and contributes to blurring clear divisions of competence.[67] Instead of bringing more discipline and predictability to the application of the economic governance framework, the expanding body of soft law has actually contributed to an increase in the complexity and opacity of the framework,[68] and the creation of a complex maze of alternative or even conflicting rules, which few understand. Rather than actually settling contentious issues of interpretation, it has pushed the substantive decisions to the stage of implementation and buttressed the institutional position of the body—the Commission—tasked to determine what kind of meaning can be attributed to each provision in each individual case. The result is, as the MIP procedure explained earlier illustrates, a prime example of discretion as the 'executive's freedom to decide and order matters for itself'.[69]

Enforcing the limits of discretion has always been difficult in EU Courts. Pleading misuse of power is rarely successful and presumes that 'on the basis of objective, relevant and consistent factors [a decision is] taken with the purpose of achieving ends other than those stated',[70] for example, that the challenged measure is founded on economic and factual premises that are manifestly erroneous or inappropriate.[71] The Court's review is geared towards the purpose of measure, rather than its content,[72] and builds on an evaluation of the scope and purpose of the delegation in light of its legal base.[73] Considering the diversity of Treaty objectives and the latitude offered to the Commission 'in its role of ensuring at all times that those various objectives are reconciled, by exercising its discretion, in order to meet the requirements of the common interest',[74] manifest errors of assessment are difficult to demonstrate. It is enough that the assessment made is 'sufficiently plausible to support the necessity' of the choices opted for.[75] In the specific context of economic governance, the

---

accessed 29 November 2017; and Commission, 'Code of Conduct: Specifications on the Implementation of the Stability and Growth Pact and Guidelines on the Format and Content of Stability and Convergence Programmes' (2016) <http://ec.europa.eu/economy_finance/economic_governance/sgp/pdf/coc/code_of_conduct_en.pdf> accessed 29 November 2017.

[65] See Case C-28/15 *Koninklijke KPN NV and Others v Autoriteit Conument en Markt (ACM)* [2016] ECLI:EU:C:2016:692.

[66] See L Senden, *Soft Law in European Community Law* (Hart Publishing, 2004).

[67] S Vaughan, 'Differentiation and Dysfunction: An Exploration of Post-Legislative Guidance Practices in 14 EU Agencies' (2015) 17 *CYELS* 66.

[68] L Eyraud and T Wu, 'IMF Working Paper – Playing by the Rules: Reforming Fiscal Governance in Europe' (2015) WP/15/67 <www.imf.org/external/pubs/ft/wp/2015/wp1567.pdf> accessed 29 November 2017. For analysis of the effect of soft law in other policy areas, see E Korkea-aho, 'Legal Interpretation of EU Framework Directives: A Soft Law Approach' (2015) 40 *ELR* 70, 87; S Vaughan, *EU Chemicals Regulation. New Governance, Hybridity and REACH* (Edward Elgar Publishing, 2015).

[69] Schwarze (n 16) 297.

[70] Joined Cases T-244/93 and T-486/93 *TWD Textilwerke Deggendorf GmbH v Commission* [1995] ECLI:EU:T:1995:160, para 61.

[71] Case T-289/03 *BUPA v Commission* [2008] ECLI:EU:T:2008:29, paras 265–6.

[72] Case T-52/99 *T. Port GmbH & Co. KG v Commission* [2001] ECLI:EU:T:2001:97, para 56.

[73] P Craig, *EU Administrative Law* (2nd ed, OUP, 2012) 430.

[74] Case T-308/00 *Salzgitter AG v Commission* [2013] ECLI:EU:T:2013:30, para 144.

[75] Case T-289/03 *BUPA v Commission*, paras 265–6.

scope for Court oversight appears particularly small. The purposes of delegations refer to such broad objectives—securing 'budgetary discipline across the Union'; 'sound government finances as a means of strengthening the conditions for price stability and for strong sustainable growth underpinned by financial stability'; the need to ensure 'sustainable growth and jobs'[76]—that a plausible argument can be built in support of almost any measure. Add to this the vast amount of discretion built into and around the rules and the highly political context in which the rules are applied, and the role of Courts in examining whether the Commission has exercised its powers in an appropriate or 'sufficiently plausible' manner is rendered practically non-existent.

These findings are particularly significant considering how the Six-Pack reforms took technocratic delegation far outside its traditional area of application and into realms where the separation of the technical from the political becomes particularly difficult or impossible.[77] Granting a body that is not directly elected by the citizens a leading role in enforcing the—still in principle, though less in practice—rules-based fiscal framework would alone be exceptional. Doing the same for the almost fully discretionary MIP was truly unprecedented. The Six-Pack regulations gave the Commission nearly unlimited freedom to intervene, with the threat of sanctions, in a euro area Member State's most politically salient matters of economic policy, and compel it to take decisions that its political system was unable or unwilling to take.

This tendency would be further strengthened if conditionality were further extended into the 'formalised and more binding convergence process based on agreed standards', as envisaged in the Five Presidents' Report. The Commission EMU Reflection Paper foresees that the new convergence code to be incorporated into the expanded European Semester would consist of 'measures to improve the quality of public spending; investment in education and training; embracing more open and more competitive products and services markets, and creating fair and efficient tax and benefit systems' possibly 'combined with minimum social standards, as envisaged in the European Pillar of Social Rights.'[78] The code would cover a wide variety of labour market, social, and tax policies, a significant part of which today fall under national competence. The EU Treaties have traditionally stayed clear of these questions and prohibited measures that would 'affect the right of Member States to define the fundamental principles of their social security systems', and

[76] Regulation 473/2013 (n 22) recital 2. For example, President Juncker has recently taken credit for the intelligent application of the SGP by his Commission, which has effectively combined the demands of fiscal discipline while being 'careful not to kill growth'. Jean-Claude Juncker, 'State of the Union Address 2017' Press Release (13 September 2017) <http://europa.eu/rapid/press-release_SPEECH-17-3165_en.html> accessed 29 November 2017.

[77] The policy areas that Majone (n 50) uses as examples—competition and health and safety—are such where there is a reasonable basis for separating technical questions from the political ones, and where delegation is the norm in most countries. Over time, the realm of policies considered suitable for delegation has expanded to also cover such major policy areas as financial supervision and monetary policy. See also PL Lindseth, 'Comparing Administrative States: Susan Rose Ackerman and the Limits of Public Law in Germany and the United States' (1995-1996) 2 *CJEL* 589, 590.

[78] Commission, 'Commission Communication - Establishing a European Pillar of Social Rights Brussels' COM(2017) 250 final (Commission Communication on Establishing an EPSR).

specified that the 'responsibilities of the Member States shall include the management of health services and medical care and the allocation of the resources assigned to them'.[79] In this way, the EU Treaties have presupposed the existence of national redistributive mechanisms,[80] which currently reflect diverse conceptions of social justice through various ideological, institutional, and financial divergences.[81] The Commission further emphasizes that, to create a truly level playing field, the standards should be 'enforceable':[82] for this reason, 'compliance could be strengthened by a strong link between related reforms, the use of EU funds and access to a potential macroeconomic stabilisation function'.[83] Since the EU lacks legislative competence in these matters, these standards would likely be set through EU executive action (such as communications, post-legislative guidance of different kinds, reports, and evaluations).

The delegation of key economic and fiscal policy choices already touches upon fundamental questions of both a constitutional and democratic nature. In any national parliamentary elections, economic and fiscal policies form the hard core of campaign platforms and are therefore a key part of the democratic process. The envisaged inclusion of labour market, social, and tax policies under the economic governance umbrella would go even further into the realm of politics. These policies are all fundamentally about the trade-offs between equality and efficiency, between protection and flexibility. They involve rights questions that touch upon some of the deepest values of society.[84] Redistribution is the most fundamental matter of politics; it involves the key societal choices that form the heart of political decision making and the primary dimension of political organization. Decisions regarding these choices are contested and legitimized through democratic elections. Deep engagement with these issues by the EU institutions would take us far beyond Majone's largely benign 'EU regulatory state'.[85] What the idea of a 'convergence process' would seem to do is to shift a considerable part of the responsibility over these choices to the EU. However, instead of a constitutional discourse on competence limits, the extension of EU powers is managed as a technical exercise, through executive discretion. As a result, instead of the (relative) Member State autonomy to decide on their own societal choices—subject to a general EU requirement of sound fiscal policies and the obligation to co-ordinate—we would have a model where the EU institutions define, through executive decision making, the convergence code and the EPSR, the desirable economic and social model, and, utilizing the European Semester, map a path for each Member State towards it. This is not a minor technical change that can be embedded in any current surveillance system in the way the Commission seems to indicate, but would affect the Member States' right to define

---

[79] Consolidated Version of the Treaty on the Functioning of European Union [2012], OJ C 326, (hereafter TFEU) Arts 153(4) and 168 (7).

[80] See Art 153(4) TFEU and Art 168(7) TFEU.

[81] K Tuori, *European Constitutionalism* (CUP, 2015) 229 and 233.

[82] Commission Communication on Establishing an EPSR (n 78) 5.

[83] Commission Reflection Paper (n 10) 28.

[84] JHH Weiler, 'To be a European Citizen – Eros and Civilization' (1997) 4 *JEPP* 495, 502.

[85] See Majone (n 50).

their own desirable economic model, including the ideological, distributional, and rights-and-freedoms questions involved, as well as to contest that model at national elections. Keeping in mind the complexity of the matters, the diverse ways in which they are currently regulated by the Member States,[86] and the fact that, unlike with the SGP, there are no Treaty-based rules to anchor the Commission's decisions, the new framework would necessarily be highly discretionary.

Whether it is, as a matter of principle, at all appropriate for the legislature to grant administrative authorities discretionary power in respect of questions involving citizens' rights and interests of this kind would seem to be the more fundamental question that has received very little attention in the EU context. In more constitutional discourses it has been argued that in a State governed by the rule of law, the administrative authorities should not be granted discretionary powers involving the determination or governance, without distinction, of all kinds of individual rights and interests.[87] If established in exceptional cases, 'such powers must be interpreted and exercised restrictively and in given situations'.[88] In a well-known and authoritative decision, the German *Bundesverfassungsgericht* found that 'revenue and expenditure including external financing and all elements of encroachment that are decisive for the realization of fundamental rights' belong to the 'essential areas of democratic formative action'.[89] The German concern—shared by various other Member States—relates especially to the substantial influence that national parliaments should enjoy in this field in order to guarantee the democratic nature of decision making.[90] Considering the limitations of EU-level democratic processes, we share the scepticism that the political structures that exist in the EU institutions would be satisfactory to guarantee the political contestation and competition that making choices of this nature would presume. The EU has no structures that would adequately replicate structures of governmental control, parliamentary accountability, or administrative responsibility that exist at the level of Member States.[91] The possibilities for the European Parliament to hold the Commission accountable for the way it uses its discretion is no compensation for the limitation of national parliamentary debates on these issues. The European Parliament has a role in adopting secondary legislation relating to economic governance, and enjoys certain powers to hold the Commission accountable, in the broad sense, for its actions and policy choices, even if the wide discretion the latter enjoys makes the enforcement of this accountability difficult. However, the European Parliament has no constitutional role in national budgetary policies or questions of redistribution. These questions

---

[86] Tuori (n 81).

[87] L Silveira, 'Administrative Discretion as Perceived by the Public' in *Administrative Discretion and Problems of Accountability, Proceedings; 25th Colloguy of European Law, Oxford, 27-29 September 1995* (Council of Europe Publishing, 1997) 55 and 59.

[88] Ibid., 74.   [89] BverfG, 2 BvE 2/08, June, 30, 2009 (Lisbon), paras 244 and 249.

[90] For example, the Finnish Parliament has stressed that economic policy needs to be examined in a much broader legal and political approach, taking into account its effects on citizens and their rights and the requirements set by democratic legitimacy: 'the principles of democracy require that member states retain their primacy in economic policy'. Statement of the Grand Committee of the Finnish Parliament, 4/2012 vp.

[91] Weiler (n 84) 512.

are still fundamentally a national competence reserve. Considering that the explicit objective of EU economic governance is to push these questions, at least to some extent, beyond the control of democratic processes, the appropriateness of delegation and the limits to executive power should be carefully considered.

4. The Emergence of a 'New Political Commission'

Above, we have traced the evolution of the economic governance framework from a narrow, rules-based exercise into a broad, discretionary one, extending far beyond the realm of normal executive discretion. In this part, we discuss the reverse causality from the discretionary powers to the self-identity of the decision maker: how these extended powers have contributed to a change in how the Commission's perceives itself and transformed it from a technocratic body into an openly political actor.

Discretion is generally reviewed through the applicable procedure or, if the review is substantive, in light of the purposes for which the discretion was used.

Since 2011, a purely mechanistic reading of the fiscal framework would have offered plenty of opportunities to escalate the procedures, possibly all the way to sanctions. However, the Commission chose, in each case, to use the considerable discretion allotted to it—through various escape clauses—to conclude that the EU requirements had been fulfilled or otherwise avoided the application of sanctions. Until very recently, no actual sanctions procedures had been launched based on any part of the EU's economic policy framework. This changed in July 2016, when the Council agreed with the Commission's finding that Spain and Portugal had failed to take effective action in response to the Council's EDP recommendations, which for the first time triggered a sanctions process. Some weeks later, fines were determined and, at the same instance, immediately cancelled.[92] Therefore, so far, no country has been fined or asked to make a deposit under the SGP, no excessive imbalance has ever been identified in a Member State, and no country has had its draft budget returned for revision by the Commission. Finally, the possibility to suspend EU structural and cohesion fund commitments as a response to a failure to correct excessive deficit has been used only once (for Hungary, a country not part of the euro area). The Hungarian government condemned the plan as 'unfounded and unfair', controversial from a legal point of view and in contradiction with the spirit of the Treaties.[93] The suspension was lifted before it came into effect.[94]

---

[92] Council, 'Council Implementing Decision on Imposing a fine on Portugal for failure to take effective action to address an excessive deficit' (2016) 11554/16 and Council, 'Council Implementing Decision on Imposing a fine on Spain for failure to take effective action to address an excessive deficit' (2016) 11555/16.

[93] N Mann, 'Hungary Slams "Unfair" EU Funding Suspension Plans', *Public Finance International* (23 February 2012) <www.publicfinanceinternational.org/news/2012/03/hungary-slams-%E2%80%98unfair%E2%80%99-eu-funding-suspension-plans> accessed 29 November 2017.

[94] Council of the European Union, 'Hungary: Council Lifts Cohesion Fund Suspension' Press Release 11648/12 Presse 278 (22 June 2012).

Perhaps the best-publicized recipient of lenience has been France, which was granted several extensions to its deadline for correcting its excessive deficit. In 2014, it announced that it would miss the 2015 deadline and that its budget deficit would fall below 3 percent only in 2017, with debt continuing on a rising trajectory. After discussions with the French government, the Commission announced, with no supporting economic elaboration or legal reasoning, that it had not found cases of 'particularly serious non-compliance', meaning that it planned to take no action regarding the French 2015 budgetary plans.[95] When asked in an interview why the Commission had repeatedly turned a blind eye to French infractions, President Juncker's answer was 'because it is France... I know France well, its reflexes, its internal reactions, its multiple facets'. Juncker argued that fiscal rules should not be applied 'blindly'.[96] One cannot help thinking that the weakness of the French government, and the risk that a harsh approach by the EU could end up benefiting the Front National, played a role. Demanding further fiscal consolidation would have been hugely unpopular in France and weakened the position of the incumbent moderate President relative to the anti-European political forces.

In the cases of Spain and Portugal, the deviations were too large to simply paper over, yet each had a convincing political story in their defence. Spain had just had its second elections in six months after a failed attempt to form a government. Any punitive actions could have had unforeseeable consequences on the government negotiations and in the looming third elections. In Portugal, after a tough adjustment program and five years of fiscal austerity, there was a wide societal consensus against further budgetary cuts. The Portuguese Prime Minister was quoted as being prepared to go the distance to make sure that the threat of sanctions was consigned to the wastepaper basket: '[t]hey simply would not be fair', Prime Minister Costa argued, '[e]veryone knows what the Portuguese people have been through in the last four years.'[97] The fines were subsequently cancelled and both countries were granted extensions to their deadlines. Similarly to the French situation, the opposite conclusion would have fuelled anti-EU sentiments that the Commission was eager to avoid.

On the side of the MIP, the first years have seen many excessive imbalances identified and articulated in the Country Specific Recommendations, but no formal procedure has been opened under the EIP. This fact has been repeatedly lamented by the ECB: '[d]espite having identified excessive imbalances in five countries, the Commission is not proposing to activate the EIP. Thus, it has again decided against

---

[95] See Commission, 'Statement by Commission Vice-President Katainen on the Draft Budgetary Plans' Strasbourg (29 October 2014) <http://europa.eu/rapid/press-release_STATEMENT-14-344_en.htm> accessed 29 November 2017.

[96] See the article by F Guarascio, 'EU Gives Budget Leeway to France "Because it is France" – Juncker' *Reuters* (31 May 2016) <http://uk.reuters.com/article/uk-eu-deficit-france-idUKKCN0YM1N0> accessed 29 November 2017.

[97] Article by N Donn, 'Brussels Threat to Impose Sanctions on Portugal Coincides with "Most Difficult Time in EU History"' *Portugal Resident* (12 May 2016) <https://www.portugalresident.com/2016/05/12/brussels-threat-to-impose-sanctions-on-portugal-coincides-with-most-difficult-time-in-eu-history/> accessed 29 November 2017.

making full use of all available measures.'[98] The Ecofin Council has also underlined that the 'the MIP procedure should be used to its full potential, with the corrective arm applied where appropriate.'[99] The Five Presidents' Report recommends that the EIP 'should be used forcefully. It should be triggered as soon as excessive imbalances are identified and be used to monitor reform implementation.'[100] Despite this encouragement, the Commission has preferred to use the wide discretionary powers granted to it by the legislation and solve problems through negotiation and interpretation, rather than entering into an open conflict with a Member State.

Exercising control—political, legal or interinstitutional—over the Commission's choices is difficult. This is by design considering the explicit objective of strengthening its role vis-à-vis the Council in the application of the SGP and reducing the political obstacles to strict enforcement of the rules through Reversed Qualified Majority Voting. In its own evaluation of the post-2011 framework, the Commission found that 'the current rules are effective and generally operate to satisfaction'. According to the Commission:

The various pieces of governance legislation have been at the core of this evolution and have significantly bolstered the existing governance setup. Overall, deficits have declined with many countries having exited the Excessive Deficit Procedure and imbalances are being corrected.[101]

External accounts of the track record are less generous. President Draghi of the ECB concluded that 'fiscal rules have repeatedly been broken and trust between countries has been strained'.[102] The IMF agreed: 'Under the SGP, noncompliance has been the rule rather than the exception'.[103] The European Parliament '[d]eplores the poor implementation of country-specific recommendations'[104] and '[c]alls on the Commission, as guardian of the Treaties, to make full use of all measures provided for in EU law to support enhanced economic policy coordination and the implementation of the CSRs so that all Member States adopt within the required time frame economic and financial policies tailored to their situation'.[105] The European Court of Auditors criticized in particular the way the Commission had used its discretion in finding that '[w]hat has been lacking is consistency and transparency

[98] European Central Bank, *Economic Bulletin* (2016) Issue 1/2016.
[99] Council of the European Union, 'Council Conclusions on Alert Mechanism Report 2016' Press Release 10/16 (15 January 2016).
[100] Five Presidents' Report (n 10) 8.
[101] Commission, 'Commission Communication – Economic Governance Review, Report on the application of Regulations (EU) No. 1173/2011, 1174/2011, 1175/2011, 1176/2011, 1177/2011, 472/2013 and 473/2013' COM(2014) 905 final, 11.
[102] Speech by M Draghi, President of the ECB, Frankfurt am Main (16 March 2015), <www.ecb.europa.eu/press/key/date/2015/html/sp150316.en.html> accessed 29 November 2017.
[103] International Monetary Fund, 'Euro Area Policies, 2014 Article IV Consultation, Selected Issues' (2014) IMF Country Report No. 14/199, 93 <www.imf.org/en/Publications/CR/Issues/2016/12/31/Euro-Area-Policies-Selected-Issues-41742> accessed 29 November 2017.
[104] European Parliament, 'Resolution of 25 February 2016 on the European Semester for Economic Policy Coordination: Annual Growth Survey 2016' (2015) 2015/2285(INI), para 33.
[105] European Parliament, 'Resolution of 22 October 2014 on the European Semester for Economic Policy Coordination: Implementation of 2014 Priorities' (2014) 2014/2059(INI), para 31.

in the application of those rules; the Commission does not adequately record its underlying assumptions or share its surveillance findings for the greater benefit of all Member States'.[106] Bofinger assessed the European Semester as having been 'a complete failure'.[107] Claeys and others found that the 'European fiscal rules are barely implemented' and that 'the threat of sanctions is not credible'.[108] However, despite all the criticism regarding the weakness of enforcement of the SGP,[109] the indeterminate character of the underlying legislation leaves factually little room to challenge the way the Commission has exercised its discretion beyond vocal protestations.

From a narrow perspective, the failure by the Commission to use all the tools granted to it by the SGP to compel a Member State to stay within the agreed rules appears to be in contradiction with the objectives and spirit of the framework. However, from a broader viewpoint, taking into account the likely consequences—in terms of electoral outcomes and the image of the EU as a positive force, of pushing a country beyond where its democratic structures are able to follow—the flexible approach and political judgment by the Commission may actually be serving the objectives of the SGP well. After all, if Eurosceptic forces seized victory as a result of EU-originated austerity policies, it is unlikely that Union objectives would have much to gain from such an outcome. To what extent it is then acceptable that the Commission *de facto* ends up calibrating its actions on the basis of the relative desirability of different outcomes in Member State elections, is a valid question. Discretion as such always involves judgments that

cannot be mapped into the available set of information, in a fully consistent manner. [...] What matters is how discretion is exercised: on the basis of economic reflections or other considerations.[110]

The simple conclusion we wish to draw here is that we take it for granted that, if such a calibration is to be made, the assessment involved is of a political, rather than a technical, nature. The use of discretion is not about the objective assessment of compliance with technical rules but about assessing the broader political situation in each Member State.

---

[106] European Court of Auditors 'Further Improvements Needed to Ensure Effective Implementation of the Excessive Deficit Procedure' (2016) Special Report No. 10/2016, 12.

[107] P Bofinger, 'The Way Forward: Coping with the Insolvency Risk of Member States and Giving Teeth to the European Semester' in R Baldwin and F Giavazzi (eds), *How to Fix Europe's Monetary Union: Views of Leading Economists* (CEPR Press, 2016) 235.

[108] G Claeys, Z Darwas, and Á Leandro, 'A Proposal to Revive the European Fiscal Framework' (2016) Bruegel Policy Contribution 2016/07 <http://bruegel.org/wp-content/uploads/2016/03/pc_2016_07.pdf> accessed 29 November 2017.

[109] Parliament, 'Dijsselbloem Concerned about Flexible Application of Stability and Growth Pact Rules', Press Release (14 June 2016) <http://www.europarl.europa.eu/news/en/news-room/20160613IPR32051/dijsselbloem-concerns-about-flexible-application-stability-growth-pact-rules> accessed 29 November 2017; T Hope and S Louven, 'Spain, Portugal Face E.U. Sanctions' *Handelsblatt Global* (13 July 2016) <https://global.handelsblatt.com/politics/spain-portugal-face-e-u-sanctions-566315> accessed 29 November 2017. See European Central Bank, 'Annual Report 2016' (2017) <www.ecb.europa.eu/pub/pdf/annrep/ar2016en.pdf?f7090bb266c06d6c8857f41220370bfb> accessed 29 November 2017, section on 'Mixed Record of Compliance with EU Fiscal Rules'.

[110] European Fiscal Board, Annual Report 2017, 4 <https://ec.europa.eu/info/publications/2017-annual-report-european-fiscal-board_en> accessed 29 November 2017.

In this way, the reforms have brought the economic governance framework deep into the hard core of political activity, opened broad discretion to the monitoring of its compliance, and left the Commission institutionally on much 'stronger footing than before'.[111] Rather than making the application of rules more automatic, the allocation of political tasks seems to have contributed to transforming the Commission's identity more clearly into a political one:[112] a 'hybrid between an independent executive agency and a political government'.[113] This development has taken place in parallel with the more general politicization of the Commission, speeded up by the reforms of the Lisbon Treaty, which tightened the ties between the Parliament and the Commission.[114] The current Commission President (reflecting his background as the 'Spitzenkandidat' for the EPP group) has been quite open about the political nature of the Commission he is leading:

The Commission is not a technical committee made up of civil servants who implement the instructions of another institution. The Commission is political. And I want it to be more political. Indeed, it will be highly political.[115]

The question of what the declaration of wishing to lead a more 'political' Commission in fact implies has provoked discussion among political scientists. A range of interpretations have been proposed, including: wishing to identify political solutions to political debates;[116] leading a Commission characterized by presidentialization and priorization;[117] examining what is politically necessary and possible;[118] staking out bold positions on pressing issues, often in contradiction to those of the Member States;[119] being party political;[120] being highly sensitive to the interests of the Parliament and its President;[121] and generally going for strategic and focused action and exerting influence on EU action in 'less intrusive ways'.[122] Among political scientists, the developments after the 2014 elections have been seen in largely positive terms: as empowering the Commission, enhancing its legitimacy and affording

---

[111] MW Bauer and S Becker, 'The Unexpected Winner of the Crisis: The European Commission's Strengthened Role in Economic Governance' (2014) 36 *J Eur Integr* 213, 226.

[112] According to Scharpf (n 12), the Commission has, to a large extent, 'lost the aura of neutrality and objectivity', 23.

[113] (n 110) 63.

[114] For the close linkages between the Commission and the Parliament, see Arts 17(7) and 17(8) TEU, and their interinstitutional framework agreement (IIA, 2010) and the 'special partnership' it aims to develop [2010] OJ L304/47.

[115] See J-C Juncker, 'A New Start for Europe: My Agenda for Jobs, Growth, Fairness and Democratic Change Political Guidelines for the next European Commission' Opening Statement in the European Parliament Plenary Session Candidate for President of the European Commission, Strasbourg (15 July 2014) 15.

[116] J Peterson, 'Juncker's Political European Commission and an EU in Crisis' (2017) 55 *JCMS* 349, 365.

[117] S Becker and others, 'The Commission: Boxed In and Constrained, but Still an Engine of Integration' (2016) 39 *West Eur Polit* 1011.

[118] Peterson (n 116) 359.

[119] D Dinan, 'Governance and Institutions: A More Political Commission' (2016) 54 *JCMS* 101, 107.

[120] Peterson (n 116) 359.   [121] Dinan (n 119) 111.

[122] Becker and others (n 117) 1026.

it greater independence from the Member States.[123] At the same time, the new stronger accountability relationship is seen to have moved the EU political system closer to maturity in creating a parliamentary government more similar to those in Member States, with a 'more political, and politicized, Commission elected as the "EU Executive" by a majority in the European Parliament'.[124] These more general findings also seem applicable to the Commission's role in economic governance: we see a Commission that is geared for targeted action rather than one focusing on the technical implementation of every single rule. However, its broad *de facto* mandate to exercise wide discretion to act in a manner that 'appears best in the public interest' provides a delegation 'without a clear structure or clear constraints', creating not only a risk of arbitrariness and unfairness,[125] but also making it difficult for the Parliament or any other actor to hold the Commission accountable for the choices made in applying the framework.

There has been limited discussion on how the emergence of a political Commission should affect our understanding of it as the technical body, the one that has been on the receiving end of many delegations justified by the need to depoliticize the matters. In fact, the only person speaking about this seems to be President Juncker, who openly recognizes the political nature of the decisions on economic governance:

> Economic governance is not about legal rules or numerical percentages: it is about people and it is about political decisions that affect them. It is about political responsibility and political accountability.[126]

President Juncker further assures that the Commission 'will continue to apply the pact not in a dogmatic manner, but with common sense and with the flexibility that we wisely built into the rules.'[127] It is difficult to find fault with this declaration of intent. After all, it is an illusion to think that a technocratic body, endowed with discretionary powers to exercise deeply political duties, could long remain a technocratic, 'benevolent agent of the public good'.[128] Rather, attempting to de-politicize deeply political tasks by delegating them to a technocratic body tends to embed the technocracy with politics, transforming it into a 'sham technocracy'.[129] Political decisions remain political, though taken in democratically less accountable fora.

Rather than prompting a reassessment of the limits of placing discretion in matters that are deeply political in nature into technocratic hands, the perception of an

---

[123] T Christiansen, 'After the Spitzenkandidaten: Fundamental Change in the EU's Political System?' (2016) 39 *West Eur Polit* 992, 1006–7.

[124] SB Hobolt, 'A Vote for the President? The Role of *Spitzenkandidaten* in the 2014 European Parliament Elections' (2014) 21 *JEPP* 1528, 1538.

[125] For a general discussion concerning such delegations, see Galligan (n 17) 33.

[126] Speech by President Juncker at the European Parliament Plenary session on the Economic and Monetary Union, Strasbourg (15 December 2015) <http://europa.eu/rapid/press-release_SPEECH-15-6328_en.htm> accessed 29 November 2017.

[127] J-C Juncker, 'State of the Union 2016' (2016) <http://europa.eu/rapid/attachment/SPEECH-16-3043/en/SOTEU%20brochure%20EN.pdf> accessed 29 November 2017.

[128] Beetham and Lord (n 13) 22.

[129] See G Davies, 'Democracy and Legitimacy in the Shadow of Purposive Competence' (2013) 21 *ELJ* 2.

increasingly political—and therefore, as its critics hold, ineffective—Commission has given impetus to take technocratic delegation one step further. We have recently witnessed the emergence of a number of expert bodies, each created for a particular purpose,[130] with the rather obvious intention to discipline the Commission and limit the ways in which it uses its powers of interpretation. Recent years have brought many examples of this deeper kind of technocratic delegation.[131] Notably, following the proposals by Five Presidents' Report, a European Fiscal Board was established to oversee the application of the fiscal framework, [132] while a system of independent national Competitiveness Authorities have been set up to monitor competitiveness and progress with structural reform.[133] Although Juncker has not criticized these innovations specifically, he has been quite clear regarding his views about attempts to move powers from a political Commission into technocratic hands:

As you know, there are some who want to weaken the role of the Commission in the management of our common economic and fiscal rules. Some even call for transferring the tasks we have under the Treaty to an agency of technocrats. I am sure I can count on this Parliament to agree with me that decisions on budgetary priorities, the balance between revenues and expenditures, the level of taxation, the performance of public administrations and social systems, these are all political decisions which require a political Commission which can account for its role and action before this Parliament.[134]

The establishment of expert advisory bodies can certainly support democratic accountability by equipping the public with independent accounts of the government's policies and assist in evaluating how the Commission has used its discretion. However, the work of independent Fiscal Boards is made difficult by the complexity and inconsistency of the applicable framework,[135] and the fact that their mandates are limited to exercising economic judgment over the Commission's choices, thus excluding political choices,[136] which the exercise of Commission discretion has increasingly relied on. At the same time, extending the role of these bodies beyond the strictly advisory one to the discretionary and fundamentally political judgments that increasingly form the European coordination framework would also involve

---

[130] On this development more generally, see RD Kelemen and AD Tarrant, 'The Political Foundations of the Eurocracy' (2011) 34 *West Eur Polit* 922, 924.

[131] Many countries—including all euro area countries as part of the Fiscal Compact and the budgetary framework directive—have established independent fiscal councils to provide an independent assessment of fiscal policies. Fiscal Compact, Arts 3 and 6(1)(b) of Council Directive 2011/85/EU on requirements for budgetary frameworks of the Member States [2011] OJ L 306.

[132] See Decision 2015/1937 of 21 October 2015 establishing an independent advisory European Fiscal Board [2015] OJ L 282/37, Art 2.

[133] See Commission, 'Recommendation for a Council Recommendation on the establishment of National Competitiveness Boards within the Euro Area', COM(2015) 601 final.

[134] Speech by President Juncker at the European Parliament Plenary session on the Economic and Monetary Union, Strasbourg, 15 December 2015, available at <http://europa.eu/rapid/press-release_SPEECH-15-6328_en.htm> accessed 29 November 2017.

[135] Presentation by JL Escrivá, President of the EU Network of Independent Fiscal Institutions, at the ADEMU Conference 'How Much of a Fiscal Union for the EMU?' organized at the Bank of Spain, 18–19 May 2017.

[136] See (n 110).

questions of the acceptable reach of technocratic delegation. For us, the reach of such delegations is the most fundamental concern.

5. Conclusions

The current economic governance framework constitutes an extraordinary experiment on the limits of delegation of discretionary powers. Discretion now reaches deeply into the political situation of each Member State, increasingly involving also questions of redistribution. The appropriateness of such delegations, justified by the need to ensure efficient implementation of the economic governance framework and the objectives it builds on by the objective, technocratic Commission, has so far gained fairly limited attention in the EU. This question becomes more fundamental against the background of the new, thoroughly and openly political Commission, which makes little pretence of acting in a technocratic manner, including in the context of applying the economic governance framework.

We do not see the Commission's track record in applying the economic governance framework as a failure. Measuring the Commission's extensive discretionary powers in this politically highly salient field against the shortage of democratic institutions available to legitimize their use, we think it is understandable that the Commission has chosen to use restraint in its application of these powers. Rather than blind confrontation and coercive enforcement of rules and sanctions that would have likely resulted in a nasty backlash among Member State electorates, EU economic governance has evolved into a discursive, context-sensitive process of guiding Member States incrementally towards better policies. We see this transformation as entirely foreseeable: a body endowed with discretionary powers in political tasks necessarily becomes politicized.

We do not see a realistic prospect of a different approach in the foreseeable future. Rather, we would advise recalibrating the expectations about what the framework can realistically deliver. The use of political power requires appropriate democratic safeguards. At present, the political accountability structures at the EU level are weak, and this weakness leaves little room for expanding the EU role in these matters. Fundamental questions relating to redistribution are not matters in which discretionary powers should be subjected to executive action at the EU level. These questions rather belong in the hands of democratically accountable parliamentary institutions where such matters can be substantively debated, contested and ultimately decided, and who also carry the political responsibility for possible policy mistakes. European democracy demands nothing less.

PART III

EU DISCRETION, LEGALITY, AND RATIONALITY—JUDICIAL REVIEW AND LEGAL PRINCIPLES

8

Judicial Review of Complex Socio-Economic, Technical, and Scientific Assessments in the European Union

*Hanns Peter Nehl**

1. Introduction

With the ongoing rise of regulatory powers and widening of executive discretion at the European Union (EU) level in areas as complex as health, safety and environmental (risk) regulation, economic and monetary policy, public procurement, competition policy, etc., administrative litigation before the Union courts and—as far as decentralized enforcement of EU law is concerned—before the national courts incrementally faces issues of high factual complexity and of controversial policy choices. It is precisely in the face of such factual complexities and difficult policy choices that EU executive/administrative bodies enjoy traditionally a large margin of appraisal or discretionary powers.[1] Yet, the EU is a union based on the rule of law—Article 19(1) TEU—in which the acts of its institutions are subject to review of their compatibility with, in particular, the Treaties, the general principles of law and fundamental rights, including the principle of effective judicial protection (Article 47 of the Charter of Fundamental Rights).[2] Judicial review of executive/regulatory measures and policy choices in complex socio-economic contexts therefore increasingly raises the question of how to define properly the scope, the degree, and the limits of such 'effective' judicial scrutiny. It is argued that, with regard to the 'institutional balance'—i.e. a system of optimal checks and balances of the powers divided between the EU institutions—the judge needs to strike a reasonable equilibrium between the protection of individual

---

* Legal Secretary at the General Court of the European Union. The views expressed in this contribution are exclusively personal.

[1] As to the conceptualization of discretion, see Section 2.1.2.

[2] Case C-583/11 P *Inuit Tapiriit Kanatami and Others v Parliament and Council* [2013] EU:C:2013:625, paras 91, 97–8.

rights and interests and the observance of the law constraining the exercise of discretion on the one hand, and the requirement to respect the core of executive/regulatory discretion on the other. Bearing in mind that the courts' office is not designed to allow the judges to substitute their own views for that of the policy maker or expert regulator, or to redo the decision-making process (*trial de novo*),[3] appropriate concepts need to be established in order to maintain a legitimate degree of judicial control without unduly restricting its effectiveness with regard to protecting individual rights. In that context, it also needs recalling that any (legitimate) concept of judicial review of the observance of EU law, as interpreted in the light of Article 47 of the Charter, may neither put into question nor exceed the constitutional framework of the Treaties in which it is embedded, in particular the parameters set out in Article 263 TFEU.[4]

The purpose of this chapter is to analyse whether and the extent to which the conceptual tools of judicial review hitherto applied to the exercise of various types of executive/regulatory discretion are sufficient to that effect, whether they are being consistently applied throughout the various fields of law and policy making, and/or whether they require further development or improvement. Those tools include the 'manifest error of appraisal' test, the emphasis on procedural legality and safeguarding procedural guarantees as a 'counterbalance' to discretion, e.g. the principle of care and/or the duty to state reasons, the required standard of evidence and the rules governing the apportionment of the burden of proof, as well as the review of breaches of fundamental rights and substantive general principles of law, e.g. the principle of proportionality. It is argued that, ultimately, whatever type of substantive or procedural legal test or concept is being applied by the courts, a meaningful and legitimate standard of judicial review requires addressing the fundamental issues of accurate and complete cognition and establishment of the facts underlying the exercise of administrative discretion and to carry out—at least to a limited extent—a value judgment on their significance or relevance to that effect (the 'relevance paradigm'). Finally, it needs to be emphasized that this chapter does not purport to deal with the Union court's unlimited jurisdiction under Article 261 TFEU to review the individual sanctions imposed by the administration, e.g. the level of fines imposed by the Commission pursuant to Article 23 of Regulation No 1/2003 in the context of EU competition law enforcement.[5]

---

[3] This is rightly emphasized by P Craig, *EU Administrative Law* (2nd edn, OUP, 2012) 435. See, e.g. Case C-510/11 P *Kone and Others v Commission* [2013] EU:C:2013:696, para 26 (EU competition law): 'the analysis by the European Union judicature of the pleas in law raised in an action for annulment has neither the object nor the effect of replacing a full investigation of the case in the context of an administrative procedure.'

[4] See, to that effect, *Inuit Tapiriit Kanatami and Others v Parliament and Council* (n 2) paras 97–8.

[5] Cf. Article 31 of Council Regulation (EC) 1/2003 of 16 December 2002 on the implementation of the rules on competition laid down in Articles 81 and 82 of the Treaty OJ 2003 L 1, 1.

2. Judicial Review of Executive Discretion: Basic Institutional and Legal Parameters under EU Law

2.1 Role of the Union courts, parameters of judicial review, and types of executive acts and discretion

2.1.1 *The GC as a general 'EU administrative court' under the ECJ's legal supervision*

Since its creation in 1988, the General Court (GC) of the EU has been conceived as a first-instance court designed to relieve the Court of Justice (ECJ) of the EU of the burdensome task to deal with voluminous cases requiring time-consuming and intense scrutiny of complex facts and evidence in areas of economic, technical, and scientific decision making, e.g. in competition matters.[6] Over the years, the GC has seen its tasks growing by the attribution of cases in other factually complex fields of law as diverse as customs, foreign trade, State aid, EU Structural Funds, economic and monetary policy, public procurement by EU institutions/agencies, health, safety and environmental regulation, emission trading, and others.[7] The GC has thus been entrusted with the task of providing (effective) judicial protection of citizens' rights within the meaning of Article 47 of the Charter by reviewing the legality of the bulk of EU administrative acts, be they individual in character (notably decisions) or of abstract and general application (regulatory or legislative acts), that are capable of affecting the rights and the interests of natural or legal persons. Today, it therefore appears justified to state that the GC has become a generalist first instance 'EU administrative court' specifically designed to review cases of high factual complexity.

The twofold role of the ECJ as the final arbiter on the interpretation/validity of EU law on appeal (Article 256(1) TFEU) or upon request for a preliminary ruling (Article 267 TFEU) in turn is limited as it does not allow a full review of the appreciation of the facts of a given case. When exercising its function as an appeal court, the ECJ's review of GC decisions is limited to points of law, while it has no jurisdiction to establish the facts or, in principle, to examine the evidence which the GC accepted in support of those facts; factual errors on the part of the GC can only lead to annulment of its decision if that error rests on a wrongful application of evidentiary rules

---

[6] See Council Decision 88/591/ECSC, EEC, Euratom of 24 October 1988 establishing a Court of First Instance of the European Communities OJ 1988 L 319, Recital 4: 'in respect of actions requiring close examination of complex facts, the establishment of a second court will improve the judicial protection of individual interests'. Cf. also M Van der Woude, 'The Court of First Instance: The First Three Years' (1992-1993) 16 *FILJ* 412 (424 et seq; 441 et seq, 460 et seq); B Vesterdorf, 'The Court of First Instance of the European Communities after Two Full Years in Operation' (1992) 29 *CMLRev* 897, 902 et seq.

[7] See, in particular, Council Decision 93/350/Euratom, ECSC, EEC of 8 June 1993 amending Council Decision 88/591/ECSC, EEC, Euratom establishing a Court of First Instance of the European Communities OJ 1993 L 144, as well as Council Decision 94/149/ECSC, EC of 7 March 1994 amending Decision 93/350/Euratom, ECSC, EEC amending Decision 88/591/ECSC, EEC, Euratom establishing a Court of First Instance of the European Communities OJ 1994 L 66.

or a manifest distortion of evidence and facts.[8] It nonetheless remains that the ECJ is called upon to sanction any error in law committed by the GC in its review of the legality of administrative discretionary decisions, e.g. where the judges have erroneously substituted their own assessment for that of the administration or have overly restricted the scope of discretion entrusted to the latter.[9] In this context, it is important to bear in mind that, according to the Union courts' case law, as a matter of principle, judicial review pertaining to issues of law, including the norms governing and constraining the exercise of discretionary powers, is supposed to be complete. This means that the judges always have the final say on the interpretation and scope of application of legal norms which, in turn, the administration is bound to respect in all circumstances without enjoying any leeway whatsoever to depart therefrom.[10] As Craig has rightly pointed out, in the EU legal order,[11] '[i]t is simply regarded as axiomatic that courts decide issues of law, in the sense of substituting judgment on the meaning of the contested term for that of the primary decision maker, and it would be seen as constitutional heresy to suggest otherwise'.[12] Similarly, when replying to requests made by national courts pursuant to Article 267 TFEU for a preliminary ruling on the interpretation or the validity of EU law/acts, the ECJ is, in principle, restricted to interpreting the relevant legal norms such as to enable the national court to apply them to the facts of the case without enjoying itself the power of finding or assessing those facts.[13] This is because the purpose of the preliminary reference procedure is limited to giving the national courts guidance as to the scope of EU law, the application and interpretation of which is needed for deciding the pending case without necessarily predetermining its outcome as regards

---

[8] Cf. e.g. Case C-623/15 P *Toshiba v Commission* [2017] EU:C:2017:21, paras 39–40.

[9] Cf. Case C-73/11 P *Frucona Košice v Commission* [2013] EU:C:2013:32, paras 88–9; *Kone and Others* (n 3) para 27: 'Indeed, when it falls to the European Union judicature to review the legality of Commission decisions imposing fines for infringements of the EU competition rules, it cannot encroach upon the discretion available to the Commission in the administrative proceedings by substituting its own assessment of complex economic circumstances for that of the Commission, but, where relevant, must demonstrate that the way in which the Commission reached its conclusions was not justified in law'. See also Case C-441/07 P *Commission v Alrosa* [2010] ECR I-5949, paras 67–8; Case C-290/07 P *Commission v Scott* [2010] ECR I-7763, paras 66, 72, 79–80, and 84; Joined cases C-247/11 P and C-253/11 P *Areva v Commission* [2014] EU:C:2014:257, para 56; Case C-603/13 P *Galp Energía España and Others v Commission* [2016] EU:C:2016:38, para 73.

[10] See, notably, the full review regarding the interpretation of the 'objective' notion of State aid under Article 107(1) TFEU in Case C-487/06 P *British Aggregates Association v Commission* [2005] ECR I-10737, paras 115 et seq. The particular authority of this legal interpretation is underpinned by its retroactive application, cf. e.g. regarding the so-called '*Altmark Trans*' criteria Case T-289/03 *BUPA and Others v Commission* [2008] EU:T:2008:29, paras 157–60; more recently in fiscal matters, cf. Case C-251/16 *Cussens and Others* [2017] EU:C:2017:881, paras 39–43.

[11] As to a more differentiated approach in US administrative law under the *Chevron*-doctrine [*Chevron v Natural Resources Defense Council*, 467 U.S. 837 (1984)], see A Scalia, 'Judicial Deference to Administrative Interpretations of Law' (1989) 3 *Duke L J* 511; more recently, Note, 'Justifying the Chevron Doctrine: Insights from the Rule of Lenity' (2010) 123 *Harv Law Rev* 2043; F Liu, 'Chevron as a Doctrine of Hard Cases' (2014) 66 *Adm Law Rev* 285; CP Schratz, '*Michigan v EPA* and the Erosion of Chevron Deference' (2016) 68 *Maine L Rev* 381.

[12] Craig (n 3), 405–6.

[13] E.g. Case C-536/11 *Donau Chemie and Others* [2013] EU:C:2013:366, paras 44 et seq.

the application of the relevant EU law as well as national procedural and substantive rules to the facts.[14]

2.1.2 Individual versus regulatory decision making and discretionary powers in EU law

In the framework of judicial review of EU administrative acts, executive discretion is relevant basically in two types of decision-making processes, the characteristics of which may well overlap. For the purposes of a rough conceptualization, 'individual' decision making aimed at adopting decisions addressed to a restricted number of clearly identified individuals or legal persons[15]—e.g. in the framework of EU competition law enforcement—needs to be distinguished from 'regulatory' decision making leading to the adoption of abstract norms or measures of general application—e.g. health and safety regulation, with, in principle, an unlimited number of addressees.[16] The prominent examples of decisions approving or prohibiting State aid schemes[17] or of anti-dumping regulations—i.e. acts of general application according to their form, yet, in substance, directed against a limited number of individuals[18]—show how difficult it may be to draw a clear line between those different types of decision making. Yet, it is submitted that the form of decision making is not necessarily determinative of the nature and scope of discretion

---

[14] See, e.g. Case C-423/15 *Kratzer* [2016] EU:C:2016:604, para 27: '[I]n a reference for a preliminary ruling under Article 267 TFEU, which is based on a clear separation of functions between the national courts and the [ECJ], the national court alone has jurisdiction to find and assess the facts in the case in the main proceedings ... In that context, the [ECJ] is empowered to rule on the interpretation or validity of EU law in the light of the factual and legal situation as described by the referring court, in order to provide that court with such guidance as will assist it in resolving the dispute before it.'

[15] As to the analogous concept of 'administrative adjudication' in common law systems, cf. the path-breaking work of LL Fuller, 'The Forms and Limits of Adjudication' (1978) 92 *Harv L Rev* 353; more recently, see KR Eyer, 'Administrative Adjudication and the Rule of Law' (2008) 60 *Adm Law Rev* 647 (US administrative law); P Craig, 'The Legitimacy of US Administrative Law and the Foundations of English Administrative Law: Setting the Historical Record Straight' (June 30, 2016) *Oxford Legal Studies Research Paper Series* Paper No. 44/2016, 27 et seq., available at SSRN: <https://ssrn.com/abstract=2802784> accessed 17 May 2015.

[16] For the various types of EU regulations, see recently Case C-183/16 P *Tilly-Sabco v Commission* [2017] EU:C:2017:704, para 88: '[A]lthough there is only one definition of "regulation" in Article 288[(2)] TFEU, the FEU Treaty distinguishes between "legislative" regulations adopted according to the ordinary or special legislative procedure in Article 289 TFEU, "delegated" regulations adopted by the Commission and intended to supplement or amend certain non-essential elements of legislative acts in Article 290 TFEU and, finally, "implementing" regulations defined in Article 291 TFEU.'

[17] See the paradigm cases on standing of competitors (Case C-78/03 P *Commission v Aktionsgemeinschaft Recht und Eigentum* [2005] ECR I-10737, paras 32 et seq.; Joined cases C-75/05 P and C-80/05 P *Deutschland and Others v Kronofrance* [2008] ECR I-6619, paras 35 et seq.; *British Aggregates Association v Commission* (n 10) paras 25 et seq.) or actual/potential aid recipients (Joined cases C-71/09 P, C-73/09 P, and C-76/09 P *Comitato 'Venezia vuole vivere' and Others v Commission* [2011] ECR I-4727, paras 53–6).

[18] The case law has recognized that, in substance, antidumping proceedings are to be equated with individual decision making rather than rulemaking, cf. e.g. for the recognition of full rights of defence of the affected manufacturers and exporters, Case C-141/08 P *Foshan Shunde Yongjian Housewares & Hardware v Council* [2009] ECR I-9147, paras 81 et seq. As to the hybrid nature of antidumping proceedings, see already Opinion of AG *Warner* in Case 113/77 *NTN Toyo Bearing and Others v Council* [1979] ECR 1185 (1246 and 1262).

assigned to the competent agency, nor does it predetermine the scope and degree of judicial oversight of the exercise of that discretion.

With respect to the way in which discretionary decision making is to be carried out by the administrative authority or regulator, as a matter of principle, 'cognitive' appraisals should be distinguished from 'volitive' appraisals.[19] Notwithstanding that basic distinction, generally speaking, it is by no means an easy task properly to define or delineate the relevant instances of discretionary powers, the categorization of which may considerably differ from one jurisdiction to the other.[20] Unsurprisingly, it is similarly hard to conceptualize discretion in the framework of EU law implementation,[21] not least because of, at times, incoherent language used by the Union courts.[22] This ultimately appears to stem from methodological uncertainty on how to draw inspiration from the various national concepts and properly to transpose them to the supranational level and its various decision-making processes. Yet, whatever the basic tenets underlying the relevant concept of discretion may be, it seems plain that the margin of manoeuvre the EU administration enjoys depends heavily on the legal criteria or the normative programme set out in statutory rules enacted by the legislature. Moreover, its actual exercise is very much affected by the legal culture and tradition, as well as the political and societal values in which the deciding body and its officials are embedded.[23] This leads to the provisional conclusion that

[19] Cf. J Azizi, 'The Tension between Member States' Autonomy and Commission Control in State Aid Matters: Selected Aspects' in H Kanninen and others (eds), *EU Competition Law in Context: Essays in Honour of Virpi Tiili* (Hart Publishing, 2009) 307–20, (310–12).

[20] Cf. e.g. German administrative law draws a fundamental distinction between the administration's margin of appraisal as to the assessment of the relevant factual/legal criteria set out in legal norms, partly made up of 'indeterminate legal notions' (*unbestimmte Rechtsbegriffe*) on the one hand (*Beurteilungsspielraum auf Tatbestandsseite*), and administrative discretionary powers as to the choice between various legal consequences on the other (*Ermessen* or *Rechtsfolgenermessen*). The opposite 'unitary' concept of discretion based on the principles of *opportunité* and *pouvoir discrétionnaire* is rooted in French administrative law. Comprehensive comparative analyses are abundant; cf. notably, C Starck, Verwaltungsermessen im modernen Staat—Rechtsvergleichender Generalbericht in M Bullinger and others (eds), *Verwaltungsermessen im modernen Staat* (Nomos, 1986) 15, (18 et seq.); JA Frowein (ed), *Die Kontrolldichte bei der gerichtlichen Überprüfung von Handlungen der Verwaltung* (Springer, 1993). As regards English administrative law, cf. the seminal work of DJ Galligan, *Discretionary Powers. A Legal Study of Official Discretion* (Clarendon Press, 1986); see also the contributions in R Allen (ed), 'Discretion in Law Enforcement' (1984) 47 *Law & Contemp Probs*; K Hawkins, 'The Use of Legal Discretion: Perspectives from Law and Social Science' in K Hawkins (ed), *The Uses of Discretion* (Clarendon Press, 1992).

[21] See A Fritzsche, 'Discretion, Scope of Judicial Review and Institutional Balance in European Law' (2010) 47 *CMLRev* 361, 362–4; for a recent comparative analysis of French, German, and Italian administrative law and the quest for a unitary concept of discretion at EU level, see J Mendes, 'Bounded Discretion in EU Law: A Limited Judicial Paradigm in a Changing EU' (2017) 80 *MLR* 443, 451–9.

[22] Craig (n 3) 403 et seq.; HCH Hofmann, GC Rowe, and AH Türk, *Administrative Law and Policy of the European Union* (OUP, 2011), 498–9 refer to Case 9/56 *Meroni v High Authority* [1957–8] ECR 133, 152, and 154 drawing a distinction between a discretionary power implying a 'wide margin of discretion' that entails the execution of actual economic policy and a more limited margin of appraisal in the exercise of clearly defined executive powers; similarly Case C-270/12 *United Kingdom v Parliament and Council (Re: ESMA)* [2014] EU:C:2014:18, para 41 reiterating the *Meroni* formula; see also the similar distinction between 'political' and 'technical' discretion made by AG *Léger*, Opinion in Case C-40/03 P *Rica Foods v Commission* [2005] ECR I-6811, paras 45–9; Fritzsche (n 21) 367 et seq.

[23] See the references in AJ Gil Ibáñez, *The Administrative Supervision and Enforcement of EC Law: Powers, Procedures and Limits* (Hart Publishing, 1999) 199–200; Galligan (n 20) 12–3.

the EU has to strike its own balance on how to make appropriate use of concepts of discretion that fit best to its own policy objectives, legal frameworks, and decision-making processes.

It is submitted that the cognition/volition dichotomy does play an important role in that respect. Insofar as the administration is granted a 'margin of appraisal' regarding complex economic, technical, or scientific facts, the exercise of discretion can broadly be described as being cognitive in nature (issue of *cognition*). However, the authority may equally or exclusively be entrusted with policy discretion or discretion proper allowing it to making policy choices among a number of legally valid options (issue of *volition*), depending on the wideness, ambiguity, or degree of precision of the normative programme provided for in the enabling legal basis. The latter mechanism can be opposed to that of 'tied competences' (*compétences liées*), where the relevant legal basis provides the authority only with limited or no leeway at all to attach certain legal effects to a given set of legal criteria and facts.[24] Moreover, those two types of discretion may be combined in a single enabling rule or delegating act. This chapter is certainly not the place to engage in an in-depth analysis of the various types of discretion that have given rise to a long-standing academic, mostly interdisciplinary, debate.[25] However, this chapter argues that this broad conceptualization provides a useful starting point for assessing the way in which the Union courts have, or should have, addressed such issues in the context of judicial review of EU administrative acts involving the exercise of discretion (see more particularly in Section 3).

2.2 Actions for annulment and damages—litigation and judicial review techniques and their limits

2.2.1 A differentiated approach for reviewing discretion under Articles 263 and 268 TFEU

The standards and concepts of judicial review applied by the Union courts to EU discretionary administrative acts vary according to the judicial remedy used by the litigants. The control of legality triggered by an action for annulment that is based on the pleas in law or grounds of review set out in Article 263(2) TFEU (see Section 2.2.2) enables the GC, in principle, to find various illegalities vitiating the exercise of discretion. On the other hand, the success of an action for damages under Article 268, read in conjunction with Article 340(2) and (3) TFEU, depends on whether the applicant is able to prove the existence of a qualified illegality, namely, a 'sufficiently serious breach of a rule of law intended to confer rights on individuals'.[26] In this

---

[24] Generally see Fritzsche (n 21) 363–4; Craig (n 3) 400–5.

[25] See Gil Ibáñez (n 23) 199; Galligan (n 20) 8 et seq., drawing, *inter alia*, on Dworkin's work. For a further attempt at categorization in EU law, see Craig (n 3) 405, who distinguishes between 'classic discretion' (the enabling norm empowers the agency to take certain action by using the term 'may'), discretion regarding the establishment of the conditions described by indeterminate legal notions (such as those referred to in Art 107(3)(a) TFEU), and discretion regarding the choice between different policy objectives (e.g. Arts 39 and 40 TFEU). For a more detailed analysis, see Mendes, Chapter 1 of this book.

[26] Case C-352/98 P *Bergaderm and Goupil v Commission* [2000] ECR I-5291, para 42.

respect, the case law draws a clear distinction between mere administrative action (i.e. where the administration is legally bound and does not enjoy discretion) on the one hand, and the exercise of discretion (in particular, in administrative or legislative rule making) on the other. According to the Union courts, it is solely where the EU agency has only considerably reduced, or even no, discretion, that the mere infringement of EU law may suffice to establish the existence of a sufficiently serious breach. Conversely, where that agency enjoys (wide) discretion, the decisive test for finding that a breach is sufficiently serious is whether it manifestly and seriously disregarded the limits on its discretion.[27] For a full understanding of the scope of the different legality tests and judicial review concepts applied in the framework of actions for annulment and for damages, it is necessary to examine the specific review techniques applied by the Union courts.

2.2.2 *Subject matter of the case, grounds of review, and their legally binding nature for the Union judge*

The action for annulment under Article 263 TFEU is by far the most important judicial remedy available to individual litigants and Member States for the purposes of reviewing the legality of administrative or regulatory discretionary decision making. Article 263(2) TFEU provides for a non-exhaustive list of pleas in law or grounds of review that may be invoked by the applicant, including lack of competence, infringement of an essential procedural requirement, infringement of the Treaties or of any rule of law relating to their application, or misuse of powers. The ground of review based on misuse of powers has lost its practical relevance in the context of reviewing the exercise of discretion because of its restrictive interpretation in the case law[28] and largely been replaced by the 'manifest error of appraisal' test (*erreur manifeste d'appréciation*), although it is not expressly provided for in Article 263(2) TFEU. The following considerations have been essentially developed in the case law related to actions for annulment, but they apply by analogy to actions for damages in particular, insofar as the criterion of illegality is concerned.

An important peculiarity of proceedings before the Union courts that is often underestimated, if not overlooked, in the academic debate concerning the scope of judicial review is the legally binding nature of the pleas in law or of the grounds of review raised against the *substantive* legality of the contested act. The case law consistently holds that it is for the applicant to determine the subject matter of a case[29]

---

[27] Case C-312/00 P *Commission v Camar and Tico* [2002] ECR I-11355, para 54; Joined Cases C-120/06 P and C-121/06 P *FIAMM and Others v Council and Commission* [2008] ECR I-6513, para 174.

[28] E.g. *Tilly-Sabco v Commission* (n 16) para 64: 'an act is vitiated by misuse of powers only if it appears, on the basis of objective, relevant and consistent evidence, to have been taken with the exclusive or main purpose of achieving an end other than that stated or evading a procedure specifically prescribed by the Treaty for dealing with the circumstances of the case'.

[29] See also Art 44(1)(c) and (d) as well as Art 48(2) of the GC's Rules of Procedure of 1991 (OJ 1991 L 136); replaced by Art 76(d) and (e), as well as Art 84(1) and (2) of the GC's Rules of Procedure of 2015 (OJ 2015 L 105). As to the parallel requirements governing actions for damages, cf. Case T-79/13 *Accorinti and Others v ECB* [2015] EU:T:2015:756, para 53.

brought before the courts by formulating in the application the requisite forms of order sought and the pleas upon which they rest.[30] In turn, the Union courts may not depart from those forms of order sought and those pleas on the substance without ruling *ultra petita* and exceeding the limits of their powers of review.[31] Thus, even a gross material defect or a blatant breach of a Treaty rule, of a general principle of law, e.g. the principle of proportionality, or of a fundamental right under the Charter, may only be taken into account by the Union judge and justify the annulment of the contested act if it has been explicitly invoked in the application.[32] However, there is a crucial exception regarding formal and/or procedural pleas in law the observance of which, as is discussed more closely in Section 3.5, is of utmost importance for guaranteeing the legality and effective judicial review of EU discretionary decision making. According to consistent case law, as a matter of public policy, the Union courts must raise of their own motion formal or procedural pleas in law, such as a lack of competence or an infringement of an essential procedural requirement like the failure to respect a mandatory time-limit[33] or the rights of the defence,[34] or a breach of the duty to state reasons,[35] provided that the annulment based on that plea does not go beyond the scope of the forms of order sought.[36] The ECJ holds that these constraints imposed on the scope of judicial review comply with Article 47 of the Charter and the principle of effective judicial protection. Compliance with that principle does not require that the Union judge—who is indeed obliged to respond to the pleas in law raised and to carry out a review of both the law and the facts—to undertake of its own motion a new and comprehensive investigation of the administrative file.[37] On the contrary, in the eyes of the ECJ

[30] See the recent clarification in the Case C-122/16 P *British Airways v Commission* [2017] EU:C:2017:861, paras 87 and 89: 'while the pleas constitute the essential basis of the form of order sought in an application, they are, nonetheless, necessarily separate from the form of order sought, which defines the limits of the dispute on which the EU courts are asked to rule.' Any unjustified failure to submit all relevant pleas in law already in the application may lead, pursuant to Art 84 of the GC's Rules of Procedure, to foreclosure at a later stage of the court proceedings.

[31] Case C-272/12 P *Commission v Ireland and Others* [2013] EU:C:2013:812, paras 28 et seq.; Case C-224/12 P *Commission v The Netherlands and ING Groep* [2014] EU:C:2014:213, para 97 (State aid proceedings); Joined Cases C-239/11 P, C-489/11 P, and C-498/11 P *Siemens and Others v Commission* [2013] EU:C:2013:866, para 340; *British Airways v Commission* (n 30) paras 81, 85, and 87 (cartel proceedings). As to the limits on the interpretation of the scope of the subject matter of the proceedings as defined by the parties' submissions, cf. also Joined Cases C-514/07 P, C-528/07 P, and C-532/07 P *Sweden and Others v API and Commission* [2010] ECR I-8533, paras 65–7 (access to documents).

[32] *Commission v Ireland and Others* (n 31) paras 29, 33, and 36.

[33] *Tilly-Sabco v Commission* (n 16) paras 114–16 and the case law cited therein.

[34] Joined Cases T-186/97, T-187/97, T-190/97 to T-192/97, T-210/97, T-211/97, T-216/97 to T-218/97, T-279/97, T-280/97, T-293/97 to T-147/99 *Kaufring and Others v Commission* [2001] ECR II-1337, paras 134–5 and case law cited therein (rights of the defence in customs proceedings). See also generally on the procedural requirements including the right to be heard Case C-304/89 *Oliveira v Commission* [1991] ECR I-2283, paras 17–18.

[35] See, in particular, *Siemens and Others v Commission* (n 31) para 321 and case law cited therein (cartel proceedings); *Commission v Ireland and Others* (n 31) para 28 and case law cited therein (State aid proceedings).

[36] This recent clarification flows from *British Airways v Commission* (n 30) paras 88 and 90.

[37] In EU competition law cf. Case C-386/10 P *Chalkor v Commission* [2011] EU:C:2011:815, para 66; Case C-501/11 P *Schindler Holding and Others v Commission* [2013] ECR, EU:C:2013:522, paras 32–6; *Kone and Others* (n 3) paras 20–6.

the analysis by the [Union courts] of the pleas in law raised in an action for annulment has neither the object nor the effect of replacing a full investigation of the case in the context of an administrative procedure. As such a limitation of judicial review is, however, inherent in the notion of the review of legality, it cannot be understood as unduly limiting the review of legality which the [Union courts are] authorised to carry out.[38]

The ECJ recently added in the same vein:

[T]he fact that the judicial review carried out by the EU courts is limited to the claims of the parties, as set out in the forms of order sought in their written pleadings, is not contrary to the principle of effective judicial protection, as that principle does not require those courts to extend their review to cover aspects of a decision that have not been put in issue in the dispute before them.[39]

Non-observance of these constraints in turn necessarily means that the Union judge exceeds the limits of his power of review by acting *ultra petita*, i.e. beyond the scope of the subject matter of the case, and commits an error of law that, on appeal, leads to annulment of the first-instance ruling. Moreover, the subject matter of the case is also determined by the contested act as such, in particular, its operative part and the essential reasons (*ratio decidendi*) set out therein in its support.[40] On account of these formal constraints, and of the fact that it is not the courts' task to redo the administrative procedure, judicial review of (discretionary) acts involving the evaluation of complex economic, technical, or scientific facts may thus not result in the GC (illegally) substituting its own reasoning for that of the author of the contested act.[41] Similarly, when reviewing the observance of essential procedural requirements, e.g. the obligation to state reasons under Article 296(2) TFEU, the Union judge is not allowed to verify the 'reasoning' or the 'reasonableness'—in other words, the merits or the substantive correctness—of the contested act.[42] It is therefore recommended no longer to use the common reference to the existence of an 'adequate' (rather than a 'sufficient') statement of reasons,[43] since the notion of adequacy, as opposed to the French expression *caractère suffisant de la motivation*, is ambiguous and can

---

[38] *Kone and Others* (n 3) para 26.   [39] *British Airways v Commission* (n 30) para 105.

[40] Ibid., para 82.

[41] *Frucona Košice v Commission* (n 9) paras 75 and 88–9; Case C-300/16 P *Commission v Frucona Košice* [2017] EU:C:2017:706, para 63 (State aid law). In the field of EU competition law cf. *Kone and Others* (n 3) para 27: 'Indeed, when it falls to the [Union courts] to review the legality of Commission decisions imposing fines for infringements of the EU competition rules, it cannot encroach upon the discretion available to the Commission in the administrative proceedings by substituting its own assessment of complex economic circumstances for that of the Commission, but, where relevant, must demonstrate that the way in which the Commission reached its conclusions was not justified in law'. See also *Commission v Alrosa* (n 9) paras 67–8; *Areva v Commission* (n 9) para 56; *Galp Energía España and Others v Commission* (n 9) para 73. As regards health and safety regulation see Case T-13/99 *Pfizer Animal Health v Council* [2002] ECR II-3305, para 169.

[42] Case C-367/95 P *Commission v Sytraval and Brink's France* [1998] ECR I-1719, paras 65 et seq.

[43] This originates in the famous *Remia* formula, cf. Case 42/84 *Remia and Others v Commission* [1985] ECR 2545, para 34, according to which, when reviewing complex economic appraisals of the Commission, the court must 'limit its review of such an appraisal to verifying whether the relevant procedural rules have been complied with, whether the statement of the reasons for the decision is adequate, whether the facts have been accurately stated and whether there has been any manifest error of appraisal or a misuse of powers'.

easily be blended with substantive value judgments. This distinction is all the more important, since a plea as to an absence of reasons or an insufficiency of the reasons stated must be raised by the Union judge of his own motion, whereas a plea going to the substantive legality of a decision can be examined only if it is raised by the applicant.[44] In addition, annulment on the grounds of a substantive defect, in accordance with Article 264(1) read in combination with Article 266(1) TFEU, normally entails that the author of the annulled act may not readopt the same act or an act with similar content. However, in case of annulment of that act on procedural grounds, the author may in principle adopt the same act or an act with the same contents again and is merely required to resume the procedure for replacing it at the very point at which the procedural illegality occurred.[45] Accordingly, annulment of EU acts involving the exercise of discretion on such procedural grounds awards both the deciding authority and the affected parties a second chance of obtaining a substantively more correct, balanced, or just decision, while annulment of acts on the same grounds but adopted in the exercise of 'tied competences' necessarily leads the authority to re-adopt the same act with the same result and content.

Last but not least, the subject matter of the case is determined by the relevant facts and evidence relied upon in support of the pleas in law, which the applicant is required to refer to in the application itself and to submit concomitantly in the form of annexes.[46] Irrespective of this requirement, it follows from established case law that, in principle, the lawfulness of an EU act is to be assessed in the light of the information available to the deciding authority at the time of its adoption.[47] Thus, in particular, posterior facts lie outside the subject matter of the case. Apart from the novel exception of judicial review of Commission decisions imposing fines in competition matters,[48] this means that an applicant will generally be unable to challenge the

[44] *Commission v Sytraval and Brink's France* (n 42) para 67; Case C-89/08 P *Commission v Ireland and Others* [2009] ECR I-11245, para 40; *British Airways v Commission* (n 30) paras 88 and 90.

[45] Case C-415/96 *Spain v Commission* [1998] ECR I-6993, paras 31–4; Joined Cases C-238/99 P, C-244/99 P, C-245/99 P, C-247/99 P, C-250/99 P to C-252/99 P and C-254/99 P *Limburgse Vinyl Maatschappij and Others v Commission* [2002] ECR I-8375, paras 72–3; Case C-390/06 *Nuova Agricast* [2008] ECR I-2577, paras 54–6, 60; Case C-308/07 P *Gorostiaga Atxalandabaso v Parliament* [2009] ECR I-1059, para 56; Case C-587/12 P *Italy v Commission* [2013] EU:C:2013:721, para 12; Case C-180/16 P *Toshiba Corporation v Commission* [2017] EU:C:2017:520, para 24; Case C-88/15 P *Ferriere Nord v Commission* [2017] EU:C:2017:716, para 42.

[46] Cf. Arts 76(f), 78(1), and 85 of the GC's Rules of Procedure, read in conjunction with Art 21(2) of the ECJ's Statute. As to the requirement to set out the essential arguments, facts and evidence relied upon in the text of the application itself, cf. Case C-382/12 P *MasterCard and Others v Commission* [2014] EU:C:2014:2201, paras 38–41.

[47] Case 114/83 *Société d'initiatives et de coopération agricoles and Others v Commission* [1984] ECR 2589, para 22 (agricultural policy). See more recently Joined Cases C-74/00 P and C-75/00 P *Falck und Acciaierie di Bolzano v Commission* [2002] ECR I-7869, para 168; Case C-276/02 *Spain v Commission* [2004] ECR I-8091, para 31; Case C-472/15 P *SACE and Sace BT v Commission* [2017] EU:C:2017:885, paras 76–7, 107 (State aid law). Cf. also Case T-358/11 *Italy v Commission* [2015] EU:T:2015:394, para 77 (EU structural funds); Case T-221/15 *Arbuzov v Council* [2017] EU:T:2017:478, para 141 and case law cited therein (restrictive measures); Case T-656/16 *PM v ECHA* [2017] EU:T:2017:686, para 36 (chemicals).

[48] *Galp Energía España and Others v Commission* (n 9) para 72; however, this statement seems to be at odds with para 73, according to which the EU courts may not substitute their own reasoning for that of the author of the contested act.

contested act on factual grounds that he puts forward for the first time in the course of the court proceedings and which were hitherto unknown to the deciding body, unless the relevant facts have already existed prior to the decision's adoption and unless that body could have taken cognizance of them if it had properly investigated the case (as to the significance of the principle of care in this context see Section 3.5).[49]

It follows from the foregoing considerations that it is of utmost importance for the applicant to prepare and conduct a careful litigation strategy, in particular, by properly drafting the pleas in law in the light of the available grounds of review and submitting the relevant facts and evidence. It is only in so doing that the applicant will enhance the courts' responsiveness to the relevant issues of fact and law that may be decisive for reviewing the legality of the exercise of administrative discretion. This is, in principle, true independently of the concepts of judicial review to be applied to discretionary EU acts and the scope and degree of scrutiny the judges will actually deploy in response to such a litigation strategy.

3. Judicial Review on Factual and Legal Grounds of EU Acts Involving the Exercise of Executive Discretion

3.1 Cognition-volition dichotomy and 'transmission belt'

As already explained in Section 2.2.2, insofar as the challenged EU act rests on appraisals of complex economic, technical, or scientific factual issues and/or on discretionary policy choices, the Union judge is, in principle, not allowed to substitute his own assessment for that of the (expert) administration. According to the ECJ's case law, the relevant constraints set out previously ultimately are the expression of an intentional decision on the part of the founders of the Treaties on how properly to separate executive decision-making powers from judicial powers of review and strike a reasonable 'institutional balance' between the administration and the judiciary. The underlying concept of separation of powers is very much influenced by the French legal tradition and system of judicial control of legality (*recours pour excès de pouvoir*) that stood as a model for shaping Article 263 TFEU.[50] However, it seems that, in EU law, the conceptualization of discretion has considerably emancipated itself from the French notion of *pouvoir discrétionnaire*, which, in its original meaning, had a strong connotation of injusticiable administrative freedom of action.[51] At the EU level, the case law generally recognizes that the administration enjoys a large margin of (cognitive) appraisal regarding complex economic, technical, and/or scientific facts and prospective analyses of chains of cause and effect on the one hand, and

---

[49] *Nuova Agricast* (n 45) para 54; *Commission v Scott* (n 9) para 91; *Commission v Frucona Košice* (n 41) paras 70–1 (State aid law).

[50] Cf. JC Bonichot, 'French Administrative Courts and Union Law' in P Cardonnel and others (eds), *Constitutionalising the EU Judicial System: Essays in Honour of Pernilla Lindh* (Hart Publishing, 2012), 167–8.

[51] Cf. D Ritleng, 'Le juge communautaire de la légalité et le pouvoir discrétionnaire des institutions communautaires' (1999) 9 *L'Actualité Juridique—Droit Administratif (AJDA)* 645, 647 et seq.

large discretionary powers regarding (volitive) political or strategic policy choices on the other. In legal practice, it is at times difficult to distinguish neatly between those two basic types of powers of appraisal and discretion, and it is submitted that the boundaries are becoming increasingly blurred in executive decision making depending on the particularities of the relevant legal framework in which the various fields of EU policy making and implementation are embedded.[52] The indeterminate legal concepts and/or broad policy objectives provided for in Article 107(3) TFEU, e.g. (a) the promotion of 'economic development' in case of 'abnormally low' living standards or 'serious underemployment' and (c) the facilitation of the development of certain economic activities/areas, are paradigmatic of this phenomenon. The implementation of those concepts or objectives not only involves the need to assess complex economic facts and the fulfilment of vague notions, but also requires the taking of a positive (volitive) policy decision on the part of the Commission for the purpose of declaring (illegal) State aid compatible with the single market.[53] Article 101(3) TFEU followed a similar precept until Regulation No 1/2003 introduced in 2004 the 'legal exception system' that entailed the Commission's loss of its 'monopoly' for exempting agreements restrictive of competition and rendered that provision directly applicable in the national legal orders.[54] This was a revolutionary step not only because the Commission definitively gave up a powerful (discretionary) decision-making tool for shaping EU competition policy, but also because it meant that indeterminate legal notions involving the assessment of complex economic and technical facts, e.g. the improvement of production or distribution of goods, the promotion of technical or economic progress, and the consumers' fair share of the resulting benefit, the appraisal of which was until then exclusively left to the Commission and subject to limited judicial review only,[55] should from then on be applied by the national courts as well.[56]

Apart from the legal and technical constraints imposed on the Union courts under Articles 263 and 268 TFEU referred to in Section 2.2, any concept of judicial review of the exercise of executive discretionary decision making needs to face a fundamental paradox known in any modern legal system that is governed by the rule of law and enjoys a minimum of democratic legitimacy. Such legal systems strive to maintain the so-called 'transmission belt' between the democratically legitimized

---

[52] For a recent, very thoughtful proposal, see Mendes (n 21) 459 et seq., pleading in favour of a unitary concept of discretion in EU law in order to tackle notably the distinction between wide policy discretion and more limited technical/executive discretion as posited, *inter alia*, in *ESMA* (n 22) para 41.

[53] Similarly, see Craig (n 3) 404, 427–9; Fritzsche (n 21) 368–9.

[54] Cf. in particular Recital 4 and Art 1(1) and (2) of Regulation No 1/2003 (n 5). The Commission has nonetheless attempted to preserve its control through its Guidelines on the application of Article 81(3) of the Treaty OJ 2004 C 101, 97.

[55] Cf. the landmark ruling in the Joined Cases 56/64 and 58/64 *Consten and Grundig v Commission* [1966] ECR 299.

[56] As to the implications of this fundamental shift in paradigm for the scope of judicial review see L Gyselen, 'The Substantive Legality Test under Article 81-3 EC Treaty – Revisited in Light of the Commission's Modernization Initiative' in A von Bogdandy and others (eds), *European Integration and International Co-Ordination: Studies in Transnational Economic Law in Honour of Claus-Dieter Ehlermann* (Kluwer Law International, 2002) 181; D Bailey, 'Scope of Judicial Review under Article 81 EC' (2004) 41 *CMLRev* 1327, 1346 et seq.

legislature on the one hand, and technocratic administration equipped with discretionary powers on the other, by guiding the exercise of executive discretion to the largest possible extent through a more or less densely shaped normative programme that also provides the yardstick for judicial review. From that perspective, when reviewing executive acts as to whether they step outside the legal bounds set by the rules contained in the normative programme, the courts, as the ultimate arbiters on legal issues, protect not only the citizens' rights, but also the legislature's will as expressed in that programme.[57] Conversely, in pursuing the objective of ensuring the rule of law, the judges also seek to protect the 'institutional balance' by safeguarding the remit of action that the normative programme has intentionally left to the administration in order to enable it properly to fulfil its tasks.[58] It is submitted that the EU legal order also rests on this understanding of 'transmission belt' by putting constraints on delegating policy discretion to executive agencies, as is evidenced by the *Meroni* doctrine and reiterated in *ESMA*.[59] On the other hand, it is a commonplace to affirm that, in modern societies, the administration needs to be equipped with the necessary discretionary decision-making powers in order to meet and solve efficiently complex socio-economic, technical, and scientific problems arising in areas such as competition, financial markets, health, safety and environmental protection, etc. Yet, those policy areas are subject to rapidly changing conditions, are replete with uncertainty and their effective regulation requires conducting open-ended procedures, such as those of risk and hazard evaluation and management, and the taking of policy choices the contents and rationality of which may no longer be sufficiently predetermined by any normative programme enacted by the legislature. In German administrative law, this phenomenon has been described as the loss of the steering capacity of the law (*Verlust der Steuerungsfähigkeit des Rechts*) that has given rise to a fundamental rethinking of some of the basic tenets governing administrative law, including the notions of procedural and distributive justice, pluralist or public interest participation, rationality and legitimacy, and, accordingly, of the functions of judicial review of administrative discretion.[60] It is arguable that this debate has even a greater bearing on EU administrative technocratic decision making, which

---

[57] As regards US law, see R Stewart, 'The Reformation of American Administrative Law', (1975) *Harv L Rev* 1669, 1671 et seq.; as to German law in a comparative perspective, see UR Haltern, FC Mayer, and CR Möllers, 'Wesentlichkeitstheorie und Gerichtsbarkeit. Zur institutionellen Kritik des Gesetzesvorbehalts' (1997) 30 *Die Verwaltung* 51, 53 et seq.

[58] Fritzsche (n 21) 381 et seq.; Mendes (n 21) 461, rightly states that 'judicial review and discretion are seen as antagonistic phenomena: if courts stray beyond the boundaries of legality, they risk annihilating the remit of discretion that administrative decision-makers would otherwise have'. See also *Commission v Alrosa* (n 9) para 67: 'By so doing, the [GC] put forward its own assessment of complex economic circumstances and thus substituted its own assessment for that of the Commission, thereby encroaching on the discretion enjoyed by the Commission instead of reviewing the lawfulness of its assessment'.

[59] *Meroni v High Authority* (n 22) 152 and 154; *ESMA* (n 22) para 41. See also M Everson, 'Administering Europe?', (1998) 36 *JCMS* 195, 200–5.

[60] Cf., e.g. the contributions in D Grimm (ed), *Wachsende Staatsaufgaben—sinkende Steuerungsfähigkeit des Rechts* (Nomos, 1990); as to the change in paradigm in US administrative law, see Stewart (n 57) 1669 et seq.

traditionally has been deeply rooted in neo-functional, expertise-driven thinking[61] and continues to be in a permanent quest for new, notably procedural, participatory, or pluralist models of legitimacy.[62] It therefore needs to be examined how judicial review of executive discretionary acts can contribute effectively to counterbalance this bias in favour of technocratic decision making.

3.2 Establishment and conceptualization of complex facts (cognition) and of indeterminate legal notions

3.2.1 *Full review of facts as a matter of principle*

At the level of the sampling and the establishment of complex facts, i.e. in the context of factual cognition, it is submitted that, as a matter of principle, the administration should not normally enjoy an unfettered or unreviewable power of appraisal.[63] It would, however, be overly simplistic to state that facts are either correct or wrong, that there is no executive margin of appraisal as to their finding, and that the courts may always double check their 'accuracy' in full. As the experience in EU merger control cases teaches, the finding of primary facts and the economic assessment applied to them are inextricably linked, because the deciding body needs to identify, evaluate, and prioritize the relevant facts in the course of its (complex) economic analysis. In such a case, the court's determination of the accuracy of the fact findings already implies a value judgment on the relevance of those facts for the purposes of the economic assessment (as to this relevance criterion see more closely in Section 4).[64] Yet, in the light of the right to effective judicial protection laid down in Article 47 of the Charter, the endeavour for guaranteeing a full review of factual findings is all the more justified in respect of adversarial or individual administrative decision making, the outcome of which may affect individual interests or rights, or even result in a prohibition or the imposition of a sanction, e.g. EU competition proceedings.[65]

---

[61] E.g. J Falke and G Winter, 'Management and Regulatory Committees in Executive Rule-making' in G Winter (ed), *Sources and Categories of European Union Law. A Comparative and Reform Perspective* (Nomos, 1996), 567–82, 569–70.

[62] Cf. the summary in HP Nehl, 'Administrative Law' in JM Smits (ed), *Elgar Encyclopedia of Comparative Law* (2nd edn, Edward Elgar, 2012), 21–36, 27–9.

[63] Fritzsche (n 21) 374–5. The overt exception to this principle—probably stemming from the French concept of *pouvoir discrétionnaire*—appears questionable, in particular in instances where judicial review is in any event limited because of wide discretionary powers enjoyed by the deciding authority; see, e.g. in health and safety decision making *Pfizer Animal Health v Council* (n 41) para 168 ('where the ... authority is required to make complex assessments ... , its discretion also applies, to some extent, to the *establishment* of the factual basis of its action'; emphasis added); in the same vein see Case C-425/08 *Enviro Tech (Europe)* [2009] ECR I-10035, para 62; Case C-343/09 *Afton Chemical* [2010] ECR I-7027, para 33; Case C-287/13 P *Bilbaína de Alquitranes and Others v ECHA* [2014] EU:C:2014:599, para 20 (see also Section 3.3.2.3).

[64] M Nicholson, S Cardell, and B McKenna, 'The Scope of Review of Merger Decisions under Community Law' (2005) 1 *European Competition Journal* 123, 145 derive from this that the courts' examination of the administration's fact-finding inevitably interweaves with its review of the substantive assessment in applying a given economic theory to the facts of the case.

[65] As to the Union courts' unlimited jurisdiction regarding the level of fines pursuant to Art 261 TFEU, read in conjunction with Art 31 of Regulation No 1/2003 (n 5), see *Chalkor v Commission* (n 37) paras 52 et seq.

In situations in which the administration actually enjoys a large margin of appraisal as to complex factual issues or even policy discretion, the Union courts have devised a number of judicial tools in order to make sure that the administration's factual findings are correct and complete, as well as to address their accuracy, coherence, and relevance to the largest extent possible. To that end, they have considerably strengthened judicial review on procedural grounds as regards the observance of basic process rights and formal requirements in the administrative procedure (see more closely in Section 3.5).[66] Moreover, they have engaged in a more intrusive style of reviewing the factual findings on the basis of the standard of proof to be met by the deciding authority, or by relying on the rules governing the apportionment of the burden of proof between the parties, and have tried to conceptualize indeterminate legal notions and typical/recurrent sets of facts in order to facilitate the application of the law to the facts.[67] All of these aspects will be considered more closely in turn.

3.2.2 Conceptualization through executive 'soft law'

In order to facilitate the application of indeterminate legal notions to complex factual situations, the EU administration itself, notably the Commission, attempts to fill vague concepts with content and to predetermine its administrative conduct by establishing and publishing 'soft law' rules, such as policy frameworks, guidelines, communications, and notices.[68] In this respect, it is important to bear in mind that the enactment of such soft law is normally based on the internal rules of organization of the deciding authority and typically relate to fields of action in which it enjoys a wide margin of appraisal or policy discretion, such as in the case of Article 107(3) TFEU.[69] In other words, the shaping of soft law rules of administrative conduct constitutes an anticipated exercise of executive discretion in abstract and general terms to an undetermined number of cases. Moreover, according to the case law, 'in adopting rules of conduct and announcing by publishing them that they will henceforth apply to the cases to which they relate, the Commission imposes a limit on the exercise of its [...] discretion and cannot depart from those rules under pain of being found, where appropriate, to be in breach of general principles of law, such

---

[66] See the extensive analyses in HP Nehl, *Principles of Administrative Procedure in EC Law* (Hart Publishing, 1999); HP Nehl, *Europäisches Verwaltungsverfahren und Gemeinschaftsverfassung* (Duncker & Humblot, 2002); HP Nehl, 'Wechselwirkungen zwischen verwaltungsverfahrensrechtlichem und gerichtlichem Individualrechtsschutz in der EG' in C Nowak and W Cremer (eds), *Individualrechtsschutz in der EG und der WTO. Der zentrale und dezentrale Rechtsschutz natürlicher und juristischer Personen in der Europäischen Gemeinschaft und der Welthandelsorganisation* (Nomos, 2002), 135–59.

[67] As to the interaction between legal conceptualization or standardization on the one hand, and the scope of discretion on the other, see Galligan (n 20) 14 et seq., drawing on Dworkin's concept of discretion.

[68] Generally, see L Senden, *Soft Law in European Community Law* (Hart Publishing, 2004); O Stefan, *Soft Law in Court. Competition Law, State Aid and the Court of Justice of the European Union* (Kluwer Law International, 2012). As to the ECB's soft law practice (Re: policy framework) see Case T-496/11 *United Kingdom v ECB* [2015] EU:T:2015:133 (not appealed).

[69] See for the various Commission frameworks, guidelines, communication, and notices in the field of EU State aid law at <http://ec.europa.eu/competition/state_aid/legislation/legislation.html>.

as equal treatment or the protection of legitimate expectations'.[70] Although such soft law rules are legally binding upon neither the Member States nor the Union courts,[71] they constitute an important yardstick for judicial review of discretion via the general principles of law, in particular, the principle of equal treatment. This requires the administration to abide by its self-imposed rules in its decision-making practice, unless those rules are not in line with superior law, such as the Treaty.[72] That technique of judicial review contributes to 'juridifying' soft law rules,[73] since the finding of a breach of the principle of equal treatment presupposes establishing that the Commission has not complied with its self-imposed rules of conduct, which implies in turn that they need to be interpreted 'as if' they were legally binding hard law rules.[74] In fact, it is at times difficult to recognize whether the Union courts merely base their judicial review technique on these criteria,[75] or whether that review ultimately amounts to granting soft law rules a legal status of their own close to that of hard law rules.[76]

3.2.3 Conceptualizing indeterminate legal notions in the case law

The case law has equally greatly contributed to the process of conceptualizing indeterminate legal notions and complex situations, either by drawing inspiration from soft law rules enacted by the EU administration for the purposes of shaping the exercise of its discretion and its course of action,[77] or by developing criteria on its own. In some cases, the Commission even enacted its soft law rules only after the case law has

---

[70] E.g. *Deutschland and Others v Kronofrance* (n 17) para 60; Case C-526/14 *Kotnik and Others* [2016] EU:C:2016:570, paras 40–1 (State aid law). On the possibility left to the Commission to depart from its guidelines under 'specific exceptional circumstances', see A Bouchagiar, 'The Binding Effects of Guidelines on the Compatibility of State Aid: How Hard is the Commission's Soft Law' (2016) 3 *JECLAP* 157.

[71] *Kotnik and Others* (n 70), paras 43–5 (State aid law); Case C-360/09 *Pfleiderer* [2011] EU:C:2011:389, para 21; *Chalkor v Commission* (n 37) para 62; Case C-226/11 *Expedia* [2012] EU:C:2012:795, para 29; *Schindler Holding and Others v Commission* (n 37) paras 37, 58, 67, and 155; *Kone and Others* (n 3) paras 24, 29, 42, and 54; Case C-428/14 *DHL Express (Italy) and Others* [2016] EU:C:2016:27, para 33; *Galp Energía España and Others v Commission* (n 9) para 90 (EU competition law).

[72] *Deutschland and Others v Kronofrance* (n 17) paras 61, 65.

[73] Cf. F Snyder, 'Soft Law and Institutional Practice in the European Community' in S Martin (ed), *The Construction of Europe: Essays in Honour of Emile Noël* (Kluwer Academic Publishers, 1994), 197–225.

[74] See e.g. Case T-551/10 *Fri-El Acerra v Commission* [2013] EU:T:2013:430, paras 27–8, 38 et seq., and 81 et seq.; Case T-319/11 *ABN Amro Group v Commission* [2014] ECR, EU:T:2014:186, paras 27 et seq. (State aid law).

[75] In this sense, see Case T-487/11 *Banco Privado Português and Massa Insolvente do Banco Privado Português v Commission* ECR [2014] (Extracts) EU:T:2014:1077, paras 82–92; confirmed on appeal by Case C-93/15 P *Banco Privado Português and Massa Insolvente do Banco Privado Português v Commission* [2015] EU:C:2015:703, paras 62 et seq.

[76] This impression is conveyed in *ABN Amro Group v Commission* (n 74) paras 25 et seq. In the field of EU competition law, the ECJ seems in the meantime to have acknowledged the risks inherent in such an approach; cf. *Schindler Holding and Others v Commission* (n 37) para 67 (Guidelines on the method of setting fines); *Kone and Others* (n 3) para 29 (Leniency Notice).

[77] Cf. *Pfizer Animal Health v Council* (n 41) paras 118 et seq., drawing inspiration from Commission Communication on the Precautionary Principle of 2 February 2000 (COM(2000)1).

managed to develop sufficiently clear criteria governing the application of broadly shaped legal concepts.[78] Judges tend to measure—either explicitly or implicitly—the degree of complexity on a case-by-case basis and, notably, where they believe to have sector-specific expertise, to conceptualize complex facts to which broadly shaped legal notions need to be applied. To this end, the judicial shaping of the contents of indeterminate legal notions appears particularly useful since those notions help describe and grasp in legal terms a given complex situation in the real world. This is particularly true in the field of EU competition law enforcement and precisely the reason for the widely shared view that, since the entry into force of the 'legal exception system', the indeterminate exemption conditions under Article 101(3) TFEU, hitherto largely seen as conferring upon the Commission a wide power of appraisal, were capable of being directly effective, *inter alia*, in the national courts (see already Section 3.1).[79] Moreover, as regards broad legal notions, such as 'concerted practice' and 'restriction ... of competition' by 'object or effect' under Article 101(1) TFEU, or 'abuse ... of a dominant position' under Article 102 TFEU, the Union courts have developed a consistent body of case law that facilitates the application of those notions to the facts irrespective of their complexity. Some commentators even have argued that the law and the degree of conceptualization in that field, including the applicable requirements of proof, have reached a level of precision such as to allow the judges to exercise a comprehensive review of the legality of the Commission's action even where it enjoys a margin of appraisal as to complex economic facts.[80] It is however submitted that such a stance overstates the programming capacity of the law in the sense that it could sufficiently steer the making of cognitive appraisals in all instances of economic complexity; nor do the judges' cognition abilities always match such complexity that would enable them to carry out a more intensive review in that respect. This is all the more true of uncertain, prospective facts or potential factual evolutions, which arguably have prevented the courts from conceptualizing any further the notion of 'significant impediment to effective competition' under Article 2(2) and (3) of the EC Merger Regulation.[81] Similarly to the process of conceptualizing Articles 101 and 102 TFEU, the Union courts have developed a dense body of case law regarding the interpretation of the (objective) State aid notion under Article 107(1) TFEU that requires a full review as to both the applicable legal concepts and the underlying facts.[82] Even where certain concepts, such as the 'private investor' test, lead to the assessment of complex economic facts in respect of

[78] Cf. in particular, after more than 40 years of case law, Commission Notice on the notion of State aid as referred to in Art 107(1) TFEU OJ 2016 C 262, 1.

[79] See (n 56).

[80] This seems to be conveyed by M Jaeger, 'The Standard of Review in Competition Cases Involving Complex Economic Assessments: Towards the Marginalisation of the Marginal Review?' (2011) 2 *JECLAP* 295; G Gryllos, 'Discretion and Judicial Review in EU Competition Law: A Technical Analysis on Sources of Discretion, Judicial Review and Implications for the Litigants' (2016) 4 *Concurrences* 1.

[81] Council Regulation (EC) 139/2004 of 20 January 2004 on the control of concentrations between undertakings (the EC Merger Regulation) OJ 2004 L 24, 1.

[82] As to the legal notion of 'selectivity', cf. *British Aggregates Association v Commission* (n 10) paras 115 et seq. See, however, also the more ambiguous language used in Joined Cases C-533/12 P and C-536/12 P *SNCM and France v Corsica Ferries France* [2014] EU:C:2014:2142, paras 14–15.

which the Commission has a power of appraisal, the Union courts have intensified their review by classifying certain types of investment as potentially falling under that test and developing the conditions under which that investment is to be carried out, including the applicable standard of evidence and the apportionment of the burden of proof.[83]

3.2.4 *The limits of conceptualization and of the courts' office in a complex world*

The attempts at conceptualizing indeterminate legal notions and complex situations referred to should, however, not conceal the fact that the more complex certain factual issues are, the less possible it is to squeeze them into given concepts, standards, or categories, let alone to make a proper judgment on their accuracy.[84] Epistemology teaches that the cognition of the real world, if not truth, is an extremely error-prone exercise and that there is not necessarily a right or wrong answer to any factually complex issue. This is particularly true in the case of evaluating complex chains of causality or uncertain, rapidly changing situations, e.g. risks for human health/safety or the environment, or the possible future evolution of a given market. Moreover, policy makers face variable degrees of factual complexity or uncertainty the evaluation of which requires corresponding cognitive capacities and economic, technical, or scientific expertise to ensure that complexity is reduced and errors of appraisal, or wrong or politically biased choices, are avoided as much as possible.[85] Expert executive bodies specifically designed to implement policies affected by such complexity or uncertainty normally possess appropriate human resources, technical equipment, and infrastructures, and suitable evaluation, management, and decision-making processes, including scientifically recognized methods or tests. These tools enable them to make adequate methodological choices and properly to gather and ascertain complex sets of facts, to weigh and prioritize them, and to carry out the necessary value judgments, e.g. for the purposes of assessing risks or prospective analyses.[86]

---

[83] Cf. very recently *Commission v Frucona Košice* (n 41) paras 58 et seq.; *SACE and Sace BT v Commission* (n 47) para 107.

[84] Similarly, A Kalintiri, 'What's in a Name? The Marginal Standard of Review of "Complex Economic Assessments" in EU Competition Enforcement' (2016) 5 *CMLRev* 1283, 1290–1, stating that the 'notion of "complex economic assessments" is a nearly all-encompassing term', which is partly 'due to the intrinsic links of competition with economics', and the 'criterion of "complexity" is immensely equivocal'.

[85] E.g. as to the ECB's role, see Opinion of AG *Cruz Villalón* in Case C-62/14 *Gauweiler and Others* [2015] EU:C:2015:7, paras 109–10: ' ... the ECB's independence is also intended to ensure that it is kept away from the political debate ... [T]hat detachment from political activity is necessary because of the extremely technical nature and high degree of specialization characteristic of monetary policy. In fact, the Treaties confer on the ECB sole responsibility for framing and implementing monetary policy, for which purpose it is given substantial resources with which to undertake its functions. On account of those resources the ECB also has access to knowledge and particularly valuable information, which permits it to perform its tasks more effectively whilst also, over time, bolstering its technical expertise and reputation. Those features are essential for ensuring that monetary policy signals actually reach the economy since ... one of the functions of central banks today is the management of expectations, and technical expertise, reputation and public communication are basic tools for carrying out that function.'

[86] AH Türk, 'Oversight of Administrative Rulemaking: Judicial Review' (2013) 1 *ELJ* 126, 140. Mendes (n 21) 462 and 464–5 has therefore rightly pointed to a blurring of the cognition and volition

This ultimately constitutes the 'technocratic' justification for granting expert agencies a margin of appraisal or discretionary power, the exercise of which is traditionally subject to marginal judicial review only.[87] Indeed, as opposed to specialized trial courts, generalist administrative courts are not normally equipped with the same level of policy-related expertise, investigatory and fact-finding powers, and cognitive methods, nor are court proceedings, in particular, when they are governed by the constraints set out in Section 2.2.2, suited for replicating the administrative decision-making process, let alone for correcting its failures or improving the rationality of its outcome.[88]

It is therefore submitted that the degree of possible conceptualization of indeterminate legal notions and of complex sets of facts and the courts' capability of reviewing them is reciprocally proportional to the degree of factual complexity, and vice versa. Put differently, the scope and the intensity of judicial review is necessarily a function of the degree of factual complexity and its justification depends on the extent to which either the executive experts or the judges are ultimately better placed to have the final say on the correct cognition and interpretation of the facts. Accordingly, it does not appear helpful when the Union courts schematically repeat their dictum of 'complex facts' or 'complex factual appraisal'. This neither reveals the real extent to which they are supposed to review the administration's factual assessment, nor how far they are actually prepared to go for that purpose.[89] On the other hand, the recurrent recourse to this empty shell in the case law does not always mean that the Union courts are deferent or unwilling to intensify their review on factual or procedural grounds via other methodological tools, such as the standard or the burden of proof. Conversely, reference to factual complexity may serve as a pretext for the judges not to engage in a more intense scrutiny of the facts, although it might be warranted.[90]

Moreover, the capacity of reducing complexity by pouring it into reviewable concepts is also impaired by the fact that there is no clear dividing line between issues of fact and law and that factual and legal appraisals tend to merge, in particular, at

---

aspects of the decision-making process that could justify recognizing a unitary concept of discretion. See also Opinion of AG *Bobek* in Case C-691/15 P *Commission v Bilbaína de Alquitranes and Others* [2017] EU:C:2017:646, para 68, considering that the (discretionary) choice and the realization of a given method 'are *parts of one and the same* highly complex scientific hazard assessment' (emphasis in the original).

[87] As to the US experience with the New Deal technocratic justification for rule making, see e.g. M Shapiro, 'Codification of Administrative Law: The US and the Union' (2016) 2 *ELJ* 26, 31 et seq.; Stewart (n 57) 1676 et seq.

[88] In the same vein, see Craig (n 3) 435; Fritzsche (n 21) 392, 395–6; Türk (n 86) 140; J Laguna de Paz, 'Understanding the Limits of Judicial Review in European Competition Law' (2014) 2 *JAE* 203, 210–12. As to an interesting empirical study purporting to show the contrary see JD Wright and AM Diveley, 'Do Expert Agencies Outperform Generalist Judges? Some Preliminary Evidence from the Federal Trade Commission' (2013) 1 *JAE* 82.

[89] Cf. also Kalintiri (n 84) 1293: '[T]he complexity of an economic evaluation should be established ad hoc. Regrettably, the practice of the EU Courts so far has been to take its existence for granted.'

[90] This seems to be the underlying message of Gryllos (n 80). See also Kalintiri (n 84) 1291, 1293, who argues that complexity should not be confused with difficulty and that 'any description of complexity must be detached from the notion of discretion'.

the stage of applying the law—and even more so if broadly shaped—to the facts (*Subsumtion* in German; *qualification juridique des faits* in French).[91] Indeed, complex factual appraisals for the purposes of implementing EU law are never performed in the abstract or in a legal vacuum, but against the background of the rules on the basis of which the administration is supposed to act, including their objectives.[92] The cognition of complex facts, their appraisal, and their legal characterization are thus essential elements of a broader cognitive process, the different stages of which are difficult to separate from each other. In addition, against the background of those rules and objectives, the Union courts are called upon to judge on the relevance of the facts established for the purpose of the administration's complex appraisal.[93] This 'relevance' criterion is accordingly situated in a grey zone overlapping the administration's factual and legal appraisals,[94] as well as the procedural and substantive legality of their exercise. And evaluating the relevance of facts always involves a value judgment on the part of the judge, thus straying into the realm of volition that is supposed to be at the core of administrative discretion.[95] Finally, it is submitted that, notwithstanding the caveats discussed in this section, there should, in principle, be no unreviewable freedom of action on the part of the administration to find, establish, and appraise the *relevant* facts necessary for its discretionary appraisal (see also Section 4).[96]

This leaves us with the somewhat unsatisfactory conclusion that, rather than the factual complexity as such, it is the degree of that complexity and the absence of its judicial command or of stricter legal conceptualization that, ultimately, prevents the judges from engaging in more intrusive scrutiny and, conversely, leads to acknowledging a more-or-less unreviewable margin of factual appraisal—and concomitantly, a certain margin of factual error—on the part of the administration.[97] Therefore, it is unsurprising that some commentators deplore the lack of coherence in the standards of judicial review of factual findings in executive decision making.[98] Yet, even if varying standards of judicial deference vis-à-vis executive complex economic, technical, or scientific appraisals are possible, depending on the degree of

---

[91] Similarly Craig (n 3) 400–3; Fritzsche (n 21) 395. [92] Cf. also Kalintiri (n 84) 1296.

[93] See Jaeger (n 80) 311: 'the first and foremost abilities required from a judge is his or her independence and capacity to discern what is relevant and to disregard what is not, whatever the complexity or the matter of the question submitted to his or her decision'.

[94] Cf. AL Sibony and E de La Serre, 'Charge de la preuve et théorie du contrôle en droit communautaire de la concurrence: pour un changement de perspective' (2007) *RTDE* 205, 244, para 49.

[95] Cf. Türk (n 86) 140; Craig (n 3) 435–6: 'It is precisely in relation to ... more complex findings, where the facts are multifaceted and difficult, requiring a greater degree of evaluative judgment that there can be real differences of view as to the facts and the possible consequences flowing from them'.

[96] Cf. the paradigmatic finding in Case C-269/90 *Technische Universität München* [1991] ECR I-5469, para 14: 'where the [Union] institutions have such a power of appraisal, respect for the rights guaranteed by the [Union] legal order in administrative procedures is of even more fundamental importance. Those guarantees include, in particular, the duty of the competent institution to examine carefully and impartially all the *relevant* aspects of the individual case, the right of the person concerned to make his views known and to have an adequately reasoned decision. Only in this way can the Court verify whether the factual and legal elements upon which the exercise of the power of appraisal depends were present' (emphasis added).

[97] In this vein, see Sibony and de La Serre (n 94) 248, para 55. [98] Türk (n 86) 139.

factual complexity and its conceptualization, judicial review on the substance[99] in cases of high factual complexity is not necessarily superficial or meaningless. In that respect, the Union courts have developed a specific review technique based on the concept of 'manifest error of appraisal', combined with certain requirements of proof, the basic tenets and limits of which are addressed in Section 3.3.

3.3 Standard of review on the substance: the linkage between the manifest error of appraisal test and the standard of proof

3.3.1 Manifest error of appraisal: a vague but flexible standard of judicial review

The principle according to which judicial review of complex assessments contained in EU administrative acts should be limited rests on the traditional *Remia* test, as developed in the context of EU competition law, which has been consistently repeated in the case law of the Union courts, albeit in different forms, in other EU policy fields.[100] Pursuant to this test, when reviewing complex (economic) appraisals of the Commission, the GC must 'limit its review of such an appraisal to verifying whether the relevant procedural rules have been complied with, whether the statement of the reasons for the decision is adequate, whether the facts have been accurately stated and whether there has been any manifest error of appraisal or a misuse of powers'.[101]

However, the repeated articulation of the 'manifest error of appraisal' test in more than 30 years of case law has not given rise to more clarity as to its actual scope and content and the way in which the Union courts are prepared to use it.[102] It is submitted that, to date, all attempts, if any, at properly categorizing that test or defining it in more detail to render it a sufficiently reliable yardstick for judicial review have failed. This is essentially due to its roots in French administrative law where the concept of *erreur manifeste d'appréciation* had been devised in the case law to grant the courts a more effective tool for reviewing—albeit in a limited manner—the exercise of hitherto unfettered administrative discretionary power.[103] From that historical perspective, the concept of manifest error of appraisal is an expression of the

---

[99] As to judicial review on procedural grounds see in Section 3.5.

[100] See, e.g. in antidumping matters Case C-687/13 *Fliesen-Zentrum Deutschland* [2015] EU:C:2015:573, para 44; Joined Cases C-376/15 P and C-377/15 P *Changshu City Standard Parts Factory and Ningbo Jinding Fastener v Council* [2017] EU:C:2017:269, para 47 (yet with a misleading reference to the broad discretion the EU institutions enjoy by reason of the complexity of the economic, political, and *legal* situations which they have to examine in the sphere of the common commercial policy and, most particularly, in the realm of measures to protect trade; emphasis added); in State aid law Case C-246/15 P *Pollmeier Massivholz v Commission* [2016] EU:C:2016:568, point 28; Case C-415/15 P *Stichting Woonpunt and Others v Commission* [2017] EU:C:2017:216, para 53; as regards mergers, see Case T-79/12 *Cisco Systems and Messagenet v Commission* [2013] EU:T:2013:635, para 50; for EU public procurement, see, e.g. Case T-514/09 *bpost v Commission* [2011] EU:T:2011:689, para 121.

[101] *Remia and Others v Commission* (n 43) para 34.

[102] In the same vein, Craig (n 3) 436.

[103] E.g. J Kahn, 'Discretionary Power and the Administrative Judge' (1980) 29 *ICLQ* 521, 528–30); JP Henry, 'Une nouvelle fonction pour l'erreur manifeste. Le contrôle du respect de l'obligation de diligence' (1979) 6 *AJDA* 17, 19 et seq.

fundamental requirement flowing from the division of powers basically to respect the margin of executive discretion and to subject its exercise to a limited judicial control only. Arguably, comparative analysis has not been very helpful either to that effect and simply shows that other jurisdictions—as shown by the 'arbitrary and capricious' standard in US administrative law[104] and that of *Wednesbury* reasonableness in English administrative law[105]—face similar problems of how to determine properly the standard of judicial review applicable to executive discretion. According to widely used, broad, tautological, and rather unhelpful descriptions, a manifest error of appraisal must be obvious, fatal, or serious, or the administration enjoys a margin of error.[106] More specific case law has held that the discretionary assessment must not be implausible[107] and that the burden lies with the applicant to substantiate and adduce sufficient evidence to that effect.[108] Beyond the finding of an arbitrary, outright irrational, or patently erroneous decision, such a plausibility check seems to require the judges to ascertain whether there are any internal contradictions, logical inconsistencies, or gaps in the administration's exercise of its margin of appraisal or discretionary power.[109] Irrespective of these attempts at further clarification, the broadness of the notion of manifest error and the uncertainty surrounding its use in litigation have rightly led a commentator to state that, ultimately, 'manifest' is whatever the judges consider to be 'manifest' in a given case.[110] This, in turn, grants the judges a very flexible instrument of control, the use of which may be fine-tuned and intensified on a case-by-case basis,[111] without overtly acknowledging it.

---

[104] For a useful comparison with EU law, cf. Türk (n 86) 138–9.

[105] In comparative perspective see G de Búrca, 'Proportionality and Wednesbury (v.) Unreasonableness: The Influence of European Legal Concepts on UK Law' (1997) 1 *EPL* 561. See more recently P Craig, 'The Nature of Reasonableness Review' (2013) *Curr Leg Probl* 1; and the contributions in H Wilberg and M Elliott (eds), *The Scope and Intensity of Substantive Review: Traversing Taggart's Rainbow* (Hart Publishing, 2015).

[106] E.g. Ritleng (n 51) 656: 'Par le contrôle de l'erreur manifeste d'appréciation, le juge interdit un usage gravement erroné de la liberté d'appréciation. Recherche d'un vice grave, évident, le contrôle de l'erreur manifeste d'appréciation ne tend pas ... à la censure de n'importe quelle violation des règles du traité dont l'application requiert des appréciations complexes. Quand elle n'exerce qu'un contrôle restreint, la Cour concède à l'autorité communautaire une marge d'erreur.' See also the criticism of Kalintiri (n 84) 1294–5: 'the "obvious error" language suffers from the same vagueness as the "manifest error of assessment" formula ... '.

[107] Case T-380/94 *AIUFFASS and AKT v Commission* [1996] ECR II-2169, para 59; *BUPA and Others v Commission* (n 10) para 221; Case T-68/05 *Aker Warnow Werft and Kvaerner v Commission* [2009] ECR II-355, para 42; Case T-282/08 *Grazer Wechselseitige Versicherung v Commission* [2012] EU:T:2012:91, para 158 (State aid law); Case T-257/07 *France v Commission* [2011] EU:T:2011:444, para 86, confirmed on appeal by Case C-601/11 P *France v Commission* [2013] EU:C:2013:465 (public health/consumer safety regulation).

[108] Cf. Case T-387/11 *Nitrogénművek Vegyipari v Commission* [2013] EU:T:2013:98, para 25: 'in order to establish that the Commission committed a manifest error in assessing the facts such as to justify the annulment of the contested decision, the evidence adduced by the applicant must be sufficient to make the factual assessments used in the decision at issue implausible.'

[109] As to the similarities with the arbitrary and capricious standard in US administrative law see Türk (n 86) 140; Craig (n 3) 440–1.

[110] F Castillo della Torre, 'Evidence, Proof and Judicial Review in Cartel Cases' (2009) 32 *World Competition* 505, 566.

[111] Cf. former president of the GC B Vesterdorf, 'Standard of Proof in Merger Cases: Reflections in the Light of Recent Case Law of the Community Courts' (2005) 1 *ECJ* 3, 18.

3.3.2 Standard of proof as a complementary judicial tool for the purposes of intensifying the scrutiny of complex facts

3.3.2.1 The fundamental distinction between standard of judicial review and standard of proof

Since, also in the context of complex assessments, the judges are in principle called upon to exercise full control over errors of fact and law,[112] it is far from being clear where to draw the dividing line between the concept of manifest error, as the primary standard of judicial review on the substance on the one hand, and the standard of proof on the other.[113] Broadly speaking, the standard of judicial review concerns the latitude and degree of control of legality that the judges may exercise on administrative acts, whereas the standard of proof relates to the quality and quantity of evidence that a party—bearing the burden of proof—needs to submit to persuade the judges that it should win the case.[114] Yet, any determination by virtue of the manifest error test as to whether the administration's appraisal is sufficiently plausible also necessarily implies a value judgment on its credibility in the sense that it is sufficiently supported by the relevant facts and evidence. Even more importantly, in respect of the issue of whether the facts and the evidence relied on are credible, the (first instance) judges enjoy an unfettered power of appraisal,[115] which enhances their capacity of faulting the plausibility of the executive's complex assessment for lack of sufficient evidence.[116] Indeed, according to consistent case law, the principle of unfettered evaluation of evidence means, first, that, where evidence has been obtained lawfully, its admissibility cannot be contested before the GC and, second, that the only relevant criterion for the purpose of assessing the probative value of evidence lawfully adduced relates to its credibility.[117] This unfettered power of appraisal of evidence in turn appears to rest on the judges' (natural) office fully to control the observance of the law (*iura novit curia*), including the legal characterization of the facts. This important overlap and complementarity between the plausibility check under the concept of manifest error and the required standard of proof, as combined with the courts' unfettered power of appraisal of evidence, is further complicated by the

---

[112] In particular in EU competition law cf. *Chalkor v Commission* (n 37) para 62; Case C-295/12 P *Telefónica and Telefónica de España v Commission* [2014] EU:C:2014:2062, para 56; *MasterCard and Others v Commission* (n 46) para 156.

[113] As to this fundamental distinction, cf. also Craig (n 3) 434–6; Sibony and de La Serre (n 94) 240 and 243–4 (paras 42, 48).

[114] As to the linkage between the apportionment of the burden of proof, the standard of proof, and the standard of judicial review, see Castillo della Torre (n 110) 512 et seq.

[115] Cf. Opinion of AG *Mengozzi* in Case C-382/12 P *MasterCard and Others v Commission* EU:C:2014:42 para 119, who acknowledges that the judges may not hide behind the Commission's margin of discretion in order not to carry out an in-depth review of the law and of the facts. However, he also raises doubts as to the 'precise scope of that dictum, which has in itself the potential to neutralise de facto the very principle of the recognition of a margin of economic assessment to the Commission ... '.

[116] In this vein, see Kalintiri (n 84) 1309–12. See also Nicholson, Cardell, and McKenna (n 64) 138: ' ... the higher the standard of proof, the closer and more extensive the degree of judicial scrutiny which is required in order to establish whether the Commission has made out its case to the necessary standard'; similarly Vesterdorf (n 111) 8.

[117] Case C-407/04 P *Dalmine v Commission* [2007] ECR I-829, para 63; *Siemens and Others v Commission* (n 31) para 128; Case C-469/15 P *FSL Holdings and Others v Commission* [2017] EU:C:2017:308, para 38; Case C-99/17 P *Infineon Technologies v Commission* [2018] EU:C:2018:773, para 65 ; Case T-392/15 *European Dynamics Luxembourg and Others v European Union Agency for Railways* [2017] EU:T:2017:462, para 50.

requirements governing the allocation of the burden of proof for which there is no general rule in the case of challenging discretionary acts.[118] It nonetheless remains that the respective concepts of standard of review and standard of proof should be clearly distinguished from each other in order to avoid fundamental misunderstandings.[119] This is not always guaranteed in legal practice,[120] since the lack of plausibility of certain assessments may also flow from a lack of convincing evidence.[121]

3.3.2.2 Standard of proof in respect of complex economic facts and assessments: the Tetra Laval test

This chapter is not the place to engage in an in-depth discussion of the various standards of proof applicable in EU administrative law the intensity of which may vary considerably depending on the nature of the policy to be implemented or the decision-making's outcome, e.g. the imposition of a sanction.[122] Yet, as regards the standard of proof to be applied to complex (economic) appraisals of chains of causality or prospective analyses in the context of factual uncertainty or of rapidly changing situations, the ECJ has set an important precedent in *Tetra Laval*,[123] a merger case whose significance for the purposes of reviewing the administration's exercise of its margin of appraisal of complex facts has strayed beyond EU competition law in the strict sense.[124] According to the ECJ, the judges have to carry out a threefold test[125] that reads as follows:

---

[118] As to the need for the applicant to show the existence of a manifest error on account of lack of plausibility of the administration's discretionary appraisal cf. (n 108). For the possible shifting of the burden of proof in the context of reviewing (former) Commission exemption decisions under Art 101(3) TFEU, see Joined Cases C-501/06 P, C-513/06 P, C-515/06 P and C-519/06 P *GlaxoSmithKline Services and Others v Commission and Others* [2009] EU:C:2009:610, paras 82–3, 85. In EU merger cases, the discussion on the requisite standard of proof seems generally to imply that, at least as regards prohibition decisions, the burden of proof lies with the Commission, see, e.g. Vesterdorf (n 111) 5 et seq. For a general account of the parameters governing the apportionment of the burden of proof see Sibony and de La Serre (n 94) 216 et seq.; Castillo della Torre (n 110) 512–9.

[119] This has been rightly emphasized by Craig (n 3) 434–6, and Sibony and de La Serre (n 94) 240 and 243–4 (paras 42, 48). See also Jaeger (n 80) 299; B Vesterdorf (n 111) 5–8, 19.

[120] See *Frucona Košice v Commission* (n 9) paras 74–6; Joined Cases C-214/12 P, C-215/12 P, and C-223/12 P *Land Burgenland and Others v Commission* [2013] EU:C:2013:682, paras 77–9 (State aid law); *Kone and Others* (n 3) paras 26–8 (EU competition law).

[121] Similarly, Craig (n 3) 434 in his comment on Case T-5/02 *Tetra Laval v Commission* [2002] ECR II-4381.

[122] See, for the various standards—stretching from beyond reasonable doubt to preponderance of evidence or balance of probabilities—Sibony and de La Serre (n 94) 212–14; Castillo della Torre (n 110) 521–8. As to the unique standard of proof to be met by the Commission for the purposes of allowing or prohibiting a proposed concentration see Case C-413/06 P *Bertelsmann and Others v Impala* [2008] ECR I-4951, paras 47–52, Opinion of AG *Kokott*, op. cit., paras 208 et seq.

[123] Case C-12/03 P *Commission v Tetra Laval* [2005] ECR I-987 para 39; cf. also *Bertelsmann and Others v Impala* (n 122) para 69.

[124] For State aid law see *Commission v Scott* (n 9) paras 64–5; *Frucona Košice v Commission* (n 9) para 76; Case C-405/11 P *Commission v Buczek Automotive* [2013] EU:C:2013:186, para 50; *Land Burgenland and Others v Commission* (n 120) para 79; *SNCM and France v Corsica Ferries France* (n 82) para 14; *Commission v Frucona Košice* (n 41) para 64. Cf. also Joined Cases T-29/10 and T-33/10 *Netherlands and ING Groep v Commission* [2012] EU:T:2012:98, para 102. For EU competition law see *Chalkor v Commission* (n 37) para 54; Case C-295/12 P *Telefónica and Telefónica de España v Commission* [2014] EU:C:2014:2062, para 54.

[125] See also EMH Loozen, 'The Requisite Legal Standard for Economic Assessments in EU Competition Cases Unravelled through the Economic Approach' (2014) 39 *ELR* 91, 102–3.

Whilst the [ECJ] recognises that the Commission has a margin of discretion with regard to economic matters, that does not mean that the [Union] Courts must refrain from reviewing the Commission's interpretation of information of an economic nature. Not only must the [Union] Courts, inter alia, establish whether the evidence relied on is factually accurate, reliable and consistent but also whether that evidence contains all the information which must be taken into account in order to assess a complex situation and whether it is capable of substantiating the conclusions drawn from it.

Interestingly, this test partly overlaps with the *Remia* test in so far as it requires the GC to ascertain whether the facts have been accurately stated, thus reaffirming the general principle according to which the judge is the ultimate arbiter of the correct establishment of complex facts.[126] More precisely, the threefold *Tetra Laval* test refers, first, to the *quality of evidence* relied upon by the deciding authority and requires the GC to review the existence of factually accurate, reliable, and consistent evidence. Second, the requirement pursuant to which the evidence shall contain all the information that must be taken into account in order to assess a complex situation relates to the *quantity* and *completeness of evidence*. Third, the judicial appraisal of the quality and quantity of evidence supplied and of its probative value consists of reviewing whether that evidence is capable of substantiating the (sufficiently plausible) conclusions drawn from it. It is submitted that the first and third parts of the test, in particular, the requirements of reliability and consistency of the evidence, are closely connected to the plausibility and/or credibility test. The first and second parts of the test overlap in turn with the requirements under the (procedural) duty of care (see Section 3.5), i.e. the need to gather and establish all—in other words, accurate and complete—information that is relevant ('must be taken into account') for assessing a complex situation. Finally, the third part of the test constitutes the very core of judicial evaluation of evidence, i.e. the establishment of its credibility and convincing nature, in respect of which the judges enjoy an unfettered power of appraisal.

Arguably, by establishing that threefold test the ECJ prepared the ground for an intensified judicial scrutiny of complex economic facts and assessments even under the heading of the concept of manifest error of appraisal.[127] In so doing, it seems that the ECJ did not wish to follow in all respects the Opinion of AG Tizzano, who advocated a more limited type of review of the Commission's economic assessment by stating the following:

---

[126] This is indirectly confirmed by AG *Tizzano*'s Opinion in *Commission v Tetra Laval* (n 123) paras 83–9. See also Nicholson, Cardell, and McKenna (n 64) 145; Kalintiri (n 84) 1311; and Section 3.2.1.

[127] Similarly Craig (n 3) 434; Kalintiri (n 84) 1310: 'the *Tetra Laval* formula has the capacity to turn marginal control in a much stricter form of judicial scrutiny, which may sometimes come very close to almost entirely eliminating any "margin of appreciation" that the Commission is said to enjoy'. Cf. *Bertelsmann and Others v Impala* (n 122) para 69: ' ... while, in the context of the control of concentrations, a field in which the Commission has a margin of assessment with regard to economic matters, review by the [GC] is limited to establishing whether the evidence relied on is factually accurate and to establishing the absence of a manifest error of assessment, it none the less remains the case that the correctness, completeness and reliability of the facts on which a decision is based may be the subject of judicial review ... '.

With regard to the findings of fact, the review is clearly more intense, in that the issue is to verify objectively and materially the accuracy of certain facts and the correctness of the conclusions drawn in order to establish whether certain known facts make it possible to prove the existence of other facts to be ascertained. By contrast, with regard to the complex economic assessments made by the Commission, review by the [Union] judicature is necessarily more limited, since the latter has to respect the broad discretion inherent in that kind of assessment and may not substitute its own point of view for that of the body which is institutionally responsible for making those assessments.[128]

Unsurprisingly, there is thus broad agreement today that the scope of judicial control of complex economic assessments, particularly in merger cases, has reached a satisfactory level. For the purpose of the following analysis, it is important to bear in mind that in any of the three stages of the *Tetra Laval* test, the Union courts need to take a clear view on the *relevance* of the facts that need to be proved, which ultimately allows them to review, according to variable degrees, the substantive soundness of the administration's evaluation of those facts. This is particularly obvious with respect to the second part of the test that seems to overlap with the requirements under the duty of care (see Section 3.5).

3.3.2.3 Standard of proof in respect of complex technical/ scientific facts and risk/hazard assessments

In respect of highly complex technical or scientific facts, notably risk and hazard assessments required by the precautionary principle that are replete of uncertainty, the Union courts have adopted a modified approach set out for the very first time in *Pfizer*.[129] It is submitted that the relevant case law describes very well the situation of scientific uncertainty and factual complexity with which expert executive bodies are faced in the framework of a decision-making process designed to implement the precautionary principle, and which, in turn, requires a further limitation of the scope of judicial review. In addition, it pertinently shows the inextricable link between cognitive processes and policy choices that increasingly blurs the cognition/volition dichotomy for the purposes of categorising discretion. In *Du Pont de Nemours (France) and Others*,[130] drawing notably on *Pfizer*, the GC summarized the case law, *inter alia*, as follows (quotations omitted):

136 Within the process leading to the adoption ... of appropriate measures to prevent specific, potential risks to public health, safety and the environment by reason of the precautionary principle, three successive stages can be identified: firstly, identification of the potentially adverse effects arising from a phenomenon; secondly, assessment of the risks to public health, safety and the environment which are related to that phenomenon; thirdly,

---

[128] AG *Tizzano* (n 126) para 86.   [129] *Pfizer Animal Health v Council* (n 41).
[130] Case T-31/07 *Du Pont de Nemours (France) and Others v Commission* [2013] EU:T:2013:167, paras 133 et seq., and 155 et seq.; see also Case T-475/07 *Dow AgroSciences and Others v Commission* [2011] EU:T:2011:445, paras 144 et seq.

when the potential risks identified exceed the threshold of what is acceptable for society, risk management by the adoption of appropriate protective measures ...

139 A scientific risk assessment is a scientific process consisting, in so far as possible, in the identification and characterisation of a hazard, the assessment of exposure to that hazard and the characterisation of the risk.

140 The scientific risk assessment is not required to provide the institutions with conclusive scientific evidence of the reality of the risk and the seriousness of the potential adverse effects were that risk to become a reality. A situation in which the precautionary principle is applied by definition coincides with a situation in which there is scientific uncertainty. Furthermore, the adoption of a preventive measure, or, conversely, its withdrawal or relaxation, cannot be made subject to proof of the lack of any risk, in so far as such proof is generally impossible to give in scientific terms since zero risk does not exist in practice ... However, a preventive measure cannot properly be based on a purely hypothetical approach to the risk, founded on mere conjecture which has not been scientifically verified ...

141 Indeed, the scientific risk assessment should be based on the best scientific data available and should be undertaken in an independent, objective and transparent manner ...

143 ... [A] preventive measure may be taken only if the risk, although the reality and extent thereof have not been 'fully' demonstrated by conclusive scientific evidence, appears nevertheless to be adequately backed up by the scientific data available at the time when the measure was taken ...

145 The responsibility for determining the level of risk which is deemed unacceptable for society lies, provided that the applicable rules are observed, with the institutions responsible for the political choice of determining an appropriate level of protection for society. It is for those institutions to determine the critical probability threshold for adverse effects on public health, safety and the environment and for the degree of those potential effects which, in their judgment, is no longer acceptable for society and above which it is necessary, in the interests of protecting public health, safety and the environment, to take preventive measures in spite of the existing scientific uncertainty ...

Moreover, as to the scope of judicial review in that field, the Union courts have re-iterated their consistent case law as to the reduced control of executive discretionary powers. In *France v Commission*, the GC accordingly relied on the *Remia* formula, the manifest error test, and the related standard of proof as recognized in *Tetra Laval*, as well as on its power to exercise an intensified review on procedural grounds, notably on the basis of the duty of care.[131]

The above considerations in the case law command the following conclusions.

First, it is striking that neither in *Du Pont de Nemours (France) and Others* nor in *France v Commission*, the GC made reference to the dictum according to which 'the broad discretion of the authorities of the European Union, which implies limited judicial review of its exercise, applies not only to the nature and scope of the measures to be taken but also, to some extent, to the finding of the basic facts'.[132] This may

---

[131] *France v Commission* (n 107) paras 84–9; confirmed on appeal by Case C-601/11 P *France v Commission* [2013] EU:C:2013:465.

[132] See also Case C-77/09 *Gowan Comércio Internacional e Serviços* [2010] ECR I-13533, para 56, relying on the *Remia* test ('whether the facts ... have been accurately stated'). See, however, more recently, in respect of REACH measures, Case T-93/10 *Bilbaína de Alquitranes and Others v ECHA* [2013] EU:T:2013:106, para 77, as confirmed on appeal by *Bilbaína de Alquitranes and Others v ECHA*

be interpreted as an attempt to intensify judicial review on factual grounds, but has largely been overruled by the more recent—in the meantime established—case law of the ECJ to the contrary.[133] It nonetheless remains that this case law does not recognize an unfettered executive discretion as to the finding or the assessment of those 'basic facts' in that field.[134] The ECJ still requires the authorities having adopted the challenged act to show that they have 'actually exercised their discretion, which presupposes the taking into consideration of all the *relevant* factors and circumstances of the situation the act was intended to regulate' (emphasis added).[135] This seems to be broadly in line with the requirements under the duty of care as established in *Technische Universität München* (see Section 3.5) and highlights once again the importance of evaluating the *relevance* of the facts for the purpose of the discretionary assessment,[136] in respect of which the Union courts seem to retain an unfettered power of appraisal.[137]

Second, the case law appears to take account of the fact that there is an important overlap between the cognition of highly complex facts and the 'volition' or policy aspects of the exercise of expert discretion, which appears much more pronounced in the field of scientific risk assessment than in complex economic—even prognostic—evaluations in EU competition law. This might also have induced the Union courts to accept a certain degree of executive discretion as to the 'finding of the basic facts' underlying the risk or hazard assessment. The required scientific assessments are particularly demanding in terms of factual complexity. They presuppose the availability of sufficient scientific expertise and knowledge to detect and recognize the reality of *primary* facts, i.e. available scientific data, to understand, prioritize, and select them according to their relevance, and to process them by using the appropriate methodology—also to be chosen among different available tests—in order to determine *secondary* or deductive (potential or uncertain) facts. The latter provide concrete meaning to or fill with content broadly shaped legal notions, such as risk, hazard, or danger under, e.g. the REACH or CLP regulations,[138]

(n 63) para 20; Case T-134/13 *Polynt and Sitre v ECHA* [2015] EU:T:2015:254, para 53; confirmed on appeal by Case C-323/15 P *Polynt v ECHA* [2017] EU:C:2017:207.

[133] Cf., in particular, *Afton Chemical* (n 63) paras 33–4.

[134] See also Türk (n 86) 139: 'seems to indicate a deferential approach based on a 'manifest error' test'.

[135] Cf. *Enviro Tech (Europe)* (n 63) para 62, still stating more ambiguously that 'where a [Union] authority is called upon, in the performance of its duties, to make complex assessments, its discretion applies also, to a certain extent, to the finding of facts underlying its action', followed by the statement of principle made in *Technische Universität München* (n 96) para 14, according to which it is the 'duty of the competent institution to examine carefully and impartially all the relevant aspects of the individual case'. The formulation has changed, as quoted in *Afton Chemical* (n 63) paras 33–4; *Bilbaína de Alquitranes and Others v ECHA* (n 63) para 20.

[136] *Technische Universität München* (n 96) para 14 and (n 135).

[137] This is confirmed by *Gowan Comércio Internacional e Serviços* (n 132) para 57, and Case C-691/15 P *Commission v Bilbaína de Alquitranes and Others* [2017] EU:C:2017:882 para 35.

[138] Regulation (EC) No 1907/2006 of the European Parliament and of the Council of 18 December 2006 concerning the Registration, Evaluation, Authorisation and Restriction of Chemicals (REACH), establishing a European Chemicals Agency ... OJ 2006 L 396; Regulation (EC) No 1272/2008 of the European Parliament and of the Council of 16 December 2008 on classification, labelling and packaging of substances and mixtures ... OJ 2008 L 353.

in particular that of 'level of risk deemed acceptable for society', whose existence is not amenable to full proof. Already the evaluation as such of the existence of a 'risk' implies the making of important value judgments going far beyond the sphere of cognition. This is the more so when it comes to assessing a given 'level of risk' and whether or not that level exceeds the threshold of what is acceptable or the appropriate level of protection for society. The latter assessment of the expert administration normally leads, quite to the contrary, to making a strategic health/ consumer protection policy choice that is typical of 'volition'. This also shows that those indeterminate legal notions are hardly amenable to legal conceptualization, as has been possible, at least to some extent, in EU competition law (see Section 3.2.3). Indeed, at various stages of that decision-making process, in the light of the legal objectives pursued and the interests to be protected, the experts will have to make appropriate value judgments on the finding of the relevant facts, the way in which they should be chosen, processed, and verified, and the conclusions to be drawn from them against the background of what they believe to be 'a level of risk deemed acceptable for society', an 'appropriate level of protection for society', or to be 'appropriate measures to prevent specific, potential risks' notwithstanding prevailing scientific uncertainty. It has therefore been rightly pointed out that the reference to scientific expertise introduces the requirement for specifically structured, rational deliberation in administrative and regulatory decision making[139] that, precisely because of the strong interlinkage between complex 'cognitive' and 'volitive' appraisals, may neither be entrusted to the judges nor be duplicated in the court proceedings. This is why the Union courts state that the responsibility for determining the level of risk which is deemed unacceptable—or in other words, the critical probability threshold for adverse effects on public health, safety, and the environment and the degree of those potential effects—and, conversely, the appropriate level of protection for society, ultimately lies with the administration. The latter enjoys broad policy discretion to that effect and for the purposes of deciding on the need to take preventive action under the precautionary principle in spite of the existing scientific uncertainty. Hence, there can be no doubt about the need to limit the standard of judicial review to the finding of a 'manifest error' in order to avoid that the judges substitute their own assessment for that of the expert administration.[140] Nonetheless, the judges have to make sure that the ultimate policy choice is being made by the rule-making institution itself, rather than the expert bodies assisting and advising it in the preparation of the rules to be enacted, e.g. via a mere 'rubber-stamping' exercise. This is rendered possible by enhanced

---

[139] HCH Hofmann, 'Inquisitorial Procedures and General Principles of Law: The Duty of Care in the Case Law of the European Court of Justice' in L Jacobs (ed), *The Nature of Inquisitorial Processes in Administrative Regimes* (Ashgate, 2013), 153–66, 162.

[140] See, e.g. *Enviro Tech (Europe)* (n 63) para 47, 'where the [Union] authorities have a broad discretion, in particular as to the assessment of highly complex scientific and technical facts in order to determine the nature and scope of the measures which they adopt, review by the [Union] judicature is limited to verifying whether there has been a manifest error of appraisal or a misuse of powers, or whether those authorities have manifestly exceeded the limits of their discretion. In such a context, the [Union] judicature cannot substitute its assessment of scientific and technical facts for that of the institutions on which alone the Treaty has placed that task'.

judicial review on procedural grounds, *inter alia*, on the basis of the principle of care that has been clothed in some broader language ('should be based on the best scientific data available and should be undertaken in an independent, objective and transparent manner').

Third, in the face of the high level of scientific uncertainty, the Union courts are supposed not only to apply a limited standard of review but also to loosen the standard of proof to be met by the deciding authority, without leaving it with unfettered discretion. Their continuous reliance on the *Tetra Laval* formula[141] should not belie the fact that they were necessarily obliged to modify or depart from the 'convincing evidence' test by holding that the scientific risk assessment as such does not require the sampling of 'conclusive scientific evidence of the reality of the risk and the seriousness of the potential adverse effects were that risk to become a reality'. The Union courts recognize that the adoption of a preventive measure 'cannot be made subject to proof of the lack of any risk, in so far as such proof is generally impossible to give in scientific terms since zero risk does not exist in practice', yet without allowing the administration to base itself 'on a purely hypothetical approach to the risk, founded on mere conjecture which has not been scientifically verified'. It is therefore necessary for the judges to double check whether, at the time of adoption of the measure at issue, the administration has gathered 'the best scientific data available' in light of the most recent results of international research and has undertaken a scientific risk assessment as completely and thoroughly as possible and 'in an independent, objective and transparent manner'.[142] According to the ECJ, the administration's assessment may not have lacunae and must contain complete, precise, and definitive findings and conclusions capable of removing all reasonable scientific doubt as to the effects of a given activity on the environment.[143] This again displays strong similarities with the obligations under the duty of care[144] and raises the question as to who should be the ultimate arbiter in deciding on the *relevance* of the (best available) primary facts that are, or should be, the subject of the scientific or technical assessment under judicial scrutiny.

---

[141] *France v Commission* (n 107) para 87: 'duty to establish whether the evidence relied on is factually accurate, reliable and consistent, whether that evidence contains all the information which must be taken into account in order to assess a complex situation, and whether it is capable of substantiating the conclusions drawn from it.'

[142] Cf. *Du Pont de Nemours (France) and Others v Commission* (n 130) paras 140–3, drawing notably on *Pfizer Animal Health v Council* (n 41) paras 142 et seq. See also *Gowan Comércio Internacional e Serviços* (n 132) para 75: 'a comprehensive assessment of the risk to health based on the most reliable scientific data available and the most recent results of international research'; similarly, Case T-333/10 *ATC and Others v Commission* [2013] EU:T:2013:451, para 85; *Dow AgroSciences and Others v Commission* (n 130) para 85, drawing on Case C-236/01 *Monsanto Agricoltura Italia and Others* [2003] ECR I-8105, paras 106 and 113.

[143] Cf. Case C-441/17 *Commission v Poland* [2018] EU:C:2018:255 para 114, as regards Article 6(3) of the Habitats Directive (Council Directive 92/43/EEC of 21 May 1992 on the conservation of natural habitats and of wild fauna and flora OJ 1992 L 206, 7, as amended by Council Directive 2013/17/EU of 13 May 2013 OJ 2013 L 158, 193).

[144] Hofmann (n 139) 164.

3.4 Judicial review of discretion proper (volition), manifest error, and proportionality

Pursuant to consistent case law, the 'manifest error of appraisal' standard of judicial review also applies to executive discretionary acts in the broad sense that imply a choice between different policies or objectives (discretion proper or pure volition) or the balancing between conflicting interests the administration is empowered to make within the boundaries of the normative programme provided for in the law. For judicial review purposes, this presents the advantage that, in principle, there is no need to draw a neat distinction between the (anyway overlapping) cognition and volition aspects of executive discretion. Hence, in an area of evolving and complex technology, e.g. the development of methods for testing the quality of petrol and diesel fuels in *Afton Chemical*, the institutions have a broad discretion not only as to the assessment of highly complex scientific and technical facts, but also for the purposes of determining the nature and scope of the measures to be adopted. Accordingly, the Union judicature's review has to be limited to verifying whether the exercise of such powers has been vitiated by a manifest error of appraisal or a misuse of powers, or whether the institutions have manifestly exceeded the limits of their discretion.[145] Similarly, in the field of EU monetary policy implementation, the case law has stressed the need to verify whether the administration exceeds the legal bounds of its discretion or, conversely, has observed the normative programme provided for in the rules framing the exercise of executive discretion. Thus, in *Accorinti* the GC held that, in the context of the tasks conferred on it for the purposes of defining and implementing the EU monetary policy, under Articles 127 TFEU and 282 TFEU and Article 18 of its Statute, in particular by intervening on the capital markets and managing credit operations the ECB enjoys broad discretion, 'the exercise of which entails complex evaluations of an economic and social nature and of rapidly-changing situations, which must be carried out in the context of the Eurosystem, or even of the European Union as a whole'. According to the GC, the exercise of that discretion implies the need for the ECB to foresee and evaluate complex and uncertain economic developments, such as the development of capital markets, the monetary mass, and the rate of inflation, which affect the proper functioning of the Eurosystem and payment and credit systems, and also to make political, economic, and social choices in which it is required to weigh up and decide between the different objectives referred to in Article 127(1) TFEU, the main objective of which is the maintenance of price stability.[146] A comparable standard of review

---

[145] This is arguably the way in which should be understood *Afton Chemical* (n 63) para 28.

[146] *Accorinti and Others v ECB* (n 29) para 68. See similarly, *Gauweiler and Others* (n 85) para 68: '[a]s regards judicial review of compliance with those conditions, since the ESCB is required, when it prepares and implements an open market operations programme ... , to make choices of a technical nature and to undertake forecasts and complex assessments, it must be allowed, in that context, a broad discretion'; Opinion of AG *Cruz Villalón* in *Gauweiler and Others* (n 85) para 111; Case C-493/17 *Weiss and Others* [2018] EU:C:2018:1000 paras 30, 73; Opinion of AG *Wathelet*, op. cit., paras 116–17.

has been recognized in respect of regulatory and executive discretion in the field of agricultural policy.[147]

It is submitted that the principle of proportionality, which is part of the general principles of EU law, constitutes by far the most common standard of judicial review to be applied in the context of policy discretion or discretion proper. This is inherent in the proportionality test that needs to be carried out in relation to a number of different measures—among which the administration has to choose—the impact of which on various, potentially conflicting interests is to be ascertained in terms of suitability, necessity, and appropriateness for attaining the objective pursued by the rules in question. In fact, according to settled case law, the principle of proportionality requires that EU measures do not exceed the limits of what is appropriate and necessary in order to achieve the objectives legitimately pursued by the legislation in question; when there is a choice between several appropriate measures recourse must be had to the least onerous, and the disadvantages caused must not be disproportionate to the aims pursued.[148] This chapter is not the place to engage in an in-depth discussion of the proportionality test for the purposes of judicial review or otherwise.[149] Suffice it to say that, in the context of policy discretion, quite ironically, a plea based on the breach of the proportionality principle only rarely succeeds in the courts. The main reason for this development is that the case law has closely connected its review to the test of manifest error by sanctioning only 'manifestly inappropriate' measures or policy choices with regard to the objective pursued.[150] This has given rise to harsh criticism because, in the absence of their outright disproportionate or arbitrary character, EU discretionary acts, in particular, those of general application, mostly escape judicial censorship, especially if the proportionality test is carried out on a stand-alone basis, i.e. disconnected from the review of the observance of fundamental rights[151] or the precautionary principle.[152] It is arguable

---

[147] *ATC and Others v Commission* (n 142) para 64: 'The exercise of that discretionary power implies the need for the EU legislature to anticipate and evaluate ecological, scientific, technical and economic changes of a complex and uncertain nature'.

[148] See, e.g. *Polynt and Sitre v ECHA* (n 132) para 104.

[149] Studies in that regard are abundant; cf. G de Búrca, 'The Principle of Proportionality and its Application in EC Law' (1993) 13 *YEL* 105; N Emiliou, *The Principle of Proportionality in European Law (A Comparative Study)* (Kluwer Law International, 1996), the contributions in E Ellis (ed), *The Principle of Proportionality in the Law of Europe* (Hart Publishing, 1999); T-I Harbo, 'The Function of the Proportionality Principle in EU Law' (2010) 16 *ELJ* 158; W Sauter, 'Proportionality in EU Law: A Balancing Act?' (2013) 15 *CYELS* 439.

[150] *Gowan Comércio Internacional e Serviços* (n 132) para 82; Case C-15/10 *Etimine* [2011] ECR I-6681, para 125; Case C-296/16 P *Dextro Energy v Commission* [2017] EU:C:2017:437, para 50. See also *Bilbaína de Alquitranes and Others* (n 132) para 115; *Polynt and Sitre v ECHA* (n 132) para 105. Similarly, in EU competition law, see *Commission v Alrosa* (n 9) paras 41–2.

[151] See the criticism raised by, in particular, German scholars in respect of Case C-280/93 *Germany v Council (Re: Bananas)* [1994] ECR I-4973; e.g. U Everling, 'Will Europe Slip on Bananas? The Banana Judgment of the Court of Justice and National Courts' (1996) 33 *CMLRev* 401, 418–19: 'By submitting the principle of proportionality to the discretion of the institutions, the Court […] grants them a carte blanche and reduces judicial control to a minimum'; N Reich, 'Judge-made "Europa à la carte": Some Remarks on Recent Conflicts between European and German Constitutional Law Provoked by the Banana Litigation' (1996) 7 *EJIL* 103, 109–10.

[152] A Alemanno, 'Annotation to ECJ Case C-77/09 *Gowan Comércio Internacional e Serviços* [2010] ECR I-13533' (2011) 48 *CMLRev* 1329, 1336 et seq.

that the proportionality test is largely unfit to induce the Union courts to engage in a more intrusive review of executive discretionary powers, the exercise of which requires choosing the most appropriate policy measure among a variety of (legally valid) options. The judges are reluctant to embark on such avenue because it takes them closer to a situation in which they need to make their own value judgment on the most appropriate measure. This, however, entails the risk of overstepping the court's office by entering the sphere of core discretionary assessment, the substitution of which is strictly prohibited by the case law. This is even more true in cases where the administration is empowered to make strategic policy choices on the basis of complex (scientific) assessments, e.g. risk evaluation, without it being possible to draw a clear dividing line between the cognition and volition aspects of the exercise of discretion (see Section 3.2.4).[153] Therefore, other tools of judicial review less amenable to such criticism, in particular, on procedural grounds, have been devised in order to increase the effectiveness of judicial review in that regard (see Section 3.5).[154]

3.5 Judicial review on procedural grounds: the principle of care and the duty to state reasons

It is submitted that, at the latest, since the landmark ruling *Technische Universität München*, judicial review of executive discretion, if not the EU system of judicial control as a whole, rests on the axiomatic understanding according to which the restrained scope of review on the substance needs to be counterbalanced by a more intense review of the observance of procedural rules and guarantees. Indeed, according to paragraph 14 of that ruling,

> where the ... institutions have such a power of appraisal, respect for the rights guaranteed by the [Union] legal order in administrative procedures is of even more fundamental importance. Those guarantees include, in particular, the duty of the competent institution to examine carefully and impartially all the relevant aspects of the individual case, the right of the person concerned to make his views known and to have an adequately reasoned decision. Only in this way can the Court verify whether the factual and legal elements upon which the exercise of the power of appraisal depends were present.[155]

It is quite safe to assume that legal theory and sociology emphasizing procedural justice in the face of uncertainty as to the just or correct outcome of a decision-making process have widely contributed to that principled statement.[156] Moreover,

---

[153] This is particularly obvious in *Gowan Comércio Internacional e Serviços* (n 132).

[154] This is also strongly advocated by Alemanno (n 152) 1339 et seq.

[155] *Technische Universität München* (n 96) para 14. See also Case C-405/07 P *Netherlands v Commission* [2008] ECR I-8301, para 56; *Gowan Comércio Internacional e Serviços* (n 132) para 57; Case C-505/09 P *Commission v Estonia* [2012] EU:C:2012:179, para 95; *Gauweiler and Others* (n 85) paras 69 and 75; *Weiss and Others* (n 146) para 30; on the specific aspect of care in this judgment, see P Schammo, 'The European Central Bank's Duty of Care for the Unity and Integrity of the Internal Market' (2017) 42 *ELR* 3, 16 et seq. Cf. also Case T-140/15 *Aurora v CPVO—SESVanderhave* (M 02205) [2017] EU:T:2017:830, paras 70 et seq.

[156] See the famous words of *R v Jhering*: 'Formality is the sworn enemy of the arbitrary, and the twin sister of freedom', cited after J Schwarze, *European Administrative Law* (Sweet & Maxwell, 1992) 1178;

even though it seemed to be inspired exclusively by 'rule of law' and dignitary considerations, including the need to enhance the protection of individual rights, this case law has been understood by many commentators as confirming concepts designed to enhance the (procedural) legitimacy not only of the Union courts' office, but also the transparency and accountability of the EU's decision-making processes and its functioning as a whole.[157] As regards more specifically executive discretion, studies analysing the enhancement of judicial review on procedural grounds in the face of limited substantive review of discretionary appraisals, as emphasized in *Technische Universität München*, have rightly focused on the principle of care, the scope of which is supposed to be commensurate with 'the duty of the competent institution to examine carefully and impartially all the relevant aspects of the individual case', as well as on the duty to state reasons.[158] Since Chapter 10 of this book is devoted to analysing the principle of care, the following indications shall suffice to highlight both its importance and potential for further evolution, jointly with the duty to state reasons, for the purpose of reviewing effectively the exercise of administrative discretion.

First, although the principle of care is not expressly mentioned in Article 41 of the Charter,[159] it constitutes a fundamental procedural device, derived from administrative investigatory powers or the inquisitorial principle (*Offizialmaxime* or *Untersuchungsgrundsatz*) and the burden of proof, in particular, in adversarial

---

and Rawls' concept of 'pure procedural justice' which 'obtains when there is no independent criterion for the right result: instead there is a correct or fair procedure such that the outcome is likewise correct or fair, whatever it is, provided that the procedure has been properly followed'; see J Rawls, *A Theory of Justice* (Harvard University Press, 1999) 75; for a more recent account, see LB Solum, 'Procedural Justice' (2004) 78 *SCL Rev* 181.

[157] E.g. L Azoulay, 'The Judge and the Community's Administrative Governance' in C Joerges and R Dehousse (eds), *Good Governance in Europe's Integrated Market* (OUP, 2002), 109, 119 et seq.; Everson (n 59) 214; C Joerges and J Neyer, 'From Intergovernmental Bargaining to Deliberative Political Processes: The Constitutionalisation of Comitology' (1997) 3 *ELJ* 273, 287. See however Nehl, *Europäisches Verwaltungsverfahren* (n 66) 143, who emphasizes that this case law should not be misinterpreted as being a first intentional step on the part of the Union courts towards fostering a pluralist deliberation model as experienced in US administrative law; cf. on this Stewart (n 57) 1711 et seq.; as to the comparison with the EU, see Shapiro (n 87) 33 et seq.; P Craig, 'Democracy and Rule-making within the EC: An Empirical and Normative Assessment' (1997) 3 *ELJ* 105, 120 et seq. More recently, see J Mendes, 'Discretion, Care, and Public Interests in the EU Administration: Probing the Limits of Law' (2016) 53 *CMLRev* 419, 427 et seq.

[158] Cf. Nehl, *Principles of Administrative Procedure* (n 66) 103 et seq.; also Nehl, *Europäisches Verwaltungsverfahren* (n 66) 323 et seq.; Hofmann (n 139) 156 et seq.; Türk (n 86) 132–4; and Mendes (n 157) 427 et seq., who emphasizes the potential of the principle of care better to include public interest considerations.

[159] See B Mihaescu Evans, *The Right to Good Administration at the Crossroads of the Various Sources of Fundamental Rights in the EU Integrated Administrative System* (Nomos, 2015) 392 et seq., with further references. As to the terminological confusion in the case law related to the so-called principle of good or sound administration, see HP Nehl, 'Good Administration as Procedural Right and/or General Principle?' in HCH Hofmann and A Türk (eds), *Legal Challenges in EU Administrative Law: Towards an Integrated Administration* (Edward Elgar, 2009), 322–51. See, however, more recently the unfortunate statement in Case C-337/15 P *European Ombudsman v Staelen* [2017] EU:C:2017:256, para 34: 'the duty to act diligently which is inherent in the principle of sound administration and applies generally to the actions of the EU administration in its relations with the public requires that that administration act with care and caution'.

decision making, ensuring that the factual basis for the exercise of discretionary powers is as complete and accurate as possible in the sense that the administration is enabled to take its decision in the best possible conditions in terms of both the quantity and the quality of the information needed.[160] Those objectives are pertinently summarized in *ATC*:

Compliance with the duty of the Commission to gather, in a diligent manner, the factual elements necessary for the exercise of its broad discretion as well as the review thereof by the ... Union Courts are all the more important because the exercise of that discretion is only subject to a limited judicial review of the merits, confined to examining whether a manifest error has been committed. Thus, the obligation for the competent institution to examine carefully and impartially all the relevant elements of the individual case is a necessary prerequisite to enable the ... Union Courts to ascertain whether the elements of fact and of law on which the exercise of that broad discretion depends were present.[161]

Second, although clothed in procedural language, the observance of the principle of care has a strong connotation of substantive review and legality of the exercise of discretion, because it necessarily implies that the judges make a value judgment on the *relevance* of the (primary) facts needed for the purposes of the discretionary appraisal. It has therefore also been described as a 'hybrid' process standard enabling the judges to quash administrative decisions that display doubts about their substantive accuracy.[162] This is particularly important in the face of hardly reviewable administrative discretion. While in such a case the judges are reluctant or even prohibited to substitute their own assessment for that of the decision maker, the principle of care grants them a flexible tool of judicial control that is, at face value, procedural in nature and shields them from being accused of illegally encroaching upon administrative discretion. From a sociological point of view this phenomenon is easily explained since, as Shapiro pertinently put it, judges consider themselves as being the experts on procedure, but not in all areas of substantive policy making in which they are called upon to exercise judicial review.[163] A closer look at the case law in US administrative law clearly shows the potential for evolution in that respect. In this context, the courts have increasingly preferred to rely on the 'adequate consideration principle'—which is broadly comparable to the principle of care—and to scrutinize the *relevance* of the facts and interests involved rather than to apply the traditional and restrained substantive 'arbitrary and capricious standard' of review.[164] Such a

---

[160] Nehl, *Principles of Administrative Procedure* (n 66) 109 et seq.; Hofmann (n 139) 156 et seq.; Mendes (n 157) 434.

[161] *ATC and Others v Commission* (n 142) para 84.

[162] Nehl, *Principles of Administrative Procedure* (n 66) 104–5, 107–9, 118–19.

[163] Shapiro (n 87) 37.

[164] Ibid., 36–8; see also Türk (n 86) 140. Cf., in particular, Stewart (n 57) 1782–3: 'Given the diversity and multiplicity of interests that may be represented as a result of increased participation rights, preparation of opinions that demonstrate "adequate consideration" of parties' contentions may impose a heavy burden on the agency [...]. In effect, the "adequate consideration" principle may become a convenient formula for reversing agency decisions which the court finds unpalatable, since it can almost always find some aspect of the controversy that has been overlooked or some contention that arguably has not been given its due. [...] Moreover, completeness in agency records and opinions alone may not be sufficient; what counts as "adequate consideration" of an issue or interest necessarily turns on the weight or value to be assigned to that issue or interest. [...] Accordingly, in applying the adequate

prospect is further confirmed by comparative analysis within the EU. In German administrative law, for instance, the lack of a proper investigation and gathering of relevant facts is constantly considered as a substantive defect in the exercise of discretionary powers (*Ermessensdefizit*) rather than a procedural irregularity,[165] whereas in France, the case law seems to hesitate between manifest error and procedural defect.[166] It is therefore unsurprising that also the Union courts sometimes tend to blend the concepts of manifest error and care,[167] notwithstanding the fundamental requirement to distinguish neatly between substantive and procedural legality (see Section 2.2.2).[168]

Third, a parallel potential has been raised with respect to the duty to state reasons[169] that may be characterized as a procedural twin or tandem-concept jointly with the principle of care, mainly because it provides a reliable material basis for double checking *ex post facto* the fulfilment of the duty of care in the course of the administrative procedure, including the way in which the relevant facts have been processed.[170] However, the scope of protection of the duty to state reasons under Article 296(2) TFEU tends to be more limited than that provided for by the principle of care. It requires the administration only to set out the *essential* reasons on which rests its decision or the reasons of decisive importance to that effect, depending on the

consideration requirement courts must employ some judgment as to the minimum weight to be accorded the relevant affected interests [...]. In the past, this judgment has been expressed and enforced through the "arbitrary and capricious" standard of judicial review which has been utilized quite sparingly by the courts to set aside agency decisions that strike a plainly unreasonable balance among relevant considerations. [...] For judges who accordingly wish to impose stricter limits on agency choice, the "adequate consideration" principle provides an alternative to the arbitrary and capricious standard that is framed in procedural terms and, since the agency on remand makes the ultimate policy decision, does not so conspicuously flaunt discretionary judicial power over policy choices'.

[165] As to the corresponding concept of *Ermessensdefizit*, see K Schönenbroicher, 'Ermessen' in T Mann and others (eds), *Verwaltungsverfahrensgesetz* (Nomos, 2014), 1346–1420 VwVfG, paras 205–9, with further references.

[166] As regards French administrative law, cf. Henry (n 103) 22 et seq., who considers a breach of the principle of diligence as a specific category of manifest error (*erreur manifeste d'appréciation*). However, English law seems to qualify such a defect as a procedural error; cf. ZM Nedjatigil, 'Judicial Control of Administrative Discretion: A Comparative Study' (1985) 14 *Anglo Am Law Rev* 97, 100 et seq.; P Neill (ed), *Administrative Justice. Some Necessary Reforms, Report of the Committee of the JUSTICE-All Souls Review of Administrative Law in the United Kingdom* (Clarendon Press, 1988), 18.

[167] Paradigmatic in this sense, see *Commission v Scott* (n 9) paras 72, 79, and 84; *Commission v Bilbaína de Alquitranes and Others* (n 137) para 35, stating, *inter alia*: 'The exercise of that discretion is not, however, excluded from review by the Court. In particular, where a party claims that the institution competent in the matter has committed a manifest error of assessment, the EU judicature must verify whether that institution has examined, carefully and impartially, all the relevant facts of the individual case on which that assessment was based.' Similarly ambiguous, see Case T-689/13 *Bilbaína de Alquitranes and Others v Commission* [2015] EU:T:2015:767, para 30: ' ... the Commission committed a manifest error of assessment in that ... it failed to comply with its obligation to take into consideration all the relevant factors and circumstances ... '.

[168] See also Nehl, 'Good Administration' (n 159) 333–5.

[169] M Shapiro, 'The Giving Reasons Requirement' (1992) *Univ Chic Leg Forum* 179, 179: a procedural guarantee 'replete with potential for development, particularly for development of a pervasive and deeply intrusive style of judicial review of administrative ... decision-making'; J Mashaw, 'Reasoned Administration: The European Union, the United States, and the Project of Democratic Governance' (2007) 76 *G Wash Intl L Rev* 99, 112 et seq., talking about the 'proceduralization of rationality'.

[170] Nehl, *Principles of Administrative Procedure* (n 66) 119–21.

factual and legal context. It is thus not necessary for the statement of reasons to go into *all* the *relevant* facts and points of law that have been raised by the parties during the administrative procedure.[171] Therefore, even though the duty to state reasons guarantees the parties a minimum '*ex post* dialogue' with the (responsive) decision maker, it appears less amenable to its transformation into a 'dialogue requirement' than some commentators have suspected.[172] It nonetheless remains that the plea based on the breach of duty to state reasons pursuant to Article 296(2) TFEU, as an essential procedural requirement within the meaning of Article 263(2) TFEU,[173] has become a powerful weapon in the hands of annulment applicants in order to overcome some of the shortcomings of judicial review on the merits. Against the background of its twofold objective—helping understand both the persons concerned and the judges the reasons for adopting the contested measure[174]—the obligation to state reasons constitutes the central nexus between the administrative procedure at the end of which the contested act is adopted on the one hand, and the exercise of judicial review by the Union courts on the other. Therefore, its ultimate goal is that of ensuring effective judicial protection within the meaning of Article 47 of the Charter,[175] which is the more difficult to attain in the face of complex assessments or the exercise of discretionary powers regarding which the intensity of judicial review on the merits is necessarily reduced.[176] These statements also rest on the fact that, in principle, a breach of that duty suffices to justify annulment of the contested decision without there being the possibility for the administration to cure that breach during the court proceedings.[177] Moreover, as already mentioned in Section 2.2.2, as a matter of public policy, the Union judicature may and even must raise a breach of the duty to state reasons of its own motion without exceeding the scope of the subject matter of the case or deciding *ultra petita*.[178] It is nonetheless submitted that the duty to state reasons presents less potential for effectively reviewing the exercise of administrative discretion than the principle of care as a judicial device displaying a strong connotation of substantive legality and review. As already recalled in Section 2.2.2, the case law has rightly emphasized that judicial control of the

---

[171] See, e.g. *Commission v Ireland and Others* (n 44) para 77; Case C-72/15 *Rosneft* [2017] EU:C:2017:236, para 122; Case C-80/16 *ArcelorMittal Atlantique et Lorraine* [2017] EU:C:2017:588, para 52. See, however, Joined Cases C-329/93, C-62/95, and C-63/95 *Bremer Vulkan and Others v Commission* [1996] ECR I-5151, para 32 ('all the relevant factors of the case').

[172] Cf., in particular, both Shapiro and Mashaw (n 169); differently, see Türk (n 86) 134–5.

[173] Its fundamental importance as a general principle of law has been underlined in Joined Cases T-265/04, T-292/04 and T-504/04 *Tirrenia di Navigazione and Others v Commission* [2009] EU:T:2009:48, para 99; cf. also more recently *Weiss and Others* (n 146) para 30.

[174] Cf., e.g. *Commission v Ireland and Others* (n 44) para 77: 'the statement of reasons required by Article [296(2) TFEU] must be appropriate to the measure at issue and must disclose in a clear and unequivocal fashion the reasoning followed by the institution which adopted the measure in question in such a way as to enable the persons concerned to ascertain the reasons for the measure and to enable the competent [Union] Court to exercise its power of review'.

[175] See, in particular, Joined Cases C-402/05 P and C-415/05 P *Kadi and Others v Council and Commission* [2008] ECR I-6351, paras 112–16. For a recent account of this protective rationale in the field of EU public procurement, see F Van den Berghe, 'L'obligation de motivation des pouvoirs adjudicateurs dans les marchés publics de l'Union européenne' (2017) 3 *CDE* 649.

[176] Cf. recently *Weiss and Others* (n 146) para 30.

[177] *Commission v Ireland and Others* (n 44) para 61.   [178] Ibid., para 34.

observance of the duty to state (sufficient) reasons may not mutate into a disguised review of the substantive correctness or the reasonableness of the reasoning of the contested act.[179] This is in line with the basic function of that formal requirement of legality, the observance of which, by definition, merely guarantees the effective exercise of judicial review on the substance, including the discovery of errors of fact, law, and of assessment.[180] Notwithstanding these caveats, ultimately, also the judges' proper grasp of the *essential* character or the *decisive importance* of a given reason presupposes a decent understanding of the overall factual and legal context in which the contested act was adopted. And this necessarily includes an at least cursory appraisal of the relevance and importance of the various points of fact and law set out in the act's statement of reasons. Yet, it appears obvious that this methodology may induce the judges to find a defect in the reasoning precisely because they have doubts as to the relevance or importance of the lacking or insufficiently explained elements.[181]

Fourth, as has already been pointed out in Section 3.3.2.2 and Section 3.3.2.3, there is an important overlap between the scope of the principle of care as defined in *Technische Universität München* and the standard and burden of proof imposed on the administration in respect of the soundness of its discretionary decision. This is obvious in the face of the *Tetra Laval* formula requiring that the administration shows to the requisite standard that it has taken into account all relevant information ('must be taken into account') for assessing a complex situation.[182] In the field of risk evaluation and regulation under the precautionary principle this is even more striking. According to the definition in *ATC*, drawing on *Pfizer*, 'a scientific risk assessment carried out as thoroughly as possible on the basis of scientific advice founded on the principles of excellence, transparency and independence is an important procedural guarantee whose purpose is to ensure the scientific objectivity of the measures adopted and preclude any arbitrary measures'.[183] The case law has also held in that context that, for the purposes of a comprehensive and thorough assessment of the risk at issue, the administration is required to gather 'the best scientific data available' in light of the most recent results of international research.[184] Moreover, the administration must be able to show that in adopting the contested act it actually exercised its discretion, 'which presupposes the taking into consideration of all the relevant factors and circumstances of the situation the

---

[179] *Commission v Sytraval and Brink's France* (n 42) paras 65 et seq. See also Case T-25/07 *Iride and Iride Energia v Commission* [2009] ECR II-245, para 76, according to which 'the absence or inadequacy of a statement of reasons constitutes a plea going to infringement of essential procedural requirements and, as such, is distinct from a plea going to the incorrectness of the grounds of the contested decision, which is reviewed in the context of the question whether a decision is well founded'.

[180] As to the risks implied in the misleading dictum in *Tirrenia di Navigazione and Others v Commission* (n 173) para 99, according to which the Union judicature is bound to examine the pleas alleging the absence or inadequacy of a statement of reasons before addressing the substantive pleas going to the incorrectness of the grounds of the contested decision, see HP Nehl, 'Direct Actions and Judicial Review before the Union Courts' in HCH Hofmann and C Micheau (eds), *State Aid Law of the European Union* (OUP, 2016), 406–49, 443–4.

[181] Shapiro (n 169) 184–9.

[182] This convergence has been rightly emphasized by Mendes (n 157) 434–6.

[183] *ATC and Others v Commission* (n 142) para 85.

[184] Cf., e.g. *Gowan Comércio Internacional e Serviços* (n 132) para 75.

act was intended to regulate'.[185] As has already been stated with respect to both the principle of care and the standard of proof, the emphasis lies on the 'relevant' facts, the appraisal of which involves a value judgment on the part of the judge as to the significance and the quality of the information provided by taking into account the overall factual and legal context in which the contested measure is embedded, including its objectives. It seems plain that such a review necessarily strays beyond the realm of pure procedure and touches upon the substantive justification for the measure taken.

These considerations underline the importance of procedural review in the face of restrained judicial control of discretion on the merits, not least because it grants the courts a very flexible tool, including the potential for overstepping the framework of mere procedure. It allows them to carry out (implicit) value judgments on the relevance of the facts and evidence forming the subject matter of the case. This 'relevance paradigm' will be addressed more closely in Section 4.

4. Conclusion: The Significance of the 'Relevance Paradigm'

Arguably, a global perception of the concepts and standards discussed in this chapter devised to structure judicial review of administrative discretion in EU law boils down to the conclusion that, whatever concept or standard is to be applied, it requires the judges to carry out an *at least* cursory value judgment of the relevance of the facts and the evidence forming the subject matter of the case. Hence, the 'relevance paradigm' seems to be an intrinsic common feature of the various concepts and standards of substantive and procedural judicial review, such as the manifest error or plausibility test, the standard and the burden of proof, and the control of the observance of the duty of care and the obligation to state reasons. Moreover, depending on the type and degree of executive discretion and the way in which it has been exercised in the contested measure (of which the statement of reasons is the most relevant account), judges tend to fine-tune their review style and carefully to choose between the different standards and concepts of review, provided they form the subject matter of the case or can be raised *ex officio*. In legal practice, it may therefore be decisive for the outcome of the litigation process before the Union courts whether the parties have put forward explicitly and in a timely fashion the appropriate plea in law concentrating on the most relevant factual issues involved, thus enabling the judges to react within the boundaries defined by the case brought before them. Under such circumstances, the judges enjoy enough flexibility to switch between or to combine the available standards and concepts that, in their view, are most appropriate to solve the legal dispute.[186]

---

[185] *Afton Chemical* (n 63) para 34.
[186] A paramount example of such a flexible, but somewhat confusing, approach is the ruling in Joined Cases C-584/10 P, C-593/10 P, and C-595/10 P *Commission and Others v Kadi* [2013] EU:C:2013:518, paras 103–110, which blends a number of process rights, including the rights of the defence, the duty of care, and the duty to state reasons, under the heading of the principle of effective judicial protection

In particular, in cases of high factual complexity, e.g. risk/hazard decision making, rather than reviewing the accuracy of complex primary and secondary facts or the soundness of the policy choice made by the decision maker, the court may be inclined to restrict itself to finding whether the administration has gathered and processed with sufficient expertise and care all the relevant or essential elements necessary for its discretionary assessment. If, for instance, the applicant argues convincingly that the plausibility of the decision-making's outcome is put into question (manifest error) because the administration has omitted to take into consideration such relevant or essential elements (e.g. certain scientific data or a given study available already during the decision-making process), the judges may reverse the burden of proof to its detriment and be willing to quash the contested act unless the administration is able—depending on the standard of proof required by the court—to provide alternative explanations for either the lacking relevance of those elements or rendering its decision sufficiently plausible on other grounds. In this connection, Mendes has rightly mentioned the judges' inclination not to interfere with the administration's policy choices as such (as to the Union courts' reluctance in that regard see Section 3.4), but to carry out their review with respect to the factual assessment forming the basis of that discretionary choice under either the *Tetra Laval* test or the principle of care.[187] It is only when, subsequent to exercising their power of unfettered appraisal of evidence, the judges are convinced of the irrelevance of the factual arguments alleged and/or, conversely, of the credibility/plausibility of the facts and evidence relied on by the decision maker, that they will be prepared to endorse the factual appraisal and policy considerations underlying the contested act as being exempt from a manifest error or a procedural defect.[188] As has been recently pointed out by AG Bobek in his interpretation of the terms 'relevant factor' under the CLP regulation,[189] the 'relevance' issue therefore lies in a grey zone comprising the assessment of issues of fact and law, the spheres of factual cognition and policy choices (volition), and those of substance and procedure. Hence, the response to the fundamental question raised in the beginning of this chapter as to whether the Union courts' approach reveals too much judicial deference or a too intrusive a style of judicial review in the face of executive discretion, or whether it ought to be intensified on the basis of any of the given standards and concepts, can neither be yes nor no. It ultimately rests on judicial policy considerations, rather than the available review standards and concepts and the judges' persuasion of the overall soundness of the contested measure whether they are willing to translate the 'relevance paradigm' into the appropriate judicial tool empowering them to review the exercise of executive discretion effectively.

laid down in Art 47 of the Charter, in order to show that the standard of judicial review in respect of (discretionary) restrictive measures is adequate.

[187] Mendes (n 157) 435–6.

[188] Kalintiri (n 84) 1311, rightly points out that the Union courts have employed evidence-related wording to retain the role of deciding themselves what is 'relevant' and what is not. Similarly, see Sibony and de La Serre (n 94) 243–5.

[189] Opinion of AG *Bobek* in *Commission v Bilbaína de Alquitranes and Others* (n 86) paras 52 et seq.

9

The Principle of Proportionality in EU Law

An Interest-based Taxonomy

Vasiliki Kosta[*]

1. Introduction

In EU law the principle of proportionality is a constitutional law principle employed to review any Union action that could be qualified as being legislative, administrative, or executive in nature. This classic tripartite categorization of legal acts is, of course, not clear cut in EU law[1] and that itself may also make more difficult an overall assessment of the role that proportionality plays in this context. It may not be possible to identify whether proportionality has a specific role in relation to EU executive action, but one can nevertheless examine how it operates as a methodological tool in judicial review and how, in general, it acts as a legal constraint on the exercise of public authority.

One way of inquiring what role the principle of proportionality plays—if at all—in a given legal order is to ask what interest it serves, since balancing competing interests is inherent to proportionality. The answer to that question is not always clear in EU law. One important factor contributing to this obscurity is that proportionality exists as a discrete and 'free-standing' head of judicial review ('*free-standing proportionality*') for all of EU action. This does not mean that proportionality relates to some particular 'free-standing' substantive value. Rather, it means that a given substantive interest served by the tool of proportionality can be considerably concealed. Take the most obvious scenario: when the ground for judicial review is compliance with fundamental rights, proportionality will be a crucial test to answer that question[2] and the interest that this tool will serve is self-evident: fundamental rights. When the ground for judicial review is compliance with the principle of proportionality, the interest served through its application could be fundamental rights, but it could also be something else. What that 'something else' is will emerge—at best—within the Courts' further reasoning only. But it can also remain unclear.

[*] Assistant Professor, University of Leiden. I am grateful for the comments of Vestert Borger, Bruno de Witte, and Joana Mendes. All errors remain mine.
[1] See Mendes, Chapter 1 in this volume.
[2] In cases where no absolute rights are at stake.

Additionally, this ambiguity on the protected interest provides room for a misapplication of the principle: the Court could employ proportionality as a ground for judicial review, while not conducting a proportionality analysis under this label at all.

This lack of clarity on the protected interest and the potential for misapplying and instrumentalizing the principle of proportionality serves to obscure its overall role as a tool of judicial review in EU law. Therefore, with the aim to map that role, this chapter proposes a taxonomy of this principle in EU law based on the interests it serves. It suggests that proportionality, as a constitutional principle, has three basic functions in EU law: it serves rights, subsidiarity, and freedom from burdens.

This chapter first briefly recalls what form proportionality takes in EU law (Section 2) before it sets out the proposed taxonomy, which will dissect the three functions proportionality has as a constitutional principle in this legal order (Section 3). It then demonstrates how a legal basis/competence review, which may employ language that sounds similar to the proportionality test, is not a proportionality review (Section 4). The final section turns to *free-standing proportionality* and the problems that may arise when it is employed, paying particular attention to the problem of its misapplication as exemplified by *Gauweiler*,[3] which involved judicial review of executive discretion.[4] This analysis shows how what is actually at stake in proportionality review may be, in specific instances, entirely unclear and, in addition, that this ambiguity may be strategically used by the Court to preserve the legality of EU acts.

2. What is Proportionality?

Proportionality is a tool that assesses the legality of the exercise of power where a legitimate aim is pursued but another interest deserving of legal protection (typically a right) is damaged. Proportionality always requires a set of *conflicting interests* that need to be 'balanced'—it is 'not an independent principle of review, since it refers not to any particular free-standing substantive value ... '.[5]

There exist slightly different variations in the formulation of this principle across legal systems, but the EU law test is in line with that of most proportionality theorists.[6] The test consists of three steps, although in some areas of Union law, e.g. the internal market freedoms, the Court may limit itself to applying only the first two steps.

First, the action must be suitable for pursuing a legitimate aim (suitability), sometimes also called 'appropriateness';[7] second, the action must not go beyond what is necessary to achieve the legitimate aim, in the sense that there are no other

---

[3] Case C-62/14 *Peter Gauweiler and Others v Deutscher Bundestag*, ECLI:EU:C:2015:400.

[4] As understood in this edited volume. See Mendes, Chapter 1 in this volume.

[5] G De Búrca, 'The Principle of Proportionality and its Application in EC Law' (1998) 13 *YEL* 105, 106.

[6] E.g. R Alexy, *A Theory of Constitutional Rights* (OUP, 2002) as referred to in K Möller, 'Proportionality: Challenging the Critics' (2012) *ICON* 709, 711.

[7] In German law, this step is split into two distinct steps: the existence of a legitimate aim as a first step and the question of suitability or appropriateness as a second one.

less-restrictive but equally effective means available (necessity); third, even if the action or measure is suitable and necessary, it must also be shown that the interference with the protected right or interest is justified in light of the gain resulting from pursuing the legitimate aim (proportionality *stricto sensu*). This latter step is often termed the 'balancing' stage in the application of the principle of proportionality. There are different ways to understand 'balancing'—an inherently vague term. Möller makes the point succinctly, saying that:

> ... there are at least two senses of balancing. The first we might call 'interest balancing'. It operates according to a cost–benefit analysis: the respective rights or interests are 'measured,' placed on a set of scales, and their weight is compared. The second kind of balancing we might call 'balancing as reasoning' [i.e.] (...) mak[ing] a moral argument as to which of the competing interests takes priority in the case at hand, and this moral argument may or may not proceed by way of interest balancing (interest balancing is one kind of moral reasoning but not the only one).[8]

It is the latter kind of balancing—balancing as reasoning—that is typically applied by courts when reviewing proportionality in (fundamental) rights-based cases.[9]

A further point needs to be made in the understanding of the principle of proportionality: it may be misleading to speak of a 'means-ends' analysis when referring to the principle, as is sometimes done in the literature. The applicable test does not only require an assessment of the relationship between the means and the ends of an action (a legitimate aim), but also between the means and their interference with the interest 'deserving of protection'.[10] In the final analysis, proportionality always seeks to balance two conflicting interests.

The following section sets out the taxonomy along the interests that proportionality serves in Union law. It demonstrates that the principle serves rights, subsidiarity, and the interest of being free from burdens.

3. The Taxonomy: The Three Functions of Proportionality in EU Law

3.1 'Rights-proportionality': the classic use

The first category is relatively straightforward and reflects the classic use of the principle in line with its historical purpose in law. *'Rights proportionality'* serves to review the interference of the measures of Member States with justiciable rights provided for in primary or secondary Union law,[11] and the interference of the measures of the Union with justiciable rights granted under primary law. Since the Charter became

---

[8] Möller (n 6) 715.

[9] E Engle, 'The General Principle of Proportionality and Aristotle' in L Huppes-Cluysenaer and NMMS Coelho (eds), *Aristotle and the Philosophy of Law: Theory, Practice and Justice* (Springer, 2014) 265, 274.

[10] A Barak (ed), 'The Nature and Function of Proportionality' in *Proportionality—Constitutional Rights and their Limitations* (CUP, 2012), 132.

[11] For an overview with reference to relevant case law, see K Lenaerts and P Van Nuffel, *European Union Law* (3rd edn, Sweet & Maxwell, 2011), at 7-034.

legally binding, whenever a situation falls within its scope, the proportionality exercise for reviewing *fundamental* rights enshrined in the Charter will be based on Article 52(3) of the Charter.[12] Proportionality as applied in the context of the internal market freedoms falls under the rights-proportionality category (as the fundamental freedoms translate into justiciable rights). It is indeed common under EU law that individuals can derive justiciable rights from (directly effective) Treaty provisions addressed to the Member States, rather than the citizens.[13]

Proportionality also applies to penalties in EU law—be they imposed by Union organs or under national law and be those of an administrative or criminal law nature. They thus include monetary penalties and deprivation of individual liberty. The need for proportionate penalties in relation to a criminal offence is enshrined in Article 49(3) of the Charter of Fundamental Rights, which states that the 'severity of penalties must not be disproportionate to the criminal offence'. The interest that proportionality serves here is not identified in the provision, but it can be understood in relation to other rights, e.g. the right to property and the right to liberty of person, which are now also enshrined as fundamental rights in the Charter (Article 17 CFR, Article 6 CFR). ECHR law, which must be followed in EU law to the extent that it is dealing with corresponding Charter rights,[14] suggests that administrative monetary penalties are to be analysed from the point of view of the human right to property.[15] As Craig and De Búrca note, 'because penalties can impinge on personal liberties, and because a court can normally strike down a penalty without undermining the relevant administrative policy', then '[c]ourts are likely to be reasonably searching in [reviewing] this type of case.'[16]

Rights-proportionality may be conducted also under the discrete heading of 'proportionality' so as to obscure the protected interest. This can be exemplified in *BAT*.[17] The Court reviewed, among others, a provision of the first Tobacco Products Directive,[18] which banned the use of certain words (such as 'low-tar', 'light', 'mild' etc.),

---

[12] See Case C-293/12 *Digital Rights Ireland*, ECLI:EU:C:2014:238.

[13] S Hölscheid, 'Abschied vom subjektiv-öffentlichen Recht? Zu Wandlungen der Verwaltungsrechtsdogmatik unter dem Einfluß des Gemeinschaftsrechts' (2001) *EuR* 376, 382.

[14] Art 52(3), EU Charter of Fundamental Rights.

[15] See ECtHR, *Konstantin v Stefanov* (27/01/2016), Application No. 35399/05, for an analysis that is sceptical of this development, and commenting on this case, see L Laurysen, <https://strasbourgobservers.com/2015/11/09/dont-open-the-floodgates-fines-and-article-1-protocol-1/>; See also Opinion AG Wathelet in Case C-255/14 *Robert Michal Chmielewski v Nemzeti Adó-és Vámhivatal Dél-alföldi Regionális Vám-és Pénzügyőri Főigazgatósága*, ECLI:EU:C:2015:475, concerning the proportionality of an administrative fine provided under Hungarian law as a penalty for breach of the obligation to declare cash pursuant to Art 3 of Regulation (EC) No 1889/2005 on controls of cash entering or leaving the EC. The AG invoked extensively ECHR case law on administrative fines penalizing failure to declare cash at the border and applied proportionality by weighing requirements of general interest on the one hand, and the right to property under Art 17 of the Charter of Fundamental Rights on the other. The Court did not cite the right to property under the ECHR and the Charter, but invoked the Charter in more general terms.

[16] P Craig and G De Búrca, *EU Law: Text, Cases, and Materials* (6th edn, OUP, 2015), 555.

[17] Case C-491/01 *The Queen v Secretary of State for Health, ex parte British American Tobacco (Investments) Ltd and Imperial Tobacco Ltd.* (hereafter *BAT*), ECLI:EU:C:2002:741.

[18] Directive 2001/37 on the approximation of laws, regulations and administrative provisions of Member States concerning the manufacture, presentation and sale of tobacco products, OJ [2001] L194, 18.7.2001.

names, pictures, and signs on cigarette packages based on the *general principle* of proportionality.[19] The Court held that this provision was proportionate in light of the public health objective of the Directive (under which the more specific objective in Article 7 of the Directive fell by ensuring that consumers are not misled as to the harmfulness of tobacco products), as 'there was no alternative measure which could have attained that objective as efficiently while being less restrictive of the *rights* of the manufacturers of tobacco products.'[20] The Court did not identify what *concrete rights* of manufacturers it was balancing,[21] but it did expressly make the point that this was at stake here.

3.2 'Subsidiarity-proportionality': confusion between Article 5(3) TEU and Article 5(4) TEU

A version of proportionality exists *within* subsidiarity (Article 5(3) TEU) in the field of shared competences, where the concern is one of balancing the protection of Member State powers on the one hand, with the achievement of Union objectives on the other. We may call this '*subsidiarity-proportionality*'.

The question of subsidiarity is asked *after* the question of competence is answered in the affirmative in order to determine '*who should act*'—the EU or the local/national level—with a preference for the latter if possible. The principle is defined in Article 5(3) TEU '... in areas which do not fall within its exclusive competence, the Union shall act *only if* and *in so far as* the objectives of the proposed action cannot be sufficiently achieved by the Member States [...] but can rather, by reason of the scale or effects of the proposed action, *be better* achieved at Union level' (emphasis added).

Lenaerts and Van Nuffel[22] suggest that the principle of subsidiarity involves a decentralization criterion ('only if') and an efficiency criterion ('better'). Additionally, the principle also includes a proportionality exercise, which is implied in the words '*in so far as*'. This proportionality exercise seeks to reconcile the protection of national powers with the achievement of the proposed Union actions' concrete objectives. The authors note that the Union action must be, first, appropriate to achieve the objective and, second, indispensable, in the sense that no other measures are available which impact less on the Member States' powers. Article 5(3) TEU, therefore, 'embodies a *specific application of the principle of proportionality* with a view to protecting the residual powers of the Member States.'[23] This proportionality exists *within* subsidiarity and can thus, I suggest, be termed 'subsidiarity-proportionality'.

Arguably, this subsidiarity-proportionality is the reason why several commentators point to the overlap between subsidiarity in Article 5(3) TEU and proportionality in Article 5(4) TEU. The latter provision states that '[u]nder the principle

---

[19] *BAT* (n 17) paras 112, 122.   [20] Ibid., para 139 (emphasis added).
[21] One may wonder whether the Court had freedom of commercial expression in mind. See V Kosta, *Fundamental Rights in EU Internal Market Legislation* (Hart Publishing, 2015), Ch 5, 172.
[22] Lenaerts and Van Nuffel (n 11) 7–028.   [23] Ibid. (emphasis added).

of proportionality, the content and form of Union action shall not exceed what is necessary to achieve the objectives of the Treaties'.

For example, De Búrca has observed 'under paragraph two [now three], the question of what kind of action the Community should take is determined by reference to the aims of the action and not going beyond these aims. But clearly, the more precisely the 'aims' of an action are defined for the purposes of paragraph two [now three], the more this overlaps with paragraph three [now four] and becomes also a question of *how* or what kind of Community power should be exercised, so that the proportionality question is subsumed into the second question.'[24]

Gutman acknowledges that there is proportionality *within* subsidiarity in Article 5(3) TEU, but that there is also a proportionality inquiry in Article 5(4) TEU after and *outside* the subsidiarity inquiry. And while she notes that they are both inextricably linked they remain in her analysis also distinct at the same time. Against these observations she calls for further research on this topic.[25] The fact that Articles 5(3) TEU and 5(4) TEU are distinct makes sense, given that Article 5(4) TEU applies also to exclusive competence, whereas Article 5(3) TEU is only applicable to the exercise of shared competence. In that context it has been suggested that the original reason for the introduction of Article 5(4) TEU was the Member States' wish for a tool that curbs the exercise of Union powers also in the field of exclusive competence.[26]

On the other hand, Schütze has argued that the principle of subsidiarity is in fact what he calls 'federal proportionality'—a principle that asks '*whether* the European legislator has unnecessarily restricted national autonomy.'[27] What role remains then for Article 5(4) TEU wherein the principle of proportionality is enshrined? Based on a historical understanding of the principle of proportionality, which is one of 'protect[ing] *private* rights [understood as an expression of liberal values] against excessive public interference' Schütze proposes that Article 5(4) TEU should be restricted to that function, while the protection of 'the collective autonomy of a people' is to be reserved for Article 5(3) TEU.[28] This proposition appears sensible, but it does not reflect the language of the Treaties, or that of current judicial practice.

3.3 'Burdens-proportionality': (how) is it different from subsidiarity-proportionality and rights-proportionality?

Article 5(4) TEU requires that the form and content of Union action shall not go beyond what is necessary to achieve the objectives of the Treaties. Proportionality thus expressed does not make much sense as it fails to identify what interest it serves. As noted at the outset, proportionality is not an independent principle of review and does not relate to a free-standing substantive value. If properly applied, it will always

---

[24] G De Búrca, 'The Principle of Subsidiarity and the Court of Justice as an Institutional Actor' (1998) 36 *J Common Mark Stud* 217, 220.
[25] K Gutman, *Constitutional Foundations of European Contract Law* (OUP, 2014), 308.
[26] T Tridimas, *The General Principles of EU Law* (2nd edn, OUP, 2006), 176.
[27] R Schütze, 'Subsidiarity after Lisbon' (2009) 68 *Camb Law J* 525, 533.   [28] Ibid.

serve some substantive interest, which is restricted by an action that pursues a legitimate objective. Article 5(4) TEU does not expressly identify this interest, which
may cause confusion as to the role that Article 5(4) plays in a given case.

However, the interest that proportionality in Article 5(4) TEU should serve is
identified in Protocol No. 2, which references the need for draft legislative acts to
'take account of the need for any *burden*, whether financial or administrative, falling
upon the Union, national governments, regional or local authorities, economic operators and citizens, to be *minimized* and commensurate with the objective to be
achieved.'[29] As Lenaerts and Van Nuffel suggest, all the legal subjects listed herein
will be able to 'plead infringement of Article 5(4) TEU where the Union unreason-
ably affects their *interests*'.[30]

The interest expressed here is one of being free from financial and administrative burdens based on Protocol No. 2. We may call this '*burdens-proportionality*'.
Moreover, the interest to be 'free from any burdens' takes on a constitutional nature
because too much interference with it would render *any* proposed action—whether
administrative, executive, or legislative—invalid. Importantly, this interest of 'being
free of burdens' continues to be served by the general principle of proportionality.
Article 5(4) TEU and the general principle exist side by side.[31]

The language of *diminishing* financial and administrative *burdens* is reminiscent of the Commission's agenda concerned with 'Better Regulation'. Thus read,
the question of proportionality under Article 5(4) TEU could be understood as
asking whether the action adopted is the most cost-effective. Of course, the terms
'burdens' or 'costs' in this context are relative and value laden—as is an assessment
of these in relation to achieving a Union objective in order to find an 'appropriate
balance'.

Moreover, such exercise is contentious. As Weatherill notes, if 'Better Regulation'
is concerned with achieving 'a more satisfactory balance between the demands of
proper protection from market failure and inequity, on the one hand, and commercial freedom and the potential for innovation on the other',[32] the complex and controversial value judgments involved in this exercise mean that ' "Better Regulation"
(...) rubs shoulders with some immensely sensitive choices about the trajectory
of the mixed economy in the modern state and in the developing transnational
European market.'[33]

If the 'better regulation ethos' has indeed been constitutionalized via Article 5(4)
TEU, it should trigger important normative questions as to whether it should be
operationalized in the name of the *constitutional* principle of proportionality as
a ground for *judicial* review. Yet before such debates can take place we must ask

---

[29] Protocol (No 2) on the Application of the Principles of Subsidiarity and Proportionality, Article 5
(emphasis added).

[30] Lenaerts and Van Nuffel (n 11) 7–040.

[31] For an older case dealing with 'financial and administrative costs' falling on Member States, see
Case C-426/93, *Commission v Germany*, ECLI:EU:C:1995:367.

[32] S Weatherill, 'The Challenge of Better Regulation' in S Weatherill (ed), *Better Regulation* (Hart
Publishing, 2007), 4.

[33] Ibid.

whether and to what degree '*burdens-proportionality*' in Article 5(4) TEU is really different from *subsidiarity-proportionality* and *rights-proportionality*.

The first difference relates to a distinction already noted with respect to the *area of application* of proportionality—that Article 5(4) TEU applies to both shared and exclusive competences, whereas Article 5(3) TEU applies only to shared competences. The second difference relates to the question as to *whose interests* are protected. *Burdens-proportionality* in Article 5(4) TEU lists both the subjects that are served through *subsidiarity-proportionality* (national governments and regional and local authorities) and the subjects that are served through *rights-proportionality* (economic operators and citizens). But in addition, it also lists the Union itself. Minimizing financial and administrative burdens falling upon the Union can be understood as an obligation to keep the operational structures of the Union to a minimum. This is reminiscent of Article 5 of the Treaty establishing the European Coal and Steel Community, which mandated that 'the institutions of the Community shall carry out these [listed in that article] activities with *as little administrative machinery as possible* and in close cooperation with the interested parties.' The third difference relates to the question *what interest* proportionality serves and brings us back to the aim of providing a taxonomy based on this criterion.

3.3.1 Burdens-proportionality vs. subsidiarity-proportionality

As mentioned, the necessity test under *subsidiarity-proportionality* asks whether there are other measures available that are less restrictive of Member States' residual powers. Is that different from asking whether there are other measures that impose less financial and administrative burdens on Member States?

A difference is visible by distinguishing between how much regulatory autonomy—in the sense of occupied regulatory space—is left to Member States (which would relate to the question of residual powers) as opposed to how many financial and administrative costs the regulation occupying that space creates (which would relate to the question of burdens). That is surely a fine line to draw; if the protected interest is framed as one of Member State autonomy more broadly (as opposed to *regulatory* autonomy), as some German authors[34] read the interest that Article 5(4) TEU is supposed to protect, this distinction fades even further.

In any event, the question of burdens can also play a role in subsidiarity when asking which level of governance can achieve the aim better, because 'better' may include considerations of keeping regulatory burdens to a minimum, depending on how the benchmark of what constitutes 'good' regulation is defined.

---

[34] E.g. J Bast, 'EUV Art. 5 Prinzipien der Kompetenzordnung' in E Grabitz, M Hilf, and M Nettesheim (eds), *Das Recht der Europäischen Union* (München Beck, 2017), 61.

3.3.2 Burdens proportionality vs. rights-proportionality

Tridimas, when commenting on the difference between the principle of proportionality as a general principle and Article 5(4) TEU-proportionality, noted that the Article did not add to pre-existing case law other than expressly granting it constitutional status.[35] He continued, suggesting that the difference between the two is just one of emphasis[36] in terms of the addressed subject/protected interest. The relevant section is worth quoting in full:

> As a general principle of law, proportionality has been developed by the Court primarily with a view to protecting the individual from action by the Community institutions and by the Member States. By contrast, Article 5(3) [now (4)] forms part of a system of provisions whose aim is to control the expansion of Community legislative action and seeks to limit *burdens* on Member States rather than *burdens on individuals*. This is not to say that the protection of *rights of the individual* is excluded from the scope of Article 5(3) [now 4].[37]

Tridimas uses the terms burdens and rights interchangeably here. However, the key question is whether that equation holds. Kokott and Sobotta have recently touched on this issue, pointing to the application of proportionality in non-rights-based cases as being peculiar from a German law perspective, where an assessment of proportionality normally requires 'a specific right that is being restricted.'[38]

Arguably, as a matter of judicial method it does make a difference whether one speaks of rights on the one hand, or of burdens/disadvantages on the other. The former requires a Court to draw the material scope of a legally protected right and then assess whether a given contested action has interfered with it. Only when that is the case will it move on to the three-step proportionality test (the questions of appropriateness, necessity, and balancing). Therefore, depending on how narrowly or broadly the scope of a right is construed, that can be a higher hurdle to overcome before proportionality review can be triggered when compared to the requirement that an action will be contestable if it creates 'any' burdens. Relatedly, it is necessary to know the concrete contours of what it is that is to be protected when applying the three-step proportionality test. Kokott and Sobotta have contended, particularly, that 'the final balancing can be performed more precisely if it is focused on a specific impact on a right and not abstractly on "disadvantages" '.[39] The consideration of burdens or disadvantages in the abstract and without a link to a right enters squarely

---

[35] Tridimas (n 26) 175.

[36] For a contrary view, see Bast (n 34) para 67: 'Dass diese Vertragsbestimmung keine spezifisch individualschützenden Gehalt hat, folgt aus dem systematischen Zusammenhang mit den anderen in Art. 5 EUV normierten Grundsätzen, bei denen jeweils die Schonung der mitgliedstaatlichen Autonomie als Schutzzweck im Mittelpunkt steht.' However, this view is not in line with current jurisprudence where the Court applies Art 5(4) TEU also in order to serve for example interests of economic operators.

[37] Tridimas (n 26) 175–7.

[38] J Kokott and C Sobotta, 'The Evolution of the Principle of Proportionality in EU Law – Towards an Anticipative Understanding?' in S Vogenauer and S Weatherill, *General Principles of Law: European and Comparative Perspectives* (Hart Publishing, 2017), 168.

[39] Ibid.

into policy considerations that are, conventionally, considered to be the premise of legislative or executive institutions.

Hitherto this problem of the distinction between rights on the one hand, and burdens/disadvantages on the other, has not been widely exposed in EU law. One reason might be that the Court has, in practice, largely adopted a hands-off approach when reviewing challenges to Union measures on the grounds of proportionality. The Court has consistently held that in areas involving economic, social, political choices and technical and complex assessments the Union institutions will enjoy wide discretion and the applicable test is whether the measure is '*manifestly inappropriate*[40] having regard to the objective which the institutions are seeking to pursue'.[41] And '[s]ince a great many Treaty articles will be of this nature low intensity review will be the norm.'[42]

In non-rights-based cases the Court has more recently taken what could be called a 'procedural approach'[43] in reviewing proportionality. Lenaerts defines 'process review' as an examination of whether 'the EU political institutions had followed the procedural steps mandated by the authors of the Treaties.'[44] An example where that was the case in relation to general legislation was *Vodafone*,[45] which challenged the 'Roaming Regulation'.[46] This was the first case where the Court relied on the Commission's Impact Assessment Report in order to review proportionality. The reliance on the Impact Assessment allows the Court to avoid conducting a substantive review that could lead it to restrict too much the discretion of the legislature. However, in the instant case, the Court did not only limit itself to reviewing whether the legislature complied with procedural guarantees when preparing the legislation, but it also relied on the substantive findings of the legislature for the purposes of its own analysis.

In relation to individual (administrative) decisions and complex technical assessments, a procedural approach to judicial review of discretion has been standard case law for much longer.[47] In these cases the duty to state reasons and the duty of care (to examine carefully and impartially all the relevant elements of the situation in

---

[40] Note that the language of 'appropriateness' might be confusing here. When applying the 'manifestly inappropriate' standard the Court does not necessarily limit itself to reviewing 'appropriateness' as the first of the three-part proportionality test, but it can go on to testing whether a measure is 'manifestly unnecessary' and 'manifestly disproportionate' in the strict sense, although it does not always do so. The word 'manifest' then is the key word indicating low-intensity review.

[41] E.g. *BAT* (n 17) para 231; C-358/14 *Republic of Poland v European Parliament, Council of the European Union*, ECLI:EU:C:2016:323, para 79; Case C-547/14 *Philip Morris*, ECLI:EU:C:2016:325, para 166.

[42] P Craig, *EU Administrative Law* (OUP, 2012), 593.

[43] See K Lenaerts, 'The European Court of Justice and Process-oriented Review', College of Europe, Department of Legal Studies, *Research Papers in Law* 01/2012.

[44] Ibid., 3; for other possible definitions of 'process review' or 'procedural review', see J Öberg, 'The Rise of the Procedural Paradigm: Judicial Review of EU Legislation in Vertical Competence Disputes' (2017) 13 *EUConst* 248, 255.

[45] Case C-58/08 *Vodafone and Others*, ECLI:EU:C:2010:321.

[46] Regulation No 717/2007, OJ [2007] L 171/32.

[47] See, in detail, the contribution of Nehl, Chapter 8 in this volume.

question) are tested and sometimes subsumed into the proportionality analysis,[48] while also the 'manifest error of assessment' standard of review can be employed, which is applied to review the finding of facts.[49]

In the post-Lisbon context, where Union legislation (of a general character) was challenged on *fundamental* rights grounds,[50] the Court has, quite reasonably, adopted a stricter fundamental rights-based proportionality test and even invalidated measures on the ground of disproportionate interference with fundamental rights protected by the Charter. The question does arise whether in this new Charter context a large variety of 'interests' can be phrased not just in rights but even in *fundamental* rights terms, given how broad of a catalogue the EU Charter of Fundamental Rights is. That approach may make especially the review of general EU legislation on proportionality grounds methodologically less contentious but it can be critiqued for amounting to 'fundamental rights-inflation' especially when considering that any economic burdens falling on private undertaking can be construed as interferences with the freedom to conduct a business (Article 16 CFR). However, in that case, the problem would lie in the catalogue and in the way the substantive scope of the fundamental right(s) would be defined by the Court, rather than in proportionality itself.

An illustration where the same question was addressed as a matter of fundamental *rights proportionality* by the Advocate General (AG) (it is no coincidence that it was AG Kokott) but in terms of *burdens-proportionality* by the Court is *Philip Morris*,[51] where a piece of general (internal market) legislation was contested. The applicants (tobacco undertakings) challenged, *inter alia*, the prohibition contained in the Tobacco Products Directive[52] to place on the market tobacco products with characterizing flavour (like menthol) or containing flavourings in any of the components. One of the questions referred was whether the articles containing this prohibition were violating the principle of proportionality. While AG Kokott reformulated this plea to read whether the prohibitions disproportionately interfered with the freedom to conduct a business (Article 16 CFR), the Court conducted *burdens-proportionality*. The proportionality *stricto sensu* stage reveals the protected interest: the negative economic and social consequences falling on certain economic operators. The interest to be free of these negative consequences was balanced against the requirement resting on the institutions to ensure a high level of human health protection in all their activities, as required by the Charter (Article 35 CFR), the

---

[48] For a case where both of these grounds were employed to review discretion *outside* any explicit proportionality analysis, see Case C-269/90 *Technische Universität München v Hauptzollamt München Mitte*, ECLI:EU:C:1991:438, where neither the term 'proportionality' nor any elements of the three-step test are mentioned. For a case where these grounds were tested under the heading of 'proportionality', see *Gauweiler* (n 3) discussed in more detail below in Section 5.

[49] See P Craig, 'Law, Fact and Discretion in the UK, EU and USA' available at: <http://www.sciencespo.fr/chaire-madp/sites/sciencespo.fr.chaire-madp/files/paul_craig.pdf>, accessed 22 June 2018.

[50] Joined Cases C-92/09, *Volker and Markus Schecke GbR*, and C-93/09 *Hartmut Eifert*, ECLI:EU:C:2010:662; Case C-293/12 *Digital Rights Ireland*, ECLI:EU:C:2014:238.

[51] See *Philip Morris* (n 41).

[52] Directive 2014/40 concerning the manufacture, presentation and sale of tobacco products, OJ [2014] L127/1.

general mainstreaming clause in Article 9 TFEU, the mainstreaming obligation in the Public Health Title of the TFEU (Article 168(1) TFEU), and in Article 114(3) as a specific mainstreaming obligation when legislating for the internal market. At this stage the Court, after referring to Protocol No. 2 and the need to minimize burdens, noted both the generous transitional period and the Impact Assessment that predicted a decrease of 0.5 per cent to 0.8 per cent in cigarette consumption over a five-year period as a result of the prohibition.[53] On this basis it concluded that the impact of the prohibition was not manifestly disproportionate. By contrast, central to AG Kokott's reasoning was the question of the hierarchical relationship between the conflicting interests, which she conceptualized as 'values'. She opined that 'the protection of human health has considerably greater importance in the value system under EU law than such essentially economic interests (see Articles 9 TFEU, 114(3) TFEU, and 168(1) TFEU, and the second sentence of Article 35 of the Charter of Fundamental Rights), with the result that health protection may justify even substantial negative economic consequences for certain economic operators.'[54] She also noted the transitional period, but did not refer to the Impact Assessment in her substantive analysis. Thus, AG Kokott conducted a methodologically very different exercise at the stage of balancing through fundamental rights proportionality, even if in the instant case she arrived at the same conclusion as the Court.

4. What is *Not* Proportionality: Questions of Suitability and Necessity as Legal Basis Requirements

The principle of conferral requires that the Union has a competence to act in a given field. Linked to that is the question whether the correct legal basis has been chosen and whether the substantive and procedural legal basis requirements have been complied with. A means-ends test may be employed in judicial review on the question of competence and choice of legal basis. But that is not proportionality,[55] even though it may be confused with such because similar language as that of the first two steps of the proportionality test can be used: the question of suitability or appropriateness, and the question of necessity.

Where the competence articulated in a legal basis is one that is formulated in terms of pursuing objectives (as opposed to one of subject matter)[56] the question

---

[53] *Philip Morris* (n 41) para 189.

[54] AG Juliane Kokott, Opinion *Philip Morris* (n 41) point 179 (quoting Case C-581/10 and C-629/10 *Nelson and Others*, EU:C:2012:657, para 81, with regard to consumer protection).

[55] It should also not be confused with what Craig labels 'competence-based proportionality review' when discussing and dismissing Davies' argument that the subsidiarity inquiry should be replaced by what Davies calls 'the competence function of proportionality' understood as an inquiry into whether 'the EU norm violates proportionality by infringing too greatly on Member State values'. See P Craig, 'A Political and Legal Analysis' (2012) 50 *JCMS* 72, 82, discussing G Davies, 'Subsidiarity: The Wrong Idea, in the Wrong Place at the Wrong Time' (2006) 43 *CMLRev* 63.

[56] On this distinction ('zielbezogene Kompetenz' vs 'sachbezogene Kompetenz') see J Bast, 'Don't Act Beyond Your Powers: The Perils and Pitfalls of the German Federal Constitutional Court' (2017) 15 *German L J* 167, 175.

of a measure's *suitability* or *appropriateness* can arise when reviewing whether it has been based on a proper legal basis. In this review the Court will look at the effects of a measure in order to assess whether it 'in fact pursues the objectives listed by the Community [now Union] legislature',[57] which in turn have to align with the objectives listed in the legal basis. If a measure goes beyond those Treaty objectives reflected in its legal basis (by doing more than what is 'necessary' to achieve these), it will be *ultra vires* for going beyond the limits of competences conferred upon the Union by the Treaties.

Tobacco Advertising I[58] may serve to illustrate the applicability of a means-ends test to the legal basis inquiry. That examination included the question whether the measure in fact pursued the objectives stated by the legislator[59] and met the legal basis requirements.[60] When exercising this review, the Court found that the Tobacco Advertising Directive at issue contained elements of regulation that did not contribute to the legal basis objective contained in Article 114 TFEU. Thus, they were not 'appropriate' vis-à-vis this objective. It also held that the Directive may include elements which, even though they did not contribute to the stated objective of the measure (ensuring free movement of goods and services and thus in line with the Article 114 TFEU legal basis requirement), they are 'necessary to ensure that certain prohibitions imposed in pursuit of that purpose are not circumvented.'[61] Note though that the language of necessity here does not amount to an inquiry about presence or absence of means that are less restrictive of Member State powers; instead, it inquires about the ability of the measure to meet the legitimate legal basis/ Treaty objective. The infamous first Tobacco Advertising Directive over-regulated by including elements that did not contribute to the legal basis objective, and thus the Union had acted beyond its competences.

Another ground for review that is distinct from the legal basis and the proportionality question but bears relevance to the question of 'pursuing in an appropriate manner a legitimate objective' is 'misuse of powers'. This ground has been invoked in cases following *Tobacco Advertising I* judgment, where tobacco control legislation adopted at EU level was challenged on competence grounds.[62] The applicable test of 'misuse of powers' is according to consistent case law the following: 'a measure is vitiated by misuse of powers only if it appears on the basis of objective, relevant and consistent evidence to have been taken with the exclusive or main purpose of achieving an end other than that stated or evading a procedure specifically prescribed by the Treaty for dealing with the circumstances of the case.'[63] The important point to note here is that it asks about the motives of the author of the measure, and is therefore—unlike the legal basis inquiry—*subjective*[64] in nature, as well as very

---

[57] Case C-376/98 *Germany v Parliament and Council*, ECLI:EU:C:2000:544 (*Tobacco Advertising I*), para 85.
[58] Ibid.   [59] Ibid., para 85.   [60] Ibid., para 95.   [61] Ibid., para 100.
[62] E.g. Case C-210/03 *Swedish Match and Others*, ECLI:EU:C:2004:802. See discussion in A Türk, *Judicial Review in EU Law* (Edward Elgar Publishing, 2010), 143.
[63] Ibid., para 74.
[64] Türk (n 62) 162. N Emiliou, *The Principle of Proportionality in EU law—A Comparative Study* (Kluwer Law International, 1996), 190.

difficult to prove. 'Misuse of powers' can and has become relevant in cases where the question is whether the legislature used a legal basis (e.g. Article 114 TFEU) for pursuing an end (e.g. health protection and promotion) in order to circumvent an exclusion of harmonizing national rules for that end as prescribed in another Treaty article (Article 168(5) TFEU). However, as Türk notes, 'this ground seems (...) residuary to the objective ground of review of the legal basis chosen by the institution.'[65] Proportionality is also an *objective* ground of review and to be distinguished on that ground from 'misuse of power'. Türk explains the difference succinctly: proportionality, and to be more precise, the first step of the three-step proportionality test, asks whether 'the institution pursues a proper objective with inappropriate means, whereas in cases of misuse of powers the institution pursues an improper objective.'[66] However, it is important to remember that in proportionality, unlike in the legal basis inquiry, that question is asked only because of the interference of the action with another protected interest, which, in the final analysis, needs to be balanced with the legitimate objective pursued.

There are provisions in the Treaty where *necessity* is an explicit legal basis requirement. That is the case with Article 352 TFEU—also known as the flexibility clause. The first paragraph of this article provides the power to pursue Union objectives set out in the Treaties and within the framework of the policies defined therein, if such action 'should prove necessary' and where the 'necessary powers' have not been granted elsewhere in the Treaties. If this condition is fulfilled, 'appropriate measures' shall be taken. The question thus arises what this requirement of 'necessity' actually entails. In German legal literature, there is a debate as to whether this 'necessity' requirement in Article 352 TFEU is constitutive of the competence (i.e. whether it serves to identify what the competence is) or whether it is a requirement that *limits* the exercise of competence instead and is thus related to Articles 5(3) and 5(4) TEU.[67] The prevailing view is that it is the former, namely, constitutive of competence[68]—a view that is convincing.

Article 352 TFEU is to be understood as a codification of the implied powers doctrine in the wide sense, i.e. that 'the existence of a given objective implies the existence of power reasonably necessary to attain it'.[69] That is different from the necessity

---

[65] See the very short reasoning of the Court in *Swedish Match* (n 62) paras 75–8, with strong reliance on its findings concerning the legal basis inquiry.

[66] Türk (n 62) 142.

[67] For example, it has been suggested that this necessity requirement in Art 352 TFEU is the *lex specialis* to the necessity inquiry in Art 5(4) TEU, but crucially, on the assumption that proportionality in Art 5(4) seeks to protect Member State autonomy. S Kadelbach, 'EUV Artikel 5 (ex-Artikel 5 EGV) [Subsidiaritäts- und Verhältnismäßigkeitsgrundsatz]' in H von der Groeben and others (eds), *Europäisches Unionsrecht* (7th edn, Nomos, 2015), RN 49–54, RN 50.

[68] See discussion in M Rossi, 'AEUV Art 352 [Flexibilitätsklausel]' in C Callies and M Ruffert, *EUV/ AEUV Das Verfassungsrecht der Europäischen Union mit Europäischer Grundrechtecharta* (5th edn, CH Beck, 2016), and in R Streinz, 'AEUV Art. 352 (ex-Art.308 EGV) [Flexibilitätsklausel]' in R Streinz, *EU/AEUV: Vertrag über die Europäische Union und Vertrag über die Arbeitsweise der Europäischen Union*, (2nd edn, CH Beck, 2012).

[69] Craig and de Búrca (n 16), 77. The authors point out that the CJEU has accepted this doctrine in the wide sense; they give case examples in relation to other legal bases but also point out that the CFI has held that such powers are only exceptionally recognized. See Case T-143/06 *MTZ Polyfilms*, ECLI:EU:T:2009:441.

inquiry under the proportionality test, which asks whether there are means available less restrictive of a protected interest.

An illustrative example is found in the EU Fundamental Rights Agency, where its founding Regulation is based on ex Article 308 EC, now Article 352 TFEU. The Union institutions have an obligation under the Charter, and thus the Treaties, not only to protect, but also to promote the EU Charter of Fundamental Rights. It is one thing to ask whether that aim requires the power to create a specialized EU body, such as an agency, in order to be fulfilled (which would be the Article 352(1) TFEU competence question). The answer could be reasonably answered in the affirmative. It is quite another to ask *how* this competence is to be exercised, i.e. what concrete form and mandate can and should be given to this body in order for it to touch as little as possible on the residual powers of the Member States while at the same time add value through its creation at Union level. That is a question of subsidiarity per Article 5(3) TEU, and serves to protect the Member States' residual powers. The second paragraph of Article 352 TFEU refers to that principle in mandating the Commission to draw national Parliaments' attention to proposals made under this article in accordance with the subsidiarity control mechanism referred to in Article 5(3) TEU.

But how do we decide what is 'required' or what is 'reasonably necessary' in the competence constitutive sense? Necessity here refers to the discrepancy between a Treaty aim and its realization.[70] Rossi rightly points out that this assertion is as clear as it is empty because it is in the very definition of an aim that it has not been realized yet, otherwise it would not be an aim.[71] He therefore points to the relative nature of this necessity requirement and suggests that the bigger the discrepancy between an aim and its realization and the longer it persists the more 'necessary' Union action will appear.[72] Of course, when aims are as broadly defined, as the Union's objectives are, Rossi's proposed additional criteria do not appear very useful in actually identifying the competence, and they do not appear to pose significant constraints on the Council. This lack of constraints is the reason why criticisms of competence creep have arisen,[73] and have also led to Declaration No. 42 annexed to the Lisbon Treaty.[74] This is a serious concern, but in search of constraining elements one should not be lead to misinterpreting the necessity requirement in Article 352 TFEU: one first needs to know what the competence is before assessing the degree to which it needs to be constrained when exercised. Therefore, the meaning that the term 'necessary' takes within this Article is one that *identifies* the competence and not one that governs the *exercise* of competence.[75]

---

[70] Streinz (n 68) para 37.   [71] Rossi (n 68) para 44.   [72] Ibid.

[73] And raised in the post-Nice and Laeken Agenda.

[74] Declarations annexed to the final intergovernmental conference, which adopted the Treaty of Lisbon, signed on 13 December 2017, OJ [2012] C 326/337. Declaration No 42 states that Article 352 TFEU 'cannot serve as a basis for widening the scope of Union powers beyond the general framework created by the provisions of the Treaties as a whole and, in particular, by those that define the tasks and the activities of the Union'.

[75] Another provision wherein a necessity requirement is expressly codified is Article 43(2) TFEU. Based on this article the legislature is required to adopt provisions, which are 'necessary for the pursuit of the objectives of the common agricultural policy and the common fisheries policy'. Again here, 'necessary' appears to be a requirement constitutive of competence.

A different scenario is where proportionality is invoked in the review of a Union measure's compatibility with a Treaty article where that sets out objectives addressed to the Union, which cannot be achieved simultaneously. A prime example is Article 39 TFEU (ex Article 33 EC, ex Article 39 EEC), which sets out the objectives of the Common Agricultural Policy. In cases where measures are alleged to breach Article 39 TFEU, the Court grants the legislature wide discretion. It has held that 'in pursuing the objectives of the common agricultural policy the Community institutions must secure the permanent harmonization made necessary by any conflicts between those objectives taken individually and, where necessary, give any one of them temporary priority in order to satisfy the demands of the economic factors or conditions in view of which their decisions are made.'[76]

5. 'Free-standing proportionality' as a Ground of Judicial Review: What it is and Why it is Problematic

'Free-standing proportionality' is not a label for yet another substantive form of proportionality serving some kind of different substantive interest from the three described previously: it is not a fourth additional category in the taxonomy proposed in this paper. Rather, here the term refers to a methodological peculiarity in the application of proportionality in EU law: proportionality is used as a discrete and 'free-standing' ground of judicial review, even though it does not relate to a free-standing substantive value. This is why the label *'free-standing proportionality'* may sound like a contradiction in terms, but the term points precisely to that contradiction.

The possibility of conducting judicial review under free-standing proportionality leads to the following problems: when it is invoked by parties to proceedings and applied by the Court, it is not always immediately clear (1) what interest proportionality is intended to serve and (2) what interest it actually does serve when applied by the Court; at best the latter becomes obvious only in the Court's reasoning. Both points lead to doctrinal confusion and are consequently problematic from the point of view of legal certainty. Moreover, as free-standing proportionality does not expose the interest served, it (3) carries a risk of misapplication and instrumentalization of proportionality. In other words, the Court could invoke the principle but in fact not conduct a proportionality exercise (a balancing of conflicting interests) without that being immediately obvious, and it could do so strategically. This is best understood by way of illustration.

To demonstrate points (1) and (2) we shall return to *Philip Morris*, where the prohibition of marketing of tobacco products with a characterizing flavour was challenged for infringing 'the principle of proportionality'.[77] And the Court conducted its review based on that free-standing ground of judicial review. The plea 'infringement of the principle of proportionality' may cover any of the three forms

---

[76] See Case C-280/93 *Germany v Council*, ECLI:EU:C:1994:367, para 47, and case law cited therein.
[77] *Philip Morris* (n 41) paras 167, 168.

of proportionality mentioned in the taxonomy here. This is why the Court and the AG could actually conduct two different proportionality exercises (burdens-proportionality and rights-proportionality, respectively) in response to the same plea. Moreover, within the Court's reasoning, it becomes only clear at the proportionality *stricto sensu* stage that the Court is actually applying burdens proportionality. That stage is revealing because it forces the Court to identify what two conflicting interests it is balancing.

The potential for misapplication (3) is illustrated by *Gauweiler*,[78] which concerns judicial review of executive discretion. Proportionality featured centre stage in this judgment, but the concrete benchmark for testing it as well as the factors that were supposedly weighed in the proportionality *stricto sensu* analysis are entirely unclear. Arguably, the reason is that the Court did not in fact apply proportionality. Given the importance of *Gauweiler* for the theme of this book, it is also subject of other contributions in this volume.[79] The discussion therefore only briefly recalls the factual background of the case and focuses only on parts of the judgment that are important for the Court's proportionality analysis.

Gauweiler concerned the legality of the Outright Monetary Transactions (OMT) programme of the European Central Bank (ECB). Under the OMT programme the ECB could buy government bonds in secondary markets to lower the market interest rates of bonds of states being subject to speculation that they might leave the Eurozone. The programme had only been announced in a Press Release and has not been used so far. However, its mere announcement contributed crucially to lowering bond yields across the Eurozone and calming financial markets.

The Press Release made the double aim of the OMT programme clear. First, safeguarding the *singleness* of the monetary policy, which is what Article 119(2) TFEU requires. Second, safeguarding an appropriate transmission of monetary policy, which, as the Court noted in *Gauweiler*, contributes to preserving both the singleness of monetary policy and to maintaining price stability.[80] The maintenance of price stability is in fact the primary objective of the Union's monetary policy under Article 127(1) TFEU and Article 282(2) TFEU.

The Court had to assess two main questions in the reference before it: whether the OMT programme violated the prohibition of monetary financing, and—the question that concerns us—whether the programme was a measure of economic as opposed to monetary policy and therefore beyond the European System of Central Banks' (ESCB) powers. The Court answered this latter question by, firstly, establishing the monetary policy nature of the OMT programme,[81] and secondly, also assessing its proportionality as per Article 5(4) TEU.

The Court's first step concerns the *delimitation* of competence, and more precisely in this case 'the delimitation of monetary policy' from economic policy.[82]

---

[78] *Gauweiler* (n 3).   [79] See, in particular, Borger, Chapter 6 in this volume.

[80] *Gauweiler* (n 3) para 49.

[81] Note that also the competence analysis of the Court is not straightforward: the Court adopted the German Constitutional Court's framing.

[82] *Gauweiler* (n 3) para 46.

As discussed, the Court's subsequent analysis on Article 5(4) proportionality should be one that concerns the *exercise* of that competence once it is established that the ESCB has the competence to act; and according to the Treaties the relevant question under Article 5(4) TEU should be whether the action (in this case the OMT programme) creates excessive administrative or financial burdens on one of the legal subjects listed in Protocol No. 2. However, in the judgment the competence and the proportionality question became confused. The remainder of this section illustrates that by considering the Court's holdings on both the delimitation of monetary policy from economic policy and the question of proportionality.

The Court dealt with the delimitation of monetary policy by referencing its findings in the *Pringle*[83] judgment.[84] It recalled that in the absence of a precise definition of monetary policy in the Treaties that issue has to be resolved with reference to the *objectives* of the measure and the *means* used for achieving the objectives.[85]

These two *Pringle* criteria could already be confused with the first two steps of a proportionality analysis as they are concerned with a means-ends analysis; namely, the establishment of permissible aims (monetary policy, price stability) and an assessment of the means in relation to permissible aims (the means should fall inside the realm of monetary policy).

On the permissible *aims*, the Court noted that a programme that aims at singleness of monetary policy and at preserving the monetary policy transmission mechanism contributes to maintaining price stability as per Article 127(1) TFEU and therefore constitutes monetary policy. On the *means* used for achieving the objectives of the programme, the Court noted at the outset that the transactions of the OMT programme use one of the monetary policy instruments provided for by primary law (Article 18.1 of the Protocol on the ESCB and the ECB). The overall conclusion is that the OMT programme falls within the area of monetary policy. The crucial reason lies in the objectives of the ESCB, which is to be contrasted to those of the European Stability Mechanism. The latter's intervention aims at safeguarding the stability of the euro area,[86] whereas the OMT programme 'may be implemented *only in so far as is necessary* for the maintenance of price stability'.[87] Note that the necessity question is clearly employed here in order to answer the competence question. If the action were to go beyond what is necessary to achieve *the aim stipulated in the Treaties*, namely the maintenance of price stability, it would be *ultra vires*. This is different from asking, as required by Article 5(4) TEU, whether the action 'does too much' in the sense of creating undue burdens, while still qualifying as monetary policy.

The Court turned after this step to review what it called 'proportionality' with reference to Article 5(4) TEU. However, it did not apply burdens-proportionality. It actually did not employ a proportionality analysis at all, but a continuation of the competence analysis by looking at whether the programme went in fact beyond the objectives of the Treaties. That is a misapplication of Article 5(4) TEU

---

[83] C-370/12 *Thomas Pringle v Government of Ireland and Others*, EU:C:2012:756.
[84] *Gauweiler* (n 3) paras 46 et seq.   [85] Ibid., paras 43, 46   [86] Ibid., para 64.
[87] Ibid., para 64 (emphasis added).

proportionality. Arguably, such misapplication is possible because of the wording of Article 5(4) TFEU when read in isolation from Protocol No. 2. Recall that Article 5(4) is formulated only in terms of the necessity of an action vis-à-vis Treaty objectives, it does not reference the protected interests (which are indicated in the Protocol). Therefore, the Court could invoke 'free-standing proportionality' with reference to Article 5(4) TEU but then falsely conduct a competence analysis thereunder, because it was not forced to identify a protected interest.

In conducting its analysis under the 'proportionality' heading, the Court started out by granting wide discretion to the ESCB as it usually does in areas that concern complex and technical assessments and policy choices. It then moved to a procedural level of review by noting that, in these areas of broad discretion, 'a review of compliance with certain procedural guarantees is of fundamental importance.'[88] These guarantees encompass the ESCB's obligation to give an adequate statement of reasons[89] and 'to examine carefully and impartially all the relevant elements of the situation in question',[90] as to whether it complied with the duty of care.

The first procedural requirement (statement of reasons) must be fulfilled in order to allow the Court to exercise its powers of review[91] and was therefore tested *before* the Court started its three-step proportionality analysis. One peculiarity of this case is that no formally adopted act was at issue—something which, as the Court notes, is required in order to test the duty to state reasons. Still, the Court found that 'the press release together with the draft legal acts considered during the meeting of the Governing Council at which the press release was approved, make known the essential elements of the programme [...] such as to enable the Court to exercise its power of review'[92] (under the heading of proportionality). The second procedural standard (duty of care) was employed *within* the proportionality test at the first 'appropriateness' stage in light of the reasons that were provided in the press release and the explanations of the ECB.[93] The inquiry was whether the announced programme was appropriate for achieving the ESCB's objectives as per Articles 119(2) TFEU and 127(1) TFEU.

The Court found that the OMT programme, which facilitates the ESCB's monetary policy transmission and safeguards the *singleness* of monetary policy, is indeed appropriate. It conducted that analysis by examining two aspects: first, the assessment that the ESCB's monetary policy transmission was in fact disrupted, and second, that the means chosen would achieve the stated aim, namely, to restore the monetary policy transmission mechanism, the singleness of monetary policy, and maintain price stability.

With respect to the first point, which concerns in essence the finding of facts, the Court employed the duty of care while applying the 'manifest error of assessment' standard of review. It held that the OMT programme was based on an analysis of the economic situation of the euro area, and this analysis of the ESCB was not vitiated by a 'manifest error of assessment'.[94] This conclusion holds, according to the Court, because of the applicable procedural standard of review that 'nothing more

---

[88] Ibid., para 69.   [89] Ibid.   [90] Ibid.   [91] Ibid., para 70.
[92] Ibid., para 71.   [93] Ibid., paras 72–80.   [94] Ibid., para 74.

can be required of the ESCB apart from that it uses its economic expertise and the necessary technical means at its disposal to carry out that analysis with all care and accuracy'.[95] The second point, that the OMT programme would achieve the stated aims based on the given analysis of the economic situation, was then easily answered in the affirmative.

The Court then turned to the next two steps in the proportionality analysis: the questions of 'necessity' and 'proportionality *stricto sensu*'. It did not, however, employ 'procedural review' in answering these particular sub-questions of investigation. That is, the Court did not review whether the ESCB complied with procedural requirements, which would show that the latter has considered and answered the question of proportionality in the affirmative. Still, low-intensity review was applied by testing—as it usually does in areas of wide discretion—whether the measure was 'manifestly' going beyond what is necessary or 'manifestly' disproportionate.

The Court found the OMT programme satisfies the requirement of necessity for two reasons. Firstly, 'the purchase of government bonds on secondary markets is permitted only in so far as it is necessary to achieve the objectives of that programme and [...] such purchases will cease as soon as those objectives have been achieved.'[96] Furthermore, implementation of the programme, which 'is strictly subject' to its objectives, will be dependent on an 'in-depth assessment of the requirements of monetary policy'.[97]

Secondly, the Court notes that the scale of the programme is limited in a number of ways. The programme is limited to (1) bonds of those states that are undergoing a macro-economic adjustment programme [*conditionality*] which have access to the bond market again, and which have a maturity of up to three years, and (2) bonds of those states that disrupt the ESCB's monetary policy [*selectivity*]. The Court also pointed out that the selection of Member States whose bonds may be purchased are identified based on criteria linked to the objectives pursued.[98]

The Court conducted the 'necessity' analysis here only by reference to the objectives listed in Articles 119(2) and 127(1) TFEU, which delimit the ESCB's powers, and not by also taking into account some other protected interest. The reasons the Court provided for demonstrating that the programme is 'necessary' overlap in part with those provided earlier to demonstrate why the OMT programme can be qualified as monetary policy and why the elements of conditionality and selectivity do not point to the contrary conclusion. These elements contribute to achieving the objective of the programme, which coincides with the ESCB's mandate while not undermining its effectiveness and at the same time ensuring the principle mandated under the Treaties that public finances of Member States must be sound. It is evident that the Court conducts at these two stages of appropriateness and necessity a means-ends analysis that relates to a competence inquiry, as explained in Section 4.

At the third—*stricto sensu*—stage of proportionality, the Court provided for only one cryptic sentence: 'the ESCB weighed up the various interests in play so as to actually prevent disadvantages from arising, when the programme in question is

---

[95] Ibid., para 75.   [96] Ibid., para 82.   [97] Ibid., para 83.   [98] Ibid., para 90.

implemented, which are manifestly disproportionate to the programme's object-ives.'[99] This is the most obscure part of the Court's analysis but it may not be sur-prising: the requirements of appropriateness and necessity can be employed to answer competence questions when used only as a means-ends analysis (without taking into account a protected interest).[100] The same is not true for the *stricto sensu* test. At this stage one has to identify the harm caused to a protected interest in order to balance it against the advantages arising from pursuing a legitimate objective.[101] Arguably, it is precisely because proportionality was actually not at stake here that the Court had not much to say on this point.

By contrast, the AG, who introduced the proportionality inquiry into the case, conducted at the proportionality *stricto sensu* stage a cost-benefit analysis, which he sees as requiring 'an assessment of *all* the benefits and costs'.[102] Apart from the diffi-culty of identifying these and weighing them in the abstract (in the form of interest-balancing or otherwise, see Section 2), this type of examination does not have room in a competence analysis that does not aim to balance two conflicting interests. That may be the reason why the Court did not replicate the AG's approach at the *stricto sensu* stage of its assessment.

There still remains the question why the Court would follow the AG to the extent that it employed *free-standing proportionality* with reference to Article 5(4) TEU, rather than limiting itself to a competence analysis. That was the concern of the German Constitutional Court, which did not ask about Article 5(4) TEU or pro-portionality more generally in its order for reference. [103] A cynical answer would be that the split between establishing the monetary policy nature of the OMT pro-gramme first and examining proportionality thereafter allowed the Court to dis-pose of the crucial and controversial question—the question of competence—more easily as unproblematic in a first step. Having cleared the ground of *competence*, the Court went on to change the nature of the inquiry and deal with the most difficult questions under 'proportionality', whereby the appearance of serious judicial review

---

[99] Ibid., para 91.

[100] Which, as we have seen herein, necessity in a real proportionality analysis however does require; in order to answer the 'less restrictive means' question, one has to know what protected interest the measure is restricting.

[101] See Barak (n 9) Ch. 12, 'Proportionality stricto sensu (balancing)', 344.

[102] Opinion AG Cruz Villalón, *Gauweiler* (n 2), point 186 (emphasis added). He went on to identify those to be taken into account: the gained 'benefit' resulting from the OMT programme is that the ECB can restore its monetary policy instruments and thereby ensure that its mandate is effective. The identi-fied 'cost' is that the ECB is exposed to a 'financial risk together with the moral hazard arising from the artificial alteration of the value of the bonds of the State concerned'.

[103] In the follow-up case C-493/17 *Weiss and Others*, ECLI:EU:C:2018:815, concerning the le-gality of the ECB's secondary markets public sector asset purchase programme ('PSPP') the German Constitutional Court picked up on the CJEU's (arguably faulty) approach of employing Article 5(4) TEU proportionality in order to answer the question of competence. In its order for reference one of the questions the German Constitutional Court asked was whether the mandate of the ECB is exceeded because the Decision formalizing the PSPP programme infringes the principle of proportionality. AG Wathelet's Opinion on this point seems confused not only because of his terminology as he conducts both the necessity and the proportionality *stricto sensu* tests under the heading 'proportionality *stricto sensu*' but also because a proportionality *stricto sensu* analysis, which attempts to identify and balance costs and benefits seems to be misplaced here.

is maintained while, at the same time, the Court has an array of tools at its disposal to adopt a 'hands off' approach and employ low intensity review. This may be mere speculation, but given how high the stakes were in this case, a strategic *ex officio* employment of free-standing proportionality is hardly implausible.

6. Conclusion

The fact that there exists proportionality as a free-standing heading of judicial review in EU law (free-standing proportionality) makes it difficult to identify what interest it serves. Yet that identification is crucial in trying to understand what role proportionality plays in EU law overall, especially knowing that the principle applies to any type of EU action, including that of the EU executive. This chapter has sought to bring some clarity on this matter. Taking as a starting point the idea that proportionality is concerned with balancing two conflicting interests—a legitimate objective that an action pursues and some other interest deserving of legal protection under EU law—it focused on this latter protected interest, 'too much' interference with which would render any Union action unlawful. This chapter provided a taxonomy based on that criterion. The taxonomy shows that there are three essential forms of proportionality applicable to any type of Union action: *rights proportionality*, *subsidiarity-proportionality*, and *burdens proportionality*. Any of these forms of proportionality can be employed, however, in the form of *free-standing proportionality*, without it being always obvious which of the three substantive categories is at stake in judicial reasoning or invoked by the parties. This is already causing confusion. That confusion is exacerbated by the fact that free-standing proportionality's ambiguity on the protected interest leaves room for, intentionally or not, misapplying it. This misapplication occurs by not conducting a proportionality analysis under this heading, but rather something that looks similar to it, namely, a means-ends analysis related to competence review. It is this ambiguity of free-standing proportionality that makes it a contentious tool for judicial review and obscures the overall role of the principle of proportionality in EU law.

10

The Interdependencies between Delegation, Discretion, and the Duty of Care

Herwig C. H. Hofmann*

This chapter looks at the development of a set of interlocking legal principles to hold the delegation of discretionary powers to account: notably the duty of care and the principle of proportionality. The relation between the concepts of delegation, discretion, care, and proportionality are not always very clearly established in EU law. Therefore, this chapter seeks to undertake a 'reconnaissance mission' and try to explain which principles of review are developing and why. This chapter then seeks to link the developments in an attempt to obtain a clearer view of the overall picture of ensuring effective yet accountable executive decision making in the EU.

This chapter first addresses the role and context of delegation of powers in EU law (Section 1) before looking at discretion and its subcategories as well as at how the Court of Justice of the European Union (CJEU) has approached different instances of discretion (Section 2). It then looks at review of discretionary powers (Section 3), concentrating on the duty of care and its role in the context of proportionality review in the context of discretionary powers (Section 4). Finally, the chapter draws some conclusions and avenues for future research regarding these complex questions (Section 5).

1. Delegation

The starting point of the observations in this chapter is that delegation of powers to executive bodies is a necessity in all legal systems. In complex modern societies, effectiveness, flexibility, and making choices adapted to future situations is not possible without delegation. The concept of delegation employed here is broad. Under the EU's concept of conferral of powers within a multilevel structure, any power to be exercised by EU institutions, bodies, offices, and agencies is delegated to them. Such delegation may take place by Treaty provisions by means of attribution of powers to the executive—essentially a delegation from Member States to individual

---

* Professor of European and Transnational Public Law, University of Luxembourg.

EU institutions. Other delegations take place by EU legislative act by which the Commission or EU agencies or also Member State bodies grant powers to executive bodies. Finally, delegation may also arise as, what might be called, subdelegation of powers. Subdelegation is delegation from one body of the executive to another, e.g. from the Commission to an executive agency of the Union or from an EU agency to a national body. These delegations may cover the full range from the development of specific policies through to the simple implementation of often highly technical regulations for the internal market.[1]

In general, however, the act of delegating powers must employ some abstract language or terms open to interpretation as well as some description of tasks for which the recipient of delegation can chose the most appropriate means. The terms of delegation of substantive decision-making leeway of the authority concerned can thus be precise or open-ended, or a mix of both. Delegation will thus appear on a spectrum. At one extreme is the idea of completely bound or pre-determined decision making having no interpretative space. Free, unlimited decision-making discretion is at the other extreme. Between these two extremes we find various shades of more or less constrained decision-making competence which, from an abstract point of view, can be understood to cover various contexts. They can concern the identification of the limits of what has been delegated; they can concern the question which input needs to be taken into account in decision making; they can define the possibilities of the outcome of decision-making process; or they can consist of a combination of these options.

The first context requires an answer as to what has been delegated. It touches upon the degree of openness and empowerment that a delegating act contains. Generally, the interpretation of an act delegating powers and thus the definition of the circumscription of powers delegated is subject to full review by Courts and no discretionary powers are afforded to the recipient of delegation in this regard. However, exceptionally, the recipient of delegation has been granted the power in the enabling act, to interpret the extent of their legal mandate. In other cases, it has been acknowledged that the recipient of delegation is required to interpret the conditions of empowerment. The interpretation of the terms of delegation and thus their concretization is then an instance of exercise of powers which are either discretionary in nature or deserve similar treatment to matters of discretion.[2]

The other three contexts of delegation of open powers can be illustrated with the empowerments of the Commission in the TFEU's provisions on State aids.

---

[1] Examples for such far-reaching delegation of powers arise from reading the Treaties and legislation, but for an example, it suffices to look at the facts underlying Case C-493/17 *Weiss and Others* [2017] ECLI:EU:2017:792, which addresses the legality of an ECB spending programme of considerable dimensions.

[2] Various legal systems approach such questions quite differently. The case law of the CJEU (e.g. German law) submits the question of interpretation of the law to full judicial review combined with the possibility of the judiciary replacing administrative interpretations. Some legal systems (e.g. outside the EU, US law) require judicial bodies to, in principle, defer to agency interpretations of legislative empowerments. This is the content of the famous *Chevron* doctrine of the US supreme court (*Chevron, U.S.A., Inc. v Nat. Res. Def. Council, Inc.*, 467 (1984) U.S. 837), which is, however, modified by several more recent cases, e.g. *Mead* (*United States v Mead Corp.*, 533 (2001) U.S. 218).

First, the Treaty has delegated to the Commission powers with respect to the input into decision making, for example, in Article 107(2) TFEU, which, *inter alia*, declares 'aid having a social character ... provided that such aid is granted without discrimination related to the origin of the products concerned' to be compatible with the internal market. The Commission, in its implementation of Treaty provisions on state aid (under Article 108 TFEU) must evaluate whether any given aid has such social character and is not discriminatory. In such a case, the Commission is then bound to regard such aid as being compatible with the internal market.

Second, it is equally possible that, under certain specified conditions, the administration will have the freedom to choose from among various possible consequences. For example Article 108(2), second paragraph TFEU states that, where a Member State has not complied with a Commission decision, the Commission 'may ... refer the matter to the Court of Justice'. In this constellation, the administration has a margin to decide about the outcome, i.e. the output of decision making. This is the constellation most frequently associated with the notion of discretion.

Third and finally, there are situations where there exists a combination of freedom to interpret the content of the empowering act, to evaluate the facts on the input side of decision-making, or to decide which of various possible consequences are to follow the final decision. For example, Article 107(3) TFEU declares that certain types of aid, e.g. 'aid to promote the economic development of areas where the standard of living is abnormally low or where there is serious underemployment', may be considered compatible with the internal market. Here we find a combination of the empowerment of the Commission to first define and then establish the existence of certain specified conditions ('abnormally low', 'serious underemployment'). Once so evaluated, Article 107(3) TFEU requires the Commission to clarify the consequence of making such findings.

Since all administrative powers are based on a delegation, contained either in primary Treaty provisions or in secondary legislation, some sort of legal framework of substantive and procedural principles and rules is always applicable to bind even apparently open-ended and broad delegations. This is not only a premise of a system under the rule of law, but also a result of a more normative requirement that legitimate delegation of administrative powers and its exercise requires moderation and binding of the exercise of public powers to a pre-defined set of constitutional values and rights.[3] The rules and principles of EU constitutional and administrative law balance the necessary delegation of administrative powers with the requirement of control over its exercise, not only from a procedural, but also a substantive, point of view.[4]

The development and application of these precepts has been a complex task, mainly undertaken through case law addressing specific problems in single policy

---

[3] See J Mendes, 'Discretion and Law in the EU Administration: Where the Courts do not Enter' in HCH Hofmann and J Ziller (eds), *Accountability in the EU—The Role of the European Ombudsman* (Elgar Publishing, 2017), 144–77.

[4] Where the applicable rules and principles are not explicit they will need to be inferred from the purpose and character of both the empowering measure and the empowerment itself.

areas and through the formulation of general principles of EU (administrative) law. In reality, the issue of the interpretation of the scope and nature of delegations and the consequent extent of substantive decision-making power is highly intertwined with practical and theoretical notions of the judicial supervision of administrative activity.[5]

How to ensure that delegation of powers is undertaken in the context of the delegating act is often a question of the forms and degree of oversight. In practical terms, therefore, delegation and discretion cannot really be seen in isolation from supervisory powers. This is well understood and described, in public choice literature, in the context of the analysis of delegation in principle-agent analysis.[6]

However, supervision takes place in the form of judicial supervision but also by means of complex administrative controls and forms of political supervision. Next to courts, therefore, a variety of bodies such as the Ombudsman[7] and the Court of Auditors review the activity of the EU's administration as to their compliance with the law and the exercise of their powers, including discretionary powers, within the law. Any such supervision thus must ask some key questions: Where is the administration best left to define its own approach, whether interpreting the confines of delegation, on the input or output-side of decision making? Where should modes of review embark upon controlling the administration's interpretation and application of a legal norm delegating power to it? What is the nature of the review which in fact takes place? The answers to these and related questions will vary according to the extent and nature of the powers delegated.

2. Discretion and Margins of Appreciation

This omnipresence of delegation in the EU legal system results in very frequent delegation of discretion. In the case of delegations of powers to the Commission, for example, the delegation of discretionary powers can cover the power whether or not to investigate a case, to start an infringement procedure, to follow up on a complaint, to decide upon which type of act to adopt if there is the choice between various forms of act, to set its priorities in its work-programme, to submit a proposal to a comitology committee, and many other more. Other institutions with far-reaching delegation of administrative powers and far-reaching discretion as to when, how,

---

[5] Art 19(1) TEU (Art 220 EC) requiring that the CJ and the GC 'shall ensure ... that the law is observed', gives a mandate for review of legal aspects, including limits to delegation. It generally does not give a mandate to review the expediency of a measure against policy considerations. See, e.g. Case C-236/99 *Commission v Belgium* [2000] ECR I-5657, para 28, with reference to Case 209/88 *Commission v Italy* [1990] ECR I-4313, para 16: '[I]t should be pointed out that under the system established by Art. 226 EC the Commission enjoys a discretionary power as to whether it will bring an action for failure to fulfil obligations and it is not for the Court to judge whether that discretion was wisely exercised'.

[6] For many, see, e.g. JL Mashaw, 'Prodelegation: Why Administrators Should Make Political Decisions' (1985) 1 *J Law Econ Organ* 81; MA Pollack, *The Engines of European Integration* (OUP, 2003).

[7] See Mendes (n 3) 144–77, 169.

and under which conditions to exercise them is the ECB (European Central Bank).[8] The CJEU has also explicitly recognized that EU agencies can be the recipient of wide discretion.[9]

The case law of the CJEU considers the question of the extent of delegation of discretionary powers, putting less emphasis on assuming the existence of clearly and rigidly delimited, abstract categories of pre-defined types of discretion, but applying instead a degree of judicial review adapted to specific constellations of delegation.[10] This arises from the CJEU case law, which has, in the past, used varied terminology to describe different types of delegation and to distinguish between certain basic modes of decision making. Identifying the extent of delegation of discretionary powers and its legal limits in EU law requires careful, contextual analysis of the underlying legal provisions.

2.1 Wide discretion

Delegation of far-reaching decision-making powers to the administration is often referred to by the CJEU as 'wide discretion'. Of fundamental importance here is the decision in *Meroni*,[11] where the Court interpreted a 'wide margin of discretion' as a delegation which 'according to the use which is made of it, make[s] possible the execution of actual economic policy'.[12] In *Meroni*, and maybe even more so in the following early cases, the CJEU often associated the notion of discretion with the delegation of quasi-legislative decision-making powers to executive bodies. In *Meroni*, for example, the Court of Justice differentiated between, on one hand, 'wide' discretion and, on the other hand, a more limited 'margin of appraisal'.[13] In the *Inland Vessels* opinion, the Court distinguished the delegation of, on the one

[8] This is brought to the foreground in cases such as C-62/14, *Gauweiler and Others v Deutscher Bundestag (OMT)* [2015] ECLI:EU:C:2015:400 as well as C-493/17, *Weiss and Others* [2017] ECLI:EU:2017:792 that both address spending programmes of the ECB, which the German Constitutional Court, in its decision on preliminary reference to the CJEU, estimated to be worth 1.8 trillion Euros by the time of its decision in May 2017 and at the time of the decision of *Weiss and Others* was estimated at 2.6. trillion Euros. See: Decision of the German Constitutional Court, Bundesverfassungsgericht of 24 May 2017, 2 BvR 859/15, 1651/15, 2006/15, and 980/16.

[9] See cases, e.g. C-534/10 P *Brookfield New Zealand and Elaris v CPVO and Schniga* [2012] EU:C:2012:813, para 51; Case C-546/12 P *Ralf Schräder v Community Plant Variety Office* [2015] ECLI:EU:C:2015:332, para 56: '…the CPVO has a wide discretion concerning annulment of a plant variety right…'

[10] The Member States 'legal systems' approaches differ widely as to the theoretical and practical approaches to the review of these powers. The literature on substantive control of administrative activity in various jurisdictions is far too voluminous to be cited and explored here. This chapter attempts, therefore, to review the background and the developments in EU administrative law only. As Schwarze points out in his comparative work on the EC and some of its Member States, a great variety of approaches to the definition and control of discretion exist. See J Schwarze, *Europäisches Verwaltungsrecht* (2nd edn, Nomos, 2005), 246–482.

[11] Case 9/56 *Meroni v ECSC High Authority* [1957/58] ECR English special edition 133. Therein the ECJ defined limitations to the possibility of delegation of administrative tasks to bodies not established by the founding Treaties.

[12] Ibid., 152 (emphasis added).

[13] Ibid. On the current tensions that this case presently raises, see also Moloney, Chapter 5 in this volume.

hand, full 'discretion' and, on the other hand, powers more clearly circumscribed, making them 'only executive powers'.[14] Today, the notion of a wide margin of discretion is also often referred to as a 'broad discretion'.[15]

Key to this notion is that the administration is thus granted powers to decide about the substance of a certain policy,[16] also with a view to future situations.[17] A broad discretion may also be granted to the institutions by the Treaties, for example, the implicit institutional right to decide upon its own organization.[18] Wide or broad discretion is also respected in areas in which complex economic or socioeconomic considerations to be taken into account.[19] It is also accepted in fields where EU agencies or the Commission have been granted the power to undertake assessments of complex economic or technical contexts.[20]

Despite its frequent use, the courts have so far not given any express definition of the notion of 'complexity'.[21] However, a review of the case law indicates that this notion is used as a shorthand for the requirement of undertaking a decision balancing up a combination of various factors, of evaluations and prognoses of future factual developments, and of interests and rights.[22] Relying on such shorthand for the definition of the areas of 'wide discretion' or 'wide margin of appreciation' can be confusing. In fact, 'complexity' might be a misnomer. After all, the fact that a matter

---

[14] Opinion 1/76 *Draft Agreement establishing the European laying-up fund for inland waterway vessels* [1977] ECR 741, para 7.

[15] E.g. Case T-54/99 *max.mobil v Commission* [2002] ECR II-313, para 58; Case 69/83 *Lux v Court of Auditors* [1984] ECR 2447.

[16] See, e.g. Case C-180/96 *United Kingdom v Commission (BSE II-case)* [1998] ECR I-2265, para 97; Joined Cases T-481 and 484/93 *Exporteurs in Levende Varkens v Commission* [1995] ECR II-2941, paras 91, 120, both from the policy area of agriculture.

[17] E.g. Case 40/72 *Schröder KG v Germany* [1973] ECR 125, para 28.

[18] See, e.g. Case 69/83 *Lux v Court of Auditors* [1984] ECR 2447: 'The Community institutions have a broad discretion to organize their departments to suit the tasks entrusted to them and to assign the staff available to them in the light of such tasks, on condition however that the staff is assigned in the interests of the service and in conformity with the principle of assignment to an equivalent post'. See also Case 19/70, *Almini v Commission* [1971] ECR 623, para 8.

[19] See, e.g. Case C-380/03 *Germany v Parliament and Council* [2006] ECR I-11573, para 145; Case C-284/95 *Safety Hi-Tech v S. & T.* [1998] ECR I-4301, para 37; Case C-86/03 *Greece v Commission* [2005] ECR I-10979, para 88; Case C-120/99 *Italy v Council* [2001] ECR I-7997, para 44; Case 113/88 *Leukhardt v Hauptzollamt Reutlingen* [1989] ECR 1991, para 20; Case C-4/96 *NIFPO and Northern Ireland Fishermen's Federation v Department of Agriculture for Northern Ireland* [1998] ECR I-681, paras 41, 42; and Case C-179/95 *Spain v Council* [1999] ECR I-6475, para 29.

[20] With respect to EU agencies, see, e.g. Case C-61/15 P *Heli-Flight v European Aviation Safety Agency (EASA)* [2016] ECLI:EU:C:2016:59, para 101; and C-270/12 *UK v EP and Council (ESMA Short Selling)* [2014] ECLI:EU:C:2014:18, paras 45–7. With respect to the Commission, see, e.g. Case C-399/08 P *Deutsche Post v Commission* [2010] EU:C:2010:481, para 97; Case C-352/98 P *Bergaderm and Goupil v Commission* [2000] ECR I-5291, para 46; Case 42/84 *Remia v Commission* [1985] ECR 2545, para 34; Joined Cases 142 and 156/84 *BAT and Reynolds v Commission* [1987] ECR 4487, para 62; and Case C-194/99 P *Thyssen Stahl v Commission* [2003] ECR I-10821, para 78 as well as Case T-271/03 *Deutsche Telekom v Commission* [2008] ECR II-477, para 185. All with further references.

[21] See, further, Nehl, Chapter 8 in this volume.

[22] See, e.g. J Azizi, 'The Tension between Member States' Autonomy and Commission Control in State Aid Matters: Selected Aspects' in H Kanninen and others (eds), *EU Competition Law in Context: Essays in Honour of Virpi Tiili* (Hart, 2009), 307–20; A Bouveresse, *Le pouvoir discrétionnaire dans l'ordre juridique communautaire* (Bruylant, 2010), 366–9; D Ritleng, 'Le juge communautaire de la légalité et le pouvoir discrétionnaire des institutions communautaires' (1999) 9 *AJDA* 645, 650.

contains economically or technically complex considerations should not necessarily put it beyond the intellectual reach of a court.[23] In fact, as AG Jacobs in *Technische Universität München* pointed out, such approach would risk violating the right to an effective judicial protection.[24] Judges are—or should be—capable of reviewing a dossier, and of reconstructing complex situations and conducting a legal assessment of the subject matter.[25] What lies behind the usage of considerations of complexity is actually the idea that policy decisions or decisions based on specific, non-legal expertise should be taken by the institutions that have both a competence and a mandate to do.[26] This is indeed the fundamental consideration underlying the notion of separation of powers. It lies at the heart of the legitimacy of actions taken and roles played by different institutions and is a result of the CJEU's mandate to ensure under Article 19(1) TEU generally the review of legality of the acts of the institutions and bodies of the Union and not the expediency of their action from a political point of view.[27] This mandate already underlay the holding in *Meroni*, where the Court referred to the 'balance of powers which is characteristic of the institutional structure of the community'[28]—the institutional balance—as a reason for its limitations upon the delegations in question there.

2.2 Reduced discretion and margins of appreciation or appraisal

Reduced discretion in other cases has been referred to as a 'margin of appreciation' and a 'margin of discretion',[29] a 'discretionary margin of appraisal',[30] a 'discretionary margin',[31] as well as 'certain discretion'.[32] The General Court is ready to qualify a delegation of administrative decision-making powers as 'reduced discretion', for example, in cases of 'the simple application of the law on the basis of the elements of fact available to the Commission'.[33] The varying terminology applied in the case law signals a lack of clear boundaries between the individual concepts and modes.

---

[23] See, e.g. the case law regarding risk assessment and risk management, in which despite the necessity of administrations to undertake 'complex technical and scientific assessments', judicial review was undertaken in a detailed fashion. See, e.g. Case 14/78 *Denkavit v Commission* [1978] ECR 2497, para 20; Case T-13/99 *Pfizer Animal Health v Council* [2002] ECR II-3305, paras 154–63.

[24] AG Jacobs in Case C-269/90 *Technische Universität München v Hauptzollamt München-Mitte* [1991] ECR I-5469, paras 10–16.

[25] V Tiili and J Vanhamme, 'The "Power of Appraisal" (Pouvoir d'Appréciation) of the Commission of the EC vis-à-vis the Powers of Judicial Review of the Communities' Court of Justice and Court of First Instance' (1999) 22 *Fordham Int LJ* 885, 890.

[26] See, e.g. Case T-187/06 *Schräder v CPVO* [2008] ECR II-3151, paras 59–63. The case is the first explicitly granting discretionary powers to an agency, potentially in conflict with the *Meroni* doctrine.

[27] Article 19(1) TEU empowers the Courts to ensure that 'in the interpretation and application of the Treaties the law is observed'.

[28] Case 9/56 *Meroni v ECSC High Authority* [1957/58] ECR English special edition 133, 152.

[29] Case C-12/03 P *Commission v Tetra Laval* [2005] ECR I-987, para 39.

[30] Case T-22/97 *Kesko v Commission* [1999] ECR II-3775, para 143.

[31] Case T-102/96 *Gencor v Commission* [1999] ECR II-753, para 165.

[32] Ibid., para 164.

[33] Case T-28/03 *Holcim (Deutschland) v Commission* [2005] ECR II-1357, paras 99–100, which draw the conclusion that '[i]t follows from those factors that the Commission's discretion was reduced in the present case'. The facts of the case are based on an antitrust decision of the Commission.

Therefore, as pointed out, far from being categorically distinct, the various forms of delegation of decision-making powers are distributed along a spectrum ranging from completely constrained to completely free. That which can be found between those extremes is indicative of the scope of the interpretative choices of the legislative basis, and of the choices contained in the decision-making parameters specifically defined in such legislation.

2.3 Bound decisions

Decision making is bound where the satisfaction of the statutory prerequisites of an administrative decision is the only matter to be determined by the decision maker. In this situation, the administration must act to comply with the statutorily speci-fied consequence, once such prerequisites have been satisfied.[34] There is no oppor-tunity in this decision-making mode to bring together relevant considerations and weigh them up in the light of statutory goals. The decision maker must (merely) establish that certain legally established elements—typically, the existence of certain kinds of facts or circumstances—are present.[35] The determination of what exactly the statutory prerequisites are (and what they mean) will often, nevertheless, require the interpretation of unclear statutory terms. Even where no discretion has been conferred on an administration, the content and meaning of a delegating provision may need to be determined by interpretation—often in light of facts, the existence of which must be established by the decision maker. An example of this exists in state aid cases, concerning the definition of an aid under Article 107 TFEU. The European courts have held that the concept of aid is objective, the test being whether a state measure confers an advantage on one or more particular undertakings.[36] Here, the Commission assesses situations in applying the law without enjoying a discretion, 'save for particular circumstances owing to the complex nature of the State intervention in question'.[37]

In the result, even where no delegation of discretionary powers has been conferred on an administrative actor, interpretations of the delegating act, the determination of the facts, and the ultimate holding that the statutory prerequisites have been met,

---

[34] C König, 'Haftung der Europäischen Gemeinschaft gem. Art. 288 Abs. 2 EG wegen rechtswidriger Kommissionsentscheidungen in Beihilfesachen' (2005) 7 *EuZW* 202, 204.

[35] However, in certain circumstances factual analysis will be submitted to the margin of appreciation category, see *Remia* (n 20) para 34.

[36] Case C-83/98 P *France v Ladbroke Racing and Commission* [2000] ECR I-3271, para 25; Case T-296/97 *Alitalia v Commission* [2000] ECR II-3871, para 95; Case T-98/00 *Linde v Commission* [2002] ECR II-3961, para 40.

[37] Case T-67/94 *Ladbroke Racing v Commission* [1998] ECR II-1, paras 52–3; Case T-358/94 *Air France v Commission* [1996] ECR II-2109, para 71; Case C-56/93 *Belgium v Commission* [1996] ECR I-723, paras 10–11. These particular circumstances have been found by the case law, e.g. in areas in which the Commission, in order to determine whether investment by the public authorities in the capital of an undertaking, constitutes State aid within the meaning of Art 107 TFEU, considers the so-called 'private investor test'. See Case C-56/93 *Belgium v Commission* [1996] ECR I-723, para 10; Joined Cases T-126/96 and T-127/96 *Breda Fucine Meridionali and Others v Commission* [1998] ECR II-3437, para 5; T-296/97 *Alitalia v Commission* [2000] ECR II-3871, para 105; T-301/01 *Alitalia v Commission* [2008] ECR II-1753, para 185; T-196/04 *Ryanair v Commission* [2008] ECR II-3643, para 41.

or not, will normally be submitted to full judicial review, underlining the point that what is involved here is a matter of objective determination and not expedient judgement, weighing up, or evaluation. The fact that a delegation of administrative tasks does not contain discretionary powers does not mean that the institution or body applying the law cannot make decisions of its own. It means merely that these are submitted to full review, and that mistakes can incur liability for damages. Also, this type of decision making can be delegated to bodies not provided for in the Treaties, such as agencies, as long as they are supervised.

Discretionary and non-discretionary decision making can, of course, be present in the same administrative procedure. As an example, one can refer to risk assessment and risk management issues. In modern regulatory regimes the 'technical' fact-finding associated with risk assessment is often a task delegated to specific bodies, such as the European Food Safety Agency, the Medicines Authority, or the European Chemicals Agency (ECHA). Such a body will, on the basis of a legal definition, establish the extent of a risk and in certain instances suggest policy approaches to address it. On the other hand, risk management decisions—decisions regarding the balancing of rights and interests—are generally reserved to the Commission.[38] This approach is problematic though, because both the distinction between risk assessment and risk management as well as, in a wider sense, the distinction between technical aspects of a decision-making procedure and the political, rights-related ones, are inherently woolly.

3. Review of Discretion

The exercise of the discretionary powers delegated to executive actors is circumscribed by legal criteria in the enabling norm identifying the purpose of the exercise and the public interest to be pursued, the general principles and values of EU law, as well as the rights of individuals. Probably the most important consequence of the European courts' finding of the existence of a discretion is that they will then, generally, exercise only marginal judicial review.[39] The courts, when finding that there has been a delegation of broad discretionary powers, tend to limit review, under the *Remia* formula, to 'verifying whether the relevant procedural rules have been complied with, whether the statement of reasons for the decision is adequate, whether the facts have been accurately stated and whether there has been any manifest error of appraisal or misuse of powers'.[40]

---

[38] See, e.g. the underlying facts and the legal assessment of the CFI in *Pfizer Health* (Case T-13/99 *Pfizer Animal Health v Council* [2002] ECR II-3305). There, the medical agency had not been delegated discretionary decision-making powers. Discretion is maintained by the Commission. That discretion by the Commission is then limited by the obligation to state reasons in case the Commission decides to divert from the proposals for risk management made by an agency.

[39] For further explanation of the French origins of these concepts developed by the case law, see Ritleng (n 22).

[40] See, e.g. *Remia* (n 20) para 34.

Reduced judicial review under the *Remia* formula should, however, be more of an exception than the rule, since it has potentially limiting factors on the legality review required under Article 19(1) TEU.[41] Accordingly, a tendency can be observed in the more recent case law of the past years of the CJEU of limiting cases of where it accepts administrative 'wide discretion'.[42] The principle–exception relation stems also from the fact that, where the delegation of policy choices is contemplated, a legislative act or a Treaty provision must clearly—explicitly or implicitly—state or indicate that is the case.[43] As a consequence, in cases held not to fall within the category of wide or broad discretion, the courts generally are inclined to raise the intensity of the review of legality to a level higher than that undertaken in applying the 'manifest error' test, used for cases of wide discretion. For example, where a delegating act confers only reduced discretion, judicial review with respect to annulment will be more thorough, and damages may be the consequence of the mere infringement of European law.[44]

Also, Article 261 TFEU clarifies that the CJEU will exercise 'unlimited jurisdiction with regard to the penalties provided for in such regulations'.[45] In these cases, despite the Commission's endowment with a delegation for the making of a discretionary decision establishing an adequate penalty for a violation of a legal provision, such penalties may be subject to full review resulting even in a *de novo* decision by the reviewing court exercising full review.

In view of the problem of the apparent lack of a clear and precise distinction along the spectrum of the different categories of wide discretion, discretion, and reduced discretion which arises from the great range of possibilities in the delegation

[41] See, further, Nehl, Chapter 8 in this volume.

[42] In *Holcim*, the GC was exceptionally explicit in that it hinted at the fact that 'it is *only* where it reviews complex economic appraisals' that the GC applies the criteria of marginal review through its formula of reducing control to only 'manifest error or appraisal or misuse of powers' Case T-28/03 *Holcim (Deutschland) v Commission* [2005] ECR II-1357, para 95 (emphasis added), with reference to *Remia* (n 20) para 34, and Case C-7/95 P *Deere v Commission* [1998] ECR I-3111, para 34. See with further discussion A Fritzsche, 'Discretion, Scope of Judicial Review and Institutional Balance in European Law' (2010) 47 *CMLRev* 361.

[43] According to the ECJ, an explicit delegation exists, e.g. in cases of decision making by the Commission in combination with a comitology procedure. See, e.g. Joined Cases C-154 and 155/04 *Alliance for Natural Health and others* [2005] ECR I-6451, para 90, in which the Court held that 'when the legislature wishes to delegate its powers to amend aspects of the legislative act at issue, it must ensure that power is clearly defined and that the exercise of the power is subject to strict review in the light of objective criteria'.

[44] This is explicitly confirmed, e.g. with respect to EU liability for damages under Article 340 TFEU. In *Antillian Rice* (Case C-390/95 P *Antillean Rice Mills and others* [1999] ECR I-769, para 58) and *Bergaderm* (Case C-352/98 P *Bergaderm and Goupil v Commission* [2000] ECR I-5291, paras 43–4, with reference to Case C-5/94 *The Queen v Ministry of Agriculture, Fisheries and Food, ex parte Hedley Lomas (Ireland)* [1996] ECR I-2553, para 28). There, the CJEU held that, where a Member State or an EU institution enjoys a discretion, a breach of the institution's obligations will lead to the obligation to make good damages where 'the Member State or the Community institution concerned manifestly and gravely disregarded the limits on its discretion'. On the other hand, it found, that 'where the Member State or the institution in question has only considerably reduced, or even no, discretion the mere infringement of Community law may be sufficient to establish the existence of a sufficiently serious breach'.

[45] F Schmidt, *Die Befugnis des Gemeinschaftsrichters zu unbeschränkter Ermessensnachprüfung* (Nomos, 2004), 19.

of administrative powers, the case law has approached the possible distinctions of the degree of review in various policy areas with great pragmatism and with great variation of the terminology used, albeit, it must be said, at the cost of a certain lack of clarity and coherence in relation to the underlying problems.

4. Fine-tuning the Degree of Review of Discretionary Powers and Respect for Procedural Guarantees

Generally speaking, the common denominator of instances where the courts find a simple or reduced discretion, as opposed to a broader discretion, seems to be that they will more fully exercise their powers to review decision making, both with respect to their interpretation of a rule-making mandate as well as, where applicable, single-case decision making. However, although there appears to be a tendency to protect individual rights in the increased intensity of such review, this will often become visible not through the initial wording of the criteria as such. Rather, the true test is the intensity by which courts review compliance with principles such as the 'duty of care' by probing whether full and impartial analysis of all relevant facts of the case has taken place. Also required is an in-depth probing into the exercise of the principle of proportionality, especially the balancing of several possible regulatory approaches in view of the least onerous choice.

The CJEU has developed its *Remia* formula stressing, since its seminal case in *Technische Universität München*, that where an institution has been granted a power of appraisal, 'respect for the rights guaranteed by the Community [now Union] legal order in administrative procedures is of even more fundamental importance.'[46] The reason for this development is linked to the heightened awareness of the CJEU as to the necessity of the protection of individual rights under EU law. Furthermore, public law concepts in general, applied throughout constitutional systems, have evolved in the past sixty years since the pronouncements in *Meroni* and others. Two factors will be analysed to greater detail in the following. One is the developing relation between facts and law and the review of scientific input versus legal analysis which is now crystallising in the 'duty of care' (Section 4.1). Another is the role of the proportionality principle, whose relation with the notion of discretion is fraught with difficulties (Section 4.2).

4.1 Duty of care and the notion of facts

Since the early 1990s, not coincidently during a phase of great expansion of the administrative law and practice of the EU, the CJEU has been developing its case law on the notion of facts and the review of these in the context of executive action under the so-called duty of care.

---

[46] *Technische Universität München* (n 24).

The concept of facts, which led to a certain degree of expansion of judicial review, was developed with respect to the classification of non-legal theories, e.g. economic theory as facts in the case law of the CJEU. Thereby, the scope of the matters subject only to limited review has become more circumscribed than in earlier case law.[47] The first wave of cases where economic theory and its conclusions (as well as technical assessments) were subject to the same review as facts was in the early 2000s in *max.mobil*,[48] *Airtours*,[49] *Tetra Laval*,[50] and *Schneider*.[51] In *max.mobil*—a single-case administrative decision on the application of competition law—the GC had distinguished the facts subject to full review and the law. The material accuracy of the facts relied on must be thoroughly examined by the Court, whereas the prima facie appraisal of those facts and, more so, the decision whether it is necessary to take action, are subject to limited review by the Court.[52]

Later, in *Tetra Laval*, the Court of Justice clarified the degree of review of broadly understood facts by holding that 'not only must the Community Courts, *inter alia*, establish whether the evidence relied on is factually accurate, reliable and consistent but also whether that evidence contains all the information which must be taken into account in order to assess a complex situation and whether it is capable of substantiating the conclusions drawn from it.'[53]

The distinction between law and fact is difficult in many legal systems.[54] In some legal systems of the EU Member States this distinction had also direct effect on the notions of judicial review of discretionary powers.[55] Nonetheless, the CJEU found an elegant way around the distinctions by declaring most factors relevant as input

[47] It has not done so, however, in the context of decision making of more legislative character. Here, the courts have been rather broad with respect to including factual concerns in the notion of discretion. E.g. in *Agraz* (Case T-285/03 *Agraz and others v Commission* [2005] ECR II-1063, para 73, with reference to Case 138/79 *Roquette v Council* [1980] ECR 3333, para 25; Case C-243/05 P *Agraz and others v Commission* [2006] ECR I-10833, para 34), the CFI and the ECJ were called upon to define the degree of discretion enjoyed by the Commission in fixing the amount of an aid to tomato growers in application of the EC Treaty. It was therein confirmed that in legislative contexts, 'when evaluating a complex economic situation, the Commission's discretion also applies to the finding of the basic facts'.

[48] Case T-54/99 *max.mobil v Commission* [2002] ECR II-313.

[49] Case T-342/99 *Airtours v Commission* [2002] ECR II-2585.

[50] Case T-5/02 *Tetra Laval v Commission* [2002] ECR II-4381, upheld on appeal in *Commission v Tetra Laval* (n 29).

[51] Case T-351/03, *Schneider Electric v Commission* [2007] ECR II-2237. On this development, see further Nehl, Chapter 8 in this volume.

[52] *max.mobil* (n 48) para 59. The ECJ on appeal found that the case before the CFI had been inadmissible, thus not further reviewing the reasoning of the CFI in substance, including the cited passage in para 59. See Case C-141/02 P *Commission v max.mobil* [2005] ECR I-1283.

[53] *Commission v Tetra Laval* (n 29) para 39.

[54] See D Simon, 'Une théorie de l'intensité du contrôle juridictionnel est-elle possible?' (2005) 12 *Europe* 3; P Craig, *EU Administrative Law* (OUP, 2006) Ch. 12; Ritleng (n 22) 648; all with further examples.

[55] See e.g. the distinction in Italian law between technical discretion (*discrezionalità tecnica*) and administrative discretion (*discrezionalità amministrativa*) and in German law between the more complete review of factual input into decision making (*Beurteilungsspielraum*) and the more marginal review of output related discretion (*Ermessen*).

to decision making, to be included in the notion of fact, subject to review. This was established and developed in the case law on the duty of care.[56]

The duty of care goes back to cases of 1991, including the seminal case *Technische Universität München*.[57] The CJEU began introducing its review of a discretionary decision in the context of a customs decision with a restatement of the *Remia* formula, under which, where the institutions have discretionary powers or powers of appraisal and thus the manifest error test is to be applied, 'respect for the rights guaranteed by the Community legal order in administrative procedures is of even more fundamental importance'. It continued to state that 'those guarantees include, in particular, the duty of the competent institution to examine carefully and impartially all the relevant aspects of the individual case, the right of the person concerned to make his views known and to have an adequately reasoned decisions.'[58] Violation of this principle would lead to the annulment of the decision.

Ever since, it has been established that an administrative decision maker, even when granted wide discretion, must therefore make the decision after considering all the relevant factors, including special circumstances affecting the instant matter. What factors may or may not be taken into account may be either expressly listed—sometimes exhaustively—in the statute or may be inferred from the statutory goals, or both. These factors will include both technical aspects, knowledge, and also public and private interests to be balanced.

The very fundamental nature of this obligation makes it applicable across various forms of administrative action in the EU—from single case decision making to the adoption of acts of general application.[59] Importantly, full and impartial assessment of all relevant facts is necessary regarding any type of discretionary powers conferred on an institution or body. The facts to be taken into account in such decision making may arise from all sources of EU administrative law applicable to the case: specific legislative or non-legislative acts, general principles of law, or Treaty provisions. This includes non-policy specific 'horizontal clauses'.[60]

---

[56] The duty of care was first explicitly identified as a principle of EU law in the case law of the CJEU by van Gerven AG and adopted by the Court in *Nölle*, an anti-dumping case. Opinion of AG van Gerven in Case C-16/90 *Nölle v Hauptzollamt Bremen-Freihafen* [1991] ECR I-5163.

[57] *Technische Universität München* (n 24).   [58] Ibid.

[59] See, e.g. *Gauweiler* (n 8) para 69 (regarding an ECB purchase programme to be implemented by individual acts under Article 18 of the ESCB Statutes); Case T-333/10, *Animal Trading Company (ATC) and Others v Commission* [2013] ECLI:EU:C:2013:451, paras 84–94 (concerning a general decision by the Commission addressed at the Member States which had negative effects on the plaintiffs). J Mendes, 'Discretion, Care and Public Interests in the EU Administration: Probing the Limits of Law' in HCH Hofmann and J Ziller (eds), *Accountability in the EU – The Role of the European Ombudsman* (Elgar Publishing, 2017), 156.

[60] See e.g. Art 11 TFEU, which requires that 'environmental protection requirements ... be integrated into the definition and implementation of the Union policies and activities, in particular with a view to promoting sustainable development', or Art 168(1), first paragraph TFEU, which requires that 'a high level of human health protection ... be ensured in the definition and implementation of all Union policies and activities'. In that respect the General Court has held, e.g. in Case T-13/99 *Pfizer Animal Health v Council* [2002] ECR II-3305, para 158 that '[t]he duty imposed on the Community institutions by the first subparagraph of Article 129(1) of the Treaty to ensure a high level of human health protection means that they must ensure that their decisions are taken in the light of the best scientific information available and that they are based on the most recent results of international research, as the Commission has itself emphasised in the Communication on Consumer Health and Food Safety'.

The duty of care to be satisfied by EU institutions thus requires the analysis of technical facts as well as interests—both public and private. It exists towards individuals, as well as towards Member States.[61] However, it also needs to be pointed out that case law developments rarely being linear, and there are examples in which principle of care does not have the power to act as limiting factor to discretionary powers. For example, in *Staelen*, the Court of Justice submitted the very compliance with the principle of care to the standard of whether an act of an institution was sufficiently serious to cause a damage to be covered.[62]

4.2 Discretionary powers and the principle of proportionality—care to the rescue

As a general principle of EU administrative law, proportionality has developed an important—yet not always well-understood—role when it comes to identifying the degree of judicial review conducted with respect to discretionary cases.[63] The principle of proportionality with its balancing requirements is specifically capable of addressing the question of whether public interests and private interests have been balanced. But the limited review in discretionary cases was often understood, such as in *Association Kokopelli*, to allow for testing only if a measure is manifestly inappropriate in relation to the objective that the competent institution seeks to pursue. This approach makes for a particularly limited reading of the criteria for review of proportionality.[64] In this context, AG Kokott's in *SPCM* criticized that the relation between proportionality review and controlling margins of discretion 'is not always clear in the case-law.'[65] She reminds the Court that statements which limit proportionality review to manifest inappropriateness à la *Association Kokopelli* '... *are liable to be misunderstood*':[66]

If there are clearly less-oppressive measures available which are equally effective, or if the measures adopted are obviously out of proportion to the aims pursued, the persons affected must be given judicial protection. Otherwise the principle of proportionality, which is part of primary law, would be deprived of its practical effect.[67]

---

[61] See e.g. C-362/14, *Schrems v DPC* [2015] ECLI:EU:C:2015:650, para 63.

[62] C-337/15 P (Grand Chamber) *European Ombudsman v Claire Staelen* [2017] ECLI:EU:C:2017:256, para 41. In *Dyson* the General Court had made the review of the duty of care subject to the same manifest error test of the exercise of discretion, thereby misunderstanding the very purpose of the duty of care (Case T-544/13, *Dyson Ltd v Commission* [2015] ECLI:EU:T:2015:836, paras 38, 39.) However, upon appeal, the Court of Justice corrected that approach. It stated that actually, that no other than the General Court itself had 'manifestly distorted' positions of the plaintiff and the facts of the case (Case C-44/16 P, *Dyson v Commission* [2017] ECLI:EU:C:2017:357, paras 49, 50).

[63] See, too, Kosta, Chapter 9 in this volume.

[64] See C-59/11, *Association Kokopelli* [2012] EU:C:2012:447, para 38. *Kokopelli* concerned a dispute between two seed dealing companies and the question whether seeds varieties not officially registered could be marketed. *Kokopelli* must be considered particularly narrow since the case actually affected rights of individuals which needed to be balanced.

[65] Kokott AG in Case C-558/07, *SPCM and others* [2009] ECR I-5783, para 73.

[66] Ibid., paras 73–7.

[67] Kokott AG in Case C-558/07, *SPCM and others* [2009] ECR I-5783, paras 73–7.

AG Kokott accordingly points to cases in which the Court also examines, in particular, whether there are obviously less-intrusive measures or even whether the burdens are proportionate to the aims pursued as models of good practice.[68] AG Kokott's statements strictly made with respect to legislative acts are, however, also relevant to the review of non-legislative activity of executive actors.

The exercise of the proportionality test requires in all matters, first, that there is a full analysis of the consequences of the limitation of a right and, second, an analysis of the various consequences of different regulatory approaches to achieve the public policy goals associated with the limitation of rights. This is where the duty of care is a valuable tool to review whether the various factors needing to be balanced in the context of proportionality have been properly analysed to be taken into account. The combination of criteria of review arising from the principle of care and from the principle of proportionality then allows for combining both a far-reaching proportionality review and a certain degree of restraint when it comes to discretionary powers.

Prominently, in *Gauweiler*, the CJEU linked the duty of care and the principle of proportionality using a joint set of tests capable of reviewing the exercise of very broadly defined discretionary powers. At stake was the making of monetary policy, which required large quantities of statistical information and economic expertise.[69] This type of highly technical, very complex, and information-intensive activity is, consequently, very difficult to monitor through 'traditional' legal means of a framework of powers and judicial review. In *Gauweiler*, the CJEU held that the institution or body exercising its broad discretion is required 'to examine carefully and impartially all the relevant elements of the situation in question and to give an adequate statement of the reasons for its decisions'. The careful and impartial examination, AKA compliance with the principle of care, emerges as a key concept in review of whether the ECB had complied with its obligations under the principle of proportionality.[70]

Linking care and proportionality review in cases of review of discretionary powers was, however, not invented in *Gauweiler*. The case law pre-dating *Gauweiler* had long begun the process of proceduralization of review criteria by placing discretion and proportionality in the context of the principle of sound administration.[71] The

---

[68] AG Kokott makes reference Case C-280/93 *Germany v Council* [1994] ECR I-4973, para 94 et seq; Case C-84/94 *United Kingdom v Council (Working Time Directive)* [1996] ECR I-5755, para 58 et seq; Case C-233/94 *Germany v Parliament and Council (deposit guarantee schemes)* [1997] ECR I-2405, para 54 et seq; Case C-17/98 *Emesa Sugar* [2000] ECR I-675, para 53 et seq; Case C-491/01 *British American Tobacco (Investments) and Imperial Tobacco* [2002] ECR I-11453, paras 123, 126, 128, et seq, 132, 139, and 140; Joined Cases C-453/03, C-11, 12, & 194/04 *ABNA v Secretary of State for Health* [2005] ECR I-10423, paras 69, 83; Case C-127/07 *Arcelor Atlantique and Lorraine and others* [2008] ECR I-9895, para 59, the latter case on the examination of the principle of proportionality in connection with the justification of different treatment. For reference to a case of whether burdens are proportionate to the aims pursued see, e.g. Case C-344/04 *IATA and ELFAA* [2006] ECR I-403, paras 88–9.

[69] *Gauweiler* (n 8). See, further, Borger and Kosta, Chapter 6 and Chapter 9 (respectively) in this volume.

[70] *Gauweiler* (n 8) paras 66–9.

[71] C-556/14 P *Holcim (Romania) SA v Commission* [2016] ECLI:EU:C:2016:207, para 80; C-534/10 P *Brookfield New Zealand and Elaris v CPVO and Schniga* [2012] EU:C:2012:813, para 51; C-47/07 P *Masdar (UK) v Commission* of 16 December 2008 [2008] EU:C:2008:726, paras 92–3.

latter requires examination of 'all the relevant particulars of a case with care and impartiality and gather[ing] all the factual and legal information necessary to exercise their discretion'.[72] Thereby, 'an institution must base its decision-making on the "most complete and reliable information possible"'.[73]

5. Conclusions and Outlook

The concepts discussed within this chapter are highly inter-related. Delegation and discretion, as well as the principle of care (the obligation to full and impartial assessment of all relevant facts of decision making), have been developed within the EU legal system in the context of far-reaching delegation of powers to executive bodies. Holding the latter to account in view of the conferral of far-reaching powers is the *raison d'être* of these concepts and the reason for their development. Delegation can confer a great variety of powers on the recipient of delegation. First, delegation can confer the possibility to interpret the conditions of delegation. Second, it can allow the recipient of delegation to establish which factors are to be taken into account to decision making and give leeway in assessing such factors. Third, delegation can allow the development of practice or rules on how to conduct fact finding and analysis. Fourth, delegation can confer powers to decide on the appropriate outcome of decisions on the basis of facts, as well as on the weighting of the input with respect to the value decisions and the balancing between public and private interests in decision making. Not all of these powers are generally conferred on executive actors in one and the same act of delegation, but several might be accumulated. In general, the conferral of such powers, under EU law, are considered as some form of discretionary powers. In that context, the question of control and supervision of the exercise of such discretionary powers is essential for accountability of the EU's institutions and bodies.

The CJEU has determined that it will, in principle, conduct only marginal review of discretion limiting itself to assessing whether in the discharge of duties an institution or body has committed any manifest errors. However, the more limited substantive review can be undertaken, the more important the CJEU's review of procedure. Where no procedural rules are formulated in positive law, either in—yet to be created—general EU regulation on administrative procedure, or in policy specific acts, the institutions and bodies receiving delegation of powers also have the powers to adopt the procedural rules. Therefore, the criteria for review have been developed by the case law in a set of principles, e.g. the duty of care and the principle of proportionality. This chapter has analysed the inter-relations and the interdependencies of these principles in the quest to ensure compliance with the obligation to ensure an effective judicial review in the EU while respecting considerations of an adequate separation of powers—the so-called 'institutional balance'. It is clear that the case law is

---

[72] *Holcim (Romania) SA* (n 71) para 80.
[73] Case C-290/07 P *Commission v Scott* [2010] EU:C:2010:480, para 90.

in full development and the concepts are developing under our gaze. The principle of care is becoming the central hub for ensuring review of discretionary powers, not least because among the specificities of the EU's legal order is the fact that delegations are ubiquitous and that it is impossible to imagine a delegation that has not a component of openness for decision making by the recipient of delegation.

PART IV
CONCLUSION

11

Framing EU Executive Discretion in EU Law

Joana Mendes*

1. Introduction

This book started from the premise that the post-2008 developments that led to restructuring the EU financial, monetary, and economic governance require an analysis of law's ability to structure executive discretion in the EU. In the aftermath of the crisis, there was a growing concern about law's normative capacity to constrain or guide the exercise of powers that, while largely dependent on technical assessments, inevitably entail policy choices, sometimes less visible in executive-led decision-making processes. As discretion took centre stage, law's normative capacity appeared to have faded before the indeterminacy of legal norms and high-profile judgments that accommodated fundamental changes and solidified the position of the EU executive institutions. The various analyses in this book move beyond the ultra vires debates that have prevailed hitherto and instead form, together, a starting point to discuss law's relationship to executive discretion in the EU. This concluding chapter gives an account of the methodological challenges, conceptual difficulties, and normative problems one faces when assessing the possible paths to secure the role of law in structuring discretion in conditions of legal indeterminacy, as they have emerged from the book's contributions.[1] This conclusion, too, is a starting point: albeit with limited ambition, it proposes possible building blocks for a conceptual–normative framework on the relationships between discretion and law in the EU.

2. Methodological Challenges, Conceptual Difficulties, and the Grey Zones of Legal Dichotomies

An inquiry into law's relationship to executive discretion obliges EU scholars to confront—once again—a familiar conundrum: on the one hand, traditional conceptual tools and analytical categories as developed in national law appear too limited to capture the complex EU institutional structures and the meanders of its

---

* Professor of Comparative and Administrative Law, University of Luxembourg.
[1] It is a self-referential piece, insofar as the analysis is limited to the book's chapters.

law (EU law itself contributes to their obsolescence); on the other, questions such as the conditions for the legitimate exercise of discretion by independent authorities or by political institutions, the problems raised by norm indeterminacy, the degree of judicial review that strikes a suitable balance between the effectiveness of public action and legality, are far from being a novelty and EU law could benefit from conceptual refinement and from normative insights that a strictly EU-driven analysis falls short of providing.[2] Notwithstanding the limitations of state public law to capture the specificity of public authority exercised in the European Union (EU), one can hardly avoid reverting to its general categories when considering how EU law should or could develop. The challenge lies, however, in reconstructing them in a way that they can anchor the development of suitable legal instruments without losing sight of the specific traits of the phenomenon one analyses and of the polity in which it emerges.[3] The analyses in this book provide some direction in this respect.

2.1　Discretion

What is discretion and, specifically, what could be a suitable concept to analyse executive discretion in EU law? Various contributions in this book have shown, both implicitly or explicitly, that discretion is a multifarious term that, in reality, largely escapes the boundaries of analytical categorization. At its core, it is a choice among possible courses of action.[4] This core focuses on the aspect of volition, inherent in a policy choice that follows from weighing different public interests.[5] It is a choice that may be influenced by other choices that executive and administrative decision makers need to make in a given decision-making process: decisions concerning the assessment of a problem entail a choice if the technical knowledge upon which such assessment is grounded does not provide clear answers; decisions concerning the scope of legal powers entail a choice, grounded on legal interpretation, if the enabling norms are indeterminate.[6] In this respect, the distinction between cognition and volition holds, but it ought not prevent us from acknowledging that they interact and that such interaction may justify a similar legal treatment of the underlying decisions. Mattarella points out that distinctions may be 'clear only in theory, but extremely uncertain in the daily practice of public administrations'. He indicates

---

[2] On this need, see, in particular, the contributions of Nehl, Chapter 8 and Moloney, Chapter 5 in this volume.

[3] On the methodological difficulties, see Nehl, Chapter 8 in this volume; on the specific traits of the EU legal order that may condition the relationship between law and discretion, see Tridimas, Chapter 3 in this volume.

[4] As expressed in the definition of Davis that Leino and Saarenheimo (Chapter 7 in this volume) cite (KC Davis, 'Discretionary Justice' (1970) 23 *J Legal Educ* 56). The concepts advanced by Galligan, which they also refer to—'autonomy in judgment and decision' (D Galligan, *Discretionary Powers: A Legal Study of Official Discretion* (Clarendon Press, 1986); and by Jürgen Schwarze—discretion is the 'executive's freedom to decide and order matters for itself' (J Schwarze, *European Administrative Law* (rev edn, Sweet & Maxwell, 2006), 297, equally referenced by Leino and Saarenheimo, are arguably considerably broader.

[5] Moloney (Chapter 5).

[6] On the different sources of these types of choices, see Mattarella (Chapter 2).

that 'it is often the law that undermines [those] distinctions', by making converge in the same instance the interpretation of indeterminate legal concepts, policy choices, and technical assessments.[7] Leino and Saarenheimo note that, in the instances they analyse, discretion occurs at the level of finding facts, setting the standards, and of applying the standards to the facts.[8] Nehl could not be clearer in this respect: in contexts of complexity, 'there is no clear diving line between issues of fact and law and that factual and legal appraisals tend to merge, in particular at the stage of applying the law (...) to the facts (...) [C]omplex factual appraisals for the purposes of implementing EU law are never performed in the abstract or in a legal vacuum, but against the background of the rules on the basis of which the administration is supposed to act, including their objectives'.[9]

Whether or not the difficulties of mapping the borders of different types of choices or of assessments devoid the ensuing distinctions of analytical value, remains a relatively moot point among the contributors to this book.[10] Yet, irrespective of whether categorical distinctions remain pertinent in certain situations,[11] it seems clear that versions of legal typologies and categorizations should not prevent the acknowledgment that discretion (conceived as the choice between policy options) may stem from the confluence of choices that, in theory, can be considered to be distinct from discretion. Moloney's analysis is particularly relevant in this respect, as it indicates how reliance on existing legal categories may lead to 'hidden' discretion. Moloney shows how the discretion of the European Supervisory Authorities (ESAs) in the field of financial services—despite the technical function of these agencies (i.e. deliver expert decision making in a highly complex area) and their legally constrained environment—involves choices with normative policy implications (the choices between the different public interests that delimit the mandate of the ESAs).[12] The problem is far from being only conceptual: as Moloney's chapter indicates, the fact that technical discretion engages public interest choices creates legitimation strains. These arise from the mismatch between this reality and the prevailing legal assumption that agencies perform a technical function.

In a different vein, but also indicating how certain classifications are unhelpful and may be normatively problematic, Nehl points out that, as much as the intensity of judicial review is a function of the degree of factual complexity, the Courts' systematic resort to 'complex factual appraisals' is (in his words) an 'empty shell': not

[7] Ibid.
[8] Leino and Saarenheimo (Chapter 7). Also pointing the difficulties of the facts/law dichotomy, see Hofmann (Chapter 10).
[9] Nehl (Chapter 8). Nehl further shows the 'inextricable link between cognitive processes and policy choices that increasingly blurs the cognition/volition dichotomy for the purposes of categorizing discretion', by reference to risk regulation cases.
[10] Nehl (Chapter 8), upholding the need to keep the distinctions; Mattarella (Chapter 2), suggesting their 'limited usefulness'; Hofmann, criticizing the lack of clarity and coherence that have resulted from the 'great pragmatism' and 'great variation' of the terminology used in the case law of the Court of Justice (Chapter 10), thus suggesting the need for keeping analytical distinctions.
[11] The argument that issues of cognition and issues of volition are intrinsically intertwined may not apply across the board.
[12] Moloney (Chapter 5).

only does it not indicate the degree of scrutiny that the Court might engage with, but also 'may serve as a pretext for the judges not to engage in a more intense scrutiny of the facts although it might be warranted'.[13] In principle, he defends, courts should not defer assessments regarding the relevance of the facts, even where that inevitably takes them into the realm of volition that is, in theory, the premise of the executive or of the administration. References to 'factual complexity', without further conceptualization, may be too easy of a way out to avoid a judicial scrutiny that the courts could and should in principle perform (and for which they have the necessary tools).[14]

These last considerations suggest that distinctions between different types of choices that are either at the core of a narrower sense of discretion—identified with an act of volition—or that overlap with that core (such as interpretation of indeterminate concepts or technical assessments) may be analytically useful, but only if they avoid too sweeping and simplistic characterizations that deny the deep interconnection between those different categories. Or, to put it differently, one must acknowledge the many grey zones between such categories, the way these interact in practice, and the normative consequences of that interaction. Such distinctions may show the multifaceted aspects of discretion and avoid dissolving them into vague concepts of freedom or autonomy that become unhelpful when devising suitable legal solutions. Nehl's analysis shows that quite clearly, by highlighting the 'relevance' element as operating a transition between factual and legal assessments, matters of factual cognition and volition, as well as of substance and procedure. From this perspective, legal dichotomies may support more pointed legal solutions. So, even if interpretation of vague or indeterminate legal concepts could deserve a treatment similar to that afforded to matters of discretion[15]—because the norms that frame discretion may only acquire meaning *ex post* through the exercise of discretion[16]— still, distinguishing what is, in abstract, a matter of interpretation from what is, in abstract, a matter of discretion may, in some cases, enable a better analysis of the type of power that executive bodies have.[17] Acknowledging the multifaceted aspects of discretion moves the discussion beyond overly simplistic assumptions: the fact that courts decide on issues of law does not mean that the EU executive does not interpret legal provisions; the fact that the EU executive has a scope of discretion that courts should preserve does not mean that courts do not perform also the value judgments that are, as a matter of separation of powers, the preserve of the executive and of the administration.

---

[13] Nehl (Chapter 8) at n 90.   [14] Nehl (Chapter 8) at n 97.
[15] Hofmann (Chapter 10) at n 3.
[16] See Borger (Chapter 6 highlighting the difficulties in distinguishing the delineation of competence and the exercise of discretion), of Leino and Saarenheimo (Chapter 7 showing how, in certain circumstances, it is simply not possible to separate the choices resulting from interpretation from a choice made under the use of discretionary powers), and of Hofmann (Chapter 10 showing the interconnection between delegation and discretion).
[17] See the discussion of the *Landeskreditbank* judgment in the introduction to this volume.

2.2 Executive

The term 'EU executive' does not refer to a coherent whole. Such a unitary term must take into consideration the different layers that compose it—the specificities of which come across in the book's contributions. 'EU executive' includes the more administrative-leaning agencies, 'non-majoritarian, technocratic, and bureaucratic institutions', designed to support the administration of the internal market, subject to tight constraints and oversight regimes, 'neither directly elected nor directly managed by elected officials';[18] the independent European Central Bank (ECB), Treaty-bound to the pursuance of monetary policy with a single predefined goal (price stability), the content of which the ECB itself gets to define through the exercise of its discretionary powers;[19] the Commission, the guardian of the Treaties often portrayed as the 'neutral trustee of the European common interest',[20] ensuring and overseeing the application of EU law (implementing and enforcing policies and norms decided elsewhere), but also a policy-making institution defining both the ends and means of public action typical of an executive, as it does in economic governance.[21]

Nevertheless, as advanced in the book's introduction, using the term 'executive' brings to the fore the functional similarities of their powers that a focus on the specific institutional characteristics risks overseeing and zooms in on law's framing and structuring capacity. Indeed, the chapters in the second part of the book deal with a problem common to these different institutions and bodies: the difficulties of legal norms in structuring discretion. Norm indeterminacy, combined with conditions of uncertainty—which these bodies and institutions face when concretizing their mandates—open the room for arbitration between different contending public interests and for discretionary choices that support their policy-making role (irrespective of the legal forms it takes), often in tension with the legal constraints to which they have been subject.[22]

2.3 Beyond conceptual difficulties: a grid for analysing EU executive discretion

Applying to the *executive* actors that are the object of this book the analytical framework of the national administrative lawyer, with its categories of norm interpretation, technical assessments and policy choices, and the corresponding legal tools and procedural constraints, could be at odds with the tenets of public law valid in a national legal system, where the executive and the administration have a different role, sometimes delineated in constitutional texts.[23] This is not the case in the EU,

---

[18] Moloney (Chapter 5).   [19] Borger (Chapter 6).
[20] Sharpf, cited by Leino and Saarenheimo (Chapter 7).
[21] Leino and Saarenheimo (Chapter 7).
[22] On this tension, see, in particular, Moloney (Chapter 5).
[23] See Mattarella (Chapter 2; in national settings, 'there is a difference between the acts of the political bodies and those of the common administrative authorities. The latter must pursue the interests established by the laws or by decisions of political bodies. The former, instead, (...) identify the public interests to be pursued', p. 36).

for the reasons advanced in the introduction to this volume. Conceptually, the discretion of the EU financial agencies, the ECB, and the European Commission can be analysed and delimited by reference to the same categories that have been developed for state-bounded public administrations (with the important caveats indicated). This approach provides a more fine-grained analysis of the type of powers they exercise. It allows us to understand what, for example, 'economic discretion' may entail.[24] By emphasizing the interconnection between different layers, it shows that, notwithstanding their institutional differences, their specific legitimacy conundrums and accountability structures, the EU financial agencies, the ECB, and the Commission all face the problem of the loss of the steering capacity of law and the lack (or impossibility) of sufficient normative determination of the norms that ground their authority.[25]

From this common point, the possible paths to support law's structuring role and their suitability may vary, as Mattarella points out, according to different criteria: the type of legal acts adopted, in particular, the way in which they affect private entities subject to their authority, or States affected by those acts; the institutional characteristics and legitimacy assets of the deciding body; and the circumstances in which it needs to act. A fine-grained analysis of the type of choices and their intertwinement in each of these instances may indicate where discretion should be constrained and where possible biases for technocratic decision making should be countered.[26] Thus, Moloney proposes changes at the level of legislative mandates. Specifically, she argues that the legislation that frames the discretion of the EU financial agencies (ESAs) 'must make a stronger attempt to identify the outcomes to be sought by the ESAs—both as an input means of structuring their discretion and, potentially, of making judicial review more meaningful; and as an output means for strengthening legitimation through accountability'.[27] Greater legislative specification, she argues, would not be intended to eliminate open-ended normative directions—both impossible and undesirable if one is to preserve the agencies' ability to perform their functions—but would be required to provide a clearer articulation of the public interest that the agencies are pursuing and of their relative importance. Borger, on the other hand, stresses the difficulties of delimiting the interests that an institution is expected to pursue and questions whether this path could ultimately lead to compromising the independence that is characteristic of the ECB. His concern stems from the possible reviewing role of the courts, once given thicker normative grounds to conduct judicial review, by way of further normative specification.[28] The conundrum of judicial review aside, Leino and Saarenheimo's conclusion is more radical: given the legitimacy concerns that underlie their analysis—in particular,

---

[24] See Dawson (Chapter 4).

[25] On the German debate on the loss of the steering capacity of law (*Verlust der Steuerungsfähigkeit des Rechts*), see Nehl (Chapter 8, n 60).

[26] On different strategies to constrain discretion, see, further, Dawson (Chapter 4), and Section 3 of this chapter.

[27] Moloney (Chapter 5).

[28] He argues that this difficulty is ingrained in the unitary conception of discretion that I have defended.

how EU discretion interferes deeply with Member States' political choices in the area of economic governance—and given the intractable indeterminacy of the legal criteria that delimit the Commission's mandates, they propose a re-allocation of authority to take decisions in the area of economic governance to democratically accountable parliamentary institutions.

This all suggests a path to overcome the difficulties in conceptualizing executive discretion in the EU framework.[29] While there are no easy solutions to the problem of law's relationship to executive discretion and no straightforward paths, the transposition of analytical categories developed in national administrative law to EU law can be a starting point to develop a framework of analysis suitable to the specificities of the EU that is mindful of the many grey zones between those categories and of the way they inter-relate.[30] Thus, for example, the statement that 'discretion begins where law ends',[31] as suggestive as it may be and despite its historical origins (mentioned by Mattarella), falls short from adequately expressing the relationship between law and discretion, given the uncertainty of law (Tridimas) and the way choices regarding the interpretation of law co-determine the executive's discretionary choices (Borger). This proposition holds both for national and for EU law.

3. The Indeterminacy and Uncertainty of EU Law

While in any legal order discretion 'depends heavily on the legal criteria and normative programme set out in statutory rules',[32] the EU's specific constitutional set-up impacts, in important respects, the ability of legal norms to steer the exercise of discretion. The EU legislative process brings together the political preferences of different states, in addition to parliamentary deliberations and views from the institution in charge of pursuing the Union's general interest. In these circumstances, the EU legislator, as Moloney points out, struggles with setting objectives, financial regulation specifically being the result of a 'myriad preferences and interests'.[33] Constitutionally, these processes take place in a constantly evolving legal order, in which legislative norms (and executive decisions, as in the case of the ECB in the OMT decision) may themselves be a vehicle for constitutional change.[34] At the same time, legislative norms are often interwoven with norms stemming from a plurality of different sources, not least of international agreements or international regulatory bodies, whose legal status and even binding effects on the EU are not always clear.[35]

---

[29] Nehl (Chapter 8, nn 21 to 23).

[30] Mattarella's analysis pointed in this direction, the other contributions of the book appear to confirm it. As Nehl argues, 'the European Union has to strike its own balance on how to make appropriate use of concepts of discretion that fit best to its own policy objectives, legal frameworks and decision-making processes' (Chapter 8, after n 23).

[31] Davis, cited by Leino and Saarenheimo (Chapter 7).

[32] Nehl (Chapter 8, between nn 22 and 23).   [33] Moloney (Chapter 5, p 166).

[34] Tridimas (Chapter 3) and Borger (Chapter 6).   [35] Tridimas (Chapter 3).

The difficulties of defining normative programmes with a sufficient degree of clarity are evident.[36]

Those legal norms apply to complex and evolving realities, while uniform application should be ensured across the various jurisdictions that compose the EU. The fact that they are meant to grasp complex realities explains that legal norms framing executive powers (both at Treaty and at legislative level) may use concepts, such as 'output gaps' or 'structural deficit', that may be 'unobservable' and require 'estimates notoriously contested among economists'.[37] The complexity of the realities that legal norms intend to shape may be such that exceptions and flexibilities multiply to the point of fragmentation. Leino and Saarenheimo point out that, in the context of the Growth and Stability Pact, 'Member States may be excused on the basis of at least bad economic times, investments, structural reforms, solidarity operations, costs of refugees, and low inflation' and the Commission, according to a legislative provision, needs to 'give due and express consideration to any other factors which, in the opinion of the Member State concerned, are relevant in order to comprehensively assess compliance with deficit and debt criteria'.[38] The Macroeconomic Imbalances Procedure is rich in providing similar examples.[39] This is, to a large extent, inevitable, as Leino and Saarenheimo acknowledge.

In these circumstances, 'soft' rules adopted by executive actors may proliferate as a means to address ambiguities and weaknesses of legal texts.[40] The proliferation of executive norms is a factor that may further weaken law's normative capacity, in at least two ways. First, bureaucratic actors, when specifying the meaning of norms, are likely to be influenced not only by the aim to complete normative programmes, but also by a variety of other factors linked to their functional role in the EU's system of government. The European Securities and Markets Authority (ESMA) Q&As on core financial market regulation, for example, have attained, as Moloney explains, 'the status of binding law given the extent to which it is followed by the market and supervisors';[41] they are likely too far removed from the normative considerations that support the legal rules that they interpret. Second, abundance of norms may both cause uncertainty and multiply the choices that executive and administrative bodies need to take in specific circumstances, causing also strains in the legitimacy of administrative action, where this is anchored in detailed legislative mandates.[42]

This brief account, extracted from the contributions of this book, shows that the challenges to the steering capacity of law in the EU are not specific to the policy areas that have been the object of the book's Part II. Financial, economic, and monetary governance are possibly particularly prone to factors that may enhance indeterminacy: the need to ensure flexibility to adjust to evolving circumstances and accommodate prognostic assessments, and the need to resort to technical concepts the meaning of which

---

[36] Dawson (Chapter 4); but see also Moloney (Chapter 5), Leino and Saarenheimo (Chapter 7), and Mattarella (Chapter 2).

[37] Leino and Saarenheimo (Chapter 7, text accompanying n 24).

[38] Leino and Saarenheimo (Chapter 7, nn 25 to 31).

[39] Dawson (Chapter 4) and Leino and Saarenheimo (Chapter 7).

[40] Moloney (Chapter 5), Dawson (Chapter 4).   [41] Moloney (Chapter 5, n 61).

[42] Mattarella (Chapter 2) and Moloney (Chapter 5, after n 27).

may be contested. Both needs weaken law's capacity to define normative programmes, but they are not unique to financial, economic, and monetary governance. There are, in addition, structural constitutional characteristics of the EU that may potentiate law's normative weaknesses in constraining discretion, as Tridimas points out: it may not be easy to delimit the competence of an entity or to determine to which institution or body a legal action is attributable. The legislature itself may foster the lack of clarity regarding legal effects. Both phenomena are particularly problematic to assert the steering capacity of legal norms.[43] Kosta's analysis, on the other hand, shows that not only the legislature, but also the Court itself, may foster ambiguity in the way law operates in constraining discretion; this results from her examination of the various functions of the principle of proportionality in EU law.

4. Inversion and Subordination: Strategies for the Law–Discretion Binomial

These considerations on indeterminacy are one important factor to consider when assessing different possible strategies to constrain discretion in the EU's specific constitutional context. Dawson's chapter maps four such strategies, which also surface throughout the rest of the book: judicial review and different degrees of deference; normative prescription; procedural rules and accountability; and inter-disciplinary justification. Their strengths and weaknesses, as they result from the various analyses of the contributors to the book, give us important indications as to the hypothesis of inversion advanced in the book's introduction.

It is clear that indeterminacy may have an impact on the role of courts in performing judicial review. As Dawson points out 'if rules (. . .) are open, nested in economic concepts, and reliant on uncertain future effects, how can judges ensure that [executive] decision-makers (. . .) have exercised their functions faithfully'?[44] Nehl guides us through the detail of how that may be possible but also of the limits within which the EU courts operate.[45] While Dawson, as well as Leino and Saarenheimo, point out the difficulties of judicial review in economic discretion, Nehl tells us that deferential review is not an inevitability. Despite the procedural possibilities to collect evidence, the cognitive abilities of judges remain a limit to the comprehensive review of facts and law that would be in principle within the purview of the EU courts, in particular, in cases that involve uncertain and prospective factual assessments.[46] At the same time, Nehl shows how tools such as standard of proof and the

---

[43] Tridimas (Chapter 3).   [44] Dawson (Chapter 4, at n 10).

[45] In his rich analysis, Nehl draws attention to an often-overlooked aspect, which merits mentioning: the applicants' litigation strategy delimits the role of the EU Courts in reviewing discretion, not least due to the procedural system of pleas in EU law, in which the substantive matters of fact and law invoked by the litigants delimit the subject matter of the case (Chapter 8, text between nn 30 and 45).

[46] Nehl (Chapter 8). See also below the observations on interdisciplinarity, the fourth strategy advanced by Dawson.

specification of the applicable requirements have enabled the EU courts to intensify significantly the degree of judicial review in areas such as competition law. Whether the assessment of complex facts and the interpretation of indeterminate legal notions opens a sphere of discretion that EU courts treat deferentially depends largely on the degree of factual complexity and on an assessment of which actor is better placed to have a final say on the correct assessment of the facts (the executive body or the court).[47] But, in making this assessment, one also needs to be mindful of the fact that not only executive decision makers, but also courts, when judging the correctness of a factual assessment, make value judgments regarding the suitability of the discretionary choice when examining the relevance of the facts.[48] For this reason, and because of the institutional implications of judicial review of discretion ('who has the final say'), in policy areas where the interconnection or overlap between cognition (factual assessments) and volition (policy choices) is more pronounced, the standard of review and the standard of proof must be loosened.[49] Such is the case in monetary policy, where, in addition, the independence of the ECB ought to be preserved (Borger) and, as results from Leino and Saarenheimo's analysis, in economic governance. In some cases, however, it is far from clear how the Court deploys those standards. The same applies to general principles of law, such as proportionality. Kosta shows in her analysis of 'free-standing proportionality' how the lack of clarity regarding what interests the Court is in fact balancing when conducting proportionality review allows for strategic uses of this principle that may ultimately lead, as Borger highlights, to equating discretion with technicity in situations where there is more at stake than just the technical correctness of the assessments made by the executive body.[50] In this sense, *Gauweiler* is an instance of a larger phenomenon: the blending of the judicial tools that the EU Court uses when reviewing discretion.[51]

Where does this analysis leave us regarding the hypothesis of inversion advanced in the introduction? It is beyond doubt that the judicial tools to avoid such inversion exist, but, as Nehl accurately shows, how they should be applied (and how deferential judicial review should be) ultimately depends on the degree of overlap between issues of cognition and volition. In turn, such overlap conditions the assessment of whether the court is the best placed institution to have the final say on the assessments and judgments that influence the exercise of discretion. These vary significantly from policy field to policy field and from case to case. They vary also according to the Court's experience and fine-tuning of its judicial tools. In this respect, at the time of writing, there is a contrast between, on the one hand, competition law and, on the other, the areas of financial, economic and monetary governance, where the EU has acquired executive competences following the post-2010 reforms (a contrast that may subside as the Court develops its tools of review in these areas, too). But, Kosta's analysis of proportionality also shows that the issue is more complex than just a progressive refinement of judicial tools of review. The taxonomy she proposes to single out the various meanings and usages of proportionality by reference to the

---

[47] Nehl (Chapter 8).   [48] See, in particular, Nehl (Chapter 8, at n 95).
[49] Nehl (Chapter 8 at nn 135 to 144).
[50] Kosta (Chapter 9, Section 5); Borger (Chapter 6, Section 2).   [51] Nehl (Chapter 8).

interests it serves in EU law shows the ambiguities of how this specific principle keeps on operating as a methodological tool in judicial review.

Moving on to the other strategies to constrain discretion, the use of soft law is normatively ambivalent for various reasons. Soft law, as is well known, may be a means of executive actors to self-bind themselves by prescribing in a general and abstract fashion how they interpret legislative norms, or at the very least, how they intend to apply them, of defining normative bounds where they consider it neces-sary for the transparency and predictability of their action.[52] But as it is apparent already from this characterization, soft law is also a means of empowering executive actors. As much is clear from Moloney's analysis of the use of soft law by the ESMA. It should be acknowledged that soft law has, in the regulatory framework of EU fi-nancial services, a very specific function: the agencies' guidance is explicitly a means of achieving supervisory coordination and convergence among national supervisors (level 3 measures, as they have been coined since the Lamfalussy reform).[53] Yet, the ESMA has also used soft law to frame its own powers in a way that has strengthened its regulatory role, allowing it to '[shape] market behaviour outside of the confines of the formal Commission-located process for administrative rule-making', bringing transformative change to the EU financial markets.[54] Soft law has been a decisive tool in supporting ESMA's 'entrepreneurial approach' that Moloney analyses, which have turned it into a 'de facto rule-maker', within the confines of Commission's re-view and the Council/Parliament's oversight.[55]

The ambiguity of the use of soft law to structure or constrain discretion has, at least, two other facets, which are also referred in the book. First, a growing body of soft law rules may lead to 'a morass of unclear obligations, unknowable to the or-dinary public'.[56] If the abundance of legal norms may be counter-productive—as Mattarella indicated, at the very least it '[multiplies] the choices regarding the iden-tification and interpretation of the law'—soft law raises an additional complica-tion: the uncertainty of their legal effects, due to their legal nature and the courts' approach thereto.[57] The result may be uncertainty and lack of clarity—the opposite of what soft law aims to achieve. This is the case Leino and Saarenheimo argue in their characterization of the EU's economic governance framework. In their view, soft law in this area has increased 'complexity and opacity' and has resulted in 'a complex maze of alternative or even conflicting rules, which few understand'.[58] In a similar effect to that detected by Moloney in the case of ESMA, they argue that

---

[52] Tridimas (Chapter 3, text accompanying nn 102 to 125); Dawson (Chapter 4, text accompanying nn 25 to 32).

[53] Moloney (Chapter 5, text accompanying nn 78 and 79), pointing out the specific legitimacy chal-lenges of these measures.

[54] Ibid., text accompanying nn 59 to 75.

[55] Ibid., text before and after n 77. Noting, too, the risk that soft law may contribute to blurring competence boundaries, Leino and Saarenheimo (Chapter 7, n 67), citing Vaughan's work on the use of soft law by EU agencies.

[56] Dawson (Chapter 4, after n 35).

[57] Tridimas refers to bindingness as a continuum (Section 4.1). On judicial review of soft law, see Nehl (Chapter 8, text accompanying nn 71 to 76).

[58] Leino and Saarenheimo (Chapter 7, text after n 68).

soft law has 'buttressed the institutional position of the body—the Commission—tasked to determine what kind of meaning can be attributed to each provision in each individual case'.[59] Second, the fact that the EU courts may bind executive bodies to their own self-imposed rules—thus placing a 'legal seal' on soft rules that binds their future action—may create the incentive to decrease resort to soft law, leading the EU institutions to refrain from making public their decision-making criteria.[60]

It follows, then, that, as much as soft law is a valuable—and, to a great extent, inevitable—means to structure discretion with significant normative advantages (among which, legal certainty and transparency), it requires delicate balances. Importantly, for the purposes of this book, the trade-offs mentioned mean also that soft law may reinforce *the hypothesis of inversion* advanced in the introduction of this book. It contributes to structuring discretion, with the limits and caveats just mentioned, but it is also a way by which executive action can determine the meaning of the legal norms that frame the exercise of discretion.

Another—third strategy—to tackle discretion is resort to procedural rules both to structure the way discretionary choices are reached and to ground a sufficient degree of judicial review. As both Nehl and Hofmann underline, that limited substantive review of discretionary powers should be counterbalanced by strengthened review of compliance with procedural guarantees is axiomatic in EU law.[61] However, here one must consider not only the procedural rules that the EU courts have progressively developed, such as careful and impartial examination and the duty to state reasons, but also procedures that could enhance deliberation and political scrutiny, such as impact assessment. Care and reasons, on the one hand, and impact assessment, on the other, have different origins, scope, and (in part) functions, but they partially overlap as means to constrain discretion.[62] Both care and reasons, as procedural guarantees, and impact assessment, as a procedure intended to rationalize policy-making in the realm of major regulatory initiatives and rule-making, ensure decision making based on evidence and on a balanced consideration of competing legally protected interests and perspectives. In this respect, both those procedural guarantees and impact assessment have an obvious impact on substance, whether at the level of primary determinations (the executive action) or at the level of secondary assessments (judicial control). If they are meant to gear the exercise of discretion towards the achievement of correct outcomes, one needs a meta-level of analysis that enables us to assess the correctness of the discretionary act beyond the very verification of procedural compliance. From a legal perspective, here again, we face the problem of legal indeterminacy and of the loss of the steering capacity of law. The more legal norms resort to indeterminate notions or objectives, the concretization of which remains largely in the hands of executive institutions and bodies—for

---

[59] Ibid.   [60] Dawson (Chapter 4, n 37).

[61] Nehl (Chapter 8, n 154), and Hofmann (Chapter 10, n 46). *Technische Universität München* remains, in this respect, a reference judgment.

[62] They overlap to the extent in which they may apply to the same type of executive acts (as is known, impact assessment analysis does not apply to individual decision making and only recently was extended to some instances of executive rulemaking).

example, in instances involving uncertain and prospective factual assessments where the latter are more difficult to disentangle from value judgments that support policy choices—the less legal norms will define a normative yardstick against which one can assess the correctness of discretionary choices, and the less procedures can structure discretion in a way that prevents the inversion of the relationship of subordination of the executive to law.

Moloney's analysis illustrates this point. Referring to the conditions to hold ESMA to account, she argues that weak substantive indications in the enabling norms may lead to accountability gaps. The lack of sufficient specification of the objectives that ESMA is entrusted with hinders the possibility of holding the agency to account for how it balances the competing interests that it needs to pursue. In these circumstances, means of holding it accountable can more easily be dominated by the institutional interests of the account-holder.[63] As a result, ESMA's enabling norms neither sufficiently constrain its discretion—they do not 'accommodate [its] current trajectory and entrepreneurial orientation'—nor provide a basis for 'more granular forms of accountability'.[64] Arguably, similar observations can be made regarding the role of procedural guarantees: in the absence of specific normative determinations, it rests largely on the decision maker and on the controlling institutions (among which courts)—the latter within the limits of their controlling function—to define the yardsticks of a correct decision. If the applicable legal norms do not provide sufficient grounds thereof, institutional interests may play a fundamental role, detached from legal normative considerations. In these circumstances, procedural rules may become weak guarantees against the hypothesis of inversion. A similar observation may be made regarding the principle of proportionality, when the concrete benchmarks to make a proportionality analysis and the factors that weigh therein are unclear, and proportionality ends up being detached from an act of balancing the harm caused to protected interests against the advantages of pursuing a legitimate aim.[65]

Dawson's analysis of the advantages and pitfalls of the 'thin' and of the 'thick' reading of procedural review of impact assessment points to a similar direction. He notes that a thin judicial review of compliance with impact assessment requirements may both support judicial scrutiny of discretion and pre-empt review, turning judicial review into little more than 'a box-ticking' exercise.[66] At the same time, a thicker version by which 'discretion is narrowed not by demanding responsiveness to substantive legal standards per se, but rather through demanding the inclusion in economic decision making of a wider range of affected actors' equally carries risks to judicial review.[67] Arguably, the lack of sufficient normative criteria provided in legal norms enhances the difficulties courts could face if they would opt for the more demanding review of impact assessment requirements.

But there are, of course, limits to the extent to which legal norms may provide 'thicker normative direction', from which one could deduce criteria for judgments on the normative correctness of the outcome.[68] Moloney suggests that clearer

---

[63] Moloney (Chapter 5).   [64] Ibid. (text after n 128).   [65] Kosta (Chapter 9).
[66] Dawson (Chapter 4, n 53).   [67] Ibid. (after n 51 and nn 57 to 60).
[68] I borrow the expression 'thicker normative direction' from Moloney (Chapter 5).

legislative articulation of the public interests that the agencies ought to pursue and indications regarding their relative importance would be possible without falling into the risks of 'a legislative list if operational targets'.[69] She therefore sees a way of strengthening the role of legislative mandates in support of more political accountability. In other areas, such legislative articulation may be impossible. Leino and Saarenheimo indicate that it may be unworkable in the area of economic governance, given the 'vast policy space' needed.[70] Borger's chapter, too, shows the difficulties of requiring a further specification of the public interests involved, both when discretion is being exercised and when it is being controlled.

Finally, Dawson proposed a fourth strategy—interdisciplinary justification—less conventional in discussions on law and discretion, but promising and alluded to also in other contributions. It is again linked to judicial review. Highlighting that judges can hardly shun ruling on economic questions and on issues that escape their legal expertise, he argues that 'mainstream economics can act as a means of guiding judicial review'.[71] The incorporation of economics into judicial review would enable courts to assess discretion exercised on the basis of economic knowledge, and possibly intensify their scrutiny. As Leino and Saarenheimo indicate, 'what might look discretionary from a legal perspective may in fact be structured from the economic perspective, and decisions that in legal analysis appear closely rule-bound may in reality be heavily discretionary.'[72] Moloney's proposal for further legislative specification—if it is to base more meaningful judicial review[73]—would arguably also require interdisciplinarity. Dawson makes clear that such an approach is far from being a novelty in EU law. In competition law, the General Court has progressively acquired the capacity to assess the economics-based claims of the Commission, having reached what is generally considered to be a satisfactory level of judicial review of complex economic assessments in this policy field.[74] Reaching the same result in monetary policy, for instance, would nevertheless not be a simply incremental development: it would require the reconciliation of economic knowledge with the normative framing set by Treaty rules and legislative frameworks, and the up-front acknowledgment that economic knowledge is contested.[75] In addition, Borger's analysis suggests that it could hamper the independence of the ECB, by potentially enabling intrusive judicial review.

Prima facie, this strategy has the advantage of levelling the role of the EU courts and that of the executive, providing the former with tools that enable them to scrutinize the expert basis of policy decisions of the latter. Arguably, courts may be well placed to reconcile economic assessments with the normative requirements of law, possibly countering to some degree the pitfalls of indeterminacy that results from resorting to open-ended or contested economic concepts. Nevertheless, the difficulties and risks are considerable. Bridging 'the gap between the legal and economic

---

[69] Ibid., last paragraph before conclusion.
[70] Leino and Saarenheimo (Chapter 7 text accompanying n 35 and n 36).
[71] Dawson (Chapter 4, text after n 67).
[72] Leino and Saarenheimo (Chapter 7, text accompanying n 19).
[73] Moloney (Chapter 5, text after n 43).   [74] See, too, Nehl (Chapter 8).
[75] Dawson (Chapter 4, text accompanying nn 68 to 71).

worlds'[76] is far from being a straight-forward exercise when the aim is to solve social problems in a way that is congruent with the normative programmes enshrined in legal norms and with the constitutional underpinnings of a legal system.

5. Moving Forward

An attempt to summarize all the above is likely to remain too superficial. The various paths discussed in this book give a rich picture of the way law (its substantive and procedural norms as well as principles) structures discretion, of its limits, and of specific challenges it faces in the constitutional context of the EU. But it is also clear that there are no straightforward solutions on future normative directions, even when considering one specific perspective on law's role, i.e. steering deliberative processes that define the way in which public interests are balanced and pursued in EU law. In addressing this question, the book engaged in conceptual discussions that, while far from complete, provide important building blocks as to how one may adequately conceive discretion in the EU and resort to the rich doctrinal repository of national legal orders (an aspect more salient in the chapters by Mattarella and Nehl). The book also considered the specific constitutional features that may condition the ability of EU law and of its legal principles to structure discretion (a discussion more prominent in the contributions of Tridimas and Kosta). Finally, the book discussed possible paths for law's role in structuring executive discretion. The contributions of Moloney, Borger, and Leino and Saarenheimo in the second part of the book, as well as those by Nehl, Kosta, and Hofmann in the third part, picked up and substantiated in different ways the strategies suggested by Dawson.

In the guise of conclusion, three final observations are pertinent and set the path for further research on the relationship between law and EU executive discretion in the EU. First, the exercise by EU executive bodies of powers that combine legal interpretation, technical assessments, and political choices is defining the meaning of the public interests that delimit the scope of their mandates and, thereby, shaping the way public interests are protected within EU integration. As much as the Court of Justice remains a crucial institution in defining the role of law and, concretely, the meaning of legal norms, it is time to start looking at the way the executive itself is shaping not only EU integration, but also EU law through the exercise of discretion. The Court undoubtedly retains its role as guardian of legality. But, in the policy fields analysed in this book, it may not be the main actor defining the way in which law may structure discretion. Second, as much as the different entities that compose the EU executive are institutionally different, a functional approach to their powers may show structural commonalties that an institutional analysis tends to downplay. Thus, despite the legacy of the *Meroni* doctrine, the nature of the executive powers of EU agencies may not be fundamentally different from the powers exercised by other executive actors, even if they are purportedly subject to stricter legal constraints.

---

[76] Ibid. (after n 68).

Identifying these functional commonalities is important when re-assessing the role law *ought* to have with regard to EU executive discretion. Thirdly, the way we conceive law's role in relation to EU executive discretion as constituting and controlling discretion, in the various ways explored in this book, or possibly also as steering the way executive actors concretize normative programmes enshrined in legal norms, shapes the type of legal order and polity the EU is and will be.

Index